Patterns of Modern Chinese History

PATTERNS OF MODERN CHINESE HISTORY

Charles A. Desnoyers

New York   Oxford
OXFORD UNIVERSITY PRESS

Oxford University Press is a department of the University of Oxford. It furthers
the University's objective of excellence in research, scholarship, and education
by publishing worldwide.

Oxford   New York
Auckland   Cape Town   Dar es Salaam   Hong Kong   Karachi
Kuala Lumpur   Madrid   Melbourne   Mexico City   Nairobi
New Delhi   Shanghai   Taipei   Toronto

With offices in
Argentina   Austria   Brazil   Chile   Czech Republic   France   Greece
Guatemala   Hungary   Italy   Japan   Poland   Portugal   Singapore
South Korea   Switzerland   Thailand   Turkey   Ukraine   Vietnam

Published in the United States of America by
Oxford University Press
198 Madison Avenue, New York, NY 10016
http://www.oup.com

Library of Congress Cataloging-in-Publication Data

Names: Desnoyers, Charles, 1952– author.
Title: Patterns of modern Chinese history / Charles A. Desnoyers.
Description: New York : Oxford University Press, 2016.
Identifiers: LCCN 2015035272 | ISBN 9780199946457 (pbk.)
Subjects: LCSH: China--History--Qing dynasty, 1644–1912. |
    China--History--Republic, 1912–1949. | China--History--1949–
Classification: LCC DS735 .D48 2016 | DDC 951--dc23 LC record available
    at http://lccn.loc.gov/2015035272

Printing number: 9 8 7 6 5 4 3 2 1

Printed in the United States of America
on acid-free paper

Brief
CONTENTS

Part 1: THE PAST AS PROLOGUE

Part 2: PATTERNS OF MODERN CHINESE HISTORY

CONTENTS

Part 2: PATTERNS OF MODERN CHINESE HISTORY

CHAPTER 3: The Apogee of Empire: The Qing Dynasty through the Qianlong Era, 1644–1795 111

List of
MAPS

PREFACE

As we move deeper into the twenty-first century, China looms so large on the world stage that all students, especially those in colleges and universities, must come to grips with understanding its modern history. As the world's second largest economy since 2010, China is increasingly making its diplomatic, cultural, and military gravity felt, particularly in its postures toward Northeast Asia, Taiwan, Central Asia, the Philippines, and, most recently, the Middle East. China's growing need for energy and markets has made it more assertive on the world stage than at any time in its history, with current interests in places as far flung as southern Sudan and Latin America. Thus, a student-friendly text, with a strong narrative line and a high level of detail without being pedantic, now seems essential for use in institutions of higher education. The need for such a text can only grow as China competes for superpower status with the United States in the coming years.

Paradoxically, given this need, there are relatively few texts specifically devoted to China's modern history, especially compared with the offerings available in world history and area studies. The majority of existing texts on Chinese history deal with the modern period—a problematic designation in itself—as part of the larger whole of China's enormous history of more than 4,000 years. Some, to be sure, privilege the modern period, although in a somewhat lopsided fashion. Some have engaging and powerful narrative lines and are beautifully written, highly detailed works, but are not classroom texts in the usual sense of the term. As for the writers who do focus on China's modern history—variously interpreted as anything from the Ming-Qing era on—the trend has been to concentrate on a relatively small period or subfield within that larger rubric, for example, twentieth-century history, economic history, or the history of imperialism. Therefore, it appears that there is ample room for an introductory text comprising a well-defined "modern" period in Chinese history, with proven pedagogical features to aid in student comprehension, written in a compelling narrative form, and versatile enough to satisfy a variety of classroom approaches.

One of the great changes that has taken place in the study of modern Chinese history over the past 30 years has been the way in which the field itself has been defined. Formerly, most historians—Chinese and non-Chinese, Marxist and non-Marxist—tended to place the beginning of modern Chinese history around 1840, a convenient decadal year that followed the opening months of the First Opium War (1839–1842). As such, it marked China's initial clash with the industrializing West at the beginning of its new era of imperialism. But as Paul Cohen pointed out in his landmark study of American historiography on China, *Discovering History in China* (1984), the approach of this "impact–response," or "Harvard School," and others that utilized such "exaggerated polarities" as "tradition" and "modernity" suffered in a number of ways from "ethnocentric distortion." Marxist approaches, and even the "world systems" paradigm of Immanuel Wallerstein, were also subject to such distortion because they all located the primary focus of their efforts on forces coming from outside of China, instead of concentrating on agency within China. Hence, they were insufficiently "China centered."

This critique has resulted over the succeeding decades in reordering approaches to Chinese history in a number of important ways. Among the most significant of these involve the chronology of modern China and the approaches to imperialism applicable to an introductory text. For example, China's early lead in advanced technologies—printing, gunpowder, paper currency, the compass, the amenities of urban living—have led some scholars to insist that China's "early modern" period might be dated as far back as the Song dynasty (960–1279). Others, citing the height of China's ability to project power—as with the great fleets of Zheng He from 1405 to 1433—place it in the Ming period. Still others start toward the height of the wealth and power of imperial China during the long reign of the Qing dynasty's (1644–1912) Qianlong emperor (r. 1736–1795).

ORGANIZATION

Although sound arguments can be made for all of these approaches, this book starts with an introductory part called "The Past as Prologue," which consists of two chapters on the origins and development of imperial China through the end of the Ming dynasty. The remaining eight chapters then comprise the heart of the text: Part II, "The Patterns of Modern Chinese History, 1644 to the Present," begins with the founding of China's last imperial dynasty, the Qing, and covers material up to contemporary times. This allows students with no background in Chinese history to acquire some grounding in the field before plunging into the modern era. At the same time, it allows students and instructors who have covered this material to skip it and start in with the Qing.

In studying modern China, a full account of the Qing dynasty is particularly important because of the peculiar character of their empire: a tiny minority of Manchu overlords dealing with a huge Han Chinese majority and dozens of other ethnicities within a vast, geographically varied territory. Thus, the *patterns* developed during the *origins* of the Qing for creating a stable polity, their *interactions* with those inside and outside their empire, and the institutional and cultural *adaptations* they make provide key benchmarks for students as they explore the histories of this dynasty and subsequent regimes. In addition, it allows us to utilize the ongoing scholarly debates about Qing efforts to preserve their ethnic distinctiveness and create an enormously diverse multicultural empire beyond the scope of their dynastic predecessors.

This approach also has the virtue of narrative symmetry. Not unlike the famous "dynastic cycle" of Chinese historiography, it begins with the Qing bringing China to its greatest historical level of imperial power by the mid-eighteenth century; follows the empire through its disastrous nineteenth and early twentieth centuries; traces the attempts of successive governments to establish strong states in the twentieth century; and then finishes with China's return to prominence—soon perhaps predominance—on the world stage.

Another challenge that this text takes on is one not only for students of Chinese history, but also for those studying the histories of non-European or non-American peoples more generally: how to conceptualize imperialism. Despite decades of criticism leveled at the Harvard School and its offshoots, most approaches still place a heavy emphasis on the impact of imperialism and the Chinese response to it. Some temper this by doing it in comparative perspective—for example, comparing imperialism in China with that in Japan or India. More recently, some world historians and area studies specialists have engaged in long-term transnational studies of the process.

Most scholars today, however, see a predominant emphasis on an impact–response approach as dated and incomplete. Thus, the problem for an introductory text becomes especially thorny. With only limited space, the narrative must give due attention to the interplay of foreign intrusion and Qing efforts to contain and absorb it, while emphasizing that imperialism throughout most of the nineteenth century had relatively little impact on most of the empire or on a majority of its subjects. Indeed, many times more people and far more territory felt the effects of the great rebellions of the nineteenth century, most of which were either unconnected or only tangentially connected to the foreign presence in China. Still, China's position by 1900 was such that the cumulative effect of its defeats and humiliation by the Western powers and Japan and the perception that the Manchu Qing were no longer competent to safeguard the interests of the country were major precipitants of revolution during the twentieth century.

This text, therefore, takes a two-prong approach to the problem: Chapter 4, "The Last Empire in Transition I: State and Society, 1795–1900," deals with Chinese history for the most part exclusive of the events of imperialism. Its initial section examines recent historiography on the Qing, developments over the past few decades in revisiting economics, land use, and stability—including the continued debate on Mark Elvin's theory of the "high-level equilibrium trap"—legal studies, perspectives on Qing "civil society," women and gender issues, and Qing "agency" on the whole. The chapter begins with a vignette of a resounding Qing victory in the 1870s establishing distinct borders and a permanent presence in the far western territory of Xinjiang. The victor, Zuo Zongtang, was hailed by European observers as a brilliant commander and his forces were considered a match for any foreign army potentially arrayed against them. It is a useful reminder that, for contemporaries, it was far from a settled issue that the Qing were in decline. The chapter then takes an extended look at the internal history of the White Lotus, Taiping, and Nian rebellions; at Qing efforts at expansion; at the structure of government, the role of the district magistrate, and his relationship with the scholar-gentry; and the structures of village and family life. The topics in Chapter 4 are thus placed before the treatment of foreign intrusion in Chapter 5 to underscore their importance in trying to create a more China-centered narrative.

Chapter 5, "The Last Empire in Transition II: Imperialism and Resistance, Reform and Reaction, 1795–1900," then covers the details of China's *guochi*: the "national humiliation" of its reduction by the Western imperial powers and Japan to nearly the status of a client state. In doing so, this chapter looks at some of the same events covered in the previous chapter, like the rebellions of the mid-nineteenth century, but more for the details of the military issues involved and especially with reference to China's efforts at "self-strengthening." As in the preceding chapter, the material is presented to emphasize Chinese agency and to again raise the point that the results in the end were by no means inevitable.

FEATURES

The enthusiasm with which so many reviewers and adopters greeted Oxford University Press's *Patterns of World History* suggests that some of its pedagogical features might work equally well here in a more tightly focused work. Thus, this book employs the *patterns* approach featured above with reference to the Qing. As an organizational tool and pedagogical aid, the text highlights *origins*, *interactions*, and *adaptations* as central components of patterns identified in the narrative. For example, the practice of smoking opium in China has its origins in medicinal practice, in the introduction of tobacco to the region by the Portuguese and Spanish, and in the Dutch transfer of the Javanese innovation of smoking a bit of the drug along with tobacco. Among significant interactions along the way were China's economic clout in the region, Western—and particularly British—initiatives to find commodities desirable for the China trade, British seizure of the lucrative opium-growing regions around Patna in India, and the loosening of the monopolies of the East India companies. The adaptations may be found in the process of war and "unequal treaties" to which Britain and other powers resorted in defense of this trade and other commercial, legal, and diplomatic issues during the nineteenth century. Equally important were China's adaptations in circumventing the strictures of these treaties by diplomacy, internal transit taxes, and a series of attempts at industrialization and modernization of its institutions.

The experience of the Taiping movement (1851–1864) marks another example of origins (Protestant Christian theology; Chinese millenarian traditions), interactions (missionary activity; Taiping leader Hong Xiuquan's visions and understanding of pre-Confucian ideas), and adaptations (Hong's version of Protestantism as the base for a revolutionary theology and movement to create a state). Similarly, Marxism, as the governing ideology of China from 1949 to the present, has its origins in the nexus of political ideas of the European Enlightenment and the hard realities of capitalism and the Industrial Revolution. The ideas of Marx and his followers filter into China after the turn of the twentieth century and interact with the intellectual ferment of the Chinese New Culture Movement, gain currency with the success of the Bolsheviks in Russia, and then are adapted by Mao Zedong and the Chinese Communist Party as tools for revolution in the specific circumstances of China's agrarian society.

As in *Patterns of World History*, examples of these patterns abound here and are woven throughout the main narrative. As with *Patterns of World History* as well, it cannot be emphasized enough that the patterns in question are not to be interpreted in any kind of deterministic or reductionist fashion. Rather, they are a flexible armature around which the shapes of many different narratives may be built up and sculpted. Indeed, their function is to provide a useable pedagogical structure for the reader, not to break new theoretical or perspectival ground. In this respect, the internal organization of the chapters follows a pattern as well, although not a rigid one. Although the narrative is fundamentally chronological, most of the chapters are also divided thematically into sections on government and politics, economics and society, family and gender, and cultural, intellectual, scientific, and technological topics, although not all of these appear in every chapter.

As in the other volumes of the *Patterns* series, each chapter of this text (with the exception of the Epilogue) begins with a vignette to set the stage or personalize the themes within it. In some cases, as with the famous Song dynasty woman poet Li Qingzhao, the world traveler Li Gui, the young woman revolutionary Qiu Jin, the American star of a Chinese soap opera Rachel DeWoskin—or, as we saw, Zuo Zongtang—they represent an exception to the expected course of events. In one respect, their exceptionalism reinforces the power and pervasiveness of the trends against which their lives and actions may be viewed. On the other hand, their stories may also be read as subtly inserting a sense of the often surprising extent of the possibilities within the strictures of their societies—of the contingent and the unforeseen in history.

In addition, each chapter contains a "Patterns Up Close" inset box—which examines a particular test case, analyzes a debate, or takes a more focused look at a larger pattern under consideration. Some of the themes include poetry about ordinary peasant life in ancient China, the private thoughts of the Qing emperor Kangxi, the enormous impact of the horse collar, wheelbarrow, and stirrup, the story of the Chinese Education Mission in America, and the ongoing debate about the compatibility of "human rights" within the rubric of "Asian values." Each chapter also contains a list of annotated sources for further reference.

The overall object has been to create an accessible, versatile text that delivers a solid factual base, nuanced analysis, scope for student discovery, and an exciting story in one medium-length volume that both students and instructors will find easy and convenient to use. As one "Patterns Up Close" subject, the artist Hung Liu, put it, "history is a verb." In the case of this text, an important aspect of this notion of continual change in historical interpretation is constant revision. We therefore hope that you and your students will find things to question and debate within it, and we invite you to contact us with your queries and suggestions.

Charles A. Desnoyers
desnoyer@lasalle.edu

ACKNOWLEDGMENTS

The process of creating a textbook and its accompanying materials is a wonderfully complex, often daunting process. I have been unusually fortunate to have had the help and guidance of a tremendously gifted and highly professional group of people at Oxford University Press to shepherd me through the process at every stage. As he did with our last project, *Patterns of World History*, vice president and publisher John Challice championed the book from its inception and provided strong support throughout the process. Development production editor, Michael B. Kopf, and editorial assistant Lynn Luecken assembled the manuscript with surpassing diligence, care, and patience, to say nothing of their unflagging good cheer, regardless of how sketchy some of my responses to their queries proved to be. Similarly, picture researcher Debbie Needleman converted what were often only vague suggestions into striking illustrations that add immeasurably to the quality of this book.

I have also received an enormous amount of help and support from a wide array of valued colleagues. I thank Jeffrey Wasserstrom, editor of the *Journal of Asian Studies*, in particular for being an early supporter of this project. The author Rachel DeWoskin and the artist Hung Liu both provided invaluable material for features in this book. My History Department chair, Stuart Leibiger, and the members of the sabbatical committee at La Salle University were instrumental in helping me receive the irreplaceable release time needed to finish the manuscript. Perhaps most of all, those who have studied, taught, and traveled with me in the classroom and abroad over the years have given me more than I can possibly repay.

Finally, I offer a special kind of thanks to my friend and editor, Charles Cavaliere. Charles had been the driving force behind our earlier effort, *Patterns of World History*, and it was his inspiration that made this book possible. Charles was indefatigable, yet flexible when illness intruded and forced me to delay the project. His insights were legion and more often than not came at a time when my own ideas were in short supply. As a master of the art and craft of producing a book, he was indeed the indispensable person in bringing this project to such a successful conclusion.

It goes without saying that I am extremely grateful to all the readers and reviewers who gave so generously of their time and expertise: Peter Worthing, Texas Christian University; Xiuyu Wang, Washington State University–Vancouver; Margaret B. Denning, Slippery Rock University; Wing Chung Ng, University of Texas at San Antonio; Carolyn Neel, Arkansas Tech; Robert Cliver, Humboldt State University–California; James Carter, Saint Joseph's University; Q. Edward Wang, Rowan University; and Jenny Day, Skidmore College. I humbly acknowledge and thank them for the advice and criticism they have shared, and I have tried to incorporate as much of it as possible. Any errors of fact or interpretation that remain are strictly my own.

NOTES ON DATES AND SPELLING

In keeping with current international standards, I am using the abbreviations BCE (Before the Common Era) and CE (Common Era) to denote dates from ancient times and the phrase "years ago" to mark dates from Paleolithic or Neolithic periods. The traditional Chinese dating system used to mark months and years based on cycles of 60 consisting of combinations of "heavenly stems" and "earthly branches" is used only to denote events that commonly contain such dates in their titles, for example, Xinhai Revolution for "1911 Revolution."

With the exception of older book titles, which use the Wade–Giles system of romanization, most of the Chinese terms in this volume are rendered in the *hanyu pinyin* system developed in the People's Republic of China, which has now become the world standard. Although exceptions to this remain among some overseas Chinese communities and in the Republic of China on Taiwan, the *pinyin* system is gaining ground there as well. In the case of well-known names or terms such as "Chiang Kai-shek" or "Canton," the *pinyin* rendering also appears in parentheses when first mentioned. The more commonly recognized form is then used throughout the text. Although spoken Chinese has many dialects and subdialects, major efforts have been underway for decades to make the northern Chinese dialect referred to as "Mandarin" the "national language" both in the People's Republic and on Taiwan. The sounds in both the old Wade and the newer *pinyin* system are based on those in Mandarin.

- Most syllables are pronounced roughly the way they would be in English. The major exception is the letter "q," which is given a hard aspirated "ch" sound. "Ch" carries a less-aspirated English "ch" sound.

- "Zh" carries a hard "j" sound and "j" a somewhat softer one.
- The letter "r" in pinyin has no direct equivalent sound in English; the best approximation is a combination of "r" and "j."
- Pronunciation of some words, particularly in the area around Beijing, carries a retroflex "r" sound so that the word shi, for example, sometimes sounds more like "shir."

ABOUT THE
AUTHOR

CHARLES A. DESNOYERS is Professor of History and Director of Asian Studies at La Salle University in Philadelphia. He has previously taught at Temple University, Villanova University, and Penn State University. In addition to serving as the history department chair from 1999 to 2007, he was a founder and long-time director of the Greater Philadelphia Asian Studies Consortium and president (2011–2012) of the Mid-Atlantic Region Association for Asian Studies. He has served as a reader, table leader, and question writer for AP European and World History. He is a lifetime member of the World History Association and served as editor of the organization's *Bulletin* from 1995 to 2001. In addition to numerous articles in peer-reviewed and general publications, his work includes *A Journey to the East: Li Gui's "A New Account of a Trip Around the Globe"* (2004, University of Michigan Press) and co-authorship (with Peter Von Sivers and George B. Stow) of *Patterns of World History* (2011, 2013, Oxford University Press). He received his PhD from Temple University.

Patterns of Modern Chinese History

An Open Empire. *Music played an important role in Tang China and was enjoyed privately as well as on public occasions. This glazed earthenware sculpture, dated to 723 CE, shows three musicians riding a Bactrian (two humped) camel. Their long coats, facial hair, and hats indicate that they are from Central Asia. Indeed, the lute held by one of the riders is a type of musical instrument that was introduced to China from Central Asia in the second century CE.*

Part 1

THE PAST
AS PROLOGUE

Timeline

ca. 780,000 BCE	"Peking Man"
ca. 50,000–20,000 BCE	Modern *Homo sapiens* Foraging Groups Established in Eastern Eurasia
10,000–8000 BCE	First Neolithic Settlements in Yellow River Valley
ca. 7000 BCE	First Evidence of Rice Cultivation in Yangzi Valley
5000–3500 BCE	Yangshao Culture Develops along Upper Yellow River
4500–1500 BCE	Longshan Culture Develops along Lower Yellow River
2852–2205 BCE	Traditional Era of "Culture Heroes" and "Sage Kings"
2205–1766 BCE	Traditional Dates for Xia Dynasty
ca. 2000 BCE	Flourishing of Erlitou, Believed to Be a City and Palace Complex of Xia Dynasty
1766–1122 BCE	Traditional Dates for Shang Dynasty
ca. 1400 BCE	Earliest "Oracle Bone" Caches with Archaic Chinese Writing
ca. 1300 BCE	Introduction of Chariot to Northern China
1122–771 BCE	Western Zhou Dynasty: Capital Located at Xi'an
770–256 BCE	Eastern Zhou Dynasty: Capital Moved to Luoyang

722–481 BCE	Spring and Autumn Period
475–221 BCE	Warring States Period
604 BCE	Traditional Date for Birth of Laozi
551–479 BCE	Traditional Date for Life of Confucius
385–312 BCE?	Life of Mencius, Champion of Confucianism
d. 233 BCE	Han Fei, Philosopher of Legalism
221–206 BCE	First Chinese Empire under Qin; First Iteration of Great Wall Begun
202 BCE–8 CE	Former Han Dynasty
ca. 200 BCE	Earliest Evidence for Wheelbarrows
24–220 CE	Later Han Dynasty
ca. 300 CE	Iron Stirrups in Use in North and Central China
220–589 CE	Three Kingdoms, Six Dynasties, North and South Dynasties; Rapid Spread of Buddhism
589–618 CE	Reunification of Empire under the Sui; Grand Canal Constructed
618–960	Tang Dynasty, China's Most Cosmopolitan Dynasty; Chang'an Grows into World's Largest City
623	Xuanzang Journeys to India
684–705	Reign of Empress Wu
ca. 750	Printing with Movable Block Type Developed
751	Battle of Talas
960–1127	Northern Song Dynasty

CHAPTER 1

ORIGINS TO 221 BCE

Heaven has rejected and ended the Mandate of this great state of Yin. Thus, although Yin has many former wise kings in Heaven, when their successor kings and successor people undertook the Mandate, in the end wise and good men lived in misery. . . . Ah, Heaven too grieved for the people of all the lands, wanting, with affection, in giving its Mandate to employ those who are deeply committed. The king should have reverent care for his virtue. . . . We cannot fail to mirror ourselves in the Xia; also we cannot fail to mirror ourselves in the Yin. . . . It was because they did not reverently care for their virtue that they early let their Mandate fall. . . .

Now let the king just earnestly have reverent care for his virtue. If it is virtue that the king uses, he may pray Heaven for an enduring Mandate. As he functions as king, let him not, because the common people stray and do what is wrong, then presume to govern them by harsh capital punishments; in this way he will achieve much . . . the little people will then pattern themselves on him throughout the world; the king will then become illustrious.

Those above and below being zealous and careful, let them say, "As we receive Heaven's Mandate, let it grandly be like the long years enjoyed by the Xia, and not fail of the years enjoyed by the Yin"—in order that [as one would wish] the king, through the little people, may receive Heaven's Mandate.

—from DeBary and Bloom,
Sources of Chinese Tradition, pp. 36–7

So asserted, by various traditions and scholarly interpretations, the Duke of Shao or the Duke of Zhou as they addressed the now former subjects of Yin, "the Many Officers" of the Shang—China's signature bronze age dynasty. The dukes were acting as regents for the young King Cheng of the ascendant state of Zhou, once on the geographical and cultural periphery of the Shang state and now its conqueror. The Zhou dynasty, which at its high point would encompass nearly all of historical North China down to the *Chang Jiang*, or Yangzi River, proved to be China's longest lived dynasty, lasting from 1122 to 256 BCE. Its novel political system of *fengjian*, sometimes, if somewhat incorrectly, rendered as "feudalism," would spawn powerful kingdoms that would eventually contend for supremacy with one another and conquer the old Zhou home state itself. One of these, Qin, would ultimately effect China's first unification in 221 BCE. During the Zhou decline would come China's greatest era of intellectual and philosophical ferment, whose leading figures included Confucius, Mencius, Laozi, Mozi, Sunzi, Xunzi, and Han Fei and generated so many different ideas that Chinese scholars dubbed it the period of the Hundred Schools of Thought.

Perhaps more enduring than any of these schools, however, was the concept outlined in the above account—the **Mandate of Heaven**. As described in China's first historical work, the *Shujing*, or *Book of History* (sometimes rendered as the *Book of Documents*), Heaven, although in most respects a neutral, rather abstract, entity, was also an agent of an essentially moral universe. The balance of Heaven, Earth, and Humanity was reliant largely on the behavior of humanity as the pivotal element. The ruler, as the Son of Heaven, bore primary responsibility for setting a moral example for his people that would then allow humanity to hold the positions of Heaven and Earth in harmony. With this condition achieved, laws would be observed, the agricultural cycle would proceed properly, and the people would be peaceful and prosperous. But, as was assumed to be the natural case of the **dynastic cycle**, morally deficient, corrupt, or weak rulers would ultimately crop up, disrupt the harmony of society through bad example and/or bad policies, and ultimately unbalance the relationship with Heaven and Earth. There would then follow a period in which human and natural disasters would provoke justified revolt among the people, the rulers would be said to have lost the *Mandate of Heaven*—Heaven's permission to rule—and, if the revolt was successful, the new rulers would acquire the Mandate and found a new dynasty.

In the quoted document, the new Zhou rulers are invoking this idea as historical justification for their conquest of the people of the Shang, or Yin, whose ruler, somewhat confusingly surnamed Zhouxin, they claim, had become degenerate and therefore lost the Mandate. The conquerors cite the experience of the Xia, whom Chinese historians have customarily placed as China's first dynasty, as losing the Mandate to the Yin, who had now lost it to the Zhou. It is widely believed that this idea was developed retroactively by the Zhou many centuries after the alleged events depicted in the *Shujing*. Regardless of its origins and provenance, the idea itself developed tremendous historical resonance for the Chinese. Every succeeding dynasty—even those coming from outside China—portrayed itself as aiming not to conquer but to reform and correct the wrongs of the preceding rulers. As propaganda it undoubtedly met with only partial success; but the idea itself—that Heaven is a moral force that favors the rulers with the greatest rectitude—has in many respects lasted to the present. In twenty-first-century China, although far removed from the old imperial dynasties, there are still many who search for signs and portents of decline and Heaven's displeasure. The rulers of China's Communist Party themselves, although viewing the concept as ancient superstition, nevertheless nervously watch the indicators of their present prosperity for clues of a downturn that could signal to many the signs of the loss of Heaven's Mandate.

In this chapter we shall explore *origins*: the general outlines of the land and people; spoken languages and dialects; and the unique system of written "characters" that represent words and morphemes, rather than the alphabetical systems with which most of us are more familiar. This system, although often incompatible with the spoken languages that adopted it, nonetheless became the first written languages of Vietnam, Korea, and Japan, as well as many of the nomadic peoples on the Chinese periphery. We will also deal with Chinese and foreign conceptions of *patterns* of the Chinese past available through archaeological and literary records. We will explore *interactions* in which different groups are exposed to influences inside and outside the various entities of "China." Finally, we will look at the *adaptations* of people and groups as a result of those interactions.

Woven through it all are the unifying ideas of the patterns by which the Chinese have interpreted history: the concepts of the dynastic cycle and Mandate of Heaven. For Chinese writers from ancient times and codified and exemplified by the pioneering court historians of the Han era (202 BCE–220 CE), these ideas remained at the core of the conceptual, organizational, and stylistic elements of Chinese history writing into the twentieth century. Indeed, one can easily find its influences in Chinese histories even today. Because history was considered the pivotal discipline in organizing, analyzing, and carrying out government and in interpreting changes in that government, its influence is of vital importance in understanding the development of imperial China and its successors.

ORIGINS: LAND AND PEOPLE

Although different states have arisen in various parts of the region that has historically been recognized as "China," the imperial and national borders of the past century have been limned according to fairly consistent natural boundaries. Along the southern border of Tibet runs "the roof of the world," the Himalayas and Pamirs. This highest and most dramatic mountain range in the world has created such a distinctive border that many past Chinese dynasties as well as the present regime have taken it as quite natural that Tibet should be considered within the Chinese purview. River systems such as the Amur and Ussuri in the north, the Salween in the southwest, and the Red in Vietnam have also represented borders at various times in the past. The northern and western deserts—the Gobi, Ordos, and Taklamakan—have served as natural boundaries, although the paths through and adjacent to them were also natural conduits for trade, as with the famous Silk Road. Indeed, control of these regions was seen as vital into the nineteenth century as successive Chinese regimes sought to thwart the incursions of nomads and exert sovereignty over various bordering peoples.

Although invaders in the nineteenth and twentieth centuries would come by sea, China's topography has tended to funnel interaction with other Eurasian cultures into a narrow corridor marked, as some have noted, by an archipelago of oases and small settlements running west of Xi'an, south of Mongolia, and north of the modern province of Qinghai, more or less along the route of the famous Silk Road. Like the Khyber Pass in India, this route, with the exception of that

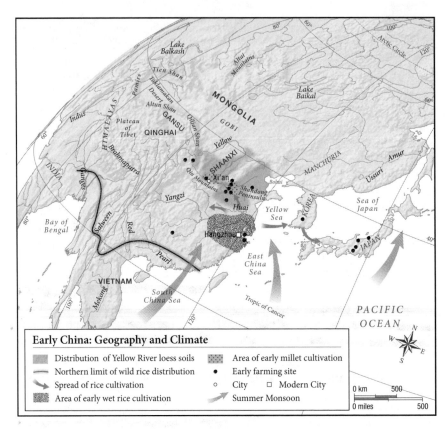

MAP 1.1

Early China: Geography and Climate

taken by the Manchus in the seventeenth century CE, has historically been the main conduit into China; unlike the Khyber, however, it has almost never been an invasion route for expansive cultural competitors. Aside from the Arabs in the eighth century moving as far as Talas to control the Silk Road, all other invaders until the nineteenth century have been nomads. The result of this has been that, on the one hand, the origins and early development of cities, towns, and villages in ancient China were somewhat more isolated than those of the other Eurasian centers of civilization; on the other hand, the absence of powerful competing civilizations ultimately facilitated both cultural and political unification.

China's climate is highly varied. The area south of the Qin Mountains marks the northern boundary of the region regulated by the *monsoon* system (from the Arabic *mausim*), with warm temperatures and abundant summer rainfall. During the summer monsoon, warm, moist winds from the Indian Ocean prevail and rainfall amounts can range from about 40 inches per year in the eastern coastal city of Hangzhou to more than 70 inches in the subtropical south. It was in these regions that the first rice is believed to have been cultivated. The suitability of monsoon-watered regions for rice cultivation resulted in rapid growth and high population density there, as it has in such varied places as India, Southeast Asia, Japan, and even southern Korea. Above the monsoon line and extending into China's modern Northeastern Provinces (historically referred to as Manchuria), temperatures and rainfall amounts are governed more by a *continental system*: that is, they are influenced by the weather patterns of Siberia and the Eurasian interior. Thus, northern China is subject to hot, dry summers and frigid winters with sparse and unreliable precipitation.

One result of these conditions has been that China's population has historically been concentrated in the plains along the major river valleys and along the coast. Three main river systems have remained the primary avenues of agriculture and commerce: the Pearl River (Zhujiang) in the south, the Yangzi River (Changjiang) in the center of the country, and the Yellow River (Huanghe) in the north. It was here where the most influential and best recorded early Chinese societies developed.

The Yellow River and Transition to Agrarian Life

The Yellow River's serpentine course takes it through a variety of regions, each of which influences its character and is in turn influenced by the river's irregular rhythms. Rising in the highlands of the northwestern province of Gansu and flowing north to the Ordos Desert, the Yellow River then turns south and east out of Inner Mongolia for 500 miles before making its great bend to the east and the sea, a total distance of roughly 3,000 miles. The river gets its name as a result of a light, dry, mineral-rich soil called *loess* deposited by centuries of strong winds carrying it from the interior, which it picks up as it flows, giving it a reddish-yellow tint. Thus, like other great river systems that spawned the first civilizations—the Tigris and Euphrates in Mesopotamia, the Nile in Egypt, and the Indus in India—the rich, easily worked soil carried by the river brought abundant agriculture to semiarid northern China. The constant buildup of silt in the riverbed, however, also causes it to overflow its banks, resulting in the devastation of fields and villages in its path through the North China, (sometimes called the Central, or Great) Plain, the vast flatlands lining the river course on its final run to the sea.

This action of loess silt in building up surrounding river banks only to have these natural barriers burst during times of heavy rains or rapid mountain snow melt, along with occasional earthquakes and direct human action—such as the dynamiting of dikes during World War II to stall the Japanese invasion—have caused the Yellow River to change course 26 times during the past 3,000 years. Its mouth has shifted several times above and below the Shandong Peninsula, assuming its present course to the north following massive floods in 1854–1855.

Not surprisingly, efforts to control the river have occupied a prominent place in the mythology, history, and political and social organization of the region from the earliest times. For example, Yu, the supposed founder of the Xia dynasty, was

Yellow River. The *Huanghe*, or Yellow River has been the site of a host of China's cultures for many thousands of years. At the top of this photo can be seen the highlands whose reddish-yellow *loess* soil gives the river its name.

said to have labored for decades to control the river's rampages. Throughout China's early period of fragmented kingdoms, the Yellow River states all had water conservancy ministries aimed at safeguarding the land and people from the Huanghe's excesses. This was even more true during the imperial era, and local officials and village headmen alike took active roles in flood prevention and relief.

Some scholars have pointed to the centralized bureaucratic structure of imperial China and suggested that it was dictated in large part by the struggle for mastery of its waterways. The most prominent of these was Karl Wittfogel (1896–1988), who in his *Oriental Despotism* (1957) characterized China, along with Egypt, Mesopotamia, India, and the large states of Central and South America, as "hydraulic civilizations." The vast numbers of laborers necessary to keep the rivers in check to safeguard the productivity of the state's agricultural base, he argued, resulted in increasingly powerful and extensive bureaucracies and ever more elaborate modes of organization, utilizing both free and forced labor. Thus, the importance of rivers in sustaining the state determined to a considerable degree the centralization of such preindustrial societies.

The deterministic air and Marxist title of the book generated more than its share of critics. The most prominent of these was the noted historian of Chinese technology and science, Joseph Needham (1900–1995). Needham felt that Wittfogel was insufficiently versed in Chinese history, that local and feudal states dealt with river matters for millennia, and that imperial China was far from despotic or static. The question of the degree to which geography is destiny, however, is still a vital issue in the social sciences. One recent commentator noted that the debate, like the late Elvis Presley, just will not go away. The question of how the search for agricultural stability has influenced the patterns of history of the peoples along China's most turbulent watercourse is one from which no student of the region can ultimately escape. Little wonder, then, that the Yellow River's gift of fertility but unpredictable nature has prompted outsiders to call it "China's Sorrow."

Neolithic Origins

One of the most important finds in twentieth-century paleoanthropology occurred in the early 1920s at Zhoukoudian near Beijing with Asia's first authenticated remains of *Homo erectus*. Although many of the original fossils of this **Peking Man** were lost during World War II, the site has been yielding remains ever since. The original finds were estimated to be 300,000 to 500,000 years old. More recent dating of nearby digs, however, put the age as far back as 780,000. Interestingly, work by Chinese and Swedish scientists in 2009 suggest that Peking Man may in fact have been a woman.

It seems safe to say that between 50,000 and 20,000 years ago modern *Homo sapiens* foraging groups had become established in eastern Eurasia. Traces of numerous human communities such as the site at Shuidonggou in Ningxia that produced small, refined stone implements such as arrowheads and knives have been unearthed. These groups repeatedly trekked across north and central China from about 30,000 years ago, marking an extensive culture that gathered local edible plants and hunted large and small game. Within a few millennia of the last glacial retreat around 12,000 years ago, the first settlements began to appear in northern China. With these modest habitations came the first traces in the region of the revolutionary transition from a subsistence forager society to an *agrarian* one, increasingly centered on the domestication of plants and animals.

The "Neolithic Revolution" of agriculture developed quickly in a number of places in China. Eastern Eurasia had a wide variety of plants that lent themselves to domestication, and the addition of others from more distant regions fostered this development as well. Among the most important developments for Chinese history was the domestication of rice, perhaps as early as 7000 BCE, making the sites of this cultivation in central China among the earliest in the world. *Millet*—a grain that remains a staple today—was already being grown in the north. Early strains of wheat and barley, perhaps originating from the region around the so-called Fertile Crescent in the Middle East and Mesopotamia, may also have been grown—suggesting the extent already of continental travel, trade, and diffusion of various items. Chickens (perhaps first domesticated in the Harappan cultures of the Indus Valley), pigs, sheep, cattle, and dogs were also widely raised, although it is unclear whether this was a regional phenomenon or possibly diffused from other areas. Although the territory along the Yellow River was certainly not the only one containing early agricultural villages, the settlements there remain among the best preserved and most thoroughly studied.

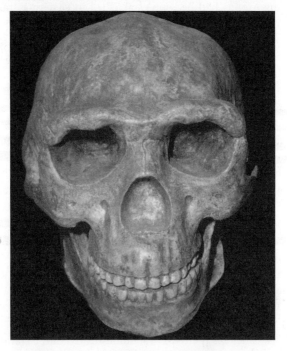

Zhoukoudian Excavation Site and Skull Reconstruction. The sensational finds in the 1920's of what came to be called "Peking Man" electrified the world of paleoarchaeology. China's first authenticated example of *Homo erectus* fossils in Asia, they were initially believed to be 300,000 to 500,000 years old. More recently, however, estimates have pushed back the date to perhaps nearly 800,000 years ago. Recent work also suggests that we should rightly call the remains "Peking Woman."

Neolithic Village Life

One of the more interesting tourist attractions in contemporary China is on the outskirts of the modern city of Xi'an: Banpo Village. The best known and most thoroughly studied of the thousands of Neolithic sites across China, Banpo is a carefully excavated and reconstructed exemplar of **Yangshao**, or "painted pottery," culture, which flourished from 5000 to 3500 BCE. Yangshao communities like Banpo had kilns capable of generating temperatures high enough to fire a wide variety of brightly painted storage pots, vases, etc., decorated with animal and geometric designs. The villagers also fashioned a wide array of stone implements to support the hunting, gathering, and fishing with which they supplemented their subsistence agriculture.

Banpo has a number of characteristics that long endured in Yellow River communities, in some cases even to the present time. Yet there are others that fell

Banpo Village. Banpo Village, near the modern city of Xi'an, remains a popular tourist stop as well as a rich Neolithic archaeological site. The photo above shows an interior view of a typical circular dwelling in the village. The photo below displays foundations, post holes and storage pits.

by the wayside, to be replaced by later variants. An example of the latter is that the settlement is surrounded by a defensive ditch, rather than the rammed earth or mud brick walls characteristic of later towns and cities. Indeed, the staple use of pounded loess as a building material in a region with little stone probably began at this time. It formed the foundations of village huts and giant palaces alike over the coming centuries. The village's dwellings, in contrast, arranged around a rectangular central structure believed by scholars to occupy some public function such as a lineage hall or early shrine, seemed to reflect regional design patterns that would be followed for millennia. Although the perishable materials are long gone, the evidence suggests that the dwellings were supported by vertical posts and had thatch roofs that, along with the walls, were plastered with mud and straw.

In addition, the Yangshao villages have yielded artifacts and structures that were to have long-standing significance in the everyday lives of Chinese villagers. Some of the dwellings at Banpo contain raised clay beds with flues laid through them—an early version of the *kang*, the fuel-efficient combination stove and heated bed still found in

Yangshao Pottery. Pot with fish motif (above) and painted pottery funerary urn, dating from 3000 BCE from Henan province. The lively, yet abstract, designs are typical of Yangshao wares. In some cases, the designs may prefigure an early writing system, although scholars are by no means unanimous that this is the case. The burial urn decorated in spirals was of a type also used for storing food.

older northern Chinese farming homes. Also, silkworm cocoons and bone needles suggest the earliest occurrence of *sericulture*—silk weaving. Perhaps more exciting—and controversial—are what many Chinese scholars feel are the first indications of a writing system. Pottery fragments bearing abstract pictures of animals and geometric figures bearing some resemblance to later Chinese characters have been found at a number of Yangshao sites. Even more intriguing, given the nature of China's early divination techniques (see below), have been shell and bone fragments with such designs apparently arranged in a systematic fashion. Some of the earliest of these, found in recent years at Jiahu in Henan province, date to 5500 BCE.

Longshan, or Black Pottery, Culture

Another Neolithic system of communities that contributed basic elements to what would later come to be recognized as a generalized "Chinese" identity was that of *Longshan*, or "Black Pottery," culture. Located to the east of the Yangshao areas, although with considerable overlap, Longshan artifacts have been dated as far back as 4500 BCE. Longshan culture was the last widespread Neolithic set of communities along the North China Plain, and branches of it survived until they were absorbed by the Shang state around 1500 BCE.

The most outstanding product of Longshan artisans was a distinctive, highly refined, often delicate black pottery, following designs and functional forms still popular in China today. Some of the pieces are so delicate and nearly transparent that they resemble the famous "eggshell porcelain" of later Chinese imperial pottery works. One of the reasons for this leap in sophistication from Yangshao forms was the introduction of the potter's wheel from western Eurasia, perhaps in the mid-third millennium BCE, which permitted unprecedented precision in molding round and curved figures. In addition, improved kilns—reaching firing temperatures in excess of 1,800 degrees Fahrenheit—and initial experimentation with kaolin clays began a long process of development that reached its high point with the matchless porcelain of the Song and Ming periods.

Longshan Pottery. Stem cups and goblet, dating to about 2000 BCE. The graceful, even elegant lines of Longshan, or Black Pottery, wares are not only distinctive but set patterns for ceramic and bronze designs that are still imitated today.

Neolithic Settlements beyond the Yellow River Basin

Despite the congenial climate and soils in the region around the Yangzi River and to the south, the remains of human societies there have been comparatively sparse. Although there are well-documented sites along the Yangzi River, including some adjacent to the modern cities of Shanghai and Hangzhou and at Dalongtan in the southwestern province of Yunnan, the most widespread culture links appear to belong to the Dapenkeng communities, named for the site on Taiwan where their artifacts were first identified. Dapenkeng culture appears to have been at its height from roughly 5000 to 2500 BCE, although recent work on Taiwan has now pushed the dating of the earliest artifacts as far back as 7000 BCE. These include a distinctive category of corded pottery, whereas arrowheads, polished stone, and bone tools and axes indicate a sophisticated Neolithic coastal and riverine society. The presence of these artifacts along a far-flung region running from the borders of modern Vietnam along the south China coast to Fujian Province and, as noted above, across the straits to the western coast of Taiwan suggest the enormous extent of this culture.

What can we infer from such a large area yielding such similar artifacts, however limited their numbers might be? Archeologists are largely agreed that it certainly suggests extensive interaction among peoples throughout the region, perhaps even more so than in North China. The origins of this culture remain obscure, although they do appear to be quite different from those of the north. Linguistic evidence points in the direction of Dapenkeng being part of a Proto-Austronesian family of languages distinct from the Sino-Tibetan language group that contains the various Chinese dialects, but one with strong links to non–Chinese speaking inhabitants of modern Taiwan. This in turn has prompted scholars studying the origins of another group of Austronesian speakers—the Polynesians—to search for possible links with ancestral peoples on Taiwan and along the China coast.

Early Rice Cultivation

It is hard to overestimate the impact of rice cultivation on the development of human life on earth. Rice has, of course, become, like corn (maize) and potatoes, a staple on every inhabited continent. Within its historic regions in Eurasia, it fed the majority of inhabitants. If we consider that the populations of East, Southeast, and South Asia when taken together have historically far outnumbered those of the western regions, we may also say that rice has been the principal staple of Eurasia as a whole.

Rice Paddies. The advent and spread of wet rice cultivation was one of the most important innovations in human history. Rice is an enormously productive grain but one that is extremely labor intensive. This photo illustrates the elaborate preparation and care required of the fields and the extensive degree of diking and water control necessary for a successful crop.

Researchers believe that there were at least two likely early regions of rice experimentation: Southeast Asia and the area roughly encompassing the eastern third of the Yangzi River and its coastal reaches. Both areas remained vital in developing increasingly productive rice strains that allowed China's food production to support its growing population through the nineteenth century. Moreover, the requirements of rice growing, particularly in regions governed by the monsoon, established patterns of agriculture that with regional variations have persisted in East, Southeast, and South Asia to this day.

Toward a "Chinese" Identity and Culture?

Over the past several decades, scholars in the humanities and social sciences have become increasingly interested in the problem of identity in studying the cultures and histories of peoples. The problem is enormously complex and can be misleading in some respects. That is, the dominance of the nation-state as the chief political entity today, with its assumptions of one's primary allegiance belonging to that state, tends to make us forget how recent a phenomenon such

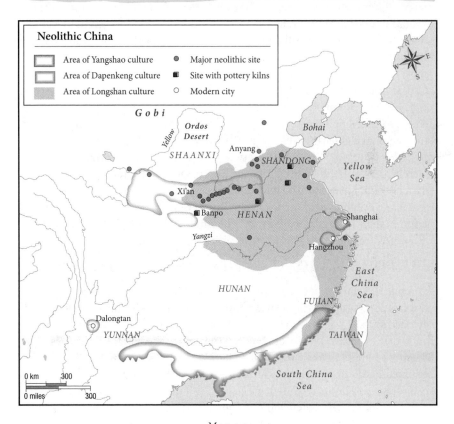

MAP 1.2

Neolithic China

political arrangements actually are. As with many current concerns, we often project them into the past and assume their continuity over long periods of time, a practice historians call **presentism.** In the past, however, family, clan, local, and regional affiliations were often primary in forming and representing one's identity. Larger ethnic, linguistic, and religious ties were crucial as well. This web of complexity can be seen in debates over what—if anything—constitutes a distinct Chinese identity or set of identities. Even today, as the leaders of the People's Republic of China work to forge an identity as a nation-state, the legacy of fragmented kingdoms, distinct regional dialects and languages, more than 50 recognized ethnic and religious minorities, and the often minimal cultural unity achieved during 2,000 years of imperial rule all continue to have an impact. In addition, the millions of overseas Chinese and those in the Republic of China on Taiwan have a multitude of ways of seeing themselves, often contesting bitterly what it means to be "authentically" Chinese.

Thus, the question of a Chinese identity as such is difficult enough. To speak of one developing in utero in the remote past becomes doubly speculative. Nonetheless, a few observations seem in order here. Although the documentary record—itself the biased product of the Shang and Zhou—suggests the centrality of those polities and the archaeological record of other regions remains sparse, scholars agree that what will emerge as a civilization with recognizable cultural links was far from being the exclusive product of the Yellow River cultures. Most scholars see a macroregion made up of agrarian communities sharing certain cultural preferences that ultimately coalesce into political units. Despite thousands of years of imperial and, more recently, national governments working to cement a unified political structure, ideology, and high culture, China still maintains regional elements visible even to the most casual observer. A loose parallel might be drawn in this respect between China and pre-Reformation Europe, wherein the Catholic Church provided a degree of cultural unity, a common written language (Latin), and attempted to enforce a considerable degree of intellectual and religious uniformity. Early Chinese writers referred to this formative period in their history as *wanguo*, the "ten thousand states."

THE FOUNDATIONS OF THE DYNASTIC SYSTEM

Although it contains a number of recurrent themes, what might be called the Chinese creation myth does not play the kind of prominent role that it does for other societies, such as those in the Judeo-Christian-Islamic tradition, or closer in proximity, that of Japan. Moreover, China's earliest known historical collection, the **Shujing**, a compilation of ancient accounts said to date from 2357 to 631 BCE, does not explore it at all. Although assorted versions of the creation—or perhaps more accurately, "appearance"—myth circulated for millennia, its most noteworthy mention takes place in the *Huainanzi*, an omnibus collection of essays on rulership dated to 139 BCE. In what some writers have compared to the modern "big bang" theory of the origins of the universe, the various gods in the story play a peripheral role while the cosmos essentially creates itself: likened to a giant egg in some accounts, the heavier elements, like the yolk, settle toward the bottom and become the dark, earthly—ultimately female—**yin** components, whereas the lighter elements rise and become the heavens and **yang**. Mediating between the two was the being Pan Gu, who, like the ruler in various Chinese political treatises, was tasked with holding both in harmony. This tripartite vision of the cosmos—Heaven and Earth with humanity occupying the pivotal middle position holding the system in balance—ultimately became a favorite model of the universe. It was often illustrated by the written character *wang*, "king" or "ruler," which consists of three horizontal lines connected by one vertical stroke.

Culture Heroes and Sage Kings

With the *Shujing* comes the long transition from myth to history. Scholars have debated its reliability for millennia, especially because, like the Homeric accounts of the Trojan War, its texts were written down centuries after the events it covers allegedly occurred. Moreover, as noted in the opening vignette to this chapter, the Zhou agenda of dynastic justification running through many of the accounts suggests that they may have been altered or even in some cases completely fabricated. Nonetheless, along with the oracle bones used by Shang rulers in divination (see below), it remains a vitally important source on China's first three dynasties: the Xia, Shang, and Zhou.

The *Shujing* claims that a series of "culture heroes" and "sage kings" reigned from 2852 to 2205 BCE. Like the gods and superhuman individuals from the extreme antiquity of other societies, these figures were said to have introduced many of China's basic elements and institutions. The first of these heroes, Fuxi, was said to have developed medicine, divination, and, according to some stories, writing. His successor, Shen Nong, was credited with developing agriculture. Huangdi, the "Yellow Emperor," brought fire and sericulture. His successor, Zhuan Xu, sometimes called the "Black Emperor," was credited with arranging the calendar and the astronomical cycles. Following Zhuan Xu were three celebrated sage kings, Yao, Shun, and Yu. Yao and Shun set the pattern for ethical rule and chose their successors from the land's most worthy men instead of from among their own family members. As for Yu,

> I [Yu] . . . opened passages for the streams throughout the nine provinces and conducted them to the seas. I deepened the channels and canals and conducted them to the streams. (*Shujing*, p. 31)

Shun therefore chose Yu to succeed him. Unlike his predecessors, however, Yu created China's first dynasty, the Xia.

Myth, History, and Religious Culture: The Xia

The centrality of history and historical writing in China and the habit of recasting it through the experiences and biases of succeeding dynasties makes it all too often deceptively slippery source material for historians. This is particularly true in

Uncertainty w/ Xia

trying to square the accounts in the *Shujing* with the archaeological record. It remains, however, the only systematic written account of the first two of the Three Dynasties to support the large but fragmentary collection of oracle bones. The problem is especially acute with regard to the Xia. Were they simply an invention of the Zhou to establish a narrative thread to their own dynasty? Was their alleged state in fact a kind of Shang mythology absorbed into the Zhou tradition?

Chinese archaeologists have been especially active in trying to peel back the mythical elements in our understanding of the Xia. Many archaeologists outside China, however, insist on a mythical explanation because the majority of the most promising sites from the period are in a cluster considerably south of the Xia's purported territory. Although still hotly debated, evidence is accumulating that perhaps some of the accounts of a culture resembling the "Xia" of the literary record may not be so mythical after all.

Excavations at *Erlitou* in southern Shaanxi Province from the 1950s on have revealed a city dating from roughly 2000 to 1600 BCE that at its height may have had as many as 30,000 inhabitants. The enclosure includes what is perhaps China's earliest palace. In addition, the plan of the structures within the city's various walled compounds resembles that of later official residences: post-and-beam construction, sloped roofs with upturned ends anticipating the famous "rising phoenix" motif, and non–load bearing curtain walls of plastered brick or masonry. Most of the larger buildings are also built along north–south axes with their courtyards and entrances facing south, a direction considered propitious even today.

Like the Shang, literary evidence suggests that Xia leaders exercised a family- or clan-based rule, and the archaeological evidence at Erlitou seems to support this to a considerable degree. Evidence indicating the role of the elites as mediators with the spirit world, and particularly with the ancestors of rulers, is also found in abundance at Erlitou. China's first bronze ritual vessels (wine beakers on tripod stands) as well as jade figurines, turquoise jewelry, the world's earliest lacquered wood items, and cowry shells—used as a medium of exchange—all testify to the leaders' religious and social roles. Some of the objects have designs on them that may be a form of writing, although it remains to be deciphered. A wide array of such items has turned up not only near Erlitou but also considerably beyond, suggesting an extensive trade network with neighboring peoples. For one leading scholar, Sarah Allen, Erlitou was perhaps the prototype for a widespread and unifying religious and cultural identity:

> My hypothesis is that the acceptance of this elite culture as a shared social and political ideal is the key to understanding the relative coherence of China in later periods, in spite of regional diversity and frequent political division. . . . Thus, Erlitou culture was not only an ancient civilization in China, it was an early form of "Chinese civilization." ("Erlitou and the Formation of Chinese Civilization." (*Journal of Asian Studies*, 66:2 (May 2007): 490)

FROM KINGSHIPS TO WARRING STATES: SHANG AND ZHOU CHINA

In the summer of 1899, at one of the low points of China's modern fortunes, a couple of Chinese scholars stumbled onto what would ultimately become one of the world's most important archaeological finds. Wang Yirong (1845–1900), the director of the Imperial Academy and an official in the Qing dynasty's Confucian bureaucracy, had been entertaining a guest at his residence in Beijing. When his friend came down with a case of malaria, Wang took him to a local apothecary to get a prescription for his ailment. As the druggist began grinding up one of the ingredients, known colloquially as "dragon bones," Wang and his friend noted with fascination that some of them seemed to have a form of archaic writing etched into them. Wang recognized it as akin to that found on old bronze ritual vessels. He excitedly quizzed the apothecary as to where he had obtained

Oracle Bones. Shang "oracle bones" used extensively for divination were first identified at Anyang a little more than a century ago and contain the earliest confirmed examples of Chinese writing. Kings or their diviners would ask questions of ancestors or gods, heat the bones, and interpret the cracks to find the answers to their inquiries. The questions and answers were then inscribed in the bones, usually the plastrons (undershells) of tortoises or (here) the shoulder blades of oxen.

the bones and so began an odyssey of inquiry that eventually led to some fields near the city of Anyang. What was unearthed there has been described as the "ritual archive" of the Shang dynasty: tens of thousands of bones used for divination by Shang kings and their spirit mediums. More than 100 years later this trove of artifacts is still yielding its secrets. More than any other single archaeological item, these **oracle bones** have opened a window on the court activities of China's bronze age. Perhaps more than that, the characters etched on the bones are China's first genuine system of writing.

With the Shang we find all of the elements of *civilization*—a highly original method of bronze casting, a substantial and diverse agricultural base, an increasingly centralized politicoreligious system, a sophisticated class structure, an independently developed written language, and, of course, cities. Although our earlier sense of their isolation has been considerably modified, more than any contemporaneous Eurasian civilization, they developed these elements with a minimum of outside interaction.

Kings and Client States

The system of dynastic rule said to have been instituted by the Xia continued under the Shang. Shang social and political organization was kinship based, with an emphasis on military power. Thus, loyalty was pledged to the Shang king and his family. Members of the king's extended family controlled political and religious power, with more distant relatives acting as court officials. Unlike other bronze age societies, there was no distinct class of priests. Rather, spirit mediums and diviners were widely used by Shang rulers and exercised considerable

influence at court. The rulers themselves, as the highest living link to the ancestors and other beings occupying a spirit realm, combined both ritual religious and secular power in their persons.

As with all agrarian–urban societies, the size of Shang territories and populations and their growing accumulation of wealth required protection. The Shang therefore fielded both defensive armies and expeditionary forces aimed at expanding their territories and forcing neighboring states to pay tribute and acknowledge their power. For the most part these forces consisted of infantry armed with spears and pikes with axe heads and were organized into companies of 100 men.

Perhaps as early as the fourteenth century BCE, however, evidence begins to appear in Shang tombs of two of the great innovations of ancient warfare: the horse and the chariot. Moreover, like the potters' wheel, these were among the items that we can authoritatively say were introduced from the outside. In this case, the evidence points to Indo-European migrants who ranged far and wide across Eurasia and spoke a language that became the parent tongue of a linguistic family that includes nearly all the European languages, as well as Sanskrit, the sacred language of Hinduism. In the history

Tarim Basin Mummy. Central Asia's Tarim Basin, one of the lowest points on earth, is also one of the driest, making it a perfect environment for preservation. It was also a place where some of the earliest interchanges took place between the peoples in China and the earliest Indo-European migrants. Remains up to 4,000 years old have been recovered. Here, the remains of a much more recent figure, "Yingpan Man" complete with mask, shows remarkably little deterioration and his clothes, though nearly 2,000 years old, look almost new.

museum of the modern city of Urumqi in China's far western province of Xinjiang, one can see today several extraordinarily well-preserved mummies of these migrants discovered in the arid Tarim Basin of Central Asia.

As at other sites in Eurasia, the use of chariots in China seems to have been shortly preceded by the widespread introduction of the horse, an innovation that had already revolutionized transport and warfare throughout much of Eurasia. Interestingly, however, the widespread use of horses as mounts for cavalry or archers did not really become important in the Chinese states until centuries later. Nonetheless, the relative scarcity of horses and suitable breeding grounds for them in China ultimately made trade with Central Asia extremely important as a source for the animals. Indeed, so great was the impact of the horse in China that eventually an immense lore pertaining to bloodlines, favored sites for purchasing horses, and the behavior and "character" of horses was created. Perhaps not surprisingly, it would be China that refined and popularized two inventions that are said by many scholars to have "created" the medieval Eurasian world: the stirrup and the horse collar.

Expansion and Interaction

The Shang were in many ways what social scientists would call today an "extraction state." Because of the system of kinship-based rule, the personal well-being of the elite and the prestige of the regime as a whole depended in large part on military power and harmony with their ancestors. Hence, Shang rulers constantly mounted campaigns for tribute and labor service from client states and allies. In addition, Shang kings continually led expeditions against settled peoples to the west, the most prominent of whom, the Zhou, based around modern Xi'an, were ultimately enlisted as allies and clients. An important aspect of these campaigns was the capture of prisoners of war for forced labor and often human sacrifice at the tombs of Shang luminaries.

As noted above, interaction between the northern Chinese states and the other Eurasian civilizational cores, although more frequent and complex than previously supposed, seems to have been irregular at best. The most direct links appear to have been through the trade and migrations of an ethnically and culturally diverse group of nomadic–pastoral peoples who ranged along a broad northern tier of Eurasia from the steppes of modern Ukraine to the area of modern Manchuria in the east. Although they left few traces and early Chinese accounts use a haphazard collection of names for them, scholars have theorized that these nomads included both speakers of Altaic languages—the distant ancestors of the Mongols, Manchus, Huns, and Turks—and the Indo-European peoples mentioned previously. In the latter group, it was the Tocharian speakers who played such an important role in spreading a host of ancient technologies throughout the eastern part of Eurasia.

Although direct mention of these nomadic peoples is almost completely absent from Shang records, a number of objects in Shang tombs carry clear signs

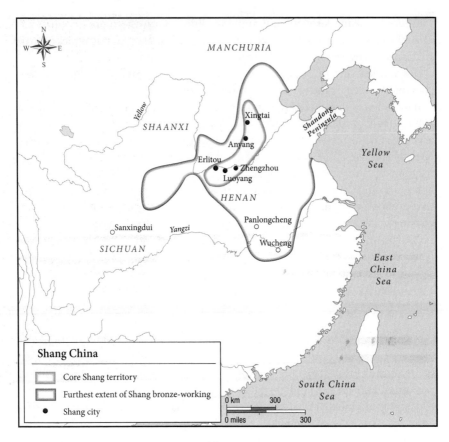

MAP 1.3
Shang China

of their foreign origins. For example, the tomb of Fu Hao (d. ca. 1200 BCE), the favorite consort of the king Wu Ding (ca.1250–1192 BCE), contains a number of bronze and jade objects—most significantly, bronze mirrors—that only later would come into widespread use in China. For their part, the Shang circulated local and foreign items such as bronze vessels, weapons, and jade throughout the region and beyond.

The picture is complicated somewhat by the recent work on cultures that show a connection to artifacts uncovered at Shang sites and even at Erlitou, but have distinct—almost exotic—regional variations. The most intriguing example is that of the strange elongated figurines of Sanxingdui in Sichuan, well out of Shang-dominated territory. On the whole, however, widespread recognition of Shang sophistication marks, with the ascendancy of the Zhou, an important pattern of Chinese history: conquerors on the cultural periphery interacting with and adapting to the culture of the conquered.

The Zhou and the Mandate of Heaven

Unlike the Xia and Shang dynasties, the nearly nine centuries of Zhou rule are extensively documented. In addition to the *Shujing*, such literary works as the *Chunqiu (Spring and Autumn Chronicles)*, *Zuo Zhuan (The Commentaries of Mr. Zuo)*, and later compilations such as the *Shiji (Records of the Grand Historian)* by the second-century BCE historian Sima Qian considerably amplify our source material. Like the *Shujing*, these Zhou accounts contain much of questionable value and uncertain origin. Nevertheless, they clearly reflect many of the same themes contained in that earlier work. They also begin to elaborate a wholesale questioning of existing values in a society that was increasingly undergoing the enormous stresses of new classes emerging and endemic warfare.

One of the revelations of the oracle bones has been to flesh out aspects of the literary record. An important example of this appears to be that by the twelfth century BCE, the Shang state had been considerably eroded by an assortment of nomadic and settled peoples to the north and west. The oracle bones suggest that in their desperation to preserve their reduced territory, Shang kings increasingly concentrated power in their own hands in a bid to keep internal order. As a later proverb about such conditions notes, however, "Disorder within, disaster without." The literary record of their successors, the Zhou, implies that Shang attempts to strengthen the control of the ruler coincided with increasing dissolution and corruption, thus letting their Mandate slip. Therefore, it appears the Zhou kings Wen, Wu, and Cheng and Cheng's regent, the Duke of Zhou, pushed their holdings eastward at the expense of the Shang from 1122 BCE. Sometime around 1045 BCE, Zhou forces captured and burned the last Shang capital and stronghold near Anyang.

Sanxingdui Figurine. One of the most intriguing finds in recent decades was the unearthing of bizarre jade and bronze figures in 1986 at Sanxingdui, near the modern city of Chengdu in Sichuan province. The strangely abstract forms, unlike anything else in Asia, suggest a wealthy and well-established culture had developed here by about 1200 BCE.

Both the literary and the archaeological record suggest that the Chinese states were atypical in that conquest by one did not necessarily mean exile, extinction, or enslavement for those defeated. There was considerable temporal and spatial overlap among the Three Dynasties, which added to the perception of shared cultural norms. The late stage of the culture at Erlitou, for example, is believed by many to have blended into an early stage of the Shang. The Zhou had been a client state of the Shang and had already absorbed a considerable amount of cultural influence from them. Given these ties, it is not surprising that the conquerors depicted their victories as acts of moral renewal for those they conquered. It should be noted as well, however, that the literary record also shows ample evidence of bloodletting in acquiring Heaven's favor.

Toward Disorder Within: Western Zhou and Eastern Zhou

By the end of the eleventh century BCE, nearly all of northern China as far south as the Yangzi River had come under Zhou rule. More precisely, a network of more than 100 smaller territories was organized under Zhou control, marking the beginning of the Western Zhou era, which lasted until 771 BCE. Zhou rulers placed family, distinguished subjects, allies, and even some defeated Shang notables in leadership positions of these territories under a graded system of hereditary ranks. By the eighth century BCE, however, the more powerful of these territories had begun to consolidate their holdings into states of their own. Although the states would continue to pledge their loyalty to the Zhou court, they increasingly

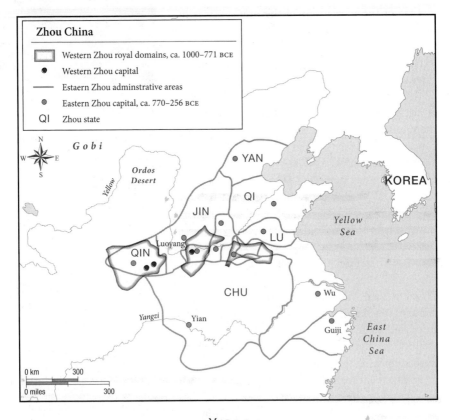

MAP 1.4
Zhou China

worked toward promoting their own interests, which resulted in a weakening of Zhou political power. A half-century of war among court factions, border struggles with nomadic peoples to the west and north, and a devastating earthquake further weakened Zhou power, resulting in the court being driven from its capital at Xi'an in 771 BCE and relocating to the east in Luoyang. This forced move began the Eastern Zhou period (770–256 BCE).

The Zhou system of decentralized government called *fengjian*, usually rendered as "feudalism," gave considerable autonomy to its local rulers and was thus an important reason for the weakening of the Zhou central government and the strengthening of its dependent states. As these states grew in power and their economies flourished, local rulers became less loyal to the Zhou leadership and some rulers even went as far as naming themselves "king" (*wang*) of their own domains. The prestige of the Zhou court was further weakened after its flight to Luoyang in 770. Continuing border problems with nomadic–pastoral peoples to the north and west around the Zhou home state and the relative isolation of its new capital drastically cut the flow of revenue from the dependent domains. This isolation was especially important since these states were in a period of tremendous economic expansion. Within a few generations of the inauguration of the Eastern Zhou in 770 BCE, Zhou control and power had significantly weakened in absolute as well as relative terms.

The Zhou decline is graphically described in the *Spring and Autumn Chronicles* and its accompanying work, *The Commentaries of Mr. Zuo*. Compiled in the Zhou state of Lu in the modern province of Shandong, these complementary works detail the maneuverings of states and individuals in northern China from 722 to 481 BCE. The world they depict is one in which repeated attempts at creating a stable political and social order among the 15 major Zhou states are frustrated by constantly shifting power dynamics and the rise of dominant states on the Zhou periphery.

Early on, the most important of these states was Qi, which dominated northeast China and much of Shandong. By shrewd diplomacy and careful use of military power, Qi became the first "senior" or *ba* state in a system of *hegemony* in which the lesser states deferred to the *ba* state as the protector of the Zhou system. The successive *ba* states mounted alliances against non-Zhou states and attempted to regulate relations among those within the system. They also presided at conferences held from the mid-sixth century BCE aimed at regularizing trade and diplomacy among the states. Qi was succeeded by Jin, which reorganized the *ba* system and, in 579 BCE, sponsored a truce and disarmament conference among the Zhou states.

By the latter part of the sixth century, a rough balance of power among the four leading states of Jin, Chu (the premier state of the southern periphery), Qi, and Qin (a rising force in the old Zhou homeland near Xi'an) held sway. Although this system functioned for several decades, new powers on the periphery, expansion into non-Zhou lands, and civil war in Jin ultimately precipitated the partition of Jin in 403 BCE, marking for some commentators the opening of the Warring States period (others use 475 or 453 BCE as the opening dates of the period). By its close, Zhou itself had been absorbed by the combatants (in 256 BCE) and Qin had emerged as not only the dominant state but also the creator of a unified empire in 221 BCE.

Zhou Era Warfare. As the Zhou states increased in wealth and ambition their wars grew more intense and deadly. As depicted in this painting, war horses drawing battle chariots were protected by disk-mail armor, iron tipped arrows and spears were in widespread use, and the composite bow with its combination of different materials gave added range and power to the archers.

SHANG AND ZHOU ECONOMY AND SOCIETY

Although the interior of the walled cities remained the province of elites and the artisans and craftsmen and women who directly served them, within the towns and villages immediately outside the larger cities a more differentiated social structure was developing. Many families and clans tended to pursue the same occupations for generations, and craft guilds and other organizations came to be dominated by family groups—such as potters and ceramics makers—as was the case later in imperial China. The constant warfare of Shang rulers and their increasing interest in monumental projects, for example, flood control along the Yellow River and its tributaries, all boosted the need for labor. Professional soldiers and local militia generally satisfied Shang military needs. Conscript labor, however, constituted an increasingly important part of the labor force.

The large size of the territory claimed by the Zhou dynasty and the enhanced trade that this expansion entailed added to the wealth and power of all the rulers of its increasingly autonomous dependencies. The expansion of these dependencies to the Yangzi River basin brought much of East Asia's most productive farmland under some form of Zhou control and stimulated increased interaction with the inhabitants of the region.

In the north, the introduction of the soybean from Manchuria, with its high protein content and ability to fix nitrogen in the soil, boosted crop yields and pushed growers to cultivate more marginal lands. The rotation of wheat and different varieties of millet allowed for more intensive farming. The use of more efficient ox-drawn plows and, from the fourth century BCE, iron-tip tools as well as increasingly elaborate irrigation and water-conservancy efforts pushed yields even further. In the south, the Zhou dependencies developed rapidly as rice cultivation facilitated population growth. With the coming of intensive rice farming, the economic and demographic "center" of China moved steadily southward. By the middle of the sixth century BCE, the Zhou kingdoms taken together constituted the world's most populous, and perhaps richest, agriculturally based urban society.

The Zhou rulers devised a system of ranks for governing their dependencies based on the size of landholdings:

- **Hou**: the title given to rulers of the Zhou dependencies;
- **Qing**: the chief functionaries of the *hou*;
- **Shi**: a general category for lower officials, eventually including talented commoners; and
- **Shuren**: commoners.

Members of the various ranks of the aristocracy were responsible for collecting taxes from their dependents and the *shuren*. They were also required to provide military service to those above them in return for support and protection. Peasant cultivators worked their own lands, with the lands of the aristocracy often scattered in plots among those of the commoners.

In an attempt to untangle the more confusing aspects of this land arrangement, the Zhou were the first among many dynasties to attempt to impose a uniform system of land tenure in China. Later writers, most notably the philosopher Mencius, would look back nostalgically on the **well-field system**—a method of land division said to have been devised by the Duke of Zhou. In this arrangement, each square *li* (one *li* is about one-third of a mile), consisting of 900 *mou* (each *mou* is approximately one-sixth of an acre), was divided into a grid of nine plots. Individual families would each work one of the eight outside plots and the middle one would be farmed in common for the taxes and rents owed the landowner or local officials. The term "well-field" comes from the Chinese character for "[water] well" (井, *jing*) which resembles a grid. Whether the system as idealized by Mencius was ever widely practiced is still a matter of debate among scholars. It did, however, remain the benchmark against which all subsequent attempts at land reform were measured, even into the twentieth century.

By the late 500s BCE, a substantial change had taken place in many of the Zhou states. The needs of individual governments to use the wealth of their states to support their militaries and developing bureaucracies prompted them to institute land taxes based on crop yields and, in some cases, commuting labor obligations to direct taxes payable in kind to the state. Depending on the state and the productivity of the land, these tended to vary from 10 to 20 percent of a family holding's yield. Then, as now, the taxes tended to affect the poor the most.

PATTERNS UP CLOSE

Ordinary Lives in Ancient China: The Classic of Odes

Despite the enhanced archaeological base and growing number of literary sources, we know relatively little about the lives of the common people during the period of the Xia, Shang, and Zhou dynasties. One of the few sources that does provide some clues is China's earliest recorded poetry, the *Shijing*, the *Poetry Classic*, sometimes called *The Classic of Odes* or *The Book of Songs*. The subject matter covers a wide range of interest and emotion, from homely observations on the cycles of rural life to protests and cleverly veiled satire. They are especially noteworthy in that women's voices figure prominently. It is believed that in most cases the verses were meant to be sung. As historical source material as well as art, the *Shijing*'s songs and poems of the lives and loves, burdens and laments, of peasants and soldiers, young wives and old men, are still striking in their immediacy today.

The *Shijing* is the third of five Zhou-era works—along with the *Yijing* (*Classic of Changes*); the *Shujing* (*Classic of History/Documents*); the *Liji* (*Classic of Rites*); and the *Chunqiu* (*Spring and Autumn Annals*)—that later came to be regarded as the Five Confucian Classics. This was partly because they made up much of the core curriculum of the *ru*, or Confucian literati, and partly because tradition held that Confucius himself had a hand in compiling or editing them—although this is doubtful. The 305 *Odes*, dating from the eleventh to the seventh century BCE, are divided into four main sections: "Airs from the States," "Greater Odes," "Lesser Odes," and "Sacrificial Odes of Zhou." Two other sections, "Sacrificial Odes of Lu," and "Sacrificial Odes of the Shang," are also appended, although the Shang *Odes* are not widely believed to be authentic to that dynasty. The last three deal principally with the Mandate of Heaven, ethical rulership, and religious ritual. The "Airs," however, are folk songs from the various Zhou states and cover the joys and tribulations of rural life, marriage, young love, and even complaints about the extractions of greedy officials.

Here, for example, a sense of duty mingled with parting sadness animates a young woman leaving home to live with her new husband's family:

> *The peach tree is young and elegant*
> *Abundant will be its fruits.*
> *This young lady is going to her future home,*
> *And will order well her house and chamber.*
>
> *The peach tree is young and elegant*
> *Luxuriant are its leaves.*
> *This young lady is going to her future home,*
> *And will order well her family.*

And here a man's parting grief for a lover:

> *The swallows go flying about;*
> *From below, from above, comes their twittering.*
> *The lady was returning*
> *And far did I escort her to the south*
> *I looked till I could no longer see her,*
> *And long I stood and wept.*

The life of the ancient common soldier carried the burdens his comrades today would surely recognize:

> *Hear the roll of our drums!*
> *See how we leap about, using our weapons!*
> *Those do the fieldwork in the State, or fortify Cao*
> *While we alone march to the south.*
>
> *Here we stay, here we stop;*
> *Here we lose our horses;*
> *And we seek for them*
> *Among the trees of the forest.*
>
> *For life or for death, however separated,*
> *To our wives we pledged our word.*

continued

We held their hands;
We were to grow old together with them.

Alas for our separation!
We have no prospect of life.
Alas for our stipulation!
We cannot make it good.

—Translated by James Legge, *The Chinese Classics, Volume 4. The She King.*
Oxford: Oxford University Press, 1898, in *Chinese Text Project.*

Perhaps the most famous of the *Odes*, at least in part because of its element of political protest, is the following:

Big rat, big rat,
Don't eat my millet!
Three years I've served you
But you won't care for me.
I'm going to leave you
And go the that happy land,
Happy land, happy land
Where I'll find my place.

Big rat, big rat,
Don't eat my sprouts!
Three years I've served you
But you give me no comfort.
I'm going to leave you
And go to those happy fields,
Happy fields, happy fields,
Who will moan there for long?

—William Theodore DeBary and Irene Bloom,
Sources of Chinese Tradition, vol. I, 2nd ed. New York:
Columbia University Press, 1999, p. 30.

The *Odes* were often one of the first works memorized by aspiring scholars and frequently quoted in other classics such as the *Xiaojing*, or *Classic of Filial Piety*. Then, as now, they were a principal window through which we can glimpse ordinary lives removed in time although startlingly contemporary in their loves, losses, aspirations, and concerns.

The New Classes: Merchants and Shi

Also contributing to the decline of Zhou rural-based feudal society was the rise of new classes. For the first time, the literary record now includes references to merchants. The growing power of this new class began, among other things, a long-term struggle with various governments for control of such vital commodities as salt and iron. It also marked the beginning of the perception of merchants as *usurpers*—a class with no ties to the land and thus no stake in the values of landholders or peasants—whose drive for profit from trafficking in the goods of others endangered the stability of Zhou social institutions. Accompanying the rise of a merchant class was the steady advance of a cash economy. The coining of money was becoming widespread by the late Zhou, including the round copper "cash" with the square middle hole—symbolically depicting heaven and earth—which remained almost unchanged for more than 2,000 years.

Although often viewed with distaste by the landed aristocracy, merchants were increasingly seen as resources to be tapped. Their rapid rise to economic prominence, however, meant that as a group their social position lay outside the traditional structures of agrarian life. Their independence and mobility, along with the steady growth of cities as centers of trade, helped spur political and economic centralization as the rulers of Zhou territories attempted to create more inclusive systems of administration. Direct taxation by the state, uniform law codes, and administrative restructuring were increasingly altering the old arrangement of mutual obligation between aristocratic landowners and dependent peasant farmers. Here, members of the new **shi** class—drawn from the lower aristocracy and wealthier commoners—who, like merchants, were divorced somewhat from the older structures of rural life, took on the role of bureaucrats and advisors. From the ranks of the *shi* would rise many of China's most famous thinkers, starting with Confucius. The duties and proper conduct of the *shi* would come to occupy a prominent place in their writings from the late sixth century BCE on.

Family and Gender in Ancient China

In marked contrast to later Chinese court life, in which the seclusion of women was a central aspect, elite women of the Shang often participated in political—and even military—affairs. We can catch a glimpse of this reflected in the objects found at the burial site of Fu Hao, discovered in 1975. The most prominent of the 64 wives of Wu Ding, Fu Hao's burial artifacts—hundreds of bronzes, jade, and bone ornaments, as well as the sacrificial skeletons of 16 people and 6 dogs—help bring to life a woman whose existence, although well established in written records, has otherwise been elusive.

For example, inscriptions on oracle bones in Fu Hao's tomb indicate that she wielded considerable power and influence even before becoming Wu Ding's principal wife. Prior to coming to court at the Shang capital of Yin sometime in the late thirteenth century BCE, she owned and managed a family estate nearby and was apparently well educated in a number of areas that would serve her well in palace life. She both supervised and conducted religious rituals at court and during military expeditions. As Wu Ding's chief confidant, she advised him on political and military strategy and diplomacy. She even conducted her own military campaigns against Shang adversaries. The king apparently considered her so wise and beloved that after her death he frequently appealed to her for guidance through divination with oracle bones.

Although elite women like Fu Hao appear to have shared a comparatively egalitarian role with male rulers, the Zhou era marks a period of transition in their status. To the extent that such literature as the *Book of History* and the *Poetry Classic* of the early Zhou era address issues of women and power, women were still depicted as occupying important positions as mentors and advisors. Women's crafts such as spinning and weaving, and especially the different skills demanded in silk production, were highly regarded. In fact, there were government offices supervised and staffed by women to oversee silk and hemp cloth weaving.

The wives and concubines of rulers in many instances had their own sets of records and genealogies as well, an important asset among the powerful in this family-conscious society. One of the most important sources we have on women's lives, though it deals entirely with women of the elite, is Liu Xiang's (77–6 BCE) *Lienu zhuan* (Biographies of Eminent Women). One of the many prominent historians of the Han period, Liu's work gives us capsule histories of 120 Zhou era women. By the late Zhou period, however, as one scholar notes, a "model" woman like Lady Ji of the state of Lu was still able to instruct her son, the high official Wen Bo (Earl Wen), in the arts of government by comparing the roles of different officials to the proper arrangement of the components of a loom in the process of weaving. In this role of advisor, her virtue was much praised by subsequent thinkers.

Yet it was also true that by this time it was Wen Bo and not Lady Ji who actually held the reins of power. Late Zhou women might be well educated and highly capable, but they seldom ruled in their own right. In fact, the treaties hammered out during the Spring and Autumn period in many cases specifically barred women from involvement in state affairs. The same general trend may be glimpsed at other levels of society as well. The enormously complex web of family, clan, village, and class associations of the Zhou era reflects considerable respect for the wisdom and work of women, but these skills were increasingly seen as best exercised in the home instead of in the public sphere. The later development of state-sponsored Confucianism, with its preponderant emphasis on filial piety, ushered in a markedly secondary role for women.

RELIGION, CULTURE, AND INTELLECTUAL LIFE

In many respects, the evolution of Chinese religion follows a similar pattern to that of other agrarian–urban societies. The first Chinese gods were local deities that inhabited a spirit world presided over by a ruling god. In some respects these spirits are still a part of Chinese folk religion, with its host of kitchen gods and hungry ghosts continuing to enjoy considerable popularity. Unlike the other religions of remote antiquity, in China the rulers' ancestors occupied the highest rungs of the spirit world and worship largely consisted of communication with them by various means. As in other places such as India, however, religion was not separate from everyday life but permeated all aspects of it. This was especially true of Shang political life.

Two aspects that mark Shang religious, intellectual, and political life as distinctive and original are oracle bones and the writing system. As we saw above in the story of the scholar Wang Yirong and the discovery of the oracle bones, divination and writing have always been closely intertwined. Scholars agree that, unless the Neolithic symbols on Yangshao pottery prove to be systematic in their application, the samples of characters found on Shang oracle bones represent China's earliest known writing.

The king seeking guidance would either himself or with a diviner ask a question of the spirit world ancestors. The bones, usually the shoulder blades of oxen or the plastrons of tortoises, were then heated and tapped with a bronze rod, and the resulting cracks were interpreted as answers. Although on some occasions the queries were incised into the bones before heating them, they were generally added later as a record of the procedure. The process of divination was at the heart of Shang politics and royal domestic life. Such matters as propitious times for battle, justifications for invasion, and the worthiness of officials are heavily represented among the oracle bones, as are matters related to royal births, deaths, marriages, and pregnancies. The gender of royal and noble children was especially important in securing male succession: as one bone predicted during a pregnancy of Fu Hao, "It is bad; it will be a girl."

Chinese Writing

Several thousand distinct symbols have been identified on the oracle bones, and many are clearly ancient versions of modern Chinese characters. More importantly, the principles on which these symbols functioned as a form of writing had already moved away from those of other hieroglyphic or pictographic languages. Although Chinese characters would became increasingly stylized and, after the Qin era (221–202 BCE), standardized, many of them retained enough of their ancient forms to be recognizable to later readers. The political and religious significance of Shang and Zhou ritual vessels, many of them with inscriptions in archaic characters, helped preserve some knowledge of them as well.

Of all the innovations commonly associated with China—paper, gunpowder, tea, the compass—perhaps the one with the longest-lasting impact was its writing system. Written Chinese has been called by the noted language scholar John DeFrancis "visible speech." Even in its archaic form, Chinese characters contained two basic elements: a semantic part, the radical element that conveys the category of meaning to which the character belongs; and the phonetic part that usually both makes the meaning more specific and offers a guide to its pronunciation. Many radicals are stylized pictures representing concrete objects: in its earliest form, for example, the Chinese character for the sun was a circle with a dot in the center. In its modern form it is still recognizable as 日. As a radical it forms a component of many characters related to light. For example, the radical for sun (日) placed with the character for moon (月) means "bright," 明. Characters combining concrete objects, such as the sun and moon here, are often used to depict abstract ideas, in this case, "brightness" or "brilliance." There are also purely phonetic characters, often used to approximate foreign words by sound, but semantically unrelated to them.

The Chinese written language had a tremendous impact on the course of Asian history. Although it requires extensive memorization compared to the phonetic languages of other cultures, it is remarkably adaptable as a writing system because the meaning of the characters is independent of their pronunciation. Thus, speakers of non-Chinese languages could attach their own pronunciations to the characters and, as long as they understood their structure and grammar, could use them to communicate. This versatility enabled Chinese to serve as the first written language not only for speakers of the Chinese family of dialects and languages on the Asian mainland but also for the Koreans, Japanese, and Vietnamese, whose spoken languages are totally unrelated to Chinese.

The pattern of interaction and adaptation prompted by the acquisition of the written language allowed the vast body of Chinese literature, philosophy, religion, history, and political theory to tie the literate elites of these states together within a common cultural sphere. In this respect, it functioned in much the same way as Latin among the educated of Europe. Even today, despite the development of written vernacular languages in all these countries, the ability to read classical Chinese is still considered a mark of superior education. Moreover, the cultural heritage transmitted by Chinese characters continues to inform the worldviews of these societies.

The close association of the written language with early Chinese religious ritual, court ceremonial functions, and individual self-cultivation and character development imbued it over the centuries with a kind of spiritual dimension not generally found among the written languages of other civilizations. The patience and discipline demanded in learning the thousands of characters necessary for advanced literacy and the artistic possibilities embodied in the brush and ink traditionally used to write them placed calligraphy at the top of Chinese aesthetic preferences. Thus, wherever written Chinese is used, skill at the three interrelated "excellences" of poetry, painting, and calligraphy is still highly esteemed as a mode of self-cultivation and expression.

Shang Bronzes and Religion

Although scholars are more or less agreed that China's earliest bronze artifacts were brought in through trade with Western Asia, the first bronze casting techniques in China likely arrived via Southeast Asia. The so-called "carved-clay" technique favored by Shang and Zhou casters—in which inner and outer molds of the object are made of clay and molten bronze is poured into the gap between them—is unique to China and radically different from the "lost wax" method of the peoples of western Eurasia. Moreover, Shang and early Zhou ritual vessels themselves, with their richly stylized *taotie* motifs—fanciful abstract reliefs of real and mythical animals incorporated into the design—are utterly unlike anything outside of East Asia.

Shang Bronze. Shang bronze-making techniques and motifs resulted in highly original designs and vessels that were often imitated by their successors. The ritual food vessel pictured here called a *li ding* is decorated with a distinctive taotie motif containing prominent eyes and scrolling horns. It was found at Anyang and dates to ca.1200–1050 BCE.

The use of bronze vessels constituted a central part of Shang religious ceremonies among the elites. Indeed, a number of Shang and Zhou ceremonial vessels passed through the hands of subsequent dynasties and came to be seen as the tangible marks of the Mandate of Heaven. Offerings of meats, grains (wheat, millet, and occasionally rice), and wine were a regular part of Shang ritual. Except for some limited references in later literature to offerings of wine and millet at local shrines and ancestral graves, we know little about the religious practices of Shang commoners.

Scholars are still unresolved as to whether *Di*, sometimes given as *Shangdi*, was the chief Shang deity or referred to a larger group or council in the spirit realm. In any case, *Di* presided over the spirit world and governed both natural and human affairs. Shangdi was joined by the major ancestors of the dynastic line, deities believed to influence or control natural phenomena, and local gods appropriated from various Shang territories. The religious function of the Shang ruler, as it appears to have been for the Erlitou culture and would be for subsequent Chinese dynasties, was to act as the intermediary between the world of the spirits and that of humanity. Hence, rituals appear to have consisted largely of sacrifices to ancestors to assure their benevolence toward the living. As the Shang state grew more powerful and commanded more and more resources, the size and scope of the sacrifices also increased. The Shang practiced human sacrifice. Excavations at both the early capital in the Erligang district of the modern city of Zhengzhou and later capitals near Anyang have yielded numerous sites containing headless skeletons along with intact ones, possibly close retainers. The evidence suggests that the death of a ruler was the occasion to slaughter hundreds of slaves, servants, and war captives, perhaps to serve the deceased in the spirit world.

Adaptations of Zhou Religion

The Zhou, like other conquerors after them, sought to give legitimacy to their reign by adopting many of the forms of art and ritual practiced by the defeated Shang. As before, the ruler maintained his place as mediator between the human and divine worlds. The Zhou era, however, marked a turn toward a more abstract, impersonal, and universal concept of religion. Di, the chief Shang deity or group of deities, began to give way to the more distant Zhou concept of "heaven" (*tian*) as the animating force of the universe. As in other religious traditions, there is a movement to go beyond the invocation of gods through proper sacrifice and divination rituals—*formalism*—to seek insight into the forces that control the universe. By the late Zhou era, this concept of heaven as the guiding cosmic force had become central to nearly every major Chinese religious and philosophical tradition. It was this more abstract heaven whose mandate gave the right to rule to all subsequent Chinese dynasties. Thus, throughout the long history of imperial China, the emperor retained the title of *Tianzi*, "son of heaven," as a symbol of his cosmic filial piety—his obligation to fulfill heaven's mandate as a son serves his father.

CONFUCIANISM AND DAOISM

Of the philosophical/religious systems that have been most influential in China's history, two, Confucianism and Daoism, are indigenous. The third, Buddhism, arrived somewhat later from India via Central Asian trade routes during the first century CE. The origins of the first two, however, may be found amid the context of the increasingly turbulent Eastern Zhou era.

This period from the move to Luoyang in 770–771 BCE until the creation of the first empire under the Qin in 221 BCE—spanning the famous **Axial Age** in so many other contemporaneous civilizations—is also considered China's most pivotal intellectual era of exploration. It marked a period in which the philosopher Karl Jaspers (1883–1969) noted a wholesale questioning of accepted values and social norms across Eurasia, running from the pre-Socratic Greeks, through the Hebrew prophets, to the development of Zoroastrianism in Persia, the Upanishads,

Mahavira, and the Buddha in India, and Confucius and Laozi in China. As we noted previously in discussing Zhou religion, in all of these places there was a movement away from religious *formalism* and toward notions of *transcendence*. Instead of propitiating gods, thinkers were increasingly searching for ways to grasp and utilize the forces animating the universe and put themselves in tune with those forces.

Not only were the origins of nearly every important indigenous school of Chinese philosophy to be found during this period, but also by the third century BCE there were so many competing ideas in play that the era is customarily referred to as the time of the "Hundred Schools." Of all these indigenous systems, the most influential in the long run were Confucianism, Daoism, and Legalism.

The Teacher: Confucius

As with so many religious and philosophical figures from antiquity, the historical Confucius is so surrounded by tradition and myth that he remains a somewhat shadowy figure. He is said to have been born in 551 BCE to a family named Kong, whose members still maintain genealogies tracing their ancestors back to him, and some descendants still live in the family

Kong Family Compound in Qufu. Though scholars still debate the authenticity of claims of authorship and descent from Confucius, the Kong family has insisted on their lineage and maintained this compound in Qufu in Shandong province. Emperors have bestowed the title of "Duke Yansheng" on the eldest male of the line since 1055 CE. The most recent holder of the title Kung Te-cheng (*pinyin* Kong Dezheng) died in 2008 on Taiwan at the age of 89. He claimed to be the 77th main line descendent of the Sage.

compound at Qufu in modern Shandong province. His given name was Qiu, or Zhongni, but in Confucian texts he is referred to as "the Master" (*zi, or fuzi*) or "the Master Kong" (**Kong fuzi**). European missionaries in the seventeenth century rendered *Kong fuzi* into Latin, where it became "*Confucius*." He was a man of the new class, the *shi*, and is said to have spent much of his early career seeking a position as a political adviser to the courts of several of the Zhou states in northern China. Although tradition has him holding a minor position in his native state of Lu, his search for employment was largely unsuccessful. He did, however, attract a group of followers as he made the rounds as an itinerant teacher. Although the writings attributed to him and his immediate disciples do not outline a systematic philosophical scheme as such, the core ideas of his vision represent a consistent view of a universal ideal of a moral order to which the dedicated may aspire regardless of their social position.

Creating a Moral Order

Confucius said he was a "transmitter" rather than an originator of ideas, which he drew heavily from his understanding of the approach and activities of ideal figures like Yao and Shun and the Zhou dynastic founders Wu, Wen, and the Duke of Zhou. As the man who first attempts to pull all of these trends together into an approach to personal ethical development, self-cultivation, and ultimately ideal rulership, he certainly breaks important ground. Indeed, it will be a core of ideas attributed to him that will form the ruling ideology of imperial China for more than 2,000 years and remain a powerful influence even today in China, Korea, Vietnam, and Japan.

As presented in the *Lunyu*, or *Analects*, the Master's ideas depict a view of human beings as inclined toward ethical behavior and of human society as a perfectible moral order. One of the key concepts shared by Confucius with many other Chinese philosophical schools is the idea of a transcendent *dao* (Tao). As we will see with the Daoists later, there are certain fundamental patterns that are manifestations of the *dao* ("the Way") of the universal order. For Confucius, one of these fundamental patterns is the relationship between parent and offspring: one owes one's life and body to one's parents. Because of this, one dares not injure oneself or others and develops one's moral character to reflect well upon one's parents; one thus serves those above as one serves one's parents. This pattern of human society as a kind of extended family exists at every level, from the ruler down to the peasant. In fact, it extends beyond human society in the sense that, through the mechanism of Heaven's Mandate, the ruler is responsible to Heaven for the state of human society. This idea is later powerfully reinforced through the Han dynasty era's *Xiaojing* or *Classic of Filial Piety*. Although this view is avowedly hierarchical rather than egalitarian, the mutual obligations present at every level serve as checks for Confucius on the arbitrary exercise of power. When asked to sum up his philosophy in one word, Confucius answered "reciprocity": "Do not do unto others what you would not have them do unto you."

Confucius believed that individuals should practice the qualities of *ren* (kindness, or humaneness toward others), *li* (the observance of rules of decorum as guides to appropriate behavior toward others), and, *xiao* (respect and devotion to parents and other elders—also known as filial piety). People who demonstrated these qualities would not only perfect their own character, but also set an example for the rest of society.

As it evolved over the course of imperial China, the Confucian canon came to include the "Four Books": *The Analects, Mencius, The Doctrine of the Mean* (*Zhongyong*), and *The Great Learning* (*Daxue*), along with the earlier Five Classics (see "Patterns Up Close") and, later, Thirteen Classics and their commentaries, which made up the major part of the curriculum of China's scholar-bureaucrats. Perhaps the best known of these is the *Analects*, a short work of 20 chapters and 497 verses ascribed to Confucius and his disciples. Below are some representative verses from the *Analects* depicting Confucius's ideas on the character of the **junzi**, or gentleman, on learning, youth and age, and the personality of the Master himself:

> The Master said: "Is it not pleasant to learn with perseverance and application? Is it not delightful to have friends come from afar?
> Confucius said: "By nature men are pretty much alike; it is learning and practice that set them apart.
> Confucius said: "In education there are no class distinctions."
> Confucius said: "The young are to be respected. How do we know that the next generation will not measure up to the present one?
> Confucius said: "When it comes to acquiring . . . *ren* (humanity), a man should not defer even to his own teacher."
> Confucius said: "Riches and honor are what every man desires, but if they can be obtained only by transgressing the right way, they must not be held. . . . If a gentleman departs from humanity, how can he bear the name?"
> Confucius said: "If a ruler can administer his state with decorum (*li*) and courtesy—then what difficulty will he have? If he cannot . . . what has he to do with rites (*li*)?
> The Master did not talk about weird things, physical exploits, disorders, and spirits.
> Confucius said: "When nature exceeds art you have the rustic. When art exceeds nature you have the clerk. It is only when art and nature are harmoniously blended that you have the gentleman."

The Model of Ethical Government

As did so many of his purported Axis Age contemporaries such as the Buddha, Laozi, and the Greek pre-Socratic thinkers, Confucius lived during a time of great social and political turmoil. Not surprisingly, many of his ideas bear on ways to restore order and improve government and society. Unlike systems that seek to create a better society by improving its institutions, however, Confucian doctrine places great emphasis on personal transformation and responsibility. In this schema, good government begins with educated leaders and officials of strong ethical character, like Confucius's frequent models, the Zhou kings Wen and Wu and the Duke of Zhou. In this sense, those who would rule should be the *junzi*. As in the examples above, the virtues embodied in the superior man are a humane temperament, courtesy, kindness, and diligence. Confucian literature is filled with descriptions of the attributes of the superior man: "he loves learning and hates sloth"; "he is broadminded and not partisan, he makes demands on himself rather than on others"; "he seeks to help people succeed in what is good but does not help them in what is evil." Since the goal of society is to create a moral order among human beings to hold the cosmos in balance—to be the "unwobbling pivot" around which heaven and earth revolve—rulers who embody these attributes would set the correct example for their subjects to follow.

One of the differences often cited between the Western political tradition, particularly in the post-Enlightenment era, and the Confucian tradition is that the former is said to be a government of law, rather than men, whereas the latter is a government of men rather than of law. Although there is some truth to this in a general sense, it is certainly not to say that Confucian China lacked for laws or a formal legal structure; far from it. But the Confucian emphasis on government and society as a kind of school of moral development created an approach that aspired to go *beyond* simply obeying laws.

Just as the *junzi* schooled himself in ethics and morals, a society run by *junzi* would spread these values to society by setting an example and encouraging proper behavior among the people. In the same way that the constant practice of scales on a musical instrument eventually makes playing them correctly second nature, the constant observance of *li*—correct ritual embodying proper behavior, sometimes rendered as "rules of decorum"—would routinize appropriate behavior among ordinary people. Not everyone would necessarily develop the high moral standards of the *junzi* but, at the least, the majority of people would almost involuntarily develop a sense of right and wrong and thus acquire a stake in the social order. A society organized along these lines would, in theory, largely police itself; and in fact, Confucian China did have a relatively small number of officials in proportion to the size of its population. The *Analects* sums this up succinctly: "Lead the people by laws and regulate them by penalties, and they will obey the laws to avoid being punished, but have no sense of shame. Lead them by rules of decorum (*li*) and they will develop a sense of shame (i.e., a collective sense of proper behavior), and moreover, will become good."

By the time Confucius died, traditionally said to be in 479 BCE, he had attracted a loyal following of adherents to his teachings. Two later students of Confucian doctrine—Mencius and Xunzi—continued to spread the teachings of the Master, with their own distinctive contributions. Both men, however, ended up moving in markedly different directions. In the long run it would be Mencius who would be seen as the inheritor of the "authentic" Confucian tradition. Xunzi's chief disciples, Han Fei and Li Si, however, would become the architects of China's unification under the short-lived and draconian philosophy of Legalism.

Mencius and the Goodness of Human Nature

By Mencius's time, the intensity of the competition and continual warfare among the Zhou states had spawned most of the Hundred Schools of Thought as thinkers questioned fundamental assumptions about private and social good. Not surprisingly, given the chaotic times, their answers varied from the radical individualism of Yang Zhu (ca. 440–360 BCE) to the arguments for universal love and altruism of

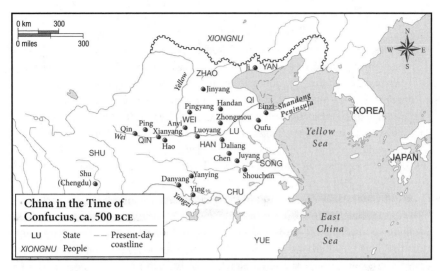

MAP 1.5
China in the Time of Confucius, ca. 500 BCE

Mo Di (ca. 470–391 BCE). Some, like Sun Zi (fl. Fifth century BCE), turned to what they considered remorselessly practical matters such as examining the nature of armed struggle in his famous *Art of War*.

For Mencius (*Mengzi*, or "Master Meng") (385?–312? BCE), people were fundamentally oriented toward ethical behavior, but must continually work to understand and refine their natural inclinations to avoid being led astray by negative influences. To illustrate this, he used the example of water, the nature of which is to flow downhill, as a metaphor for human nature. It is possible, of course, to force water out of this natural tendency, said Mencius, but once such artificial means are removed, it reverts to its original course. Hence, the way to proper behavior is to cultivate the Confucian virtues as a hedge against temptations toward "unnatural" behavior.

Mencius traveled throughout China spreading Confucian ideals, especially as a basis for government practice. The *Mengzi*, or Book of Mencius, is written in more of a narrative form than the *Analects* and fleshed out by stories, parables, and debates with advocates of other schools, particularly those of Yang and Mo. Since China's Warring States period was approaching its peak during his time, some of the *Mengzi*'s most powerfully argued sections deal with the obligations of rulers to their subjects—starting with the famous opening dialogue between Mencius and King Hui of Liang:

> [King Hui:] "Venerable Sir, since you have not considered a thousand *li*
> too far to come, may I presume you bring something that may profit
> my kingdom?
> [Mencius:] "Why must Your Majesty use that word 'profit?' I bring only
> humanity [*ren*]
> And righteousness [*yi*]!"

He went on to say:

> A king . . . is he who gives expression to his humanity through virtuous conduct. To be a true king, one does not have to have a large estate. . . . When men are subdued by force, it is not that they submit from their hearts but only that their strength is unavailing. When men are won by virtue, then their hearts are gladdened and their submission is sincere, as the seventy disciples were won by the Master, Confucius. . . . States have been won by men without humanity, but the world, never.
>
> —DeBary, ed. *Sources*. 20–33 passim. and 89, 93

As the center of both power and moral authority, the ruler had a primary duty to maintain the "people's livelihood" (*min sheng*) and uphold the social order. Mencius revived the old well-field system as a model of just land tenure to support this idea. A ruler who abused or neglected his subjects, however, upset not only the social order but also the cosmic order. In such a case, the people had not only the right but also the obligation to invoke the Mandate of Heaven and depose him. For many, however, Mencius's calls for leadership based on humanity and benevolence were out of step with the turbulent times. As we will see in the next chapter, it will be the teachings of another Confucian scholar, Xunzi, that set the basis for ancient China's most radical approach to political and social reform.

The Natural as Transcendent: Laozi and Daoism

Although most Chinese philosophical schools accepted the concept of the *dao* as the governing principle of the universe, they varied as to the best means of achieving harmony with it. For Confucians, study and self-cultivation to the point of intuitive understanding put the individual in tune with the *dao*. For followers of the Daoist tradition attributed to Laozi (Lao Tzu), the Confucian path *prevented* genuine understanding of and harmony with the *dao*.

Laozi, to whom the founding of Daoism is usually attributed, is an even more obscure figure than Confucius. In fact, many scholars believe him to be a mythical being. Chinese tradition cites his birth date as 604 BCE and his name as Li Er. The honorific title "Laozi" is translated as either "the Old Master" or "the Old Child." The translation Old Child captures something of the Daoist belief that only a return to childlike simplicity will lead to union with the *dao*. Daoists rejected the Confucian emphasis on personal responsibility and ethical social behavior because that emphasis implied following a specific course of good behavior. Because, according to the Daoists, the "way" encompasses the *entire* universe—including all opposites and paradoxes in the world—no single path of action would lead an individual to union with the *dao*. To choose the good as the Confucians do is therefore to follow only a limited part of the universal *dao*. Instead, the Daoists taught that only through a life of quiet self-reflection and contemplation of opposites and paradoxes might an individual come to know the *dao*. As did

[handwritten margin note: modern democratic ideal?]

Mencius later on, the Daoists used water to illustrate how the "weak" will overcome the "strong": water flows around rocks in a stream but eventually erodes them down to nothing. A classic tale that expresses the paradoxical aspect of Daoist thought is the story of the philosopher Zhuang Zhou (Zhuangzi), who awoke from a dream unsure of whether he had dreamed he was a butterfly or whether he was a butterfly dreaming he was Zhuang Zhou.

Laozi Delivering the *Daodejing*. Laozi as a painting subject, often depicted as an immortal among other immortals, was a favorite of many artists. In this ink on paper, done by a Ming era (1368–1644) artist, he is shown delivering the most famous Daoist work, often attributed to him.

Daoist political theory held that the best government is one that governs least. Here, the key idea is one from the most famous Daoist work, the *Daode Jing* (*The Classic of the Way and Its Virtue*): "By non-action there is nothing that is not done" (*Wuwei er wu buwei*). This is not to say that the ruler literally does nothing; rather, his role is to create the conditions that *naturally* lead to a society in which everyone spontaneously acts in accordance with the *dao*. The ruler should not push specific policies but should let all things take their natural courses. This natural course would lead to union with the *dao* and restore equilibrium in the world. For Daoists, the ruler is thus like the field that provides the essential conditions for flowers and plants to grow according to their own natures.

Both Daoism and Confucianism advocated self-reflection and a striving toward personal growth as means toward good government. However, neither of these philosophical schools could restore order during the Warring States period. Only through the harsh policies of Legalism did political and social order return to China.

CONCLUSION

The period from the first Neolithic settlements in the Yellow River valley through the Warring States period witnessed the beginning of many of the foundations of the cultures of China and, through interaction with Chinese influences, East and Southeast Asia. Like the other agrarian–urban cores in Mesopotamia, along the Nile, and in the Indus valley, the society that emerged in northern China was very much a product of its major river system. As early as 8000 BCE, the Yellow River basin saw the rise of self-sufficient agricultural villages, marking the transition from forager to agrarian society. It was the early states that developed here that came to dominate the Chinese historical record. With the rise of the Erlitou culture—perhaps the mythical Xia dynasty—late in the third millennium BCE, the first evidence of Chinese cities and the first people, places, and events traceable through later literary sources all make their appearance.

The Shang conquest of the Xia, traditionally held to be in 1766 BCE, marks the first flowering of China's "bronze age." The centering of political, military, and religious authority in one ruler; the development of a unique and versatile form of writing; the growth of cities; and the widespread use of bronze under the Shang in many ways run parallel to developments in the other early centers of civilization. In their casting techniques and design motifs of bronze ritual vessels and their system of writing, however, Shang contributions were original and long lasting.

The theme of moral renewal and the Mandate of Heaven came with the rise of the Zhou after 1122 BCE and was perhaps made retroactive by them as well. Nearly all of China from the Yangzi River basin north was incorporated into a decentralized governmental system centered on the Zhou court at Xi'an. But the growing power of the largest Zhou territories eventually eclipsed that of the court, and this began a prolonged era of struggle between the states. The increased wealth and power of rulers, aided by the drive of new social classes such as merchants and the *shi* to share in it, contributed to the breakdown of older feudal social patterns during the Spring and Autumn period from 722 to 481 BCE. Continual warfare stimulated both a drive for political consolidation and a questioning of the foundations of society. As the late Zhou dynasty dissolved into the chaos of late Spring and Autumn and Warring States periods (722–221 BCE, collectively), Chinese intellectuals sought practical ways to restore political and social order. The quest for unity and harmony led to the development of three major indigenous schools of philosophy—Confucianism, Daoism, and Legalism—and a host of minor ones. The period was so fertile in the development of Chinese thought that it is sometimes referred to as the time of the One Hundred Schools of Thought.

With the ideas of Confucius, a radical direction in conceiving the nature and aims of society took place. His ideas, adopted by a Chinese imperial system that would last more than 2,000 years, profoundly affected hundreds of millions of people inside and outside of China in the centuries to come. In the immediate future, however, it would be Legalism that would create an empire.

FURTHER READING

Chang, Kwang-chih. *The Archaeology of Ancient China*, 4th ed. New Haven, CT: Yale University Press, 1986. Sophisticated treatment of recent archaeology of Shang China. Prime exponent of the view of overlapping periods and territories for the Sandai period. Erudite, yet accessible for experienced students.

Ebrey, Patricia Buckley, ed. *Chinese Civilization: A Sourcebook*, 2nd ed. New York: Free Press, 1993. Wonderful supplement to the preceding volume. Some different classical sources and considerable material on women and social history. Time frame of this work extends to the modern era.

Keightly, David N., ed. *The Origins of Chinese Civilization*. Berkeley: University of California Press, 1983. Symposium volume on a variety of Sandai topics by leading scholars. Some exposure to early Chinese history and archaeology is necessary to best appreciate these essays.

Liu, Xiang. *Exemplary Women of Early China: The Lienu zhuan of Liu Xiang*. Edited and translated by Anne Behnke Kinney. New York: Columbia University Press, 2014. Translation and treatment of one of the only accounts of the biographies of women of the Three Dynasties. Liu Xiang (77–6 BCE) writing during the Han period covers the lives of 120 Zhou women, mostly wives and concubines of noted rulers.

Lowe, Michael, and Edward L. Shaughnessy, eds. *The Cambridge History of Ancient China. From the Origins of Civilization to 221 B.C.* Cambridge, U.K.: Cambridge University Press, 1999. The opening volume of the Cambridge History of China series, this is the most complete multiessay volume on all aspects of recent Chinese ancient historical and archaeological work. The place to start for the serious student contemplating in-depth research.

Raphals, Lisa. *Sharing the Light. Representations of Women and Virtue in Early China*. Albany, NY: SUNY Press, 1998. Reexamines the stereotypes of ancient Chinese women as oppressed by patriarchal society and argues the women had considerable influence and agency, particularly in the era before the Han.

Schirokauer, Conrad. *A Brief History of Chinese Civilization*. New York: Harcourt, Brace, Jovanovich, 1991. Readable one-volume text on Chinese history up to the present. More thorough treatment of Sandai period than is generally the case with other one-volume texts.

Thorp, Robert L. *China in the Early Bronze Age: Shang Civilization*. Philadelphia: University of Pennsylvania Press, 2006. Comprehensive yet accessible survey of recent archaeological work on the period 2070–1046 BCE, including traditional Xia and Shang periods under the heading of China's bronze age.

Wang, Aihe. *Cosmology and Political Culture in Early China*. Cambridge, U.K.: Cambridge University Press, 2000. Part of the Cambridge Studies in Chinese History, Literature, and Institutions series. Wang argues that control of *cosmology*—how the world and universe operate—was a vital key to the wielding of power among the Shang and Zhou rulers. Recommended for serious students.

Watson, Burton, trans. *The Tso Chuan. Selections from China's Oldest Narrative History*. New York: Columbia University Press, 1989. Elegant translation by one of the most prolific of scholars working today. Excellent introduction to Zhou period and politics. Appropriate for beginning students, although more useful for those with some prior introduction to the period.

Yao Xinzhong. *An Introduction to Confucianism*. Cambridge, U.K.: Cambridge University Press, 2000. Sound, scholarly overview of the Confucian tradition as it has developed through the centuries in imperial China and in its impact today.

CHAPTER 2

IMPERIAL CHINA
BEFORE THE QING,
221 BCE–1644 CE

We were happy together in those years,
Our lives like incense filling sleeves.
By the fire we made tea.
We traveled on beautiful horses, by flowing streams, in light carriages,
Undaunted by sudden storms,
So long as we could share a cup of warm wine and sheets of fine paper.
Now embracing each other is impossible.
Can there be times like those ever again?

—(From Li Qingzhao, "A Reminiscence," in her
ci poetry collection, *Shuyu ci ("Jade Rising ci")*

For the writer and poet Li Qingzhao (1081–1151; some sources say 1084–1155), the times had indeed been extraordinary. The poem she had just composed mourned her recently deceased husband, the scholar and official Zhao Mingcheng (1081–1129), and the end of their life together in China during the Song dynasty. The marriage of Li and Zhou seemed to defy convention at almost every turn. At a time when marriage in China—as in most agrarian societies—was driven by patriarchal standards in which women were unequal to men and where most of their efforts were expected to be aimed at producing sons, theirs was a passionate, childless, and intellectually engaging union between two accomplished literary figures. Moreover, it was Li's work that was best known and received the most acclaim among her contemporaries and whose intellectual legacy was celebrated long after her death. Even today, she is recognized as China's greatest woman poet.

Although the relationship between Li and Zhao was unusual for their time and place, many of the aspects of their union that strike us as modern—even contemporary—reflect the society in which they lived. The Song dynasty (960–1279) has often been designated as the beginning of China's early modern era. Many of what historians consider the essential ingredients of modern society were already present during this period. Song China had the world's largest cities,

[handwritten margin note: Song Ching – big advances]

a burgeoning economy, and an unsurpassed diversity of consumer goods and had made significant advances in technology and industry. This remarkable period also boasted the world's highest literacy rate—as reflected in the careers of Li and Zhao—the result of mass education and the development and perfection of the printing process. All of these advances were supported by the world's largest and most productive agrarian state.

As we saw in the previous chapter, the Zhou dynasty fragmented into a number of small states continually battling one another for advantage. During the mass chaos of the Warring States period (variously given as 475, 453 or 403–221 BCE), the goal for both rulers and scholars of the new *shi* class had been to construct a political system that would reunite the region, although the mode of what constituted proper rule varied widely across the writings of the Hundred Schools of Thought. The political system that eventually prevailed in China blended the ideology of three philosophical schools—Confucianism, Daoism, and Legalism—with Confucianism ultimately exercising dominant influence. From the cultural core of a unified China, the Chinese imperial system, commercial contacts, and the ideologies of the three philosophical schools—with the later addition of Buddhism—spread to the periphery: Korea, Vietnam, Japan, and beyond. The pattern of each dynasty seeking to justify its seizure of the Mandate of Heaven continued as well.

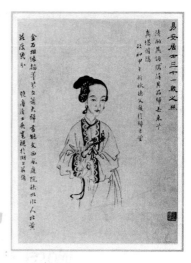

Li Qingzhao. Li Qingzhao (1084–1151) was China's most famous woman poet, a renowned writer, and admired calligrapher. Many of her works mourn the loss of her husband, the official Zhao Mingcheng, with whom she shared a passionate interest in art and literary pursuits. According to some accounts she later remarried a man named Zhang Ruzhou, but his ill treatment of her pushed her to divorce him in a few months—both considered transgressive acts for Chinese women. In this portrait, her pseudonym Yi'an Jushi, is used and the large character title reads "A picture of Yi'an Jushi [age] 31 years."

QIN LEGALISM AND THE ORIGINS OF EMPIRE

As we saw previously, the continuum of philosophical and political speculation generated by the Hundred Schools thinkers marked what was unquestionably China's greatest outpouring of original thought. The systems ran the gamut from the passive approach of the Daoists to the hard-eyed *realpolitik* and practical military advice of Sunzi and from the universal love of the Mohists through the family-centered loyalties of the various Confucian schools to the radical individualism of Yang Zhu. In the end, the dominant ideology for China's 2,000 years of empire would be a synthesis with a reinterpreted Confucianism at its core and with elements of Daoism and, later, Buddhist cosmology blended in as well. But the immediate future would briefly belong to the extreme utilitarian vision of *fajia*, or **Legalism**. Moreover, long after the philosophy of the Legalists had been repudiated, its vision of centralized imperial government and the structures of that first government's organization remained vital.

A Darkening View of Human Nature

As the struggles of the Warring States period settled into their final phase, the views of Mencian Confucianism, with its emphasis on the essential goodness of people, seemed less and less appealing to many rulers confronted with the prospect of being conquered and struggling to survive. The many collateral branches of the Confucian philosophical tree now began to produce ideas that seemed radically at odds with those of the earlier sages, although formally adhering to their tenets.

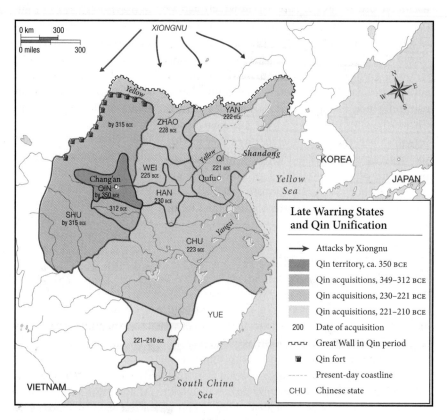

MAP 2.1
Late Warring States and Qin Unification

The most influential of these was Xunzi (ca.310–219? BCE). He believed that individuals were self-involved creatures whose interest in societal well-being was tenuous at best. People have the capacity to understand what is good, he asserted, but are able to regulate themselves only through immense and constant effort. Moreover, government must take an active role: "People must await ordering by the sage kings and transformation through ritual and rightness, and only then do they attain order and accord with goodness" (DeBary and Bloom, 1999, p. 182). Thus, by the third century BCE, Confucian thinkers had come to disagree about such basic ideas as the authentic nature of human beings. Although it would be the more moderate views of Confucius and Mencius that ultimately became the predominant ideals of imperial China, it would be Xunzi's vision that informed the foundations of the Legalist school founded by his two students, Han Fei (d. 233 BCE) and Li Si (d. 208 BCE). It was the Legalists who would provide the power and ideology to conquer China's first empire.

Although the immediate development of Legalism as incorporated by the state of Qin came from Han Fei and Li Si, its roots may perhaps be traced back much further. Here the pre-Confucian ideas of Guan Zhong in the seventh-century BCE state of Qi are often cited, although the work attributed to him, the *Guanzi*, is undoubtedly of more recent vintage. More directly connected to the Legalist school was the *Shangjun shu* (*The Book of Lord Shang*), detailing the ideas of Gongsun Yang (Shang Yang, d. 338 BCE), the architect of the state of Qin's rise to prominence during the late fourth century BCE. In the *Book of Lord Shang* one sees most of the elements that would be refined and completed during the creation of China's first empire: strict impartial law; severe punishments for small infractions as inducements to avoid greater crimes; an emphasis on only "practical" subjects in education; and the sanctioning of war as an instrument of state policy. Indeed, the *Shangjun shu* states flatly that "the means whereby a country is made prosperous are agriculture and war" (ibid., p. 194).

The chief architects of Legalism in its mature phase were Han Fei and Li Si. Both accepted their teacher Xunzi's view of human beings as inclined toward evil: Han Fei himself may have met his end through the aegis of Li Si when Li was the pre-imperial state of Qin's prime minister. In the system they created, all old *fengjian* privileges of rank were leveled in favor of uniform laws and practices based on the will of the ruler in a highly centralized state. Order would prevail in the state only through the institution of strict, detailed, and explicit laws diligently and impartially enforced. In keeping with the idea that obedience on small matters led to compliance on larger ones, they imposed harsh punishments—forced labor, mutilation, and in some cases death—for even the tiniest infractions.

It followed that all subjects be required to serve the state through productive activities. As the *Book of Lord Shang* had insisted, agriculture and military service were central to the well-being of the state. Individuals were encouraged to take up either or both of these as their livelihood; any other occupation was discouraged or prohibited, and work was compulsory for all. To suppress dissent and encourage approved thinking, only government-approved history and literature were tolerated. In short, says Han Fei, the government must be like a mother lancing a boil on her infant: although the baby screams from the immediate pain, he or she is better for it in the end. Thus the fully developed Qin state anticipated many of the features of the totalitarian regimes of the twentieth century. The price exacted during its short duration was considered by many contemporaries and nearly all succeeding generations of Chinese commentators to be far too high. Yet its ruthless concentration of power and resources finally made possible the forced march to empire that no preceding regime had been able to effect.

The Qin Dynasty, 221 to 206 BCE

Qin's position as a small, poor, far western frontier state made it in many ways deceptively unlikely as a candidate for empire. Yet, as has sometimes been the case in other areas in world history, territories on the periphery can grow in the shadows, unnoticed by potential rivals, until they are powerful enough to strike. In the case of Qin, its position and relative poverty provided what at the time were unrecognized advantages over its opponents to the east. As a frontier society, encouraged by its emphasis on agriculture, it adopted a policy not unlike that of the American Homestead Act of the 1860s: promising land to peasant cultivators as the state seized territory from nomadic peoples to the west. Qin's relative isolation also kept it out of many of the internecine fights that plagued the interior Zhou dependencies and eroded their resources. At the same time, policing its expanding territories encouraged military preparedness. By 350 BCE, Qin rulers began reorganizing the state along the lines envisioned in Lord Shang's treatise. In less than a century they had eliminated the rump state of Zhou itself in 256 BCE and began the final subjugation of the remaining Northern Chinese states.

With its strong economy, expert military, and the centralizing policies espoused by Han Fei and Li Si, Qin took advantage of the war-weary northern Chinese states and conquered them with stunning swiftness. They then drove south and eliminated the opposition of the many tribal peoples below the state of Yue. From there they drove into *yuenan* (south of Yue)—the northern part of modern Vietnam—thus beginning a long and often bitterly contested relationship with Southeast Asia. China would attempt to rule the area with limited success for more than a thousand years and claim it as a protectorate until ousted by the French in 1885. In the north and west, Qin armies fought a series of campaigns to drive nomadic peoples from newly established borders and secure the trade routes into Central Asia. The most prominent of these groups was the *Xiongnu*—a people whose ethnicity is uncertain but whom DNA testing and linguistic evidence has linked to both the Mongols and the Siberian Yakuts, and who some scholars believe are the ancestors of the Huns.

The First Emperor

In 221 BCE,

Qin shi; Huangdi - 1st Emp. of Qin

> came the First Emperor who, carrying on the glorious spirit of his six predecessors, cracked his long whip and drove the universe before him, swallowed up the Eastern and Western Zhou, and overthrew the feudal lords. He ascended the throne of honor and ruled the six directions, scourging the world with his lash, and his might shook the four seas. (Sima Qian, *Records of the Grand Historian: Qin*, Burton Watson, trans. [New York: Columbia University Press, 1993, p. 79])

So wrote the Confucian scholar, Jia Yi (201–169 BCE), quoted by the famous Han historian Sima Qian, of the ascension of the Qin king Cheng (r. 246–209 BCE), who now proclaimed himself *Qin Shi Huangdi*, the First Emperor of the Qin. With Li Si as his chief minister, he instituted the Legalist system throughout the newly won empire. With virtually unlimited resources available to this centralizing state and the ruthless drive of the First Emperor to expand and fortify it, the new regime began a series of projects during the next dozen years that are still astonishing today in their scope and ambition. The Chinese writing system was standardized, as were all weights, measures, and coinage. The people were organized in a standard way as well. Under Li Si an initial version of the famous **baojia** system (see later) of mutual responsibility was set up. Hundreds of thousands of laborers worked on roads, canals, and a multitude of irrigation and water-conservancy projects. As a safeguard against attacks by the Xiongnu and other nomadic peoples ranging across the Mongolian plains, tens of thousands of forced laborers were conscripted to cobble together the numerous defensive walls of the old Zhou states along the new empire's northern tier. Stretching more than 1,400 miles, this massive project under the direction of Meng Tian (d. 210 BCE), would become the first iteration of the Great Wall of China.

goals of Qin

Beginning a pattern that was to become almost routine under subsequent dynasties, the First Emperor "in the south seized the land and the lords of the hundred tribes of Yue and of it Guilin and Xiang provinces" (ibid.). Indeed, he kept going farther south into the northern part of modern Vietnam and established a Chinese presence there that would last off and on for more than a thousand years. As late as the 1970s, China would invoke historical precedent and invade northern Vietnam to punish it for its invasion of Khmer Rouge–controlled Cambodia (Kampuchea).

What most people remember the First Emperor for, however, is the massive tomb complex he ordered built for himself, which, according to the *Records of the Grand Historian*, would signify "a rule that would be enjoyed by his sons and grandsons for 10,000 generations" (ibid.). Long thought to be a legend, the tomb was discovered in 1974 by a peasant digging a well outside the modern city of Xi'an. Excavation of the First Emperor's tomb unearthed an army of thousands

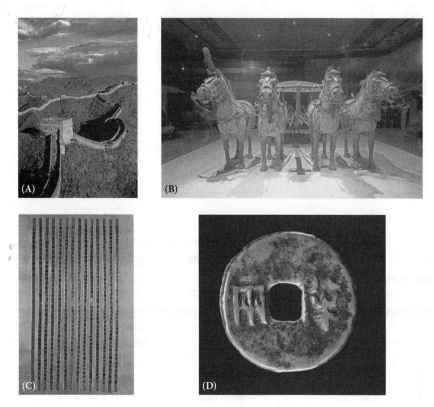

The Qin. Examples of the immense ambition of the First Emperor, and his urge to standardize. **(A)** The Great Wall at Jinshanling pass, northeast of Beijing. Though these sections of the wall were rebuilt in the early fifteenth century CE, this prospect shows some of the detail and intricacy of its fortification and also gives an idea of the immensity of the structure. **(B)** Many of the most important Qin artifacts have been recovered from the First Emperor's tomb complex at Xi'an. Here in the site's Qin Shihuangdi Museum is pictured the Emperor's number 2 bronze chariot in one-half scale pulled by four-horse team. **(C)** The urge to standardization extended to writing and coinage, among other items. Here bamboo slips, used as writing media before the advent of paper, are inked with official script handwriting from Qin dynasty tomb found at Shuihudi in Yunmeng County of Hubei province. **(D)** Banliang coin, Chinese, 3rd century BC. The Chinese inscription reads 'banliang', with 'ban' to the right of the hole and 'liang' to the left. Banliang means 'half-ounce.' In 221 BCE, the First Emperor announced that banliang coins would be the new standard throughout the empire. This type of coin, including lower denominations later on made of copper, would be standard throughout the history of imperial China. The shape may be symbolic; it was believed that the earth was square and heaven was round. Some have argued that the shape could be an aid to mass production: the coins needed to be filed down after casting and their square holes allowed a stack of these coins to be slid onto a square-shaped rod, and all filed down at the same time.

of life-size terracotta warriors with removable heads and individualized features marching in timeless close-order drill to protect Qin Shihuangdi after his death. The dig, now the site of a large park and museum, has become China's most popular tourist destination after the Great Wall.

Terracotta Warriors. One of the most important archeological finds of the 20th century was the tomb of the First Emperor on the outskirts of modern Xi'an in 1974. Over the last four decades, thousands of life-sized terracotta warrior guardians of the tomb complex have been unearthed, as well as bronze model chariots (see previous illustrations) and other artifacts. Theories abound as to the reasons behind the individualized faces on the removable heads: One holds that they were taken from real soldiers; another is that they were symbolic of the emperor's universal rule over China's many peoples. The immense museum complex now at the site is one of China's most popular tourist attractions.

From his palace in Xianyang, now the modern city of Xi'an, which, under various names, was destined to be the capital city of no less than 13 Chinese dynasties, the First Emperor tightened his control over anyone who might potentially challenge his rule. Scholars who objected to government policies were buried alive. Any literature not officially sanctioned by the government was destroyed. In 213 BCE, Minister of State Li Si suggested that "all books in the imperial archives, save the memoirs of Qin, be burned." Moreover, "anyone referring to the past to criticize the present should, together with all members of his family, be put to death" (DeBary, Bloom, 1999, p. 210). Given that the accounts of the First Emperor's reign are drawn from the writings of Han dynasty historians, whose condemnations of the Qin excesses were meant in part to justify their own dynasty's ascension, they should not be accepted uncritically. Nonetheless, although it is difficult to assess the extent to which the book burnings actually took place, it is believed that a great many works that existed before the Qin were put to the torch.

After a reign of a dozen years as emperor, Shi Huangdi died. If the *Records of the Grand Historian* may be believed, for many, if not most of his subjects, the First Emperor's death must have been a relief. His strict laws, severe punishments, and huge construction projects had angered and exhausted the people. Soon after Qin Shihuangdi's death, the empire erupted in rebellion. Ironically, the government's severe laws and punishments now worked against it as officials attempted to conceal the revolt's extent for fear of torture and execution. At the same time, Minister Li Si provoked additional discontent by conspiring to keep the First Emperor's death a secret to rule as regent for the monarch's son. He was captured attempting to flee the rebellion and executed in 208 BCE. In an attempt to make the punishment fit the crime, "Li Si was sentenced to undergo the five penalties [tattooing of the face, amputation of the ears, nose, fingers and feet, flogging, and exposure of his severed head] and to be cut in two at the waist in the market place of Xianyang" (Sima Qian, *Records of the Grand Historian*, p. 204). After a brief civil war and an attempt to revive a version of the old Zhou system of decentralized government, a general named Liu Bang put an end to the fighting and restored order to the region. He proclaimed himself emperor in 202 BCE and called his new dynasty the Han.

THE HAN DYNASTY, 202 BCE TO 220 CE

It is often said that the Qin forced the structure of empire on China, whereas the Han continued it behind a more benign ideology. The **Han Synthesis**, as it is sometimes called, retained the centralized political system of Qin ministries and *commanderies*—districts under military command—but combined these with more moderate Confucian ideals of government as a moral agent. Although there were some key differences in this new model of government-sponsored Confucianism from some of the ideas of Confucius and Mencius, the basic model of rule endured with some interruptions and modifications for more than 2,000 years and still retains considerable cultural power in East Asia today.

One consequence of Qin social leveling was to break the power of the old aristocratic families. In this sense, Liu Bang, who had taken the reign name Gaozu (r. 202–195 BCE), represented a new kind of ruler. He had been a peasant and so had little stake or interest in bringing back the old feudal system of the Zhou. Having received from the Qin an administrative structure more or less intact, he retained it for ease of pacification and control. Within that structure, however, he enacted a number of reforms that contribute to our understanding of this system as a synthesis: token distributions of land were made to some members of the upper ranks; taxes and labor obligations were widely reduced and the most severe punishments under the Qin were rescinded.

As the Han empire expanded—reaching a population recorded in 2 CE comparable with that of Rome at the time of just under 60 million—so did its

MAP 2.2
The Han Empire

bureaucracy. Within little more than a century of the Han ascension, the number of government officials had swollen to 130,000—a number comparable to that of several subsequent and much more populous dynasties. Setting a pattern for the administration throughout much of the history of imperial China, officials were divided into graded ranks ranging from the heads of imperial ministries to district magistrates. Below these officials were clan leaders and village headmen. Landowners were responsible for collecting taxes for themselves and their tenants, whereas the lower officials recorded the rates and amounts, kept track of the labor obligations of the district, and mobilized the people during emergencies.

The Rise of Confucian Education

The first Han rulers tended to be fairly eclectic in their ideological preferences. Their approach to government combined the more lenient aspects of Legalism with those of other surviving schools. Of these, however, Confucianism, with

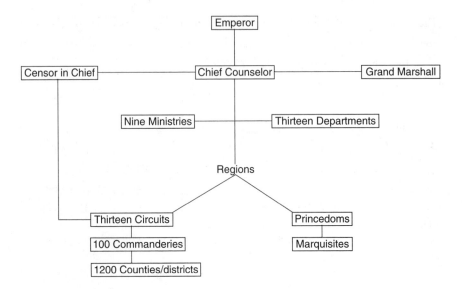

Diagram of Han Governmental Structure.

its emphasis on the ethical correctness of officials, caring for the people, filial piety, and the study of history, tended to make it a good fit for Han administrators. By the second century CE, the steadily growing popularity of Confucian academies led to their subsidization by the state, in effect placing all official education in their hands. Ultimately, knowledge of the Confucian canon became the centerpiece of entrance into state service. Although other branches of knowledge, sometimes including practical elements of administration, were occasionally added to the entrance exams, knowledge of the Confucian classics would remain the primary standard of admission until the opening years of the twentieth century.

Although Confucianism served as the foundation for the Han educational curriculum, Confucian doctrine had changed in some significant ways from the early teachings of Confucius and his disciples. During the Warring States period and the era of Qin rule, much Confucian thought—along with that of other philosophical schools—had been altered to suit the times, and a great many texts had also been lost along the way. Thus, the Confucianism that finally received state approval included a number of elements reflecting the new realities of Han rule.

This so-called Han Synthesis of Confucian philosophy is evident in the era's chief treatise on government, the *Huainanzi*. In this document, a number of Confucian ideals—humane, righteous, filial behavior by the powerful—are linked with Daoist ideas of the ruler as divorced from day-to-day administration and Legalist notions of centralization and the role of officials. As we saw earlier, the structure of the cosmos with the ruler as intermediary holding Heaven, Humankind, and Earth in balance was retained and given new emphasis.

a little bit of everything in every aspect

The predynastic ideal of passing rulership on to the country's most able men was again set aside: for stability and continuity's sake, it was felt that a dynasty had to be hereditary. The ideas of Heaven's Mandate and the dynastic cycle, however, were retained and strengthened. As we will see below, it became the central principle around which the patterns of Chinese historiography would be set.

Han Expansion

During their brief interval the Qin had established a pattern that would be repeated through many later dynasties: like the idealized interpretation of the dynastic cycle favored by Chinese historians, the initial part of their reign was marked by expansion and consolidation. This was true of the Han as well, with a significant part of that expansion happening during the reign of the emperor Wudi, whose reign name means "Martial Emperor" (141–87 BCE). In addition to once again driving into the Korean Peninsula and south into Vietnam, the Han under Wudi moved deep into the interior of Asia.

As had the Qin, and like many of his successors, Wudi faced the difficulty of defending the empire's long, sparsely populated northern and western boundaries from diverse groups of nomadic peoples, especially the Xiongnu. Hoping that a strong Chinese presence would discourage potential invasion, he encouraged the emigration of settlers to the region—a practice many of his successors would follow down to the present. He also extended and fortified the Great Wall. Because the Han had also expanded into the narrow corridor in the west adjacent to the Central Asian trade routes marking the developing Silk Road, Wudi and his successors mounted repeated expeditions into the area, built numerous guardhouses, and stationed garrisons along the way. In 89 CE after a lengthy conflict, the Han finally succeeded in destroying the Xiongnu state.

As did many of his successors, Wudi employed strategies that later became famous as the "loose rein" and "using barbarians to check barbarians": he tried diplomatic efforts, offering the Xiongu food and other necessary supplies, but when those efforts failed, he mounted military campaigns against them. He also doled out favors to some groups as a way to cement

Han Guardhouse. Han expansion into Central Asia and expanded trade along the routes of the Silk Road required garrisons and fortifications at key points beyond the Great Wall to protect travelers and settlers from attacks by nomadic peoples like the Xiongnu. Typical of such outposts was that depicted by the ceramic model illustrated here. The upper stories have protected balconies for archers and spearmen, while the lowest story provides a place for domestic animals like the ducks depicted here. Note the crossbowman barely discernable in the left rear of the upper story.

their loyalties to use them to guard the frontiers against other, less pliable groups. In this, they were not unlike the Romans in their policy of employing as *foederati,* some Germanic tribes to guard the frontier against others. Like the Romans as well, the Han adopted the practice of culturally assimilating, or "sinicizing," nomadic peoples. Along with the imposition of Han rule came the Chinese writing system and the infusion of Confucian ideology and practices.

The Wang Mang Interregnum and the Han Decline

As imperial China's longest dynasty, the Han era has traditionally been divided into the Former or Western Han (202 BCE–8 CE) and the Later or Eastern Han (24 CE–220). During a brief interval between 8 and 24 CE, the dynasty was temporarily interrupted when a relative of the royal family, Wang Mang (45 BCE–23 CE) seized power. According to the *Hou Hanshu* (*The History of the Later Han*), Wang attempted to nationalize the land and redistribute it according to the old well-field system to reduce the abuses that had crept into land tenure practices as well as the growing gap between rich landowners and peasants. This precipitated a rebellion by a secret society based in Shandong called the Red Eyebrows. The rebels killed Wang Mang and sacked the capital of Chang'an. Although an imperial relative restored the dynasty, the capital was moved to a safer location in Luoyang, but the empire, now reduced in size and resources, never fully recovered.

For a time, however, the general prosperity of the regime continued to mask its weaknesses and Chinese historians would label the Later Han as one of China's four great "Restorations" (see Chapter 4). By the late second century CE, however, the restored dynasty was showing signs of strain. In a pattern that would be repeated a number of times in future dynasties, ambitious internal improvements ordered by Han emperors were increasingly carried out by *corvee* labor in a manner uncomfortably reminiscent of the Qin. Like Rome during its "crisis of the third century," the increased costs of defense, growing labor obligations for peasant cultivators, and the loss of arable land led to an accelerating decline. As if to underscore the rhythms of the dynastic cycle, internal battles within the imperial family, aggravated by the increasing regional power of Han generals and the rise of the Daoist Yellow Turbans after 184 CE, finally brought the Han dynasty to an end in 220 CE.

Despite a number of attempts at reunification over the next four centuries, it seemed that China had permanently fallen back into the disorder of the late Zhou period. Yet even as political chaos prevailed, a number of new standards in calligraphy, aesthetics, and literary style emerged. Perhaps it was the lack of central authority that allowed a number of outside influences to permeate China. For example, Buddhism, first mentioned in Han documents in 65 CE, grew to be a major force not only in China but also in East Asia. The spread of Buddhism brought China into a vastly enlarged and united cultural and economic sphere. Political reunification, however, would prove another matter entirely.

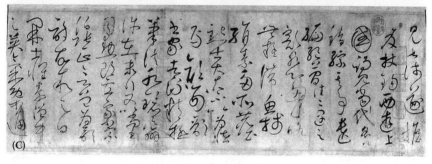

Samples of Excellence in Painting and Calligraphy. Painting, poetry and calligraphy are even now considered to be the highest forms of artistic expression in China. The early master of these arts was Wang Xizhi (303–361) whose work remained the great model for subsequent followers of the calligrapher's brush. In the examples here, all the artists flourished during the Tang Dynasty, considered one of China's greatest periods of artistic flowering. There are a number of recognized formal styles and substyles of calligraphy. **(A)** In the sample on the top left, is the most ancient form called "seal script," a variant of which is called "tadpole script" because of its shape. These characters are close to the forms found on the oldest bronze vessels, seals, and oracle bones. The sample here comes from Li Yangbing, a high-ranking Tang Dynasty government official, noted calligrapher, and relative of the famous Chinese poet Li Bai. Li Bai (701–762), has generally been regarded as one of the greatest poets in China's Tang period, which is often called China's 'golden age' of poetry. Around a thousand existing poems are attributed to him, but the authenticity of many of these is uncertain. Thirty-four of his poems are included in the popular anthology, 'Three Hundred Tang Poems'. **(B)** Top right, Li's calligraphy is shown in a semi-cursive form called "running hand." **(C)** In the sample below Li Bai's is an excerpt from the autobiography of the monk Huaisu (Huai Su) (737–799) who was famed for his wildly cursive style of calligraphy within the larger stylistic category of "grass hand." Huaisu would become so intent on spontaneous cursive self-expression that after a burst of creativity he sometimes could not read what he had written. His fondness for alcohol inspired the nickname of "drunk monk."

(Continued)

(D)

(D) Wang Wei (699–759), along with Li Bai and Dufu, was one of the Tang Dynasty's most famous poets, as well as a musician, painter, and statesman. It was said later that in his work there was a painting in every poem and a poem in every painting. Many of his poems are preserved, and twenty-nine were included in the highly influential 18th century anthology, 'Three Hundred Tang Poems'. Here is a portrait attributed to Wang of the scholar Fu Sheng (268–178 BCE).

FROM THE FALL OF THE HAN THROUGH THE SUI DYNASTY, 220–618 CE

The long period of turmoil and fragmentation between the end of the Han era and reunification under the Sui dynasty (589–618) is traditionally divided into the era of the Three Kingdoms (220–280), the overlapping Six Dynasties period (222–589), and the also overlapping period of the North and South dynasties (317–589).

Throughout this period the aim of reconstituting the empire was always present. Many of the factors that had undermined the Han, however—the growing power of landed elites, the increasing weakness of the bureaucracy, the chronic defense problems of the north and west—continued and even multiplied. Like the Western Roman Empire in the fifth and sixth centuries, the absence of effective centralized administration, the crumbling infrastructure, and the collapse of the once interdependent internal economy into self-sufficient regional units proved powerful deterrents to reunification, and warfare, famine, and banditry plagued the land.

As it had been with the Zhou and the Qin, it would be a people on the periphery of the Chinese world that would ultimately create the next dynasty and recreate the empire. In this case it was an eastern Mongolian people known as the Toba, part of a larger group the Chinese called *Xianbei*, who established the state of Northern Wei (386–585) along the old Northern Chinese heartland of the Yellow River basin. Here again was another instance of an historical circumstance that

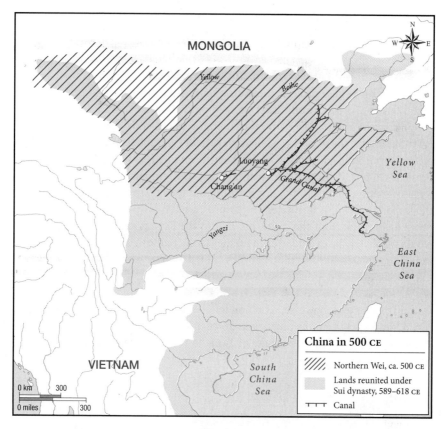

MAP 2.3
China in 500 CE

had already established itself as a pattern over time: the power of Chinese civilization to attract and ultimately assimilate newcomers. With varying degrees of success, this pattern would be invoked with regard to the Mongols of the Yuan dynasty (1279–1368), the Manchus of the Qing dynasty (1644–1912), and the Europeans and Americans who would come in the nineteenth century.

By the beginning of the sixth century, the descendants of the Toba and nomadic groups ranging across the borders of Northern Wei and neighboring states had formed a kind of ethnically hybrid society. They developed a policy of interacting and adapting to Chinese culture—taking Chinese names, marrying into the leading families, reviving old imperial rites, and taking on the perennial problem of land reform. In organizing a program of land redistribution to the peasants, they helped pave the way for the return of centralized administration, military service, and tax collection. In this respect, Northern Wei in particular provided a prototype for a renewed bid for empire. In 589 a general named Yang Jian succeeded in uniting most of the old Han territories and called the reunified dynasty the Sui.

The Sui Dynasty, 589–618 CE

Like the Qin and Han before them, the Sui pushed into Korea in their zeal to re-build the empire. Like the Qin as well, the forcefulness with which they pursued empire building prompted unrest among the people. Moreover, their use of forced labor for these projects, including huge palaces, roads, and perhaps most ambitious of all, the **Grand Canal**, created unrest as well.

Linking the Yangzi River with the Huanghe, the Grand Canal has been called, "without doubt, the grandest navigation system ever undertaken by a single sovereign in pre-modern history" (John Keay, *China: A History*, New York: Harper Press, 2008, p. 230). Actually several canals and accompanying natural water systems stretching for 1,550 miles, it is still in use today. Through the remainder of the imperial period it facilitated the shipment of large quantities of tax rice and other food crops from the south directly to the capital at Chang'an. The canal would ultimately be extended even further to the Beihe to service the later capital at Beijing. Over time, this mode of moving tribute and tax grain and provisioning the ballooning population of the capital would render both the waterway and the cities it served vulnerable to attack and siege.

For the moment, however, rebellion following the death of the second Sui emperor, Yangdi, brought the precocious 16-year-old Li Shimin to power. Li encouraged his father, Li Yuan, the Duke of Tang, to rebel and, with him, had the new

Grand Canal. One of the most extensive excavation and construction efforts of the pre-indusatrial world, the Grand Canal was begun under the Sui Dynasty, and refined and extended over the following centuries until it reached the Beihe so as to allow tribute grain and supplies to reach Beijing. In terms of the greater agricultural output of the south, it played a vital role in supplying all the northern capitals, especial Chang'an and Kaifeng. Here, ships and barges move down the Grand Canal near its early terminus at Hangzhou.

Sui emperor killed. Supporting his father's bid for the throne, he cofounded the Tang dynasty in 618. After a few years, he forced his father, who had taken the reign name of Gaozu, to abdicate and took power in his own right in 627 as the emperor Taizong.

CHINA'S COSMOPOLITAN AGE: THE TANG DYNASTY, 618–907

The position of Tang China, and especially its capital at Chang'an, made it in a sense a pivot in the fortunes of not only trade but also the circulation of ideas and beliefs around Eurasia. The lucrative Silk Road trade now grew richer and more diverse with the traffic of Buddhist travelers, pilgrims, and missionaries, as the Tang pushed deep into Central Asia. Indeed, the shape of their empire ultimately resembled a dumbbell, with a large Central Asian bulge at one end, a narrow strip of territory around the Silk Road, and the traditional territories of earlier Chinese states as the other bulge. By the end of the seventh century, they had expelled many of the major nomadic groups from the empire's western borderlands, pushing them west to Anatolia, Eastern Europe, and the Mediterranean. They invaded Korea yet again and opened diplomatic relations with Yamato Japan, which, through its 645 Taika (Great Reform), made itself over along the lines of the Tang: Japanese imperial institutions, Buddhism, Confucian bureaucracy, record keeping, and even architecture were faithfully copied from their Chinese counterparts. Even the new Japanese capitals of Nara and Heian-Kyo were faithful copies of the urban plan of Chang'an.

Enhanced Interaction

As noted in the previous chapter, scholars of China used to make a point of emphasizing its relative isolation from other Eurasian centers. Recent work by both China scholars and world historians, however, has considerably moderated this outlook. A sizable degree of interaction and connection had already taken place as far back as the second millennium BCE with the contributions of such Indo-European speakers as the Tocharians. In terms of imperial China, the Han extensively documented the activities of groups outside China, such as the Xiongnu, the Koreans, and the Yamato Japanese, as well as more shadowy peoples such as those of "Da Qin"—Rome.

Chang'an's position as a center of the Buddhist cultural sphere and the eastern terminus of the Silk Road and Tang China's enhanced maritime trade with India, Japan, Southeast Asia, and even Africa now led to China's first direct encounters with the major societies to the west. During the seventh century, Arab conquests in Southwest Asia brought China into contact with the rapidly expanding world of Islam. In 674, members of the Sasanid Persian royal house fled the advancing Arab armies and arrived in Chang'an. In their wake came merchants who established a taste among the Tang elites for Arab, Persian, and Central Asian musical

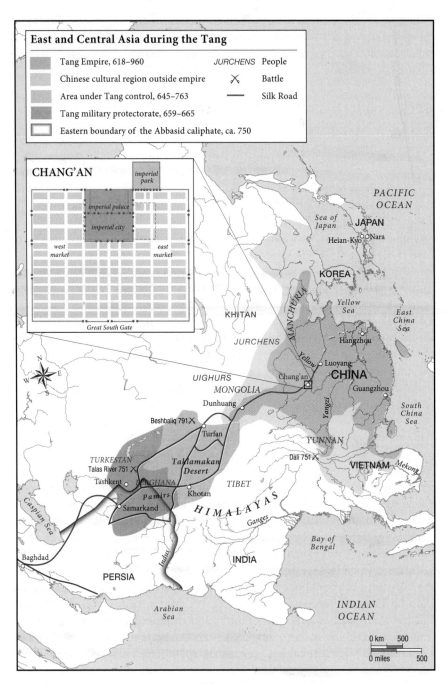

East and Central Asia during the Tang

- Tang Empire, 618–960
- Chinese cultural region outside empire
- Area under Tang control, 645–763
- Tang military protectorate, 659–665
- Eastern boundary of the Abbasid caliphate, ca. 750

- *JURCHENS* People
- ✕ Battle
- —— Silk Road

CHANG'AN

imperial park

imperial palace

imperial city

west market

east market

Great South Gate

MAP 2.4

East and Central Asia during the Tang

forms—China's first real orchestral music—dance, silver artwork, and a host of other items. China's major cities now had quarters set aside for foreign traders, which by the end of the Tang era included Jews, Nestorian Christians, Zoroastrians, members of the major Indian traditions, and the beginnings of what would one day be a substantial Muslim minority. Arab and Indian intermediaries extended trade from China all the way to the East African coast and past the Mediterranean to the developing lands of Europe. With the expanding empire, flourishing trade, and large bureaucracy the capital of Chang'an grew into perhaps the world's largest city, comparable in size to Baghdad or Constantinople, with as many as 2 million people living in its metropolitan area. Its streets, official buildings and residences, and the south-facing imperial palace dominating the center became the model for urban planning throughout East Asia.

Buddhism in China

The growth of Buddhism in China is to some extent a surprising phenomenon. It is the first and, with the exception of Islam in some areas, the only foreign religion to strike deep roots in China. In addition to the occasional stigmatizing of its foreign origins, many of its practices—monasticism, egalitarianism, celibacy, the missionary impulse—have been regarded as going against the grain of traditional family life and Confucian virtue. Why then has it retained its attraction in not only China but also East Asia as a whole over two millennia?

Part of the answer may be found in its character as a universal missionary religion. Indeed, it may be argued that in its original form it resembled less a religion and more a kind of philosophy of self-help. The story of the Buddha is well known. Around the mid-sixth century BCE, the prince Sakyamuni, having emerged from his palace and observed human suffering, came, after much religious searching, to the conclusion that human suffering comes from craving. Humans search for stability in an ever-changing world and so attach themselves to things that provide the illusion of permanence. At Sarnath, near the Indian city of Varanasi (Benares), the Buddha ("Enlightened One") preached the Four Noble Truths: that all life is suffering; that suffering comes from craving; that one can eliminate suffering by eliminating this craving; and that one can eliminate this craving by following the Noble Eightfold Path. The Path consists of a middle course between the ordinary pursuits of civilized life and extreme asceticism and calls for nonviolence toward sentient beings, kindness, right conduct, and "mindfulness" to reach a state of calm nonattachment to the things of this world. One may then transcend the state of constant death and rebirth as one apprehends universal truth and the karmic soul "blows out" like a candle—the origin of the term *nirvana*.

Although born of the Indian religious traditions that developed into Hinduism, followers of the new belief insisted from the beginning that it was applicable to all. Thus it was actively propagated by its adherents and by the brotherhood of monks of the rapidly multiplying schools of Buddhist practice. By the mid-first century CE, when it is initially mentioned in Chinese accounts, Buddhism had already split into the major divisions of Theravada (Hinayana), which had established itself in southern India and Sri Lanka and was moving into Southeast Asia; and Mahayana, which would be established in China, Korea, Vietnam, and Japan.

As with Christianity in Rome, there were considerable obstacles to the introduction of Buddhism to China. The incompatibility of the Chinese written language with the Sanskrit and Pali Buddhist scriptures meant that missionaries had to rely heavily on transliterations, borrow extensively from Daoist terminology, and invent a new and diverse vocabulary of Chinese terms. Over the next several centuries, this eclecticism resulted in a proliferation of sects and a growing need on the part of Chinese, and later, Korean, Japanese, and Vietnamese converts to travel to India for study and guidance.

The travel account of the Chinese monk and early pilgrim Fa Xian, who journeyed throughout Central Asia and India from 399 to 414 in search of Buddhist works, contributed greatly toward understanding the growing Buddhist world.

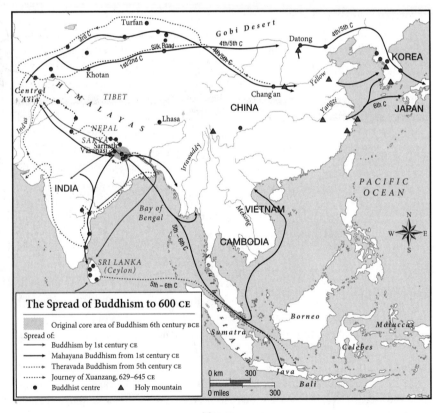

MAP 2.5

The Spread of Buddhism to 600 CE

It was the more famous pilgrim, Xuanzang (Hsuan Tsang) (596–664), however, who was destined to have the larger impact. Xuanzang journeyed through Central Asia and Afghanistan to India in 629 and remained for 16 years. His travels took him nearly 10,000 miles and he brought back an extensive collection of scriptures written in Pali on palm leaves, many of which are still housed in the Great Wild Goose Pagoda he had built just outside Chang'an (Xi'an). Much of what we know about India in the seventh century, including firsthand accounts of the Buddhist king Harsha Vardhana, comes from his account, *A Record of the Western Regions*. His travels were later immortalized in the popular sixteenth-century collection of fabulous tales called *A Journey to the West*.

The four centuries between the collapse of the Han and the ascendancy of the Tang were also marked by the founding of several of the most important schools of Buddhism. By the fifth century, a school of popular devotion to Amida, the **Buddha of the Pure Land**, was spreading rapidly in China. For Pure Land adherents, no immersion in the texts is necessary for enlightenment: merely invoking Amida's name is sufficient for salvation. Even today, it remains the most popular Buddhist sect in both China and Japan. Amida is often pictured with the bodhisattva Guanyin—Kannon in Japan—the Goddess of Mercy who, like the Virgin Mary in Catholicism, is frequently invoked during times of peril.

Another influential Buddhist school, Tiantai, centered on a scripture called the Lotus Sutra. Tiantai emphasizes contemplation of the Sutras as the vehicle to enlightenment and later inspired several schools of *esoteric*, or "secret," paths to enlightenment. These schools exercised considerable influence over both the Tang and the Japanese court at Heian during the eighth and ninth centuries.

Finally, one rather demanding Buddhist school that later achieved fame, if not widespread popularity, was Chan—more widely known by

Amida Buddha. Originally incorporating aspects of both male and female, Guanyin (also spelled Kuan-yin) came to be depicted as female as Buddhism became firmly established in China. For Pure Land adherents, she was the bodhisattva invoked in times of extreme peril, and "the miracles of Guanyin" was a favorite theme of Chinese and Japanese artists.

its Japanese name: Zen. Chan departs from both the devotional and the scriptural paths of Pure Land and Tiantai in that enlightenment comes through a tightly supervised program of carefully regulated activities under the guidance of a master. The intense give and take between master and pupil, the discipline involved in performing humble tasks, the contemplation of paradoxical questions, and, in some cases, meditation are all meant to generate an intuitive flash of enlightenment. Although limited in its influence in China, the emphasis on discipline and obedience made Zen the preferred Buddhist school of Japan's warrior aristocracy after the twelfth century.

The Cycle of Expansion: Emperor Taizong

Having killed his two brothers and forced his father to abdicate, Li Shimin acceded to the throne as Taizong in 627 and began a reign of more than two decades. Dynamic in nearly every area, he was especially effective as a military leader. He led expeditions into Central Asia where he defeated both eastern and western branches of the Turks and forced them to recognize him as their *khan*, or leader. He mounted successful forays into Tibet. During his reign Tang China was arguably the world's most powerful and prosperous empire.

Taizong was also central to the development of China's long-standing law code, the *Tanglu*, major portions of which are attributed to his brother-in-law, Zhangsun Wuji (d. 659). The code's 502 articles, each with commentaries, subcommentaries, and model questions, tied together the large but less systematic corpus of edicts and customary law accumulated over the years and inherited from the Han and Sui and became a model for similar codes throughout East Asia. As the *Tanglu* preface notes,

> A statute is similar to a measure or a model. The *Classic of Changes* states: "The regulation of resources, the rectification of pronouncements, and the sage's preventing the people from doing wrong we call 'rightness.'" Therefore the lawmaker must measure the gravity of offenses; he institutes statutes in accordance with rightness. The *Great Commentary* on the *Classic of Documents* speaks of Heaven's great statute. The commentary explains: "We receive Heaven's great law. Law is also statute. Hence we use the term "statute." (DeBary and Bloom, 1999, p. 549)

One of the most important group of statutes was meant to address the perennial land problems of the empire and prevent the creation of a landed aristocracy. The code forbade primogeniture, the practice of the oldest son inheriting the land of the father; instead, it mandated equal distribution. Thus, it proved a powerful impediment initially to the rapid accumulation of large estates by the wealthy. Instead, over time a different kind of elite emerged that would dominate rural politics in imperial China into the twentieth century.

As we noted earlier, the Han had set up a bureaucracy and subsidized Confucian academies to help provide able administrators for it. The Sui had revived the practice of examinations for government posts and the process was extended and strengthened under the Tang. Although the Song examination system is often cited as the model for that of the imperial system as a whole, the Tang routinized the process and laid out its basic curriculum and format. The test was open to all males whose fathers were not artisans or merchants. The curriculum for the first test was based on the Five Confucian Classics (see Chapter 1, "Patterns Up Close"), whereas that of the second exam was oriented more toward practical elements of administration as well as such aesthetic skills as essay and poetry writing. Appearance and deportment were important as well; candidates were often vetted by the court. Buddhist subjects for the most part were not part of the tests. Because Taizong's family claimed a tenuous line of descent from the philosopher Laozi, some Daoist material occasionally appeared on the tests as well.

Taizong's death in 649 was followed by the rule of his son, who took the name of Gaozong and reigned until the end of 683. Historians generally view him as consumed with court intrigues and not particularly effective. His initial years bore some promise, however. Gaozong built on his father's conquests with additional territories of his own. By the 670s, however, many of those territories had been whittled away. In his last years he appears to have suffered a stroke and was increasingly reliant on his remarkable wife, Wu Zetian.

Empress Wu

Wu Zetian (r. 684–705) was one of the most intriguing figures of the Tang era. She is the most noted exemplar of both the influence of Buddhism and the wide degree of agency possible for elite women of the era. Tour guides in present-day Xi'an celebrate her as a feminist figure, especially for their European and American visitors. The daughter of a public works official, she spent a brief period as an imperial servant before becoming a Buddhist nun, only to return to the palace as a concubine of Taizong. Soon after, she caught the eye of the emperor's son, the future Gaozong. By all accounts she was beautiful, highly educated, and ruthless in exploiting opportunities for advancement at court. Like Cleopatra in Egypt, hostile chroniclers in subsequent dynasties tended to downplay her genuine skills as a ruler and attributed her success to her powers of seduction and sexual exploits.

After the death of her husband, the emperor Gaozong, in December 683, she ruled as Empress Dowager and as regent for her son, the emperor Ruizong. In reality, however, she had effectively held power since Gaozong's later years. To maintain it, she kept Ruizong isolated in the palace. He is said to have spurned an offer to rule in his own right in 686, feeling his position might be even more precarious if he accepted. Wu's position was precarious as well, but her many years at court had made her an adroit political maneuverer. Realizing that the

Empress Wu. The Empress Wu Zetian, one of the most powerful Tang dynasty rulers and perhaps the most colorful. She reigned from AD 684 to 705 and successfully fought off several attempts to unseat her. In her devotion to Buddhism, she declared Buddhism the new state religion and took the title of "Divine Empress Who Rules the Universe." In 690 she declared the founding of a new Zhou Dynasty though the new regime died with her in 705.

only sure way to keep power was to rule in her own right, in 690 she inaugurated a new Zhou dynasty. This was risky in a number of ways, not least of which was that no woman before her (and none since) had ever ruled as an empress, let alone a claimant to the Mandate of Heaven as a dynastic founder. A devout Buddhist, she took the bold step of declaring Buddhism the state religion, another precedent-shattering act. The final move came in 693, when she took the Buddhist title "Divine Empress Who Rules the Universe."

Even the most hostile chroniclers of her reign admit that she was a highly capable ruler. She was careful to pick able administrators and widened the pool of examination candidates to classes that had previously been excluded. Although her military record was spotty, the policy of establishing farmer–soldier colonies added a degree of stability to a number of frontier areas. Her practice of dispensing relief to the common people also ensured her general popularity. She also maintained a highly efficient secret police apparatus and encouraged informers from all classes. On several occasions she launched massacres of real and alleged conspirators. Such enemies multiplied as her reign continued because the act of creating her own dynasty and new titles for herself was considered usurpation by many of her subjects. It ultimately provoked a rebellion, which she handily suppressed until her death from natural causes in 705. Following the Confucian backlash of the Song era, no woman in imperial China would wield this kind of power again until the reign of the Qing Empress Dowager Cixi in the late nineteenth and early twentieth centuries. Still, the noted Song historian, Sima Guang (1019–1086), grudgingly admitted:

> She grasped the powers of punishment and award, controlled the state, and made her own judgments as to policy decisions. She was observant and had good judgment, so the talented people of the time also were willing to be used by her. (From Sima Guang, *Zizhi Tongjian, Comprehensive Mirror in Aid of Governance*, vol. 205)

The Tang in Decline

The first half of the eighth century is often seen as a golden age both for the Tang and for imperial China itself. Following a half-dozen years of court maneuvering,

Empress Wu's son, Ruizong, and his consort, Princess Taiping, enjoyed a brief reign before abdicating to his son, Xuanzong, whose 43-year rule (712–756) proved to be the dynasty's longest. The prosperity of the Tang empire expanded, but toward midcentury many of the problems of uneven growth that had plagued the Han dynasty began to reassert themselves. For example, as the center of population continued to move south, the northern regions languished in relative poverty and the capital grew economically isolated. The agriculturally productive subtropical areas south of the Yangzi now yielded about 90 percent of the empire's taxed grain and contained as much as 70 percent of the population. Moreover, as maritime trade grew and ports increased in size and number, the connecting infrastructure of roads, courier stations, and especially canals required ever more investment and attention. This was a particularly acute problem in the case of communication with the capital. As an administrative center and trade crossroads, the capital city of Chang'an had ballooned to a size that was now unsustainable without constant grain shipments from the south—and its isolation made it particularly vulnerable to attack. Since the capitals of succeeding dynasties tended to be in the old northern heartland as well, this problem of maintaining communication and provisioning them remained chronic throughout the imperial era.

Xuanzong's efforts to control military outposts along the Silk Road, with its lucrative trade and Buddhist shrines, brought the empire into conflict with Arab expansion as the century wore on. Despite some early successes, Tang armies suffered a decisive defeat by the Arabs in 751 at Talas in Central Asia. This loss followed a series of setbacks at the hands of the Tibetans and Uyghurs from 745 to 750 and simultaneous uprisings in the border areas of Manchuria, Korea, and the southern province of Yunnan. From 755 to 762 a revolt led by Tang general An Lushan devastated large sections of the empire and resulted in heavy land taxes after its suppression. As with the later Han, the dynasty was now in a downward spiral from which recovery seemed increasingly unlikely.

For the next century and a half some economic and political recovery did in fact occur, but the problems of rebuilding and revenue loss persisted, accompanied by a questioning of a number of the premises of the regime, particularly by the Confucians. For example, Confucians questioned Buddhism, which received support from the Tang, and its "foreign" ideas and practices such as monasticism, celibacy, and personal enlightenment, which, as noted earlier, contradicted the Confucian standards of filial piety, family life, and public service. At the same time, Buddhist monasteries, which paid no taxes, were tempting targets for an increasingly cash-strapped government. In 845, the Tang forcibly seized all Buddhist holdings, although followers were allowed to continue their religious practice. Despite renewed campaigns against border peoples and other attempts at reinvigorating the empire, sporadic civil war continued for the remainder of the century, leading to the collapse of the Tang dynasty in 906. China again entered a period of disunity as regional states battled for ultimate control. None of these states would be victorious until the emergence of the Song in 960.

THE SONG AND YUAN DYNASTIES, 960–1368

The Song era is considered by many to mark the beginning of the "early modern" era of Chinese history. During the Song dynasty China in many ways achieved its greatest degree of sophistication in terms of material culture, technology, ideas, economics, and the amenities of urban living. Its short-lived incorporation into the huge empire of the Mongols again opened the country to foreign influence and helped to spread Chinese influence westward, most famously through the accounts of the travelers Marco Polo and Ibn Battuta.

The Song Dynasty

Like the Tang, the Song instituted a strong central government based on merit rather than heredity. The Song, however, again broadened the eligibility of those seeking to take the civil service exams, and with increased opportunities to join government service, a huge bureaucratic network emerged. This unwieldy system placed an enormous financial burden on the state, which, to secure revenue, placed heavy taxes on individuals outside the bureaucracy. This constant demand for revenue by the state would ultimately lead to rebellion.

The need for administrative reform spurred the official Wang Anshi (1021–1086) to propose a series of measures designed to increase state control over the economy and reduce the power of local interests. Wang proposed state licensing of both agriculture and commercial enterprises, the abolition of forced labor, and the creation of a system of government pawnshops to loan money at reduced rates to break the power of usurers and middlemen. He also urged greatly reducing the number of bureaucratic positions to lessen the power of local officials and clan heads. Opposition to his proposed reforms forced Wang from office in 1076. The question of government involvement in commerce and the economy has been the subject of vigorous debate throughout the history of imperial China, particularly during times of national crisis. In many respects it is a debate that continued through various regimes in the twentieth century and reached its most dramatic phase in the 1970s, when Deng Xiaoping in effect repudiated Mao Zedong's collectivism in favor of the market reforms of the Four Modernizations.

In addition to internal problems, such as the financial strain of maintaining a huge bureaucracy, the Song faced external problems. Because the Tang had lost much of northern China, including the Silk Road, to nomadic groups, Song lands from the start were substantially smaller than those of their predecessors. Although the new dynasty spent a great deal of treasure and energy to maintain a professional army of more than 1.5 million as well as a formidable navy, this massive force ultimately proved ineffective against the expert and more mobile militaries of invading nomadic groups. The Song also tried careful diplomacy and bribery to maintain its stronghold; such efforts, however, were unable to keep the northern part of the empire from falling to the nomadic Jurchens in 1127.

Focus on economy

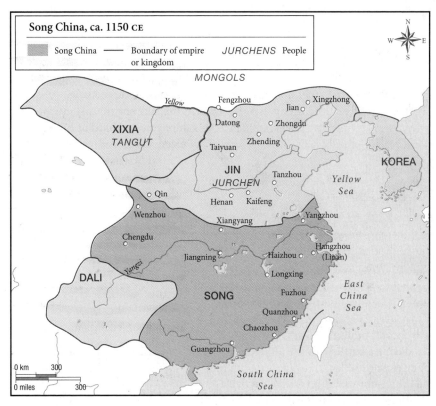

MAP 2.6
Song China, ca. 1150 CE

Forced to abandon their capital at Kaifeng on the Grand Canal just south of the Huanghe, the Song created a new capital at Linan, the modern city of Hangzhou.

The decreased size of this Southern Song empire resulted in an even more southern-oriented and urbanized economy. The new capital at Hangzhou, described by Marco Polo as the most beautiful city in the world, may also have been the largest, with a population estimated at 1.5 million. Despite the bureaucracy's disdain for the merchant and artisan classes, the state had always recognized the potential of commerce to generate revenue through tariffs, export taxes, and internal transit fees. Thus, while attempting to bring the largest enterprises under state control, the government pursued measures to facilitate trade, such as printing the world's first paper notes, minting coins, and restraining usury. These practices, combined with an excellent system of roads and canals, fostered the development of a national market. The Song conducted a lively overseas trade, and Chinese merchants established colonies in major ports throughout Southeast Asia and the Indian Ocean.

楼船

Song Naval Technology. The Song navy had a wide array of weapons at its disposal, including gunpowder, which undoubtedly gave it a technological edge over its adversaries. The use of "fire arrows"—rockets mounted to arrow shafts—was recorded during a battle with the Mongols in 1232. Song naval vessels were equipped with missiles and even employed ships with detachable sections filled with explosives with which to ram opponents.

The Mongol Conquest

Commercial success, however, could not save the Song from further invasion by neighboring nomadic peoples. For centuries, disparate groups of nomadic Altaic-speaking Mongols had lived as loosely organized tribes and clans in eastern Central Asia. There was no real push to unite these groups until the rise to power of the Mongol leader Temujin (1167–1227). Combining military prowess with diplomatic strategy, Temujin united the various Mongol groups into one confederation in 1206. He was given the title "Chinggis/Genghis Khan" (Universal Ruler) of the united Mongol confederation.

Following confederation, the Mongols launched a half-century of steady encroachment on northern China. The Mongols had several advantages over the huge but unwieldy infantry-based armies of their opponents. Their skill at horsemanship and archery began at a young age; they were unsurpassed in their ability to fire arrows at pursuers while galloping away from them at full speed; and they employed terrain effectively for concealment along with repeatedly successful tactics of feigned retreat. In fact, all of these advantages were in evidence whether their opponents were Chinese infantry, the light cavalry of the western steppes, or the heavily armored knights of Europe.

Chinggis Khan's grandson, Khubilai Khan, resumed the Mongol offensive in southern China after the Southern Song unwisely attempted to enlist Mongol aid against the Jurchens. In 1267 he moved his capital from Karakorum to Khanbaligh, called by the Chinese Dadu—the future city of Beijing—and steadily ground down the Song remnant. Hangzhou fell to the Mongols in 1276. The dynasty ended with the death of the young Song emperor in 1279 as he attempted to flee by sea.

The Yuan Dynasty

In 1280 Khubilai proclaimed the Yuan dynasty. This short-lived dynasty now placed China in an empire spanning all of Eurasia from Korea to the interior of

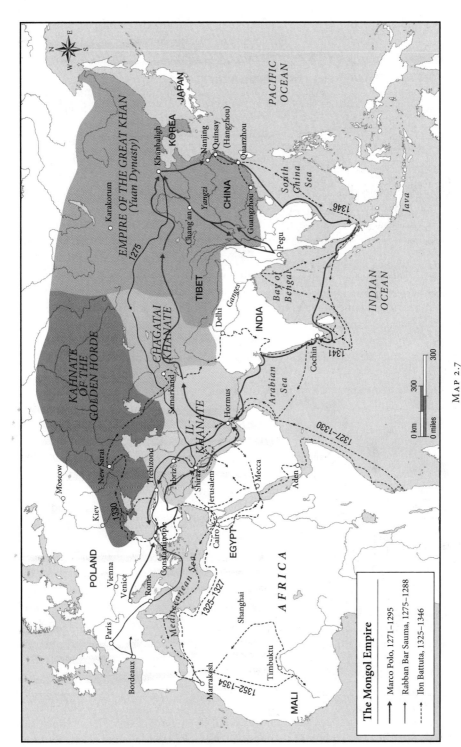

MAP 2.7

The Mongol Empire

The Mongol Empire

— Marco Polo, 1271–1295
→ Rabban Bar Sauma, 1275–1288
---- Ibn Battuta, 1325–1346

Poland and probing as far as Vienna, Java, and Japan. Like their predecessors in the Northern Wei and Sui dynasties, however, the Mongols found themselves reluctantly adapting to Chinese culture to administer the densely populated and complex society they had wrested from the Song. Unlike the Toba and earlier nomadic groups, however, the Mongols kept their interaction to a minimum and were scarcely affected by "sinicization." Thus, although some senior Song bureaucrats resigned in protest of the new Mongol government, many carried on with their posts. The examination system begun under the Han, expanded and refined under the Tang, and, put in its mature form under the Song, was half-heartedly reinstated in 1315. It had been discontinued in the interim as the Mongols utilized the many different peoples in their empire as officials, many of whom were rotated into positions in China.

Now that China was part of a much larger empire, its culture was for the first time widely diffused throughout Eurasia. Conversely, China was open on an unprecedented scale to a variety of foreign goods, ideas, and travelers. Such Song-era innovations as paper money, gunpowder, coal, the compass, and dozens of other important Chinese developments circulated more widely than ever, while emissaries and missionaries from the developing states of Europe traveled east to the Chinese capital city of Khanbaligh. Rabban Sauma, a Turkish Nestorian Christian who had been born in China, traveled from Khanbaligh to Paris and Rome, even celebrating a Mass with the Pope in 1278. The two most famous travel accounts of the era, those of the Venetian Marco Polo (1254–1324) and Ibn Battuta of Tangier (1304–1377), who lived and traveled throughout the Mongol empire, are testament to the powerful impact of Mongol rule on facilitating travel over such a vast area. Indeed, it was during the brief rule of the Mongols that the European image of China as a fairyland of exotica, fabulous wealth, and wondrous inventions was firmly set.

For Chinese historians, however, the Yuan period is almost universally regarded as one of imperial China's darkest times. Although the Mongols quickly restored order and allowed a relative tolerance of religious practice and expression, the Yuan period was seen as an oppressive time of large standing armies, withdrawal from service of many Chinese officials, ineffective administration, forced labor, and heavy taxes. One group that did relatively well under the Mongols was merchants. Given their desire to foster trade as a means of integrating their empire, this is not surprising. The Mongols set up

Khubilai Khan. Kublai Khan (1260–94), Founder of the Yuan Dynasty of China under the reign name of Shizu and reigned from 1260 till 1294 in the Mongol empire overall and 1280 to 1294 in China. He was a grandson of the founder of the Mongol Empire, Genghis Khan (c. 1162–1227).

merchants' associations called *ortogh* in which traders could pool their investments in a caravan and reduce their personal losses if the caravan met with misfortune along the way—a kind of early limited liability corporation

Compounding the intensity of the tensions between Mongols and Chinese was perhaps the single worst disaster of the fourteenth century, the bubonic plague. Although scholars have only recently begun to examine Chinese mortality rates resulting from the plague, Chinese accounts suggest that they were in all likelihood similar to those of Europe in some areas, with perhaps one third of the population of about 100 million being carried off from the 1340s until the end of the century.

By mid-century, all of these factors contributed to outbreaks of rebellion in China. Moreover, the Mongol empire spanning Eurasia had now begun to dissolve into a series of increasingly squabbling regional *khanates*. By 1368, the coalition led by the soldier-Buddhist monk Zhu Yuanzhang had driven the Mongols from the capital at Khanbaligh and proclaimed a new dynastic line, the Ming. A final measure of revenge came when the last Mongol pretender to the throne was physically driven into the sea—just as the last Song emperor had been by the Mongols.

THE MING: THE QUEST FOR STABILITY

The "Pig Emperor," as Zhu was sometimes derisively called because of his ungainly features, took the reign name of Hongwu and spent much of his rule driving the remaining Mongols out of his empire. Under Hongwu's leadership, Chinese politics and customs were restored and a powerful centralized government was put in place. This new imperial state Hongwu and his successors created would, with minor modifications, see China into the twentieth century.

During the 88 years of the Yuan dynasty, Chinese political and cultural traditions had been compromised in a number of ways. As previously noted, Mongol overlords relied on their own administrative practices and even placed foreign administrators from Persia and other countries in official positions. Marco Polo, for example, claimed to have worked as an official in China. In doing so, the Confucian educational and examination system that had been a mainstay in China since the Han dynasty had been considerably devalued by having outsiders placed in key positions at the top. Ming emperors, however, reinstated a number of Chinese institutions and renewed the primacy of the Confucian bureaucracy.

Recovery

Hongwu sought to streamline this newly reconstituted bureaucracy by concentrating power and governmental functions around the emperor—a practice that had been common during the Qin, Han, and Tang dynasties. Thus, one of his first steps in reshaping the government was to create the Grand Secretariat in 1382. This was a select group of senior officials who served as an advisory board to the emperor on all imperial matters. The Grand Secretariat became the highest level of the bureaucracy and the most powerful level of government after the emperor. Although military needs eventually moved much of its power to the Grand Council set up by the Qing in the mid-1700s, the Secretariat remained at the apex of imperial Chinese power into the twentieth century. With a powerful, centralized government in place, Ming emperors now had a base from which to take measures to protect the empire from incursions by Mongols and other nomadic groups in the north. One step to protect against invasion was taken in 1421, when the capital of the empire was moved from Nanjing in the south to the old site of Kambaligh, now renamed "Beijing" (Northern Capital), so that a strong Chinese presence in the region would discourage invasion. Further safeguards against invasion included the upgrading of the fortifications along the Great Wall.

While the country fortified its borders and reinstated political systems that had been dismantled by the Mongols, it also had to contend with a sharp drop in population caused by warfare and the lingering effects of the bubonic plague that ravaged the country in the 1340s. The population rebound, however, did not assume significant proportions until aided by the introduction of a number of new food crops in the sixteenth and seventeenth centuries, which boosted agricultural productivity.

The Interlude of Naval Power

Thanks to the foundation laid by Hongwu, the dynasty's third emperor, Yongle (r. 1403–1424) inherited a state in 1403 that was already on its way to recovering its economic dynamism. Taking advantage of this increasing prosperity and fearful of potential usurpers, he ordered China's first and last great naval expeditions to seek them out. These voyages, sent out from 1405 to 1433 under the command of his childhood friend and imperial eunuch, Zheng He, were perhaps the most remarkable feats of their day.

The story of Zheng He himself was equally remarkable. Born to a Muslim family in the southern province of Yunnan in 1371, Zheng was taken captive when Ming armies conquered Yunnan in the bloody war to recover the last Mongol strongholds in the region. Ten-year-old Zheng's quick wit impressed a Ming general, who spared the boy's life and placed him as a servant in the household of the future Yongle.

Although Zheng's life was not taken, he suffered the fate of all captured males in the region: castration. His genitalia were taken and his traumatized urethra was capped with a wooden plug. Unlike many of his fellow captives, however, Zheng survived the after-effects of his castration and grew into a physically imposing man, with his boyish face and high-pitched voice the only outward signs of his ordeal. His condition also allowed him a privileged place in the inner precincts of the imperial household. Emperors often placed considerable trust and power in the hands of their court eunuchs because they could not produce heirs and thus were unable to build a power base that could challenge imperial

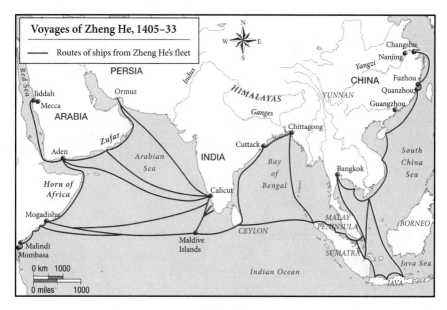

MAP 2.8
Voyages of Zheng He, 1405–33

authority. Zheng He's steadfast loyalty won him particular favor when Yongle ascended the throne.

The vast fleets Zheng now commanded were the largest amphibious forces the world would see for centuries to come. With a length of more than 400 feet, the largest of Zheng's "treasure ships," as they were called, were more than four times the length of Columbus's *Santa Maria* and many times its bulk and were accompanied by a diverse array of smaller vessels that carried cargo, supplies, and troops. There were even tankers that carried fresh water for the fleet, while the larger ships grew fruits and vegetables on their aft decks. Zheng's ships also carried a formidable arsenal of cannon, bombs, rockets, and other weaponry and a force of nearly 30,000 men. In addition, they featured such technological innovations as watertight compartments, sternpost rudders, magnetic compasses, and paper maps marked with navigation grids.

The first voyages were expeditionary forces aimed largely at overawing any nearby foreign powers that might be harboring pretenders to Yongle's throne. As the realization set in that this threat was nonexistent, the voyages became focused on trade and exploration and ranged further and further afield, ultimately covering the Indian Ocean, the Persian Gulf, and the East African coast. Along the way they planted or reestablished contact with Chinese merchants in South and Southeast Asia. Of particular interest were the first direct Chinese contacts with the Swahili-speaking states of East Africa. In one famous exchange of gifts, the King of Malindi sent Yongle a giraffe, which found the emperor among the

Zheng He "Treasure Ship" with Christopher Columbus's *Santa Maria*. The huge fleets and enormous ships of Zheng He expeditions from 1405 to 1433 were the largest amphibious forces in the world for centuries. With dozens of ships, some over 400 feet long, and up to 30,000 men they were also technological marvels with their cannon, rockets, stern post rudders, water-tight bulkheads and gridded maps for navigation. In this picture the relative sizes of Zhong He's largest "Treasure Ships," as they were called, and Columbus's flagship "Santa Maria" are shown in dramatic relief. The Santa Maria was barely 100 feet long and a fraction of the capacity of the Chinese ships.

awestruck admirers of the creature at the imperial court. Even today one can still see the stone markers left by the Chinese along the East African coast where their ships put in.

The End of Maritime Exploration

Although Zheng He's explorations firmly established Chinese predominance in naval technology and power, Yongle's successors put an end to the expeditions. The reasons for this abrupt turnabout were both political and strategic. By the 1430s the Mongols, having regrouped from their defeats, were again threatening the northern frontiers. The huge expense and the realization that there were no significant naval rivals nearby were therefore convincing arguments to discontinue the voyages in the face of the Mongol threat. In addition, Confucian officials, always suspicious of the influence of the merchants and court eunuchs,

Confucian belief

argued that maritime trade was not vital to the over-all welfare of the empire.

With maritime travel ended, China's main contact with the outside world came through so-called tribute missions in which representatives from other countries would visit the imperial court with native gifts for the emperor and apply for a trade license. The emperor would then usually allow those countries' merchants to trade in China for a set period of time. Although a more secure China was the ultimate goal of the ban on maritime travel and the system worked reasonably well until the nineteenth century, this decision would have far-reaching consequences when China faced the advanced naval technologies of the industrializing West—technologies that, in a number of cases, the Chinese themselves had developed.

Ming Decline

The activist style of Hongwu and Yongle proved to be the exception rather than the rule during the nearly three centuries of the Ming. As had so often been the case in Chinese history, a degree of weakness at the center of power encouraged probes of the frontier by nomadic peoples on the empire's periphery: "disorder within, disaster without." A disconcerting foretaste of this occurred in 1449, when the emperor was taken prisoner by the Mongols following the defeat of his expeditionary force. Through most of the sixteenth century, a succession of weak emperors eroded the stability of the reformed Ming imperial system, which had been based on enhancing the emperor's power. To compensate for the chronic weakness at the center, power was increasingly diffused throughout the system. Over time, much of it was acquired by the Grand Secretariat and provincial governors, whereas at the village level, magistrates and village headmen assumed the bulk of power and responsibility.

Scroll with Yongle's giraffe. The nearly 30 years of Zheng He's voyages resulted in, among other things, a constant stream of exotic items coming into the empire. One of the more striking of these was a gift of a giraffe by the king of the East African trading state of Malindi. The arrival of the animal caused a sensation and was immediately added to the emperor's menagerie and became the subject of this commemorative scroll.

China and the World Commercial Revolution

China's rapid recovery, particularly as the 1500s brought with them the new crops from the Americas, placed the late Ming in the center of an increasingly extensive and complex worldwide commercial revolution. China's immense production of luxury goods, the seclusion policies of Japan and Korea, and the huge and growing demand for porcelain, tea, silk, paper, and cotton textiles made the empire the world's dominant economic engine until the productive capacity of the Industrial Revolution vaulted Great Britain into that position in the nineteenth century.

In the midst of this growth, the government took steps to simplify the system of land taxation. As in previous regimes, land was assessed and classified according to its use and relative productivity. Land taxes were then combined into a single bill, payable in silver by installments over the course of the year: the so-called "single-whip" tax system. The installment plan allowed peasants to remain relatively solvent during planting season when their resources were depleted, thus reducing the need to borrow at high rates from moneylenders at crucial times of the yearly cycle. Significantly, the requirement that the payment be in silver also played a crucial role in the increasing monetization of the economy.

Regulating the Outer Barbarians

Ming China by the late fifteenth century had made considerable progress toward the long-standing goals of peace and stability traditionally sought by Chinese regimes. In practical terms this meant defending the traditional avenues of invasion in China's remote interior. Psychologically, the view of the empire cultivated by China's elites placed it at the center of a world order defined by Neo-Confucian philosophy and supported by a host of Chinese cultural assumptions. Like the Tokugawa Shogunate in Japan in the seventeenth century, the Ming, and later the Qing, had come to view foreign influence as less "civilized" and far too often injurious to the social order. Hence, successive rulers placed strict regulations on maritime trade and conceived of diplomatic relations primarily in commercial terms. "All the world is one family," imperial proclamations routinely claimed, and the emperor was conceived as the father, in Confucian terms, of this world-family system. The so-called tribute missions sent from Korea, Vietnam, the Ryukyu Islands, and occasionally some of the outer *han* (feudal domains) of Japan worked reasonably well within the long-standing hierarchy of the Confucian cultural sphere. By the late eighteenth century, however, it came into direct conflict with the more egalitarian system of international trade and diplomacy that had evolved in the West.

The End of the Ming

Despite the increased attention directed at the Mongol resurgence of the 1440s, periodic rebellions in the north and northwest punctuated the late fifteenth and sixteenth centuries. The huge commitment of Chinese troops in Korea against the forces of the Japanese leader Hideyoshi Toyotomi during his attempted invasion of Korea and China from 1592 to 1598 weakened the dynasty further during a crucial period that saw the rise of another regional power: the Manchus. As we will see in the next chapter, the Manchus soon took advantage of the "disorder within" and become involved in the factional fighting of the late Ming. They then formed their own dynasty, the last of China's imperial regimes: the Qing.

ECONOMICS, SOCIETY, AND GENDER

Throughout Chinese history, the various dynasties actively encouraged and supported agriculture as the basis of the domestic economy, yet from the Han dynasty on, China exported far more in luxury goods and technology than it imported. Unlike the various regimes in India, which actively sought to foster trade, the Confucian view of the pursuit of profit as corrupting meant that Chinese governments seldom encouraged merchants and generally preferred to adopt a passive, but controlling role. Although merchants were held in low esteem, the state recognized that trade was indispensable to the financial health of the empire and saw it as an expandable source of tax revenue.

Industry and Commerce

Goods made in and distributed throughout the empire by the time of the Han included some of the best known items of Chinese production. By the first century CE, Chinese manufacturers were making paper using a suspension of mashed plant fibers filtered through a fine-mesh screen and set aside to dry—a method still considered to produce the highest quality product for painting or literary work. By this time, too, artisans were producing a kind of "proto-porcelain" that, with increasing refinement, would be known in the succeeding centuries to the outside world as "china." The use of lacquer as a finish, as well as in artwork created by sculpting built-up layers of it, was also well established. By the second century CE, the Chinese had perfected silk production techniques developed over millennia and had become world leaders in textile weaving. Both treadle and water-powered looms were in widespread use, and bolts of silk of standardized sizes and designs were produced for export. Supply could barely keep pace with demand, especially in Persia and Rome—both of which ultimately acquired the skills and materials to start their own industries.

As noted earlier, by the Han period, the Chinese were also producing cast iron in huge foundries. According to one estimate, by 2 CE, there were no less than 48 major ironworks in north China, and the mining industry as a whole may have employed as many as 100,000 people. The foundries, which produced ingots of standardized sizes and weights, used sophisticated systems of forced-air control, including water-powered bellows. Salt mines employed complex gearing for lifting brine from deep wells, systems of bamboo piping for transferring it, and evaporators fired by natural gas for extracting the salt. Because of the enormous productivity of the iron-making and salt-mining industries, the government continually sought ways to regulate and control them.

As we saw before, the opening of the Silk Road under the Han and the infrastructural improvements such as the Grand Canal had vastly expanded the internal and external connections of the Chinese economy. The dramatic expansion of maritime and caravan trade from the seventh century on under the Tang, particularly within the huge Buddhist cultural sphere, spread Chinese technology further abroad and brought new products into the empire.

Tea, imported from Southeast Asia, quickly established itself as the beverage of choice during the Tang and vied with silk for supremacy as a cash crop during the Song. Tea had a profound effect on the overall health of the population in China, Vietnam, Korea, Japan, and Central Asia. The simple act of boiling water renders it potable, and the tea itself contains a number of healthful, even medicinal, properties. By the height of the Song period, tea, silk, porcelain, paper, and cotton cloth had all become major industries and China dominated—in some cases, monopolized—production and distribution of all of them. An increasingly sophisticated infrastructure of commercial credit, paper money and specie, and insurance for merchant houses and their agents supported and secured China's vast network of industry and trade.

Agricultural Productivity

A number of technical and systemic improvements steadily increased agricultural productivity. In addition to such staples as wheat, millet, and barley in the north and rice in the south, a wide variety of semitropical fruits and vegetables were also cultivated within the empire. New strains of rice introduced during Tang and Song times resulted in larger harvests on more marginal land. Champa rice, a key variety imported from Southeast Asia in the eleventh century, allowed three crops per year in suitable areas. The vastly expanded productivity of the land enabled by the introduction of Champa rice helped prompt a huge increase in the empire's population, perhaps topping 100 million during the Northern Song era. Trade with Central Asia had introduced wine grapes, and fermented grain beverages had become a substantial industry. New techniques of crop rotation, fertilization, and plowing were gradually introduced, as were the breast-strap harness for draft animals and the wheelbarrow; oxen-drawn, iron-tip plows; treadle hammers; undershot, overshot, and Pelton-type waterwheels; the foot-powered "dragon" chain pump for irrigation; and the *fengche*—a hand-cranked winnowing machine with an internal fan to blow the chaff from the grain. With this basic, reliable technology, China led the world in agricultural productivity until the eighteenth century.

During the late fourteenth and early fifteenth centuries, while the country was rebuilding from the war to drive out the Mongols, the chronic problems of land distribution and tenancy had abated somewhat. As in Europe, the depopulation of some areas from fighting and banditry and the lingering effects of the Black Death, which had reduced China's population from perhaps 100 million to about 60 million, had raised the value of labor, depressed the price of land, and increased

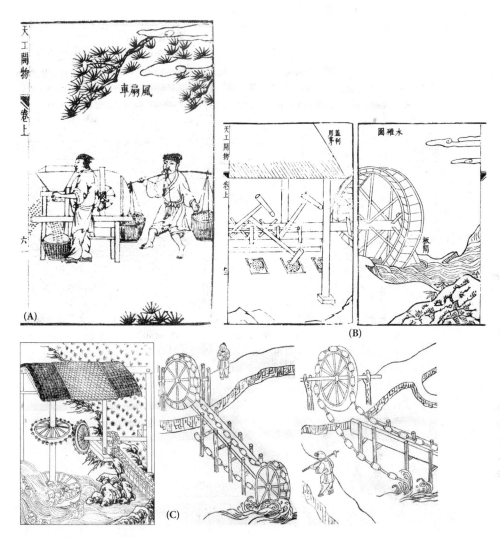

Agricultural Innovations. By the first century CE, Chinese sophistication in crafts and labor-saving devices could be seen in a number of areas. While the illustrations here are from the famous seventeenth-century compendium of technology, *Tiangong kaiwu* (*The Works of Nature and Man*), all of them depict techniques that go back to the Han dynasty: **(A)** *fengche* winnowing machine; **(B)** undershot waterwheel driving hammers in a pounding mill; **(C)** vertical and horizontal waterwheels driving chain-bucket "dragon pumps" for irrigation

the proportional amount of money in circulation. Another factor in play came indirectly from the creation of overseas empires by the Portuguese and the Spanish in the sixteenth century. This resulted in the circulation of a number of new food crops on a global scale that would soon have a substantial impact on the world's agricultural productivity.

Land Reform

The Qin had gone a long way in a short time toward eliminating the old Zhou aristocratic order. By the time of the late Han, China's old aristocracy had largely died out, its place at the top of the social hierarchy taken by the so-called *scholar-gentry*—the educated large landholders who constituted the Confucian bureaucracy. Despite the elimination of the old aristocracy, however, landlord holdings continued to expand. Since the upper ranks of the landowners and bureaucracy either were exempt from taxes or paid reduced amounts, the tax burden fell increasingly on tenants and owners of small parcels of land. Poor harvests or bad weather, particularly in the arid north and west, made the situation even worse for those already heavily taxed. Because the north, despite its elaborate irrigation works, was far less productive and more prone to crop failure than the south, it was also proportionally more heavily taxed.

Such problems made land reform and redistribution an ongoing concern, as we saw with Mencius and the attempted reforms of Wang Mang. The Tang, for example, continued the policy of land redistribution begun during the brief Sui dynasty by allotting each peasant family a tract of 100 *mou*, only one fifth of which was inheritable, while the remainder reverted to the state for redistribution. Although the Tang land redistribution policy resulted in a relatively high level of prosperity, absentee landlordism, tenancy, and usury also rose again, particularly during times of economic stress. Conditions were similar under the Song and Yuan, especially as the bubonic plague reduced production and tax revenues in many areas after the 1340s. The continual cycle of landlordism and tenancy, followed by attempts at land reform and redistribution, remained a chronic problem for every Chinese regime deep into the twentieth century.

Visions of Rural Life: The Scholar-Gentry

Although China boasted some of the world's largest cities, more than 85 percent of the country remained rural during the period from the Qin through the Ming. At the top of the local structures of power and influence from the development of the Confucian bureaucracy during the Han were the *scholar-gentry*. As a class, they were by definition the educated and included all ranks of degree holders, whether in or out of office, and their families. By imperial edict and custom they were expected to exercise leadership over the classes of peasants, artisans, and merchants and, along with the district magistrate, take the initiative during times of trouble in safeguarding the lives and property of the community. Like the magistrate as well, they were expected to set a high Confucian moral tone for their villages and districts.

In theory, scholar-gentry membership was open to most males and their families, although in practice it seldom exceeded 1 to 2 percent of the population in most areas of the empire. As the system reached its mature phase from the Song period onward, the chief qualification was attainment of at least the lowest official degree, which enabled the bearer to attend a government-sponsored academy for further study and draw a small stipend. The demands of memorizing the classical canon and learning to write in the rigid format of the "eight-legged essay" required for the exams, however, were such that the wealthy had a distinct advantage in the leisure time, access to tutors, and the connections required to pass the exams. Still, there were enough poor boys who succeeded by hard work and the sacrifices of their families and neighbors to provide a surprising degree of mobility within the system.

Since prestige within the scholar-gentry derived from education even more than wealth, it was not uncommon for individuals to purchase degrees, although technically they were barred from doing so in the upper three categories. Thus, there was considerable snobbery among the upper gentry of advanced degree holders and officials toward the lower gentry. This was reinforced by an array of sumptuary laws and a court-directed protocol of buttons worn on the hats of officials signifying to which of the nine official grades—each with an upper and lower rank—they belonged. Individuals could also attain honorary ranks, awarded by the emperor, for meritorious service in the military, outstanding ability during times of emergency, decades of diligent study unaccompanied by success in the exams, and even for living to a ripe old age: Commoners reaching the ages of 80, 90, and 100 were awarded official ranks of the ninth, eighth, and seventh grades, respectively, and given the honorary title of "elder."

In keeping with their role as the informal administrative apparatus of the magistrate, the scholar-gentry enjoyed a number of privileges as well as responsibilities. At the same time, their position as community leaders and their grounding in Confucian ethics frequently placed them in tension with the official bureaucracy, especially when local interests appeared at odds with regional or imperial ones. For example, the general reverence for education ensured that the scholar-gentry were exempted from the labor tax of the Ming, as well as from judicial torture and corporal punishment. If convicted of felonies or capital crimes, elaborate procedures had to be followed to strip gentry of their degrees before the sentence could be carried out. By a variety of stratagems available only to the wealthy, they were frequently able to conceal the amount of taxable land they possessed and generally paid lower rates than the commoners. Along with the district magistrate, they presided over all ceremonies at Confucian temples, and the ones holding the highest ranks led all clan ceremonies. In addition, they mingled with the official authorities more or less as social equals; in the case of those in between appointments to high office, they frequently outranked the local magistrate.

Their privilege and wealth, however, also meant that they were expected to function as community leaders. As with all those in positions of power in imperial China, it was assumed that they would live up to the moral authority invested in them as teachers and exemplars. They were expected to engage regularly in philanthropic activities, such as raising subscriptions for schools, temples, public works, and other local needs. In times of famine, they raised funds for relief; during times of unrest, they organized militia and paid for and supervised defensive works. As local leaders, they settled small disputes and lawsuits. They also wrote the local histories and gazeteers of their districts—even today, among the most important primary sources for Chinese social history.

Many of these things, however, also led to tensions within the system and thus serve to illustrate the fluidity within the hierarchies of Chinese society. Local government relied to an extraordinary degree on the cooperation of the gentry and people with the magistrates, subprefects, and prefects to function. Because the presiding officials were moved so frequently, the gentry represented a consistent network of people to carry out the day-to-day work of government. They took seriously the Confucian injunction to remonstrate with officials, especially when their complaints coincided with local interests. Thus, they could—and did—rally the people to subvert the policies of unpopular magistrates. Moreover, as influential men themselves—and often officials with national connections—they could force the resignation of officials and sometimes even bring about changes in regional or imperial policy.

The Baojia System

The tendency toward greater centralization under the Ming also reverberated within the structures of Chinese village life. Although much of local custom and social relations among the peasants still revolved around family, clan, and lineage—with the scholar-gentry setting the pace—institutions perfected and revived under the Ming had a lasting impact into the twentieth century.

Originally conceived during the Qin and continued in one form or another during most of the succeeding dynasties, the *baojia* system of village organization called for families to register all members and be grouped into clusters of 10. One family in each cluster was then assigned responsibility for the others. Each group of responsible families would then be grouped into 10 and a member selected from them to be responsible for the group of 100 households and so on, up to the 1,000 household level. The *baojia* headmen at each level were to be chosen by the families in the group, although they received their office from the magistrate. They reported to the magistrate on the doings of their respective groups and were held accountable for the group's behavior. The system was especially important in that it allowed the authorities to bypass potential scholar-gentry resistance to government directives and guaranteed a network of informers at all levels of rural life.

Gender and Family

As we saw previously, with the rise of the imperial bureaucracy during the Han and the increasing emphasis on filial piety within its new Confucian curriculum, a more rigidly hierarchical, patriarchal model of proper women's behavior gradually developed in imperial China. Along the way, the emphasis on sons within the extended family as carriers of the ancestral line and their potential to win admission to official state service led to a gradual devaluing of daughters. In times of severe economic stress when families had difficulty supporting several children, young girls were the first to suffer. Despite the greater flexibility among elites during the Tang period, families, especially in rural areas, would sometimes sell their daughters into prostitution or even kill female infants. By the Song era problems relating to the treatment of young girls had become so acute that China's first foundling hospitals were opened in 1138.

Other tensions in the patterns of both rural and urban life tended to be intensified in the lives of women and girls as well. Although recent work has shown that the experiences of Chinese women of all classes was considerably less oppressive in many respects than previously supposed, it was generally more circumscribed than that of men. On the one hand, the education of upper-class women tended increasingly toward those areas aimed at making them more marriageable. Study of proper Confucian etiquette—as outlined in Ban Zhao's *Admonitions for Women* (see later)—light verse, and a heavy dose of filial piety occupied a large portion of their curriculum. Among the ideals for women one finds chastity, loyalty, and obedience high on the list. Marriage and property laws were set up to reinforce these qualities—although during the Tang, Empress Wu attempted to equalize them.

There was remarkable continuity in the ideals express in Ban Zhao's Han-era *Admonitions* and the Song and Ming *Nuerjing*, or *Classic for Girls*. In this work, the author of which is unknown, proper girls' and women's behavior is given the sanction of nature and the Dao. Its structure in couplets is reminiscent of that of the boy's primer and guide to behavior, *Sanzijing*, or *Three Character Classic*. Here proper Confucian behavior was set out in simple, easy to memorize three-character aphorisms. *The Girl's Classic* lines are more elaborate and are meant to be memorized as a handy guide of behavior from young childhood to old age. At every stage, one's behavior is expected to be restrained, modest, submissive to authority, but assertive in teaching and educating one's children—though with very different ends in mind:

> *When he grows to years of boyhood*
> *Then a teacher call at once,*
> *Who will books and manners teach him that he may not be a dunce.*
> *Lazy habits in his study will good people all annoy,*
> *And his indolence the prospects of his future life destroy.*
>
> *For your daughter in her girlhood,*
> *To learn fancy-work is best.*
> *Ne'er allow her to be idle, lolling to the east or west,*
> *If in youth you do not teach her, when full grown 'twill be too late,*
> *When she marries it will bring her only shame, disgrace, and hate.*

> (From Robin R. Wang, ed. *Images of Women in Chinese
> Thought and Culture.* Indianapolis/Cambridge: Hackett,
> 2003. Pp. 445–6)

In addition to the premium placed on mourning by both sexes, widows were expected to remain single out of duty and loyalty to their departed and obedient to the eldest son. Indeed, widows who remarried forfeited all inherited property to their husbands' closest male relative—including what remained of the dowry they had originally brought with them. The painful custom of **foot-binding**, originating during the Song, gained ground during the Ming and, despite initial attempts to ban it by the Qing, stubbornly continued even in the face of Republican prohibitions until its final suppression under the People's Republic after 1949. Though often viewed by men through a lens of erotica, the *Girls Classic* ties this custom to the more prosaic rationale of homebound modesty and discouragement of easily showing oneself in public:

> Have you ever learned the reason
> For the binding of your feet?
> It's from fear that it will be easy to go out upon the street.
> It is not that they are handsome when thus like a crooked bow
> That ten thousand wraps and bindings are bound around
> them so.

(Ibid., p. 444)

Even within these strictures, many women were highly educated and dynamic and exercised considerable resourcefulness and agency. The noted Han historian Ban Zhao, for example (45–116), came from the most prominent family of historical scholars of her time, including her father Ban Biao and her brother Ban Gu. It was she who, following the death of her brother, was made chief court historian and finished his work, the *Han Shu*. Ban Gu's daughters also became noted historians. As we saw, too, in the opening vignette of this chapter, the poet Li Qingzhao lived, worked, and loved in a way that seems strikingly modern to us today. For much of this time woman's education may have centered primarily on cultivating the domestic virtues of devotion and obedience, as well as mastering crafts such as spinning and weaving. In farming households, for example, women monopolized textile production. They sorted silkworm cocoons, boiled them and extracted the threads, spun and wove. During the Tang and Song, treadle looms grew quite sophisticated, so much so that some have suggested that they lacked only a reliable power source to trigger an industrial revolution. The introduction of cotton spurred further production, and its processing and weaving was also widely practiced on Chinese farmsteads. The commercialization of textiles and commodities for the internal economy and increasingly for export drove the demand for these crafts. Yet it does not appear that such skills enhanced the position of women in society—indeed, some commentators at the time felt the physical demands of textile production for trade diminished women's agency and left them exhausted. From the fifth century on, however, the popularity of monastic Buddhism also created alternatives for women and men fleeing family pressures. Those engaged in Buddhist schools that required extensive scriptural study became highly educated, and the communities themselves, like Christian monasteries in Europe, often owned large tracts of land and wielded considerable local influence. Especially after the advent of block printing in the eighth century, Buddhism became a powerful force for spreading literacy. At the same time, the relative strictness of the practices regulating sexual and family life varied, particularly among the high officials and the growing urban commercial classes. Foreign influences and fashions also affected behavior, particularly in Chang'an and places involved in international trade. Tantric Buddhist and Daoist sexual practices, which were used by their followers as means of spiritual liberation, undoubtedly contributed to a more relaxed approach to relations between men and women during the Tang and Song as well.

THOUGHT, AESTHETICS, SCIENCE, AND TECHNOLOGY

One of the signal developments of the imperial period was the institutionalization of the writing of history. Control of the past was an important preoccupation for Chinese rulers because it spelled out their present relationship to the dynastic cycle and Mandate of Heaven.

The Legacy of the Han Historians

For the men and women charged with writing about the past, much like modern historians, the aim was the accurate transmission of information—often with verbatim copies of important documents—and analysis of the events portrayed in terms of a larger vision of the direction and purpose of human history. For the Han historians, as for Chinese historians throughout the imperial era, history was cyclical: human events, as manifestations of the great universal cycles of being, are a constant succession of birth, growth, decay, death, and rebirth, in which older ideas of the Mandate of Heaven, dynastic cycles, and *yin* and *yang* theory are imbedded. The moral lessons learned are therefore tied to actions taken at various stages of these cycles.

The basic format of long-term history was laid out by the father and son team of Sima Tan (d. 110 BCE) and Sima Qian (145–86 BCE). Their *Shiji*, *The Records of the Grand Historian*, attempts the first complete history of the Chinese people from the mythical Yellow Emperor to their own time. One particularly valuable section that became a staple of later histories was a survey of non-Chinese peoples encountered along with their habits, customs, religions, geography, and other significant traits. Hence, the Han records give us our first written accounts of Japan and other places on the Chinese periphery.

Like other Chinese officials, the historians took their role of "conscience" of the government seriously, sometimes at severe peril to themselves. As historian to the powerful Emperor Wudi, for example, Sima Qian offended the ruler by exonerating a general in his writings whom the emperor and court had accused of cowardice. Given the choice between execution and castration, Sima chose the latter; if he were dead, he explained, he could not finish his history, which he believed was his highest duty.

Several generations later, the Ban family comprised another dynasty of Han court historians. Writing after the Wang Mang interval, Ban Biao (3–54 CE) and his son, Ban Gu (32–92 CE), pioneered the writing of dynastic history with their *Hanshu* (*The History of the Former Han*), which laid out the format that all subsequent dynastic histories followed. As we noted above, Ban Gu's daughters were also scholars and writers and his sister Ban Zhao (48–116 CE) carried on the family tradition of history writing and contributed her treatise on proper women's behavior, *Admonitions for Women*.

Admonitions for Women. A handscroll painting from the Tang Dynasty.

Accounts of the historians' activities themselves may be found in the *Hou Hanshu, The History of the Latter Han*, written after the fall of the dynasty by Fan Ye (398–446 CE) Another epic historical compendium, in this case extending from the Warring States period to the time of the author (1076), came from the brush of Sima Guang in his *Zizhi Tongjian* of the Song dynasty. The long period of the intermingling of Confucianism with Buddhist, Daoist, and other systems of thought forced an extensive reformulation of its core concepts. By the twelfth century, this reformulation had matured into Neo-Confucianism, which combined the moral core of Confucian and Mencian ethics with a new emphasis on speculative philosophy.

Neo-Confucianism

Neo-Confucianism holds that one cannot sit passively and wait for enlightenment, as the Buddhists were said to do, but must actively "seek truth through facts" to understand correctly the relationships of form (*li*) and substance (*qi*) as they govern the constitution of the totality, or Great Ultimate (*taiji*). Concerned with answering the Buddhist doctrine of impermanence, Neo-Confucianism taught that just as self-cultivation of the Confucian virtues is the means of discovering one's true *li*, so investigation of the physical world is a means of discovering one's place in the larger *li* of the Great Ultimate. Hence, knowledge is a cumulative, unified whole, with the moral dimension of such understanding taking precedence over mere observation. One experiences the ethical and epistemological strands of this exploration holistically in a manner beyond mere reason and more akin to a Buddhist flash of enlightenment. Exploration of the physical universe undertaken in this spirit is thus the ultimate act of Confucian self-cultivation in that one apprehends the Way (*Dao*) on every level.

This vision of Neo-Confucianism was propounded by the Cheng brothers, Hao (1032–1085) and Yi (1033–1107), and perfected by Zhu Xi (Chu Hsi, 1129–1200), generally recognized as the leading Neo-Confucian thinker. Not surprisingly, these ideas came to prominence during the Song period, riding a wave of anti-Buddhist reaction in the wake of the fall of the Tang. The incorporation of Buddhist approaches to cosmology made the philosophy attractive to those who were intrigued by inquiries into the nature of the universe while retaining the Chinese ethical precepts of family relationships and behavior.

Zhu Xi's speculative Neo-Confucianism lost favor somewhat in part because of a Buddhist revival of sorts during Ming. A modified view in favor of more direct ethical action favored by Wang Yangming (1472–1529) now came to the fore. For Wang, as for Zhu Xi, truth, whether in terms of epistemology or ethics, was unitary. He believed that all people carry within them an "original mind" in which rests an intuitive sense of the fundamental order of the universe. It is out of this instinct toward the right that one investigates the physical and moral universe to refine one's conclusions.

Wang, however, departed from Zhu Xi's emphasis on a rigorous "investigation of things" as the necessary route to understanding the nature of the world. Instead, he insisted that such investigation merely hones one's existing instincts in these areas to a higher degree. For example, the innate feelings one has toward one's parents naturally lead one to see filial piety as a fundamental condition of the universe; further investigation allows one to grasp its subtleties.

Wang's other area of emphasis, nurtured by a long study of Buddhism—especially *Chan* (Zen)—and Daoism was the unity of knowledge and action. Although everyone has the spark of intuition, he argued, true understanding is inseparable from active pursuit and cultivation of that spark. Moreover, the sage must act in the world as his knowledge becomes increasingly refined, both to be a moral example to others and to complete his own self-cultivation

The endpoint comes when, like Confucius at 70, one can "follow one's heart without transgressing what is right." Thus, for Wang, "knowledge is the beginning of action, and action is the completion of knowledge." Although Wang's school remained a popular one, especially because of its implicit critique of some of the more speculative areas of Zhu Xi's Neo-Confucianism, Zhu Xi's school remained the orthodox one, and with later support from the Qing continued to be so until the last years of the imperial era. During the Qing dynasty (1644–1912), however, it was resurrected by the Emperor Kangxi (1662–1723) and made the official school of Confucian orthodoxy, where it would remain until 1905.

Poetry, Painting, and Calligraphy

To a considerable degree, Chinese concepts of aesthetics, especially those developed during the Tang and Song periods, became the founding principles for the arts throughout East Asia. The most important developments during this period were the maturation of three disciplines: poetry, painting, and calligraphy. These three disciplines are considered closely interrelated and governed by the same overriding principles. Central to each discipline is the idea of spontaneous creation as a reflection of the inner state of the artist. The artist in each of these media seeks to connect with the Dao by indirectly suggesting some aspect of it in the work itself. For example, Song and Yuan landscape paintings often feature misty mountains, lone pines, and tiny human figures, with the action and occasion implied rather than detailed, because too much detail would place limits on the illimitable. Some of the best examples of this concept may be found in the work of the painters Zhao Mengfu (1254–1322), and Ni Zan (1306–1374).

Tang and Song poetry, especially the compressed "regulated verse" of eight five-character lines, and the terse four-line "cutoff line" poems, attempt to do the same thing: suggest powerful emotions or themes in minimalist fashion. For example,

Minimalism. In *Twin Pines, Level Distance*, painted around 1310, Zhao Mengfu rejects illusionistic representation and reduces the landscape to a set of calligraphic brush strokes. Zhao also chose a traditionally significant subject. In Chinese art, pine trees have long symbolized survival. By representing them here, Zhao may be referring to his own political survival under the Mongol yoke, as well as to the endurance of Chinese culture under foreign rule.

Zhao Mengfu (1254-1322). Colophon writer: Yang Zai, Chinese, 1271-1323. Twin Pines, Level Distance, ca. 1300. Handscroll; ink on paper, Image: 10 9/16 × 42 5/16 (26.8 × 107.5 cm.). Overall with mounting: 10 15/16 × 307 11/16 in. (27.8 × 781.5 cm.). Ex coll: C.C. Wang Family, Gift of The Dillon Fund, 1973 (1973. 120.5). The Metropolitan Museum of Art. Image copyright © The Metropolitan Museum of Art. Image source: Art Resource, NY.

the deep Confucian sensibilities of the Tang poet Du Fu (712–770) are often detectable in his emotionally charged poems such as "Mourning Chen Tao." Li Bai (or Li Bo, 701–762), his friend, was in many ways the opposite, both in the way he lived his life and in the emotions he sought to stir. Carefree, witty, and a lover of wine and women—according to legend, Li Bai drowned after a drinking bout attempting to "embrace the moon" reflected in the water—his poetry evokes happier moments, but frequently conveys them as fleeting and thus bittersweet. Wang Wei (701–781) was a third renowned Tang poet. Of him, it was later said that "in every one of his poems is a painting, and in every painting a poem."

Often an artwork combined all three disciplines: for example, a painting with a poem done in the appropriate calligraphic style for the occasion. Often, too, successive owners of such works added their own poems or comments to them, thus continuing the conversation. The calligraphy used on such occasions would properly complement the style of the painting by means of a personal version of one of the four approved main styles. Frequently, the master they sought to copy in this regard was Wang Xizhi (303–361), who remains to this day the supreme stylist of "running script" (*xingshu*) calligraphy. The most distinctive calligraphy, however, was often done in the ultracursive *caoshu* ("grass hand") style, which occasionally proved so idiosyncratic that a calligrapher could not later on make out what he had written. Such an occasion was considered a transcendent seizure of the artist by the overpowering creative urge of the Dao.

Technological Leadership

From the Tang through the Southern Song, China was the site of an unprecedented number of technological innovations that would have a profound effect inside and outside the empire. The horse collar, moldboard plow, wheelbarrow (see "Patterns Up Close"), advanced iron casting, compass, gunpowder, porcelain, and paper diffused widely throughout Eurasia and the Indian Ocean basin. By the height of the Song period, tea, silk, porcelain, paper, and cotton cloth had all become major industries, and China dominated—in some cases, monopolized—production and distribution of all of them. An increasingly sophisticated infrastructure of commercial credit, printed paper money, and insurance for merchant houses and their agents supported and secured China's vast network of industry and trade.

PATTERNS UP CLOSE

Three Transformative Technologies

As is evident from the many impressive inventions and breakthroughs mentioned in this chapter, China has been a world leader in a variety of technologies for millennia. Indeed, it has become a cliché to cite things like paper,

continued

block printing, the compass, and, of course, gunpowder as Chinese inventions that changed the world. In this *Patterns* feature we will concentrate on three humble devices that not only contributed mightily to China's wealth and power, but also altered Eurasian society for more than a thousand years and ultimately the world: the wheelbarrow, the horse collar, and the stirrup.

The earliest of these devices is perhaps the wheelbarrow. Although some scholars speculate that there may have been a version of a single-wheel vehicle in ancient Greece, the first images of what is recognizably a wheelbarrow turn up in second-century BCE Han-era tombs. Isolated references to the vehicle appear by the first century CE, and at least one Chinese history, *The Record of the Three Kingdoms*, credits the statesman Zhuge Liang (181–234) with the invention. Early Chinese versions, like Zhuge Liang's "wooden ox," featured a large central wheel around which the load box was built. Large later versions even featured small sails to add power to the human or animal muscle moving the vehicle.

Although early Chinese wheelbarrows were used extensively as convenient means of carrying military supplies, their real contribution came in construction and family agriculture. A wheelbarrow functions as a second class lever and thus allows a mechanical advantage to the operator, allowing him or her to carry far heavier and bulkier loads than would be possible without the device. In the case of the ancient Chinese barrows, the weight was centered over the wheel, requiring only enough force to move the vehicle forward or backward and allowing the load to be easily dumped. It thus multiplied human power and efficiency as it spread throughout the continent all the way to Europe.

Similarly, the horse collar allowed for unprecedented gains in transportation and agricultural productivity. Yoked oxen and water buffalo had long been used for pulling loads and plowing, but it was recognized that the animals were relatively slow and tired fairly easily. Horses were a much better choice, but the harnesses used tended to choke the animals. Sometime around the first century BCE, the Chinese developed the breast-strap harness, which allowed the horse's load to be more evenly distributed. Not long after, the "ridged full collar" familiar to us today emerged on the scene, which distributed the load efficiently across the horse's upper breast and shoulders.

This proved to be a crucial advance in agriculture. One draft horse with the new collar could do the work of 50 men. It could pull a moldboard plow through tough sods and open up new lands for cultivation. It not only transformed agriculture in China and East Asia, but also its arrival in Europe between 700 and 1050—along with the system of three-field crop rotation—allowed a surge in population, economic development, and cultural maturation that continued until the Black Death of the 1340s.

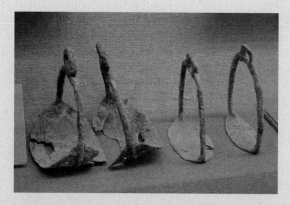

Iron Stirrups from the Jin Dynasty. Widespread use of the stirrup not only brought the deployment of cavalry to the forefront of warfare, it led to a resurgence in power of Eurasian mounted nomadic peoples. Stirrups such as the ones depicted here helped the nomadic Jurchen people displace the Northern Song dynasty and set up their own Jin Dynasty, which lasted from 1127 to 1234. Their downfall was brought about by another nomadic people, the Mongols, whose short-lived super empire spanned almost all of Eurasia in the late thirteenth and early fourteenth centuries.

The final transformative innovation was the stirrup. Although the horse had occupied a prominent place in Eurasian warfare for more than 2,000 years, its utility had been limited to pulling chariots and providing mounts for archers and riders with light spears. The problem was that the back of a horse is a precarious perch: it was difficult to mount a horse when one was weighed down with armor and weapons but easy to be knocked from one, especially when engaged in close combat and swift maneuvering.

Around the beginning of the Common Era the first attempts at saddles with straps for supporting ones feet began to appear in Northern India. But these employed only a simple toe loop and the saddle concentrated the rider's weight on a small area of the horse's back, making it sore and tiring the animal. The basic idea, however, appears to have spread via the Silk Road, and by the early 300s CE a recognizably modern iron stirrup with a flat bottom and semi-circular top began be used in north and central China. At about the same time, saddles with rigid frames to distribute the rider's weight more evenly and better padding to cushion its effects on the horse began to be employed.

The effects of these changes were swiftly apparent in a China now dominated by feuding states and marauding nomads in the post-Han era. With his legs secured to his mount and a high saddle back to cushion him in combat, a mounted warrior could use a long lance to charge directly into enemy formations without fear of being immediately unhorsed. Further, he

continued

could wear a full complement of armor and also armor his horse. The combination proved so effective that by the fifth century the armies of all the states in China had adopted and refined the technology. In China, it helped pave the way for the Sui reunification.

It was western Eurasia, however, where the new technology saw its greatest impact after its arrival in the seventh century. The ability of a heavy cavalry of armored warriors to break infantry formations and fight effectively at close quarters from horseback placed a premium on refining the new armor and weapons, training warriors, and breeding bigger, faster, and stronger horses. The politically fractured eras of post-Roman and post-Carolingian Europe meant that local elites and regional strong men had to mount their own defenses and keep order. The stirrup and the military innovations it spawned allowed them to do this without heavily equipped armies, whereas the expenses necessary to adopt the new technology ensured that it would remain a monopoly of the rich and powerful. Indeed, one can argue not only that all three of these devices were central to China's material pre-eminence for the next thousand years but also that the feudal society of Europe was ultimately derived from them.

Printing with movable block type had been developed as early as the eighth century, ensuring that the literatures of China, Japan, and Korea would have wide circulation. The compass, invented by the Chinese and routinely used on their trading vessels, guided ships throughout the Indian Ocean and Southeast Asia. China's early sophistication in iron production continued to grow: during the Song, the empire's annual production of steel, at 150,000 tons, surpassed that of all of Europe in 1700.

The techniques involved in generating the extremely high temperatures required for steel were also transferable to porcelain production. Although there is debate about when the breakthroughs resulting in true porcelain first occurred, by the Tang period, distinctive brown and green glazed figures, often depicting the colorful parade of peoples and animals of the caravan trade, were widely traded. Following centuries of experimentation with *kaolin* clays, glazing mixes, and extremely high firing temperatures, Song craftsmen hit on the formula for creating the world's most celebrated pottery. Elegant white and *celadon* (a shade of green) porcelain vessels were manufactured in great numbers and the surviving examples of Song wares today are among the world's most valued art treasures. Techniques for using distinctive blue cobalt oxide pigments were introduced from Persia toward the end of the fourteenth century and were soon being utilized by Ming potters to brighten their porcelain ware. Government sponsored and run kilns, notably at the Jingdezhen works in Jiangxi province, allowed for unprecedented volume and quality control.

If fine porcelain, lacquerware, landscape painting, poetry, and calligraphy marked the refined side of Song life, the most momentous invention to emerge from the era was gunpowder. Perhaps arising from Daoist alchemy as early as the eighth century, its use in rockets, bombs, and primitive types of cannon routinely appear in twelfth-century accounts. It undoubtedly gave the Southern Song a critical, although temporary, technological edge over their northern adversaries, perhaps prolonging the life of the beleaguered dynasty. Its rapid

Fire demon. The earliest representation of a gunpowder weapon, discovered in 1985 among a group of figures carved in high-relief on the walls of a cave temple in Sichuan, dating from 1128.

spread through India and the Arab world has suggested to some scholars the possibility of a simultaneous development for it. By the late thirteenth century, its appearance in the writings of the English Franciscan monk Roger Bacon marked its diffusion throughout Eurasia.

The period from the Tang to the Ming was marked by unsurpassed technological prowess. Indeed, according to the leading scholar of China's record of innovation, Joseph Needham, China remained the world's leading producer of new inventions until roughly 1500. So striking is this record and so suddenly does it subside after this time that historians sometimes refer to the problem of why it took place as "the Needham question." One possible answer may be simply that the Chinese considered that they had achieved a degree of perfection in so many areas that, like their great naval expeditions, there was simply no pressing need to advance them further. Within a few hundred years, however, the momentum of technological innovation had shifted decisively to the small, feuding states of Europe. Zheng He's ships, with their dazzling array of innovative features in the fifteenth century, remained unsurpassed triumphs of Chinese naval architecture until the mid-nineteenth century, when the Qing dynasty's first steamships were launched.

CONCLUSION

The political and social turmoil of the late Zhou era also marked an enormously important period in Chinese intellectual and cultural history. During this era the most important schools of Chinese thought and philosophy developed: Confucianism, Daoism, and Legalism. Although Confucianism ultimately triumphed as the ideology of imperial China, it was the Legalist state of Qin that created the empire itself.

When the Qin dynasty fell in 206 BCE, much of the infrastructure of the early empire—including the Great Wall—was in place. The Han dynasty, from 202 BCE to 220 CE, retained the administrative structure of the Qin, but softened the harsh laws and punishments of the Legalists. Eventually, the form of Confucianism practiced by the empire's administrators was taught in the imperial schools, becoming in effect the imperial ideology. By the end of the Han, China had created a solid alliance between the state and this all-encompassing philosophical system.

Perhaps more important than even the structures themselves, however, was that, like the Egyptians and Romans, the Chinese had become accustomed to what has been called the "habit of empire." Four hundred years of unity under the Qin and the Han had conditioned them to believe that empire was the natural state of Chinese political organization and that any interruptions would be but brief interludes in the dynastic cycle. Thus, Chinese history has been marked by rhythms of inwardness and outwardness, outside usurpation and inward renewal. Following reunification under the Sui and the Tang came a period of relative inwardness and renewal under the Song. Foreign invasion briefly placed China within the world's largest empire, controlled locally by the Yuan dynasty.

Recent scholarship suggests that, by the time of the Ming "restoration" in 1368, the economic center of the Eurasian world had shifted markedly toward China, although China's technological lead over its competitors was beginning to narrow. Ironically, the persistence of China's apparent supremacy in wealth and power over its neighbors convinced Chinese leaders that their institutions had been largely perfected, one proof of which was that so many representatives of the "outer" world vied for Chinese products. China therefore grew more insular even as representatives of the outer world grew more aggressive.

For China during the fourteenth century, the basic political structure changed relatively little and reemerged with greater centralization than ever during the Ming dynasty. Culturally, the Mongols influence on China was negligible, and they in turn did little by way of interaction and adaptation to Chinese norms, preferring instead to maintain their ethnic autonomy. Through it all, however, not only did Chinese leadership in technical innovation in so many fields keep up its former pace, but also the brief unity of the so-called Pax Mongolica spread Chinese advances throughout Eurasia. In China, however, the dominant political structures of empire and cultural assumptions of Confucianism not only resisted Mongol attempts to circumvent them, but also outlasted them and reemerged more strongly than ever. Unlike the Muslim conquerors in India, the Mongols did not adhere to a powerfully articulated universal religion. In fact, they proved receptive to several of the religious traditions they encountered in their conquests: Islam, Buddhism, and Nestorian Christianity all gained Mongol adherents. Even before this, however, the real tensions between Buddhism and Confucianism in China resulted not in persecution of the Buddhists, but in Confucian thinkers reacting to their speculative philosophy and creating an expanded synthetic ideology: Neo-Confucianism. The Chinese, firm in the belief that all outsiders could ultimately "become Chinese," continued to pursue this policy. Its next test was to come with another outside group of conquerors, the Manchus. It was the interactions and adaptations of Manchus and Chinese that created China's last imperial dynasty, the Qing.

FURTHER READING

DeBary, William T. and Irene Bloomeds. *Sources of Chinese Tradition*, Second Edition, vol. I. New York: Columbia University Press, 1999. Excellent introduction to major Chinese philosophical schools. Extensive coverage of Buddhism and Neo-Confucianism with accessible highly informative introductions to the documents themselves.

Ebrey, Patricia Buckley, ed. *The Inner Quarters. Marriage and the Lives of Chinese Women in the Sung Period*. Berkeley: University of California Press, 1993. Pioneering study of women's participation in Song commercial enterprises, urban life, and the institutions of early modern China. Extensive source materials.

Gernet, Jacques. *Daily Life in China on the Eve of the Mongol Invasion, 1250–1276*. Stanford, CA: Stanford University Press, 1962, 1970. Pathbreaking popular social history of Southern Song China. A wealth of detail with somewhat dated conclusions.

Graham, A. C. *Disputers of the Tao: Philosophical Argument in Ancient China*. La Salle, IL: Open Court, 1989, 1990. Complex exploration of modes of philosophical expression by one of the field's most noted scholars. Most useful for advanced students.

Henricks, Robert C., trans. *Lao-Tzu, Te-Tao Ching. A New Translation Based on the Recently Discovered Ma-wang-tui Texts*. New York: Ballantine Books, 1989. Fresh scholarship on Daoism. Includes several textual variations with Chinese characters. Sound, accessible overview.

Huang, Ray. *China: A Macro History*. Armonk, NY: Sharpe, 1997. Readable, entertaining, and highly useful one-volume history. Particularly good on the complex politics of the post-Han and Song-Yuan periods.

Loewe, Michael. *Everyday Life in Early Imperial China during the Han Period, 202 B.C.–A.D. 220*. New York: Harper & Row, 1968. Short, highly useful one-volume survey of Han social history by a preeminent scholar. Especially good on details of peasant and elite daily existence.

Nylan, Michael. *The Five "Confucian" Classics*. New Haven, CT: Yale University Press, 2001. Reinterpretation of the place of the core classics in the tradition of the *ru*, or scholarly class. The author emphasizes the importance of the non-Confucian part of this canon in forming the intellectual framework of China's scholarly elite. Best for older students.

Sima Qian. *Records of the Grand Historian*, Burton Watson, trans. Revised Edition, New York: Columbia University Press, 1993. Vital primary source for the Qin and Han period by perhaps ancient China's most prominent historian.

Weatherford, Jack. *Genghis Khan and the Making of the Modern World*. New York: Broadway Books, 2004. Revisionist history of the Mongol empire and its founder by a leading anthropologist. Sees the Mongol interval as breaking down feudal structures, increasing trade, and abetting religious tolerance well in advance of its European counterparts.

Freedom and Power. *Tens of thousands of people flock to Tiananmen Square at dusk on June 3, 1989. In the background, the Goddess of Democracy statue confronts the portrait of Mao above the Gate of Heavenly Peace. In less than 24 hours, the square would be filled with blood after People's Liberation Army troops opened fire on the demonstrators.*

Part 2

PATTERNS OF MODERN CHINESE HISTORY

Timeline for Part Two

1368–1644	Ming Dynasty
1557	Portuguese establish first European colony in Macau
1577	Matteo Ricci, first Jesuit missionary in China
1600–1800	England and the Netherlands import 70 million pieces of porcelain from China
1644	Qing Dynasty proclaimed
1664–1722	Reign of Kangxi emperor
1689	Treaty of Nerchinsk sets border between China and Russia
1699	Qing permit overseas trade at Canton
1727	Protectorate over Tibet established
1733	Yongzheng creates Grand Council
1736–1795	Reign of Qianlong Emperor
1793	Macartney mission to Beijing
1794	Outbreak of White Lotus Rebellion
1839–1842	First Opium War with Great Britain
1851–1864	Taiping Rebellion

1851–1868	Nian Rebellion
1856–1860	Second Opium War
1860–1895	Self–strengthening era
1877–1878	General Zuo's campaign in Xinjiang
1894–1895	Sino–Japanese War
1898	Hundred Days of Reform
1900	Boxer Rebellion; population of Shanghai reaches 1 million
1904	Confucian academies closed
1912	Last Qing emperor abdicates; Republic of China founded
1919	May Fourth Movement
1921	Founding of Chinese Communist Party
1931	Japan annexes Manchuria
1934–1935	The Long March
1937	Rape of Nanking
1949	Founding of People's Republic of China
1950–1953	Korean War
1958–1961	Great Leap Forward
1964	China detonates its first thermonuclear device; first "Little Red Book" published
1966–1969	Cultural Revolution

1972	Richard M. Nixon travels to China; diplomatic relations between China and US restored
1976	Deaths of Zhou Enlai and Mao Zedong
1978	Four Modernizations inaugurated
1979	China invades Vietnam
1980	Trial of Gang of Four; first Special Economic Zone established
1983	Campaign against "spiritual pollution" launched
1989	Tiananmen Square massacre
1990	Shanghai Stock Exchange opened
1997	Hong Kong ceded to China by United Kingdom
1999	Macau returned to China by Portugal
2001	China joins World Trade Organization
2006	Completion of Qinghai-Lhasa Railway
2008	Beijing hosts Summer Olympics
2010	China surpasses Japan as second-largest economy
2013	"Airpocalypse" across several Chinese cities

CHAPTER 3

THE APOGEE OF EMPIRE: THE QING DYNASTY THROUGH THE QIANLONG ERA, 1644–1795

The Russians, Dutch, and Portuguese, like the other Europeans, are able to accomplish whatever they undertake, no matter how difficult. They are intrepid, clever, and know how to profit themselves. As long as I reign there is nothing to worry about from them for China, I treat them well, and they like me, respect me, and attempt to please me. The kings of France and Portugal take care to send me good subjects who are clever in the sciences and arts, and who serve our dynasty well. But, if our government were to become weak, if we were to weaken our vigilance over the Chinese in the southern provinces and over the large number of boats that leave every year for Luzon, Batavia, Japan, and other countries, or if divisions were to erupt among us Manchus and the various princes of my family, if our enemies the Eleuths [the Oirats, the westernmost group of the Mongols] were to succeed in allying with the Tartars of Kokonor, as well as our Kalmuk and Mongol tributaries, what would become of our empire? With the Russians to the north, the Portuguese from Luzon [sic] to the east, the Dutch to the south, they would be able to do with China whatever they liked.

—(Quoted in Laura Hostetler, *Qing Colonial Enterprise:*
Ethnography and Cartography in Early Modern China.
Chicago: University of Chicago Press, 2001, p. 40)

So summarized the Qing Kangxi emperor (r.1662–1722) in a conversation recalled later by the Jesuit missionary Antoine Gaubil and recorded in a letter to a colleague in 1752. Much of the commonplace view of the Qing inherited from their later clashes with some of the same European powers mentioned above depicts them rather differently. Two centuries later they are routinely stigmatized as reclusive, hidebound, inept at warfare and diplomacy, unwilling and unable to "modernize"—with the result that by 1900 China under Qing rule had been reduced to what Mao Zedong famously called a "semicolony." Viewed through this lens, Kangxi's observations—despite placing the Portuguese rather than the Spanish in Luzon—seem rather prescient.

They also, however, support a perspective that has recently attracted increasing numbers of scholars and one to which we have referred several times in this volume: that China was never so isolated as had once been supposed and indeed, had for most of its long history been involved—often as a major player—in world politics and economics. Kangxi had extensive contact with European travelers and especially Jesuit missionaries. He employed them as advisors and took an active interest in the information they brought with them. He even considered converting to Catholicism at one point. Perhaps more importantly, he was keenly aware of his empire's strengths and vulnerabilities and how it fit into the complex mosaic of the new world systems of trade and colonization emerging during his lifetime. His reflections show a similarly acute awareness of the power positions and ambitions of his potential rivals.

The China that develops under the Qing is in one sense a "regulated society," not unlike its contemporaries Japan and Korea. In economic terms, they sought to strictly control trade and foreign influence, export luxury items, and import little except cash. In this sense, as recent scholarship has suggested, China—and to a somewhat lesser extent, India—was the primary economic engine that drove the Eurasian economy behind the scenes. However, it was also an empire that was expanding throughout the seventeenth and eighteenth centuries and through nearly all that time was widely respected and admired by Western observers as prosperous, powerful, and well governed. In this chapter we will examine the period of consolidation and expansion in the Qing's dynastic cycle bracketed by the dynasty's two most dynamic and effective emperors: Kangxi and Qianlong (r. 1736–1795). It was toward the end of the latter's reign that the first foreshadowing of the woes of the following century would manifest themselves: the British mission of Lord Macartney to establish diplomatic relations along European lines and the White Lotus Rebellion, which would smolder for years (see Chapter 4). In retrospect, it can be seen as an indicator of military slippage and ultimately as a harbinger of the bloodiest civil conflict in human history: the Taiping and Nian rebellions, which together took perhaps 30 million lives.

DISMOUNTING AND RULING

As we saw toward the end of the previous chapter, the Qing dynasty, as had the Zhou and Qin as well as the Toba, Jurchens, and Mongols, emerged from the periphery of the Chinese cultural sphere. Like so many of the northern nomadic peoples migrating along a tier running from Manchuria to Xinjiang, the Manchus periodically raided a wide area on both sides of the Great Wall, but by the fifteenth century had largely settled in the region bounded by Siberia, Mongolia, and Korea. Linguistically, they were speakers of the Tungusic group of languages within the larger Altaic family, which includes Mongolian and the Turkic languages such as Uyghur. Ethnically, it is believed that they are descended from some of the major Jurchen groups, which had formed the Jin dynasty (1115–1234) that had eliminated the Northern Song.

With the Mongol revival during the 1400s the Ming sought to "use barbarians to check barbarians" and so looked for allies among the ever-shifting nomadic groups beyond the Great Wall. The Jurchens seemed a good fit and so were recognized and courted by the Ming, who were anxious to pry them away from both Korean suzerainty and relatively close relations with the Mongols. At the time, however, they were relatively weak and disunited, although increasingly influenced by Chinese culture and Confucianism. With Ming fortunes on the downturn in the wake of the costly defense of Korea again the Japanese invasions of Hideyoshi in the 1590s, an opportunity for expansion seemed to present itself. By the turn of the seventeenth century, under the leadership of Nurhachi (1559–1626) and Abahai (1592–1643), the Jurchen groups united and founded a second Jin dynasty in 1616. They abandoned the old Jurchen script derived from the Khitans in favor of one based on the Mongol alphabet and began to call the united group "Manchus" (*pinyin*: *Manzu*), a name whose origins are uncertain. By 1636, the newly united Manchus controlled the area including and adjacent to the Liaodong Peninsula and declared the foundation of a new dynasty: the Qing (Pure).

By 1642 a civil war wracked the Ming. Among other difficulties, the regime's attempts to check Manchu power in Liaodong lessened its hold on the western regions around Shaanxi province already reeling from famine and a smallpox epidemic. Out of these hardships came two rebel armies. One advanced on Beijing; the other moved south to the wealthy regions around the Yangzi River and the cities of Hangzhou and Nanjing. The northern group, under Li Zicheng, who claimed descent from one of the Ming pretenders once sought by Zheng He's fleets, had captured Luoyang and the old capital of Xi'an by 1643. By April 1644 he had entered the outskirts of Beijing. On hearing this news, the Chongzhen emperor (r. 1628–1644) committed suicide: some accounts indicate he hanged himself from a beam in a pavilion on a hill in the imperial gardens.

Although apparently secure in the **Forbidden City**, Li received information of an impending counterattack from the east by the loyalist general Wu Sangui. Li took his army to launch a preemptive strike on Wu and the two forces met at the pass at Shanhaiguan, where the Great Wall approaches the sea. In desperation, Wu had invited the Manchu leader Dorgon (1612–1650) to cross the Wall and join forces with him. For the Chinese, this event would come to carry the same sense of finality as Caesar's crossing of the Rubicon. Wu Sangui prevailed and pursued the remnants of Li's army. Dorgon, however, led his forces unopposed into Beijing where, on June 5, true to historical precedent, they announced that they had come to avenge the Ming and correct the mistakes of the past. There the new regime would remain until 1912. Like the outside invaders before them, the Manchus now found themselves in the position of having to "dismount and rule."

Manchu Bannerman. The Manchu fighters of the early Qing Dynasty were much feared as expert horsemen and highly competent marksmen with either firearms or bows. This rendering shows a bannerman archer, with the characteristic cap, and curved broadsword in a scabbard by his side.

The Banner System

The **banner system** under which the Manchus were organized for military and tax purposes was now expanded under the Qing to provide for segregated Manchu elites and garrisons in major cities and towns. Under the banner system, the Manchu state had been divided into eight major military and ethnic divisions (the five ethnicities recognized as Manchu, Han Chinese, Mongolian, Tibetan, and *Hui*, or Muslim), each represented by a distinctive banner. Within each banner division, companies were formed of 300 fighters furnished by their constituent families. Originally a mode of organization for a mobile warrior people, the system became the chief administrative tool of the Manchu leadership. Now it was introduced into China in such a way as to constitute the Manchus as a hereditary warrior class occupying its own sections of major Chinese cities. The Han, or ethnic Chinese, forces were organized into their own "Armies of the Green Standard," so named for the color of the flags they carried.

Creating the New Order

As were all nomad conquerors of China, the Manchus were acutely aware of their position as a tiny ruling minority. With their numbers comprising only about 2 percent of the population, they struggled to maintain a balance between a minimum degree of administrative and cultural adaptation and the kind of thoroughgoing assimilation characteristic of previous invaders like the Toba. The struggle among scholars to understand the complexities of Qing rule is well illustrated by the ascendency of different theoretical perspectives over the past half-century. In the 1960s the dominant school, associated with Mary Wright, Ho Ping-ti, and John K. Fairbank, was based on the idea of sinicization. What made Qing rule successful, they argued, was the degree to which the Manchus interacted and adapted to Chinese norms. Wright in particular stressed that the Taiping Rebellion of the mid-nineteenth century both enhanced Manchu notions of their ethnicity—because of their identification by the rebels as foreign "demons"—and pushed Han and Manchu closer together because of the government's use of the cultural identity of Confucianism as propaganda.

In the 1980s, however, Pamela Crossley and Evelyn Rawski challenged this prespective on several fronts. The older perspective, they charged, was driven in part by a residual Han Chinese nationalism that had pushed Sun Yat-sen and other revolutionaries to see Manchu rule as the root of China's problems. The access to Manchu archives under Deng Xiaoping allowed scholars to develop a much deeper understanding of the nuances of Qing policy and how it had differed in its approaches to the hierarchies of imperial rule and especially to the multiethnic character of the Qing empire than had been possible before. As opposed to the sinicization model, this was sometimes called the "northeastern" model.

Yet even this enhanced understanding of the inner workings of the goals and worldview of the Manchu elites did not completely satisfy a new generation of scholars who felt that the sinicization model should not be completely abandoned and that perhaps a more synthetic approach was required. Here Mark Elliot has been at the forefront of the "New Qing History" (*pinyin: Xin Qing shi*), conceptualizing a dialogic approach that places due emphasis on the concept of "identity."

Thus, any generalized characterizations we make about Qing rule must be seen as provisional. In terms of the mechanics of Qing policy, we can say that Han Chinese and Manchus were recruited in equal numbers for high administrative posts. Manchu quotas in the Confucian examination system were instituted, and edicts and memorials were issued in both Chinese and the Manchu written language. Always with an eye toward projecting legitimacy, Qing emperors also sought to control the empire's high culture. As we have noted, Manchu "bannermen" of the various garrisons were kept in their own special quarters in the towns and cities. Manchus were forbidden to intermarry with the local population and Manchu women were enjoined from foot-binding.

As a means of instilling loyalty to the new order, the Manchu conqueror Dorgon instituted the infamous "queue edict" in 1645: all males, regardless of ethnicity were now required on pain of death to adopt the Manchu hair style of shaved forehead and long pigtail in the back—the *queue*—as the outward sign of submission to the dynasty. This distinctive hairstyle can be seen in early photographs taken of Chinese men until the Qing dynasty fell in 1912. As it was put with a kind of sinister whimsy, "Keep the hair, lose the head; keep the head, lose the hair." The results, however, were bloody and long lasting. The edict provoked revolts in several cities and the attendant casualties in its suppression may have numbered in the hundreds of thousands. For the remainder of the Qing era, rebels and protestors routinely cut their queues as the first order of business. During the Taiping Rebellion (1851–1864), for example, the insurgents were known as "the long-haired rebels" from their immediate abandonment of the Qing hairstyle. Yet over time the population also became surprisingly routinized to the style. In a number of cases in the wake of the 1911 revolution, many men resisted cutting their queues. It is worth mentioning, too, that the Qing made several efforts to eliminate foot-binding, not only for Manchus but also for all the empire's women.

Manchu Hair Styling. (A) A Manchu lady having her hair prepared in the elaborate and ornamented style that was customary at the time. Married women often wore elegant gold, silver or jade hairpins, in a style called "the golden head." Since Manchu women did not bind their feet it was often said that they had "a golden head and heavenly feet." (B) The more familiar men's hairstyle of the *bianzi*, or queue shown in this early photograph, was imposed on all Chinese males as a symbol of loyalty to the regime.

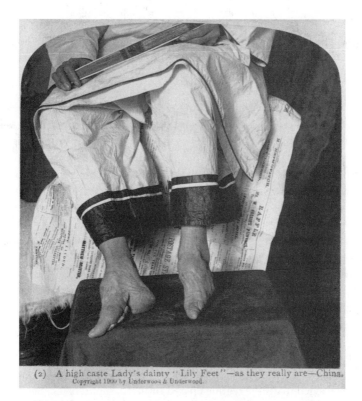

(2)   A high caste Lady's dainty "Lily Feet"—as they really are—China.
Copyright 1900 by Underwood & Underwood.

Bound Feet. Begun in the Song Dynasty, the practice of tightly wrapping the feet of young girls to reduce their size and create the "lily buds" of male erotic fantasy would continue halfway into the twentieth century.

As a number of scholars have suggested, the situation of the Qing represents a curious relationship between a cultural core and its periphery, in which the conquest of the core by the periphery brings the core temporary renewal, but the interests of stability loom so large for the newcomers that they become the ones who cling most tenaciously to the forms of the old order. In this view, by the end of the Qing period, when the empire was faced with foreign pressure and domestic agitation for reform, the Manchu court and nobility were willing to risk the collapse of the empire to retain the power of their dynasty and position. In contrast, it might also be argued that it was precisely the threat to the old elites represented by the Qing reforms of the early twentieth century that deprived the dynasty of crucial support (see Chapter 6).

At the same time, recent scholarship has increasingly shown that from the beginning of the dynasty there was a powerful ideological element to Qing rule that insisted that the empire was not merely the Manchus ruling the Han, but that it was an enormous multicultural entity. As we will see shortly, for example, conquest in minority areas was generally accompanied by efforts to reconcile the conquered to their distinctive place in the new order. This was particularly true of the Mongols and the Tibetans in the eighteenth century. Although the Qing conquest of Xinjiang and the quelling of the revolt of Yaqub Beg in the 1870s were bloody affairs accompanied by what today would be termed "ethnic cleansing" and "cultural genocide" among the Muslims in the region, Qing propaganda always insisted that all the peoples in the empire—even those outside the wall or China's formal borders—were part of the Qing family. Such expressions as "inner and outer" and "Chinese and foreigners" as "one family" routinely appear in official documents. This was even carried into the larger diplomatic world: China's first representatives to Europe, Japan, and the Americas routinely presented credentials that read in part that the emperor considers that "all the world is one family." As one historian notes,

> Thus in China's empire, as in other colonial empires, marginalized minorities were already being portrayed in a context calculated to advertise the distinction and the all-embracing dominion of the ruling power. Replicated in print and paraded on the podium, such attitudes . . . would be adopted by later regimes, whether chauvinistically Nationalist, patronizingly Maoist, or tourism-minded market-socialist. (John Keay, *China: A History*, New York: Harper Press, 2008 p. 453)

The Three Emperors

Since they needed to get the regime up and running, suppress incipient rebellion in the provinces and Taiwan, and consolidate gains already made, the Qing had little incentive to change the centralized imperial system of the Ming. Indeed, they had little choice but to keep it since they lacked the personnel to force wholesale changes down to the local level. They did, however, impose the banner system as a kind of parallel administrative organ to go along with the Manchu garrisons occupying their separate quarters in the larger cities.

Over time they also made one significant addition to the uppermost level of the bureaucracy. While retaining the Ming Grand Secretariat, the emperor Kangxi's successor Yongzheng set up an ad hoc inner advisory body called the *Grand Council* in 1733. Over the succeeding decades the Grand Council became the supreme "inner" advisory group to the emperor, whereas the Grand Secretariat was relegated to handling less crucial "outer" matters of policy making and implementation. By the nineteenth century, nearly all important matters were decided by the Grand Council.

As if in harmony with the rhythms of the dynastic cycle, the Qing had the good fortune to have three highly capable rulers in succession: Kangxi, Yongzheng, and Qianlong. Known as "the **Three Emperors**," they reigned collectively from 1664 to 1795 and presided over what was arguably imperial China's greatest era of global power and influence. During their reigns China's territory doubled, expanding to most of its "natural borders" and incorporating Mongolia, Tibet, Taiwan, and most of Xinjiang, as well as exercising suzerainty over Korea and

Vietnam. With the new territories and the global trade in new food crops, the population doubled to perhaps 300 million. Moreover, as we noted previously, the empire's enormous internal economy and burgeoning export trade drove that of all of Eurasia, although this was not well understood at the time. China's military forces dwarfed those of any potential competitors, although toward the end of Qianlong's reign, the use of improved drill and flintlock firearms saw the technological edge in weaponry move toward Europe. Finally, nearly all observers during this period remarked on the peace, prosperity, and excellence of Confucian government, some even seeing it as a model for their own countries.

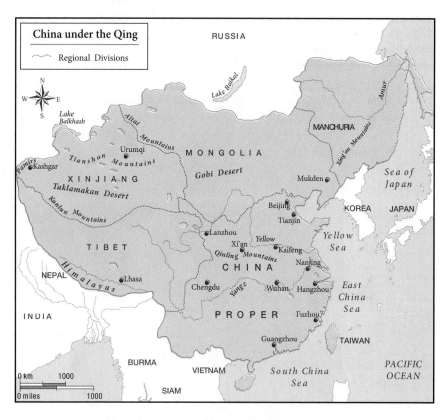

MAP 3.1
China under the Qing

The Age of Kangxi

For most of the seventeenth century, however, the pacification of the empire remained the primary task. Much of this was accomplished under the able leadership of Nurhachi's great-grandson, the Kangxi emperor, who reigned from 1661 to 1722. Kangxi's reign, the longest of any Chinese emperor, was well documented with memorials from provincial officials, accounts by European travelers and missionaries who had access to him at court, and his own writings. Indeed, Kangxi began the palace memorial system—in which any official of any rank could send a message (memorial) to the emperor—to receive unfiltered information from his realm. The practice continued throughout the Qing era, and the tens of thousands of memorials from various imperial reigns have constituted some of the most important source material for later Chinese imperial history. Kangxi was a "hands-on" ruler, physically active, often leading military campaigns, and traveled extensively through his realm. A series of commemorative scrolls depict his southern tours and, like those of his grandson, Qianlong, his real activities found their way into popular literature and local folklore. Both emperors were often depicted as touring their realms in disguise, righting wrongs and ferreting out and punishing abusive officials. Indeed, a recent made-for-television movie series on Kangxi's legendary exploits found eager audiences in the People's Republic of China.

Emperor Kangxi. The long reign of Kangxi (1661–1722) began a period of unprecedented power, wealth, and influence for both the Qing and imperial China more generally. Here the emperor sits in his study, perhaps in his forties, at the peak of his powers.

Throughout the 1640s and 1650s various remnants of Ming loyalists attempted to create regimes in the south, although these were summarily crushed. More serious was the maritime threat posed by the formidable Zheng Chenggong (1624–1662), more popularly known as "Coxinga" or "Koxinga." Zheng's family had been merchants in Japan (his mother was Japanese) with powerful maritime connections in China. He had been adopted by one of the Ming pretenders in the south and by the early 1650s had a headquarters in Fujian province, from where he directed the most powerful fleet on the China coast. In 1659, in an attempt to restore the Ming to Nanjing, his ships sailed up the Yangzi but were soundly defeated by the Banner land forces and their heavy cannon. Following this setback, Qing armies advanced on Fujian and, in an attempt to halt any assistance to Zheng's forces, tried to remove the population from the coast of the southern seaboard provinces. Zheng, however, and a number of emigrants now moved to Taiwan.

Taiwan was very much a frontier territory, with a significant aboriginal population and no formal Chinese claim on it at this point. The Portuguese had established a trading base on what they called "Formosa" but had been expelled by the Dutch, who set up a base called Fort Zeelandia. The base was an important entrepot for the Dutch, who were at this point the only Europeans allowed to trade in Japan. Moreover, they hoped for trade concessions from the Qing and so felt obligated to support them against Zheng's forces. The result was a siege of Zeelandia by Zheng in 1661, from which the Dutch were expelled. Zheng soon died and his son then held their island redoubt for another two decades before his defeat by Qing naval forces. From this point on, Taiwan, despite periodic revolts and later attempts by Europeans and even Americans to establish bases on the island, remained part of Fujian Province until being ceded to Japan in 1895 as spoils of the Sino-Japanese War. It would remain in Japanese hands until 1945. In one of the more ironic historical parallels of the region, the Nationalist regime, like Zheng's Ming loyalists, would flee to Taiwan in 1949—where their descendants remain today.

Although the threat posed by Zheng's naval power was troublesome, a more serious problem developed for Kangxi in the interior of the empire. Moreover, it was a problem caused not by Ming loyalists but by regional leaders who had served the Qing. Indeed, the most powerful of the three "feudatories" in question was none other than Wu Sangui, who had invited the Manchu forces into China. Wu had served the new regime well. He had driven the Ming remnant out of Yunnan and Guizhou and into Burma. He had also been well rewarded with command of the area and effectively created a military dictatorship in the region. The Qing had similarly rewarded two other commanders with such feudatory powers in Guangdong and Fujian. The south and west had traditionally been regions that fomented rebellion; the seaboard provinces of Guangdon and Fujian, likewise, had been the recent site of "Koxinga's" exploits, so it made sense to impose a system of martial law there.

Divorced from the oversight of the Confucian bureaucracy, however, the three feudatories were unconstrained by the normal checks and balances of the administrative system and proceeded to enrich themselves and accrue civil and military power. As had many officials during times of weakness at the center, they had become regional warlords. In 1673, Kangxi accepted pro-forma requests from two of the feudatories to resign their official posts. They had expected their requests to be ceremonially turned down and to be given their rewards and positions permanently. When this was not forthcoming, they rose in rebellion in what became known as the Revolt of the Three Feudatories (1673–1681). Although the rebels enjoyed some initial success as a result of their local power and calls for the overthrow of the Qing and restoration of the Ming, many distrusted them because they had originally been defectors from the Ming to the Qing. Wu himself belatedly tried to found yet another "Zhou" dynasty without success. The inability of the Feudatories to work together allowed the Qing to crush them piecemeal and the threat was subdued by 1683.

Expanding the Empire

As had been the case in past dynasties, the Qing sought to safeguard and expand the borders of the empire by bringing peoples on the periphery into the imperial system through a judicious application of the carrot and the stick or, as we have noted previously, the "loose rein," and "using barbarians to check barbarians." In practical terms, this meant a final reckoning with the Mongols. Many Mongol groups had allied themselves with the Manchus and there had long existed a Mongol Banner division. But the disorder accompanying the dynastic change and pacification, including the recent Revolt of the Three Feudatories, had produced a new drive for unity among the Oirats of northwestern Mongolia. Kangxi himself, in the vignette at the opening of this chapter, had noted the danger posed by the possibility of the "Eleuths"—the Oirats—uniting with other Mongol groups.

In the final decades of the seventeenth century, that danger seemed particularly acute to the Qing. Under the Khan Galban (r. 1671–1697), a group of the Oirats variously called the *Zunghars*, *Junghars*, or *Dzungars* seemed to be on the verge of just such unification. With religious links to the Tibetans and the Yellow Hat sect of the Dalai Lama and connections and influence within Wu Sangui's feudatory, a religiously and politically reunified Mongol threat combined with simmering anti-Qing sentiment seemed imminent. Kangxi therefore pursued a strategy that reached out to the expansive Russian state in the Treaty of Nerchinsk in 1689 (see later) to blunt any further expansion below Siberia and into the Manchu homeland and then turned his attention to the Zunghar threat. In 1696 and 1697 Kangxi accompanied his large and well-equipped army on a war of extermination against Galban's forces. He and his successors—Yongzheng and Qianlong—took more than 60 years to finish it. With the help of an accompanying smallpox epidemic, they accomplished their end. Along the way, they pushed the borders of the empire deep into Xinjiang, where Qianlong's forces defeated the Muslim Khojas in 1759.

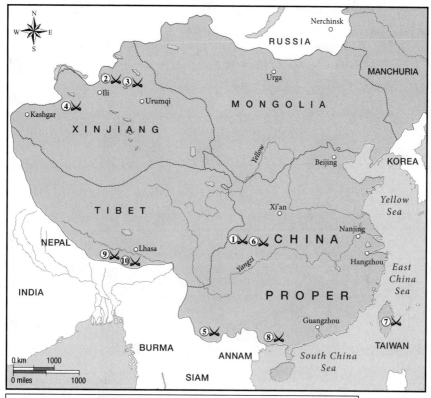

Campaigns of Qianlong

① First Jinchuan campaign (1747–49)
② First Zunghar campaign (1755)
③ Second Zunghar campaign (1756–57)
④ Suppression of Khoja rebellion (1757–59)
⑤ Burma campaigns (1767–71)
⑥ Second Jinchuan campaign (1771–1776)

⑦ Suppression of Lin Shuangwen rebellion, Taiwan (1787–88)
⑧ Vietnam campaign (1786–89)
⑨ First Gurkha campaign (1790)
⑩ Second Gurkha campaign (1792)

MAP 3.2
Campaigns of Qianlong

Meanwhile, by means of improved cannon and small arms, along with bribes and presents to friendly chieftains, and the intervention of the Qing in religious disputes regarding Tibetan Buddhism, the Yongzheng emperor established a protectorate over Tibet in 1727. The Dalai Lama was sanctioned to rule as the approved temporal and religious leader. To cement the relationship further, the emperor built a replica of a Tibetan *stupa* just outside the Manchu quarter in Beijing and a model of the Dalai Lama's Potala Palace at the emperor's summer retreat in Jehol.

Tibetan Stupa and Temple, Beijing. This marble *chorten*, the Tibetan interpretation of the Buddhist stupa, or reliquary, was built by the Qianlong emperor for the visit of the Panchen Lama in 1779, to cement the new relationship growing from the establishment of the Qing protectorate over Tibet.

PATTERNS UP CLOSE

Qing China Through The Emperor's Eyes

"Heaven is high and the emperor far away" is an expression that is in many ways appropriate for historians as well as ordinary people in imperial China. Of course, we know a great deal about court protocol, about the memorials they answered, about palace intrigues, and about the events recorded in dynastic histories and other formal records. What of the inner man, however? What kinds of quotidian things interested a man who was often the most powerful person in the world? How did he think about his realm? About the world? Was he able to see through the agendas of courtiers and read between the lines of flowery formal language in his contacts with them?

Fortunately, we have a number of private musings from the scattered fragments of the personal records of Emperor Kangxi (1661–1722), China's longest reigning ruler, whom we met in the opening vignette of this chapter. As we have seen briefly already, Kangxi defies the stereotype of a Chinese emperor as a shy, retiring presence, cosseted by eunuchs and protocol in the Forbidden City, insulated from the actual running of his empire. He was instead a remarkably involved ruler, not only well informed about the inner workings of his realm but also probably more knowledgeable about the realities of the outside world than most of his successors would prove. Moreover, he was an extremely vigorous man, both physically and in his intellectual pursuits. He enjoyed riding, shooting, hunting, and fishing. Indeed, his strategy in personally pursuing Galban, he noted, was one he had employed on many hunts. He strove to be impartial in his dealings with Manchus and Chinese, although he could not resist commenting that he found the former bolder and more forthright. He was also frank about his own shortcomings and more often than not willing to accept good advice, regardless of its source. His mind was eclectic in its inquisitiveness, and he had a constant urge to notice and understand things ranging from animal and plant species to astronomical phenomena to foreign religion and politics. In the following excerpts one can see his devotion to justice and Confucian morality distinctly evident—as is his impatience with fawning officials:

> For his part, the emperor has to withstand the praise that showers upon him and fills his ears, for it is of no more use to him than so-called "restorative medicine"; these banalities and evasions have all the sustenance of dainty pastries, and one grows sick of them. (p. 44)[1]

> On tours I learned about the common people's grievances by talking with them, or by accepting their petitions. In northern China I asked peasants about their officials, looked at their houses, and discussed their crops. In the South I heard pleas from a woman whose husband had been wrongfully enslaved. . . . But if someone was attacked in an anonymous message, then I refused to take action, for we should always confront a witness directly; and if someone exaggerated too stupidly, then too I would not listen. A man swam toward my boat in Hangzhou with a petition tied around his neck, shouting out that he had a certain enemy

continued

who was the number-one man in the world for committing evil acts—and I simply had my retainers ask him, "Who then is number two?" (p. 43)

Kangxi blamed himself in part for the outbreak and duration of the *Sanfan* conflict (the Revolt of the Three Feudatories) and it colored his approach in extending mercy toward dissent and discontent:

There had been eight years of bitter war and, though peace had come, the scars were not yet healed. I refused, and continued to refuse, all requests that I be granted new honorific titles as a victor, because this war had resulted from my miscalculations, and the responsibility for it—for all of it—was mine. I had not expected Wu Sangui to revolt in 1673 when I accepted his retirement pleas. I had not expected so many to follow Wu when he did revolt. And this I wrote out and gave to the Grand Secretary Ledehun to read to all my officials before the Qianqing Gate that victory winter. They would have to see that I couldn't claim the name of victor in good heart, since the victory sprang from so much error. (p. 37)

He saw himself not as a figurehead but as a true commander in chief and while campaigning he took pride in living like his troops:

While on the move I'd live roughly and without formality—those passing in front of me didn't have to dismount, and as on the hunts we would cook fish or food we caught in a simple way, and sit sometimes in the herders' tents and eat, and drink kumis (a mildly alcoholic drink made from fermented mare's milk) as we talked. . . . And in the frontier towns I would not have the streets cleared, but would pass by particularly slowly, so that all would have a chance to see me; or I'd let the common people gather round and watch me as I ate and give them millet and meat.

Wherever I went among the rank and file, I would call some of the soldiers forward and chat with them, for after a longish period of peace men forget about fighting, and the youngsters need to learn from the veterans. . . .

The frontier areas can be cold and damp and remote, with deserts that seem to stretch forever, with a few wild sheep and asses but no people, no houses, and no birds flying. I have seen with my own eyes men having to boil up a few nuts and eat them to keep alive, with no knowledge of how they might get through the winter; and cattle so thin that, though living, they soon must starve to death. (pp. 19–20)

Even as his vigor declined, his mind stayed sharp—although his insight was also sufficiently keen to sense that it was far from what it had been in its voracious youth:

When you are young your mind is sharp and penetrating—after you grow up the thoughts scatter and gallop away. So you must not lose the chance to study while you are still young. The books I read when I was seven or eight were not forgotten after fifty or sixty years; those read after I was twenty are forgotten unless I review them after a few months. If you had no chance to study when young, then certainly you should still do so when you are grown up—but things you studied as a child are the light of the rising sun; the studies in your maturity, a candle. (p. 112)

—[1]All excerpts from Jonathan Spence, *Emperor of China: Self-Portrait of K'ang Hsi*, New York: Vintage Books, 1975.

The Late Summer of Empire: Qianlong

With the traditional threats from the borders now quashed the reign of the Qianlong emperor, the period from 1736 to 1795, marked both the high point and the beginning of the decline of the Qing dynasty—and of imperial China itself. As we have seen, the period witnessed China's expansion to its greatest size during the imperial era. This was accompanied by a doubling of its population to perhaps 300 million by 1800. By almost any measure, its internal economy dwarfed that of any other country and equaled or surpassed that of Europe as a whole until the Industrial Revolution was well under way.

Although the Qing army had already been eclipsed in terms of efficiency of drill and probably weaponry by the leading nations of Europe, Qianlong wielded this power successfully a number of times during his reign, with expeditions against pirates and rebels on Taiwan and in punitive campaigns against Vietnam, Nepal, and Burma between 1766 and 1792. During his long life, he also tried, with limited success, to take up the writing brush of a scholar and connoisseur, creating the collection of art that is today the core of the National Palace Museum's holdings on Taiwan. As it had under Kangxi, the state under Qianlong sponsored monumental literary enterprises on a scale still awesome to contemplate today (see later). Through the small but steady stream of information on the empire circulating around Europe, it seemed to some that the Chinese had solved a number of the problems of good government and might provide practical models of statecraft for Europeans to emulate.

When he stepped down in 1795, stopping short of equaling the 61-year reign of his grandfather out of filial devotion, he had unknowingly moved into a new phase of the dynasty's and the empire's fortunes. For the moment, the empire was at peace, its economy never larger or stronger, foreign nations

Portrait of Qianlong. Qianlong (1736–1795) was the third in the line of emperors (Kangxi and Yongzheng) who presided over imperial China at its height. As had Kangxi and Yongzheng, he employed European technical advisors in various areas. One of the more intriguing cultural interactions between China and Europe resulted in this portrait by the Italian Jesuit painter and architect, Giuseppe Castiglione (1688–1766). Castiglione served Kangxi, Yongzheng and Qianlong and absorbed Chinese painting styles while influencing his Chinese colleagues in the used of vanishing point perspective. The interaction of these influences can be seen in this portrait of the young Qianlong, portrayed in court dress but gazing confidently full on toward the viewer.

never more cultured or submissive, foreign trade never more prosperous, and foreign relations never better managed. Although it scarcely seemed like a harbinger of things to come, the bizarre envoy from the king of far-off Great Britain and his large entourage, despite their lack of understanding of proper protocol, had been handled appropriately and dispatched home two years before with a message to his ruler that China really had no pressing need of any of his country's goods or for an ambassador to take up residence in Beijing and that trade would go on as before. In less than 50 years all of this would change.

Early European Contacts

Ironically, it was precisely at the time that China abandoned its oceanic expeditions that tiny Portugal on the Atlantic coast of Europe surmounted its first big hurdle in pursuit of what would become the first worldwide maritime trade empire. By the 1440s, Portuguese navigators had rounded the bulge of West Africa and opened commercial relations with the coastal kingdoms there. Scarcely a decade after Vasco da Gama arrived in Calicut in 1498, their first ships appeared in Chinese waters. By 1557, these *Folangqi*—the Chinese transliteration of "Franks," a generic term for Europeans transmitted by the Arabs to Malacca, where it was transformed into "*Ferenghi*"—had wrested the first European colony from the Chinese at Macao (pinyin Macau). It was destined to be the longest lived European colony as well, remaining under Portuguese control until 1999. From this point on, through merchants and missionaries, the contacts would frequently be profitable and sometimes disastrous. Ultimately, they provided some of the most far-reaching interactions of world history.

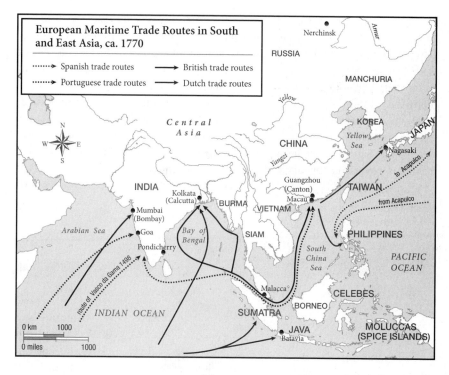

European Maritime Trade Routes in South and East Asia, ca. 1770

········▸ Spanish trade routes   ⟶ British trade routes
········▸ Portuguese trade routes   ⟶ Dutch trade routes

MAP 3.3
European Maritime Trade Routes in South and East Asia, ca. 1770

The first Portuguese and Spanish traders were less than impressive to the Chinese officials charged with handling commercial affairs. As we have seen, Confucian tradition had long maintained that merchants were generally a disreputable, if necessary, class. The outlandish appearance, disagreeable smell—from months aboard ship with primitive sanitary facilities—and aggressive, self-confident behavior of these so-called "men of the Western Ocean" only solidified this impression. Additionally, trade restrictions imposed by the Ming had only partially reduced the network of Chinese merchants long established in the ports of Southeast Asia, Malaya, and the Moluccas. In these areas they often traded in contraband goods and competed for markets with Arab, Malayan, and Japanese merchants and pirates. In short, the Europeans had now entered a region of trade where the lines were quite fluid between legitimate and illegitimate enterprises and both they and the Chinese authorities reacted accordingly.

The Canton Trade

Although China's commerce with the maritime Atlantic states grew rapidly in the eighteenth century, the Europeans had not yet been fully incorporated into the Qing diplomatic system. During the preceding century, the expansion of Russia into Siberia and the region around the Amur River had prompted the Qing to negotiate the Treaty of Nerchinsk in 1689. Under its terms, negotiated with Kangxi's Jesuit advisors acting as interpreters and go-betweens (with Latin as the negotiators' *lingua franca*), the Russians agreed to abandon their last forts along the Amur and were given rights to continue their lucrative caravan trade in the interior. Formal borders were established in Manchuria, and the first attempts at settling claims to the Central Asian regions of Ili and Kuqa (Kholjia) were made. Significantly, because trade relations with Russia were at this point exclusively overland through Central Asia, Russian envoys were also permitted to reside in Beijing but in a residence like those used by the temporary envoys of tribute missions.

Canton Factories CA. 1800. Under the "Canton System" all maritime trade with Europeans, and after 1784, the Americans (note the U.S. flag in the center of the painting), was tightly regulated and controlled through the port of Guangzhou (Canton). Foreign merchants were not allowed within the city walls and were confined to their "factories"—offices and warehouses along the Pearl River waterfront, as depicted here.

The situation among the European traders attempting to enter Chinese seaports, however, was quite different. The British East India Company, having established its base at Calcutta in 1690, shortly sought to expand its operations to China. At the same time, the Qing, fresh from capturing the last Ming bastion on Taiwan and worried about Ming loyalists in other areas, sought to control contact with foreign and overseas Chinese traders as much as possible while keeping their lucrative export trade at a sustainable level. Their solution, implemented in 1699, was to permit overseas trade only at the southern port of Guangzhou, more widely known as Canton. The local merchant's guild, or **Cohong** (*pinyin:gonghang*), was granted a monopoly on the trade and supervised by a special official from the imperial Board of Revenue (*pinyin: Hubu*). The official was referred to by the European merchants as the Hoppo.

Much like the Tokugawa in seventeenth-century Japan, the Qing permitted only a small number of foreigners, mostly traders from the English, French, and Dutch East India Companies, to reside at the port. They were confined to a small compound of foreign **factories** (not places where goods were manufactured, but sites where the various "factors" involved in trade lived and worked), were not permitted inside the city walls, and could not bring their wives or families along. Even small violations of the regulations could result in a suspension of trading privileges, and all infractions and disputes were judged according to Chinese law. Finally, since foreign affairs under these circumstances were considered a dimension of trade, all diplomatic issues were settled by local officials in Canton—hence Qianlong's refusal to permit a British embassy in Beijing.

The eighteenth century proved to be a boom time for all involved in the trade, and the British in particular increasingly viewed it as a valuable part of their growing commercial power. By 1770 the "Canton trade" was perhaps the most profitable of the British East India Company's many concerns. Among the items most avidly sought was porcelain. Highly distinctive blue-and-white ware—the result of employing pigments with cobalt oxide from the areas around modern Iran and Iraq—set the world standard for elegance. The artistic excellence of Chinese porcelain had spawned imitators throughout the Chinese periphery. By 1500, porcelain works in Korea, Japan, and Vietnam supplied a burgeoning market both at home and throughout East and Southeast Asia. Thus, there was already a highly developed regional market for what was, at the time, arguably the world's most highly developed technology. The period from 1500 to the mid-nineteenth century, however, brought about another great innovation in which China was the driving force: the world market for porcelain.

China's wares had found customers for centuries in nearly every corner of Eurasia and North and East Africa. Before the sixteenth century, however, only a trickle of Ming porcelain made its way to Europe. With the setting up of the first European trade empires, however, the demand for porcelain skyrocketed. Portuguese, Spanish, and later Dutch, French, English, and, after 1784, American merchants all sought porcelain in ever-increasing amounts. From 1500 to 1800 porcelain was arguably the single most important commodity in the world commercial revolution that was unfolding. Although estimates vary, economic historians have suggested that between a third and a half of all the silver produced in the Americas during this time went to pay for porcelain. Vast quantities were shipped to Britain's American colonies. Incoming ships often used the bulk cargoes as ballast, and foreign merchants sent custom orders to their Chinese counterparts for Chinese-style wares designed for use at Western tables. Such was the prominence of this "export porcelain" in the furnishings of period homes that scarcely any family of means was without it.

With the prominence of mercantilist theory during the seventeenth and eighteenth centuries, it is not surprising that foreign manufacturers sought to break the Chinese porcelain monopoly. The Japanese, for example, forced a group of Korean potters to work at its famous Arita works to turn out Sino-Korean designs; the Dutch marketed "delftware" as an attempt to copy Chinese "blue willow" porcelain. It was not until German experimenters in Saxony happened on a workable formula for hard-paste porcelain—after years of trial and error and melting down Chinese wares for analysis—that their facility at Meissen began to produce true porcelain in 1710. Chinese manufacturers, however, would still drive the market until the later nineteenth century.

Export Porcelain. By the 18th century, export porcelain—items either made to order by Chinese porcelain works for the European market or generic items made to suit Western tastes—had become such big business that cargoes of them were sometimes used as ship's ballast on homeward voyages. Shown here is a European style candlestick with Chinese motifs in the much desired cobalt blue of Ming and Qing wares.

Taperstick. Made in China for export to Europe. 18th century (ca. 1700). Hard-paste porcelain, H. 5 1/4 in (13.3 cm.). Purchase, Winfield Foundation Gift, 1970 (1970.266.3). The Metropolitan Museum of Art. Image copyright © The Metropolitan Museum of Art. Image source: Art Resource, NY.

By the 1770s Europe's and especially Great Britain's enormous thirst for tea had grown to challenge porcelain for supremacy among the Canton traders. The quantity of tea shipped by the British East India Company alone rose fivefold from 1720 to 1730, surpassing a million pounds; between 1760 and 1770 it tripled from 3 million to 9 million pounds. Silk also grew in importance, as well as lacquer ware, wicker and rattan furniture, and dozens of other local specialties increasingly targeted at the export market. After 1784, the United States also joined the Canton trade, but despite the growing American presence, it was the British East India Company that dominated the Canton factories. Both the Cohong and the foreign chartered companies carefully guarded their respective monopolies, and the system worked reasonably well in keeping competition low and profits high on all sides.

Missionaries

Shortly after the arrival of the first European merchants in East Asia came the first Catholic missionaries. Although the crusading impulse was still very much alive in Christian dealings with Muslim merchants in the Indies, the Franciscan, Dominican, and, later, Jesuit missionaries were quick to realize the vast potential for conversions in China and Japan. The various missionary orders set up headquarters in Malacca and in 1549 the Franciscan Francis Xavier landed in Japan. The endemic conflict among the *daimyo*, or feudal lords, of Japan as they struggled to unify the islands and hold the shogunate helped create a demand for Western goods, especially firearms, and the association of these with Christianity allowed considerable progress to be made in gaining conversions. China, however, seemed to require a vastly different strategy.

Wary of potentially disruptive foreign influences, the Ming at first refused entry to missionaries. Once admitted, the Franciscans and Dominicans, with their limited training in Chinese language and culture, made little headway. Additionally, their efforts were largely aimed at seeking conversions among the poor, which won them scant respect or influence among China's elite. The Jesuits, however, tried a different tack. Led by Matteo Ricci (1552–1610) and his successors, Adam Schall von Bell (1591–1666) and Ferdinand Verbiest (1623–1688), they immersed themselves in the classical language and high culture of the empire and gained recognition through their expertise in mathematics, astronomy, cartography, military science, and other new European skills sought by the imperial court. Jesuit advisers served the last Ming emperors as court astronomers and military engineers and successfully made the transition to the new dynasty.

The high point of their influence was reached during the reign of the Kangxi emperor. Indeed, the interval of the strong Jesuit presence in Kangxi's court marks one of the most intriguing instances of cross-cultural exchange of the early modern era. Schall had been a tutor of Kangxi and served in his last years as his official court astronomer and mathematician. Chinese emperors were habitually on the lookout for astronomical phenomena that might be interpreted as ominous for the dynastic cycle. Kangxi's habit of canvassing reliable officials for weather information and

Matteo Ricci. Matteo Ricci, (1552–1610) Italian Jesuit priest, was one of the founding figures of the Jesuit China Mission. Unlike his colleagues from other missionary orders, his strategy was to educate himself in the classical language, absorb Chinese high culture, and use his knowledge of mathematics and astronomy to win influence at court, which he did with great success. Jesuit advisors served in various capacities at the Ming and Qing courts until 1837 and at one point prompted Kangxi to consider adopting Catholicism.

crop reports—in hopes of anticipating crop failures or other similar signs of Heaven's displeasure—had helped spawn the palace memorial system. Now he commissioned an entire European-style observatory to be set up in Beijing. Because of such efforts on the part of his Jesuit advisors, Kangxi actively considered conversion to Catholicism—an act that would have potentially netted the Church tens of millions of adherents.

The papacy, however, had long considered Jesuit liturgical and doctrinal adaptations to local sensibilities problematic. In China, the Jesuits' use of tea and rice during the Eucharist instead of bread and wine was looked upon with disfavor by Rome. More difficult still was the Jesuits' tacit acceptance of their converts' veneration of family shrines and ceremonies at Confucian temples. No doubt many of the annual rites the emperor himself maintained at the Temple of Heaven and the Temple of the Earth in Beijing would have proved problematic for officials in Rome as well. The imperial court and the Papacy thus became involved in the so-called Rites Controversy. In the end, after several decades of intermittent discussion, Kangxi's successor, Yongzheng, banned the Jesuit order's activities in China in 1724. Christianity and missionary activity were driven underground, although the Qing would retain a Jesuit court astronomer into the nineteenth century. It would not be until after 1860 that missionaries and Chinese Christians would be allowed to venture openly beyond their treaty port enclaves.

China and the European Enlightenment

Although the European intellectual influence on China was limited to a small circle at court, the reports of the Jesuits and other foreign observers from the empire had a considerable effect on several of the important figures of the European Enlightenment and on creating an overall image of China in the West. For the *philosophes* Voltaire, Liebnitz, Diderot, and Montesquieu, the vision of a vast, wealthy, and powerful empire governed by a highly developed bureaucracy according to a pragmatic and secular system of ethics provided much ammunition for critiques of European monarchies. A Chinese Christian convert, Hoange, who secured a minor position in the French government as a cataloger of its Chinese works, provided a wealth of information to the young Montesquieu, who incorporated it into his satire of French life, *The Persian Letters*. The emphasis placed on the importance of land by Chinese officials was also reflected in the arguments of the Physiocrats, whose chief exponent, Francois Quesnay, was sometimes called "the Confucius of Europe." Philology was also greatly enhanced by the production of the first Chinese dictionaries for use with European languages. Finally, the growing trade in luxury goods spurred both a fashion for **chinoiserie** (items done in Chinese styles, real or imagined) among the elite and a desire among European manufacturers to develop domestic industries in such items as silk and porcelain. Although viable silk industries were created in both France and Italy, the manufacture of true porcelain in Europe would not be seen until the innovations of Meissen and Wedgwood.

Chinoiserie. The favorable image of China in the West during the 18th century created by missionaries, merchants, and the handful of travelers who went there—as well as the tremendous popularity of porcelain, tea, and luxury goods, prompted a fashion for imitation Chinese items known as *Chinoiserie*. The European ability to make real porcelain by the 1700s stimulated this copying as did the growing market for lacquer ware. The two items here are typical products of this fad.

VILLAGE, FAMILY, AND SOCIETY

As with other agrarian–urban empires, much of what little we know about Chinese peasant life comes through literary sources. Most of these were compiled by the scholar-gentry, although starting in the seventeenth century a small but influential number were also produced by Westerners traveling in China. The local histories and *gazetteers* (local atlases with demographic, genealogical, and historical information) with their reliance on unusual events—famines, revolts, riots, spectacular feats, and exemplary wives—generally fit peasant experiences, when they are addressed at all, into the mold of history as Confucian morality. It should be noted, however, that this was also a period when the expansion of the empire and the inclusion of new minority peoples, as well as Han Chinese emigrants into new regions, were also extensively documented. As we noted earlier, the way these newly colonized people were portrayed was generally in keeping with Qing official ideology of inclusion and diversity in the service of enhancing the dynasty's image of universal domain.

More authentic, although still fragmentary, pictures of village life emerge from the works of popular writers like Pu Songling in his rich depictions of folk myth and religious syncretism. Even with these limitations, however, some generalizations can still be made about rural and family life in Qing times. First, although the introduction of new crops during the period had brought more marginal land under cultivation, allowed for a huge increase in the population, and helped lend momentum to the trend toward more commercialization of agriculture, the work, technology, and overall rhythms of peasant life had changed little over the preceding few centuries. Second, as with the gathering political tensions, some early signs of economic stress were already present toward the end of Qianlong's reign. Chief among these was the problem of absentee landlordism. This would grow increasingly acute as the vitality of the commercial networks and market towns of central and southern China increased and the gentry were drawn by the opportunities and amenities of the cities. In addition, successful tea, cotton, silk, and luxury goods traders frequently retained their compounds in the cities while buying land and degrees and becoming scholar-gentry, further increasing the incidence of absenteeism in the countryside. During the next century, with the dislocations of the Opium Wars, Taiping Rebellion, and the foreign Treaty Ports, the problem of absentee landlordism greatly accelerated.

Third, as we have seen before, pressures on patterns of village life tended to be magnified in the lives of women and girls. Elite women were routinely educated to be as marriageable as possible; their level of literacy was among the highest in the world's preindustrial societies. Study of proper Confucian decorum, writing model essays and chanting poetry, and a firm grasp of the *Xiaojing* (*Classic of Filial Piety*), and as we saw earlier, the *Nuerjing*, were central to their lessons. As noted earlier as well, women were expected to be modest and obedient and were usually separated from and subordinate to men.

Yet among women themselves, there was, as noted earlier, considerable scope for agency. It should be remembered that, as in previous Chinese dynasties, the dominance of women over the "inner realm" of the family remained largely complete. Moreover, as is often the case, the presence of laws, models of behavior, and valorization of these idealized representations can itself be interpreted as an indication of how frequently such norms were circumvented. For example, marriage and property laws were set up to reinforce these idealized qualities and relationships. The premium placed on mourning by both sexes was accompanied by the expectation that widows were to remain single and be subordinate to their oldest sons. Sometimes, however, the desire of a widow to remarry coincided with the ambition of male family members to control the family wealth. Thus, widows were occasionally encouraged to defy filial piety and loyalty and remarry, thus surrendering their wealth to their sons. Moreover, as Dorothy Ko has noted, elite women, even those predominantly occupied with domestic chores, were often intensely involved in artistic and literary pursuits. It was not uncommon for women to venture out of the home to sell their painting, poetry, and calligraphy to connoisseurs.

Women's assertiveness was more pronounced among Manchus, especially in the early years of the dynasty. Chinese commentators saw the newcomers' forthrightness with male strangers, unbound feet, and less attention paid to the "inner" and "outer" realms, as markers of barbarity and lack of assimilation to Confucian norms. Early European commentators saw the inquisitiveness of Manchu women in much more favorable terms and closer to the norms their own societies observed.

As with the wider debate on Manchu "sinicization" and identity, there is considerable disagreement on what practices continued by Manchu women deep into the Qing period actually represent. Many see the evolving Manchu identity as heavily gendered: Men forcing newly acquired Confucian norms (with the conspicuous absence of footbinding) on reluctant spouses and daughters determined to retain their own modes of dress and deportment. A number of scholars have explored the different ways Han and Manchu have viewed the concept of the "virtuous" (e.g., chaste) widow: On the surface seen in similar terms but more subtly as a mark of traditional nomadic honor among the Manchus and as an expression of filial piety by Han Confucians. Here again, the less understood role of minority practices in the Qing empire promises a number of rich areas for scholarly exploration.

Domestic Life. This 1873 photograph illustrates a pattern in Chinese history that has endured for millennia, namely, the centrality of the family and its Confucian hierarchy. In this portrait of the well to-do Yang family of Beijing, the father and eldest son occupy the places of honor under the central window of the ground floor, while the wives, concubines, infants, and servants look down from the upper veranda. In most cases, wealthy women such as those of the Yang family were nearly completely secluded from the outside world. The photographer reported, however, that these women frequently moistened their fingertips and rubbed them on the paper windowpanes to make them transparent so they could secretly watch events outside.

Social Mobility and the Scholar-Gentry

In the long sweep of world history, the many-layered system of examinations for entry into imperial China's bureaucracy seems unique in its scope and impact. Sifting at every level through vast numbers of test takers for the best and brightest in terms of their understanding of the Confucian Classics, the official class was not only able to perpetuate itself, but also ensured ideological orthodoxy and monopolized the surest route to both wealth and power. One of the proudest claims of the system's proponents was that it was open to all males—with some minor restrictions. Through the first part of the twentieth century, most scholars accepted this claim at face value. After World War II, however, the advent of improved statistical methods and increased access to local records brought the system under closer scrutiny. Pioneering studies of the Chinese scholar-gentry by Ho P'ing-ti and Chang Chung-li in the 1950s and 1960s ushered in an entirely new arena in Chinese social history. The result has been a divergence of opinion on both the relative openness of the system and its actual impact on social mobility in China.

One of the first to take up the issue in the postwar years was the sociologist and anthropologist Francis L. K. Hsu. For Hsu, one impediment to a more thorough-going understanding of the issue was that so much of the evidence brought to bear on it was anecdotal. In this regard, he asserted that those who claimed that the so-called "*yin* privilege" of allowing the son of an official to enter service without taking the exam undercut the openness of the system, had seriously overstated their case. Hsu's careful combing of the examination records and gazetteers of districts, prefectures, and provinces convinced him that there was instead a cycle of "rags to riches to rags," or "downward mobility," as he termed it.[2]

A study by Adam Yuen-chung Lui, done more than 30 years after Hsu's, produced similarly counterintuitive results. In analyzing factors that would be likely to affect the scores of the highest candidates in the metropolitan exams, Lui found that "only a very small portion of the . . . group whose fathers or uncles were themselves senior officials of the third rank or above benefited from their family influence."[3]

But does the mere fact of different families and ethnicities moving in and out of the system represent widespread accessibility or simply the circulation of elites within the few positions available at any given time? The Japanese scholar Ichisada Miyazaki, in his *China's Examination Hell* (1963), comes down firmly in favor of the second option: "The examination system actually dealt with this class [the wealthy], which had the surplus resources to meet the expenses of education and of the many different examinations." Hence, "seen in this light, the contention that the doors of the examination system were open to all applicants was an exaggeration, of course." Still, one must look at the prevailing conditions of the time and place to avoid the problem of *presentism*:

> But here, too, we must not lose sight of the historical context: the very idea that everyone should be eligible for the examinations, regardless of family

background or lineage, was incomparably forward-looking in its day. None-theless, from Sung times until very recently, the Chinese social structure changed very little, and the discrepancies between the rich and the poor continued to be extreme. During that long interval the examination system, too, continued with minimum change. Compared with European institutions, it was extremely progressive at its beginning—and very far behind the times at its end.[4]

Today the perception that "the Chinese social structure changed very little" has been challenged on a number of fronts. And so we come back to some basic questions: How should we measure change over time? Should those standards be different at, or for, different times? How does something so "incomparably forward-looking in its day" become "very far behind the times at the end?"

[2]From Francis L. K. Hsu, "Patterns of Downward Mobility," in Joanna Menzel, ed. *The Chinese Civil Service.* Boston: Heath, 1963, p. 41.

[3]Adam Yuen-chung Lui, *The Hanlin Academy.* Hamden, CT: Shoestring Press, 1981, pp. 167–8.

[4]Ichisada Miyazaki, Conrad Schirokauer, trans., *China's Examination Hell.* New Haven, CT: Yale University Press, 1963, 1976, 1981, pp. 119.

SCIENCE, CULTURE, AND INTELLECTUAL LIFE

As we have seen in other sections of this chapter, although China still confronted regional peoples as an expanding imperial power and cultural exporter, by the Qing era the scientific and technological prowess that had once led the world seemed to be slackening along the lines we explored in the so-called Needham Question: Why this slowdown from around 1500? Although various causes have been suggested for this, not the least common of which is that a kind of psychological paradigm of perfection had been reached, there was still plenty of scope for innovation.

Science and Literature

In geography, mathematics, and astronomy a fruitful exchange was inaugurated with European Jesuit missionaries in the seventeenth and eighteenth centuries among a small but influential group of Chinese officials. The most lasting legacy of this meeting was the European-style observatory in Beijing and a number of new maps of the world based on sixteenth and seventeenth-century explorations. Unfortunately, by the nineteenth century these were all but forgotten, and the inadequacy of the geographical knowledge of Chinese officials in policy-making positions was soon all too apparent.

The Beijing Observatory. One of the ways the Jesuits were able to gain favor at the imperial courts of two successive dynasties was through the New Sciences of the West. Jesuit mathematicians, technical advisors, mapmakers, and astronomers found an eager reception among their Chinese counterparts, the fruits of which included armillary spheres (shown on the left and right foreground in this illustration), and the celestial globe (middle foreground). The instruments were cast, in the 1680s, by Chinese artisans to the specifications of the Jesuit court mathematician Ferdinand Verbiest.

As in seventeenth-century France, the centralizing tendency of the government of China exercised considerable control in the cultural realm through patronage, monopoly, and licensing. As Manchus, the Kangxi, Yongzheng, and Qianlong emperors strove to validate their reigns by being patrons of the arts and aspiring to high levels of connoisseurship and cultivation of the best of the literati. As in other absolutist realms, they not only set the tone in matters of aesthetics, but also used mammoth cultural projects to direct the energies of scholars and officials into approved areas. At the same time, they sought to quash unorthodox views through lack of support and, more directly, through literary inquisitions. Kangxi, for example, sponsored the compilation of a huge dictionary of approved definitions of Chinese characters—still considered a primary reference work today. Under his direction, the commentaries and interpretations of Neo-Confucianism championed by the Song philosopher Zhu Xi became the approved versions. Kangxi's Sixteen Sacred Edicts, embodying maxims distilled in part from Zhu Xi's thought, became the official Qing creed from 1670 on. Anxious to legitimize themselves as culturally "Chinese," Kangxi and Qianlong sponsored huge encyclopedia projects. Qianlong's effort to catalog every literary effort of China's long history ran to 36,000 volumes: perhaps the most ambitious undertaking of its kind ever attempted.

THE SACRED EDICTS OF KANGXI

At the age of 16, Kangxi published the following 16 maxims, each given in seven character couplets of terse literary Chinese. These were posted throughout the empire and meant to be read twice a month by a local scholar, who would translate the literary language into a colloquial version in the appropriate dialect. These were later used as the base for a much amplified 10,000-character version by Kangxi's son, Yongzheng, written in a more colloquial style and issued in Chinese, Mongol, and Manchu versions in keeping with the Qing vision of universal multicultural empire.

1. Esteem most highly filial piety and brotherly submission, in order to give due importance to the social relations.
2. Behave with generosity toward your relatives, in order to illustrate harmony and benignity.
3. Cultivate peace and concord in your neighborhoods, in order to prevent quarrels and litigations.
4. Recognize the importance of husbandry and the culture of the mulberry tree (i.e., as food for silkworms), in order to ensure sufficient food and clothing.
5. Show that you prize moderation and economy, in order to prevent the lavish waste of your means.
6. Give weight to colleges and schools, in order to make correct the practice of the scholar.
7. Banish strange principles, in order to exalt the correct doctrine.
8. Lecture on the laws, in order to warn the ignorant and obstinate.
9. Demonstrate ceremony and deference, in order to improve popular customs.
10. Labor diligently at your proper callings, in order to stabilize the will of the people.
11. Instruct sons and younger brothers, in order to prevent them from doing wrong.
12. Put a stop to false accusations, in order to preserve the honest and good.
13. Warn against sheltering deserters, in order to avoid being involved in their punishment.
14. Fully remit your taxes, in order to avoid being pressed for payment.
15. Unite in hundreds and tens (i.e., the baojia system), in order to end thefts and robbery.
16. Remove enmity and anger, in order to show the importance due to the person and life.[5]

[5]Translated by Victor Mair, in "Language and Ideology in the Sacred Edict," in David Johnson et al., *Popular Culture in Late Imperial China*. Berkeley: University of California Press, 1985, pp. 325–59.

Neo-Confucian Philosophy

Although the urge to orthodoxy pervaded both the Ming and Qing dynasties, considerable intellectual ferment was also brewing beneath the surface of the official world. As we saw in the previous chapter, in the sixteenth century, the first major new directions in Neo-Confucianism were being explored by Wang Yangming (1472–1529). Although Wang's school remained popular, his emphasis on intuition, on a kind of enlightenment open to all, and, increasingly, on a unity of opposites embracing different religious and philosophical traditions placed his more radical followers increasingly on the fringes of intellectual life. In addition, the Qing victory ushered in an era of soul searching among Chinese literati and a wholesale questioning of the systems that had failed in the face of foreign conquest.

Two of the most important later figures were Huang Zongxi (1610–1695) and Gu Yanwu (1613–1682). Both men's lives spanned the Qing conquest and, like many of their fellow officials, concluded that the collapse of the old order came in part from a retreat from practical politics and too much indulgence in the excesses of the radicals of the Wang Yangming school. With a group of like-minded scholars, they based themselves at the Donglin Academy, founded in 1604. Here, they devoted themselves to reconstituting an activist Confucianism based on rigorous self-cultivation and on remonstrating with officials and even the court. One outgrowth of this development, which shares interesting parallels with the critical textual scholarship of the European Renaissance, was the so-called "Han Learning Movement." Convinced that centuries of Buddhism, religious Daoism, and Confucian commentaries of questionable value had diverted Confucianism from the intent of the sages, Han Learning sought to recover the original meaning of the Confucian works through exacting textual scholarship and systematic philology, or historical linguistics. The movement, although always on the fringe of approved official activities, peaked in the eighteenth century and successfully uncovered a number of fraudulent texts, while setting the tone for critical textual analysis during the remainder of the imperial era.

Novels and Popular Literature

Although the novel during Ming and Qing times was not considered high literary work by Chinese scholars, the form, as with Europeans in the eighteenth and nineteenth century, proved immensely popular. During the mid-eighteenth century, what many consider China's greatest novel, *Hong Lou Meng* (*The Dream of the Red Chamber*), was written by the shadowy Cao Xueqin (1715?–1764?). Almost nothing is known of Cao, including exactly when he was born and who his actual father was. The novel itself chronicles the decline and fall of a powerful family over 120 chapters. Some scholars see in it a loose autobiography of Cao's own family and a thinly veiled account of events in the early days of the Qing. In fact, the novel has been so closely studied and analyzed that there is an entire field called "Red Studies" or "Redology" (*hong xue*) devoted to examination of the work.

Another popular work, and one that as a satire has a great deal to tell us today about family, status, and social world of the examination system, is Wu Jingzi's (1701–1754) *The Scholars* (*Rulinwaishi*). Written around 1750 with incidents perhaps based on Wu's own experiences, the book is actually a series of loosely linked short stories in which certain characters make repeat appearances. Widely recognized stereotypes are played for humor—the retiring scholar, the ambitious aspirant who never quite passes the examination, the social climbing family. Confucianism itself, however, emerges as a system with strong roots and abiding ideals. Significantly, especially in light of Confucian patriarchal practices, women also emerge as fully realized characters who are treated with a degree of equality, especially the wife of the character Du. One other noteworthy aspect of the work is that it is written in a more accessible, even colloquial form than the *wenyan* literary language animating the vast majority of literature of the time.

Urban and village China were populated by storytellers, corner poets, spirit mediums, diviners, and a variety of other sorts of entertainers. Although village social life revolved principally around clan and family functions, popular culture was also dominated by Daoism, Buddhism, and older traditions of local worship, all with their own temples, shrines, and festivals. The oldest beliefs of the countryside involving ancestral spirits, "hungry ghosts"—roaming spirits of those not properly cared for in death—fairies, and demons were enhanced over the centuries by a rich infusion of tales of Daoist adepts and "immortals," *yijing* diviners, Buddhist Bodhisattvas, and underworld demons. Stories incorporating all of these, like *A Journey to the West* (see Chapter 2), continued to be popular fare for the literate as well as for storytellers and street performers.

One of the richest glimpses into local society comes from Pu Songling's (1640–1715) *Strange Tales from the "Make-Do" Studio*, sometimes given in English as *Strange Tales from a Chinese Studio*. Although considered a master stylist among his circle of friends, Pu never progressed beyond the provincial-level examinations and spent most of his life in genteel poverty. He traveled extensively collecting folktales, accounts of local curiosities, and especially stories of the supernatural. Considered an unparalleled interpreter of the *pinghua* style of literary versions of popular tales, which had originated during the Song period, his stories are available to us today thanks to the foresight of his grandson, who published them in 1740. In Pu's world, "fox-fairies" appear as beautiful women, men are transformed into tigers, the young are duped into degenerate behavior—with predictable consequences—and crooked mediums and storytellers take advantage of the unwary.

The slow movement of popular literature away from the classical and toward more current, colloquial language would grow during the nineteenth century. Later, with an infusion of literature from the West and the westernizing Meiji culture of Japan, it would burst forth during the so-called "Literary Renaissance" of the New Culture Movement at Peking University from 1915 to 1921. This increasing emphasis on "*baihua*," or "plain speech," would ultimately force the classical language aside. For most of the twentieth century, the great stylists would be stylists of colloquial literature.

The Arts of the Brush

Although China's literati clung to an amateur ideal of the "three excellences" of poetry, painting, and calligraphy, increasing official patronage ensured that approved schools and genres of art would be maintained at a consistent, if not inspired, level of quality. Here, the Qianlong emperor was perhaps the most influential force. Motivated in part by a lifelong quest to master the fine arts, he collected thousands of paintings—to which he added, in the tradition of Chinese connoisseurs, his own colophons—rare manuscripts, jade, porcelain, lacquer-ware, and other *objets d'art*. Because the force of imperial patronage was directed at conserving past models rather than creating new ones, the period is not noteworthy for stylistic innovation. One interesting exception to this, however, was the work of the Jesuit painter Giuseppe Castiliogne (1688–1766). Castiliogne's access to Qianlong resulted in a number of portraits of the emperor and court in a style that merged traditional Chinese subjects and media with Western perspective and technique. Evidence of this synthesis can also be seen in the Italianate and Versailles-inspired architecture at the emperor's Summer Palace just outside of Beijing.

Summer Palace. During the middle years of Qianlong's reign, he decided to build a pleasure garden in honor of his mother's 60th birthday. He had three smaller lakes consolidated into the present large artificial Kunming Lake, and had dozens of halls, galleries and pavilions built to provide views of various prospects of the lake and the three islands constructed in it to represent three mythical lands from Chinese tales. In 1860, the invading British and French burned and looted the Palace in retribution for the treatment accorded some of their men captured by Qing forces. The palace was rebuilt in the latter nineteenth century and the notorious marble paddle-wheel boat was added to replace a wooden vessel destroyed during the looting.

CONCLUSION

The trend we have noted among the Qing, continued from the Ming, toward greater regulation and centralism in politics and diplomacy, economics, social institutions, and even literary pursuits may be seen more generally as part of a regional—even a global—trend during the seventeenth and eighteenth centuries. In the case of China and, for that matter, Japan, Korea, and Southeast Asia, governments emerging from internal or external conflict naturally sought to emphasize stability—even to the point of severely limiting foreign contact, banning foreign religions, and imposing new regulations aimed at limiting social mobility. In this sense, Qing China at its height may be seen as what we have termed a *regulated society*. The cross-cultural comparisons may be drawn even further: many of the governments of Europe, led by France under Louis XIV, came to adopt a governmental system of *absolutism*, in which the state attempted to eliminate disruptive tendencies among the nobility by creating professional armies and centralized bureaucracies as well as pursuing mercantilist economics. We can also see this in the form of the "fiscal military states" that include the famous "gunpowder empires": those of the Ottomans, Safavids, and Mughals.

In terms of Chinese history more specifically, the Qing through the 1790s represent another example of a peripheral people, the Manchus, who, taking advantage of weakness at the center, seize the opportunity to strike at the top and defeat their divided competitors piecemeal. Once again, however, they are immediately faced with the prospect of having to "dismount and rule." The adaptations they make in their attempt to navigate the treacherous waters of ethnic preservation and utilizing existing institutions worked reasonably well during this period. Regardless of where one stands on the "Sinicizing," "Northeastern," or "synthetic" discussion on the Qing approach to rule, we can certainly say that the "three emperors" who dominated the era—Kangxi, Yongzheng, and Qianlong—were models of adopting certain Chinese cultural elements, while preserving what they considered the most important aspects of the Manchu–Jurchen heritage. In terms of enhancing the size and strength of the empire, expanding its vast internal economy, maintaining a lucrative and well-regulated foreign trade, and spreading the prestige of the empire's cultural, political, and social institutions, this was indeed a golden age for imperial China.

Yet as we will see in the following two chapters, cracks had already begun to appear in this idyllic picture. China's population would continue to expand through the next century. Demographers are still debating about what kind and how much of an impact this had on Qing policies and social institutions. The foreign presence would grow in Canton, increasingly trafficking in dangerous contraband. Legal and diplomatic disputes would multiply and China would find itself humiliated in war by the newly industrializing states of Europe. Christian proselytizing would bear unexpected fruit in contributing to an ideology that drove the biggest civil war in human history. Finally, the Manchus would find themselves whipsawed by the increasing need to reform their technologies and institutions to defend themselves from imperialist encroachment and the need to keep the structures of control they had put together intact. The ultimate result would be revolution.

FURTHER READING

Crossley, Pamela K. *A Translucent Mirror: History and Identity in Qing Imperial Ideology.* Los Angeles: University of California Press, 1999; paper, 2002. Pioneering study with an emphasis on the transition of the Qing from an ideology of conquest in the seventeenth century to one of universal emperorship under Qianlong.

Elliott, Mark. *The Manchu Way: The Eight Banners and Ethnic Identity in Late Imperial China.* Palo Alto, CA: Stanford University Press, 2001. With access to newly opened Manchu archives, Elliott is a leader in the synthetic, identity-based "New Qing History" that seeks to break out of the standoff between the "sinicization" and Northeastern" approaches.

Hostetler, Laura. *Qing Colonial Enterprise: Ethnography and Cartography in Early Modern China.* Chicago: University of Chicago Press, 2001. Path-breaking study on the crafting of a Qing ideology of inclusive multiculturalism with less emphasis on the concept of the Mandate of Heaven.

Ko, Dorothy. *Teachers of the Inner Chambers: Women and Culture in Seventeenth Century China.* Palo Alto, CA: Stanford University Press, 1994. Pioneering work that challenges the stereotype of late Ming and early Qing women as simply hapless victims of Confucian patriarchy.

Lach, Donald F., and Edwin J. Van Kley. *Asia in the Making of Europe.* Chicago: University of Chicago Press, 1993. Classic, magisterial account of Asia's impact on late medieval and early modern Europe. Especially good on early contacts. Volume Three, *A Century of Advance*, and Book Four, *East Asia*, deal most directly with China and its immediate neighbors.

Miyazaki, Ichisada, and Conrad Schirokauer, trans., *China's Examination Hell.* New Haven, CT: Yale University Press, 1963, 1976, 1981, Classic study of the workings of the Confucian exam system, of the cramming and aids often available, and the often unbearable pressures brought to bear on aspirants to office.

Mungello, David E. *The Great Encounter of China and the West, 1500–1800.* Lanham, MD: Rowman & Littlefield, 1999. Short, handy volume that serves as a solid introduction to the role of China and Asia more generally in the opening centuries of global empires.

Rawski, Evelyn S. *The Last Emperors: A Social History of Qing Imperial Institutions.* Berkeley: University of California Press, 1998. (See next)

Rawski, Evelyn S. "Presidential Address: Reenvisioning the Qing: The Significance of the Qing Period in Chinese History." *Journal of Asian Studies* 55, 4 (November 1996). With the elaboration of her argument in the previous volume, this address represents the critique of the sinicization school of Qing studies and outlines the Manchu-centered identity approach of the "Northeastern" school.

Shuo Wang. "Manchu Women in Transition: Gender Relations and Sexuality," in Stephen A. Wadley, Carsten Naeher, *Proceedings of the First North American Conference on Manchu Studies.* Wiesbaden: Otto Harrassowitz GmbH & Co. KG, 2006. Pp. 105–130.

Pioneering study in the area of studies of the status of Manchu women, particularly over the early period of Chinese cultural influence and the pressures of assimilation. Argues for the centrality of Manchu women in resistance to the imposition of Chinese norms and the preservation of Manchu identity.

Spence, Jonathan. *Emperor of China: Self-Portrait of K'ang Hsi*. New York: Vintage, 1975. Spence is arguably the finest stylist and most interesting writer among twentieth-century China scholars. Here (as presented in this chapter's "Patterns Up Close"), he attempts to reconstruct the interior world of Kangxi using translations of the emperors own accounts.

CHAPTER 4

THE LAST EMPIRE IN TRANSITION I: SOCIETY AND STATE, 1795–1900

It is some of the bleakest territory on earth. For centuries the Tarim Basin and Taklamakan Desert—the site of one of the lowest elevations on the planet—had marked the place where the famed Silk Route divided into northern and southern branches in an effort to skirt these fabled badlands. During the Tang dynasty, the Chinese had controlled a vast stretch of this area of Central Asia, with the empire's shape, as we have seen, often likened by scholars to a dumbbell whose western bulge encompassed the lands all the way to Talas, where Tang forces met their initial defeat at the hands of Arab armies in 751 CE. Over the intervening centuries, the lands had passed through the hands of an assortment of nomadic peoples, many of whom had converted to Islam, as well as being a part of the great Mongol empire and its successor states.

The Qing, however, had made expansion into the area a priority in the eighteenth century in their efforts to quell rebellion and propagate their idealized vision of a universal empire with an equal place for its many minorities. Now, in 1877, they were attempting to reclaim and expand their hold on the region called "Xinjiang"—the "New Territories." The man at the head of their forces was perhaps China's most effective general of the nineteenth century, Zuo Zongtang (1812–1885).

The perception of a growing decline in the power of the central government from foreign encroachment and the disastrous Taiping and Nian rebellions during the 1850s and 1860s had encouraged regionalization in the west and sparked an Islamic movement to create an independent state of "Kashgaria" under the Tajik adventurer Yaqub Beg. In Beijing, it sparked a debate about whether the government's efforts should be directed toward coastal defense against the Western powers—and now Japan—or toward eliminating this threat on the interior periphery. Although, as Zuo vigorously argued, this was strictly speaking a domestic affair, the Russians, British, and Ottoman Turks, involved in their own Great Game for control of the territories north of India, saw in

Kashgaria a useful buffer state and had already extended Yaqub Beg tacit recognition. If this were allowed to stand, the Qing would lose vast territories that would dwarf the coastal foreign concessions and Hong Kong. Thus, Zuo and his armies were on the march to forestall any further foreign interference and decisively crush the rebellion.

General Zuo (Tso), who is remembered by most Americans today for the chicken dish attached to his name, suppressed the rebellion, conducted a bloody mop-up operation in the region, and made it possible for the Qing to effectively limn and secure the borders of their New Territories. Even though negotiations with an expansionist Russia remained fraught, the incident marked for many observers what appeared to be a key turning point in Qing fortunes, although one that in the end would prove to be a false dawn.

For our purposes, Zuo's experiences in the extreme west mark an important departure in modern Chinese history. The nineteenth century is generally seen as one of repeated disaster for the Qing. Foreign imperialism, the Taiping movement, and growing stresses on rural society are all seen as markers of note for histories of the period. Chinese commentators often use the term "century of humiliation" to define the interval from the 1840s to 1949. Yet for much of this period, although accounts of imperialism long dominated the historiography of the era, far more was happening in the empire than foreign encroachment. For example, despite the influence they wielded, the number of foreigners in China was far smaller than the number of Chinese living just in the Americas by the 1870s. Even in military matters, far more men and much more materiel were involved in Qing efforts to crush the Taiping and in Zuo's expeditionary force than were involved in conflicts with the Western powers. Thus, the above vignette is meant to reinforce the point that if one is to empathetically enter the world of nineteenth-century China, one must pay due attention to what the Chinese themselves considered important, where the government and people put their efforts, and how much agency still existed in the hands of the Qing.

This chapter and the following one attempt to explore a persistent problem in recent history writing about modern China. The phenomena of foreign influence and imperialism and Chinese steps to confront it are obviously of key importance, but for most of the nineteenth century this was largely restricted to coastal and riverine regions and more broadly to the economics of foreign trade. For the empire as a whole, imperialism was most important after the war with Japan in 1894–1895, when the gap between China's power and that of the West and Japan became dramatically evident. Therefore, we begin the section addressing this period with a chapter that looks at the history of the nineteenth century largely in terms of the interior of the country, exploring its various political and economic regions, examining family and gender relations, community life, and the activities of state and local governments—all with a minimum of reference to China's "response" to the Western "impact."

The following chapter then deals with imperialism and its role in accelerating the idea that Qing rule had become bankrupt, beyond reform, and that a revolution was called for to resurrect China.

HISTORIOGRAPHY AND THE LATE QING

As noted in the Preface, modern Chinese *historiography*—the history of its history writing—has undergone profound changes in recent decades. This is true among Chinese historians as well as non-Chinese writers. In the case of scholars in the People's Republic, the requirement of seeing Chinese history through a tightly focused lens of Marxism-Leninism-Mao Zedong thought that marked the period from 1949 through the late 1970s has increasingly given way to one that borrows far more widely from current international perspectives and methodologies. Political restrictions on certain topics such as Tibet notwithstanding, the kinds of social history pioneered by the *Annales* School and long since firmly established in the United States and Western Europe have recently come to the fore in Chinese historical studies in the People's Republic of China (PRC) as well.

"China-Centeredness"

Among the writers outside the PRC, the changes have been somewhat more subtle but no less profound. As noted in the Preface, the size and scope of the field in temporal and spatial terms has been radically altered in recent decades. In the 1950s and 1960s the tendency among scholars—Marxist and non-Marxist; inside and outside the PRC—had been to consider that "modern" Chinese history properly began with the First Opium War (1839–1842), with the beginning date often cited for convenience's sake as 1840. Here the nexus was the dramatic opening clash between two radically different civilizations: one whose industrial revolution and post-Enlightenment ideologies were helping to create the self-defined "modern" world and the other seen as the last of the "great traditions" of agrarian empires. The subsequent history of China was then presented as an ongoing struggle to come to grips with a modernity forced on it while attempting to survive revolutions, fragmentation, civil war, and authoritarian rule.

Although critiques were mounted against this perspective, especially in the late 1960s by younger scholars more receptive to Marxist approaches and often opposed to American involvement in Vietnam, the methodological and perspectival problems of American writing on China as a whole were most effectively raised by Paul Cohen in his landmark 1984 book, *Discovering History in China*. For Cohen, all of the extant approaches of American scholarship on modern China were marred by what he called "ethnocentric distortion."

Cohen began with the most prevalent variant of the model of modern China outlined above, often called the impact–response or Harvard School approach after the institution of prominent American scholar John King Fairbank and his students. In his influential sourcebook of translations of Chinese documents tracing China's experience with modern imperialism, *China's Response to the West*, written with Ssu-yu Teng, Fairbank posits a China situated in what he later termed "change within tradition." This China was only able to break out of this relatively static condition by means of the shock of its encounter with the industrializing West. Thus, modern Chinese history is presented as a series of problems dealing with various "responses" to this Western "impact."

Cohen saw this as essentially asking questions of Chinese history based on an understanding of what had been important in the European and American past. In addition, he considered what the impact–response advocates saw as China's failure to develop historical phenomena similar to those in the West, or to resist their influence, as problematic in that they were interpreted as hidebound resistance not only to the West but also to "modernity" itself. Thus, from the impact–response perspective, China's responses, such as "self-strengthening" (see Chapter 5), were seen as failures attributable to Chinese cultural, intellectual, psychological, and social biases. Japan, faced with similar intrusive forces, was on the other hand "successful" because it adopted Western norms in a more thoroughgoing way and thus became modern.

An additional problem with the impact–response model was that it assumed that China's problems with Western imperialism were the central focus of the empire's activities from 1839 into the twentieth century. Yet, Cohen argues, throughout most of this time the Western threat was seen by the imperial government as largely confined to the coastal ports and their immediate littoral areas. Indeed, in the preface to an 1880 summary of the empire's foreign relations during the reign of the Tongzhi emperor (1861–1875), it was reported that the foreign residents in China had been "soothed and pacified" and were moving toward acculturation to Confucian norms.

A related perspective Cohen identified was based on what he called the "exaggerated polarities" of tradition and modernity. Here there were strong parallels with many of the points made by Edward Said in his influential and controversial book, *Orientalism* (1979). For Said, Europeans and Americans had created a comprehensive "repertory" of descriptions and images of "the Orient" in literature, art, and even the social sciences that, although consistent with itself, bore little resemblance to the "real" Orient—here meaning the Middle East, India, and the Islamic world in general. It was a picture of a static world mired in tradition, almost ahistorical, a kind of "antimodernity" in which outsiders could project bizarre vices and practices as well as some elements of their own past they felt they had discarded.

Chinese Sawmill

A World Mired in Tradition? Chinese Sawyers. The prevalence and abundance of hand labor in China at a time when Western Europe and the United States were undergoing their industrial revolutions was cited by contemporaries as proof of China's alleged "backwardness." Twentieth century scholars tended to view China in more nuanced terms as undergoing "change within tradition," and awaiting the shock of the Western "impact" in order to develop a Chinese "response," that included the first steps toward industrialization. More recently, however, students of Chinese history have felt this "impact-response" model to be both too narrow in scope and insufficiently "China-centered." In the photo here, two Chinese sawyers use a two-man rip saw to cut boards from a log.

Although Said did not extend his critique to imperialism in China, Cohen sees distinct parallels with him in many of the difficulties raised by the tradition/modernity dyad. The idea of the impact–response approach, with its assumption of a comparatively static China, is one striking parallel. Like Said's Orient, it is at least in part a function of a profound change in the way Europeans and Americans looked at China across the divide of the Enlightenment and, especially, the Industrial Revolution. China, which had seemed so well governed, wealthy, and philosophically enlightened to European observers in the eighteenth century, was now portrayed as "barbaric" and "semicivilized" by the mid-nineteenth century. Its technologies that once led the world were now seen has having lain fallow for centuries until taken up and exponentially improved by the West. In short, the gap between the patterns of history characteristic of agrarian–urban empires and those of the new and expansive factory-driven nation-states was seen as almost insurmountable.

In Cohen's view, much of the problematic of American scholarship on modern China revolved around the cluster of issues arising from this situation: How compatible were Confucian culture and society with modern science and technology? Could they be successfully merged as the "self-strengtheners" argued or would the Western imports ultimately undermine "traditional" Confucian society as their opponents argued? Indeed, was it possible to become modern without becoming "Western?" And what about the actual distance between the problematic constructs of tradition and modernity? Where does one start and the other stop? Are they distinct polarities or part of a continuum? Don't both conditions evolve over time? If so, how does one measure the relative amount of either condition within a particular society as well as among different societies? Do extreme cultural differences—"otherness"—essentially make measuring such things meaningless?

For Cohen, Marxism, as essentially a materialist interpretation of the idealized European historical experience, was equally problematic as a template for understanding Chinese history. Complicating this further was its dogmatic linkage with Mao's ideas of peasant revolutionary potential and "mass-line" (see Chapter 7) politics among PRC historians. Here, China's society before 1949 is invariably described as "feudal" or "semifeudal" and its political status as "semicolonial." In addition to conceptual problems posed by such terminology, Marxism more generally tends toward class-based reductionist and determinist modes of analysis.

In this respect it is reminiscent of the approach critiqued by Herbert Butterfield in his *Whig Interpretation of History*. That is, Chinese history becomes narrowed into a search for origins of certain present phenomena, often with reference to historical incidents or situations that are seen as anticipating them. To cite one example, the Taiping Rebellion (1851–1864) is celebrated as a proto-socialist peasant revolution, but one doomed to failure because the feudal economic and political conditions of the time had not been sufficiently developed to make the leap to socialism. Thus the "conservative" or "reactionary" forces of the Qing were able to quash it.

This brings up a second difficulty, not only with Marxism but also with all such "Whig" interpretations that judge the past by the standards of the present: the practice, as we have seen, frowned upon by historians as *presentism*. The act of reading the present as the perfection of the past suggests that the past can never live up to the present in any meaningful way. Moreover, it establishes a kind of pervasive historical morality in which those who champion ideas or events that appear to advance the causes of "progress" toward our more perfect present are seen as good, whereas those who oppose them are bad—regardless of any other qualities they may possess. Thus, the Taipings are seen as heroes and Qing officials who fought them are seen as villains. This, of course, leaves little scope for trying to understand the complexity of how these issues appeared to contemporaries. Indeed, one could also see the impact–response approach in similar terms since it subordinates modern Chinese history into a narrow search for the foreign origins of China's decline.

Similarly, Cohen sees "World Systems" theorists like Immanuel Wallerstein as acting in a reductionist and determinist mode in assessing imperialism. Here, the degree of integration into the worldwide economic and political systems of the growing European empires is seen as the determinant of how independent and successful a country's defensive policies were likely to be. Thus, despite their cultural similarities, China and Japan had different historical trajectories because China had been much more thoroughly integrated into the capitalist world system, whereas Japan's later "opening" allowed it the breathing space to successfully adapt to the new order and shortly become an imperial power itself.

Again, the "one-size-fits-all" approach of this perspective is problematic for those who see the cultural differences between the two countries as profound. As one observer put it, "China reacted as a culture under attack; Japan as a nation under attack." Japan's different societal hierarchy and its long-time emphasis on military prowess did make its response different, as did the striking unity of its government and people from the time of the Meiji Restoration (1868).

Writing on China since the 1980s

Although Cohen was the most comprehensive and trenchant observer of these trends and in mounting his critique of them, many historians of China since the 1980s have tackled directly or implicitly this problem of "ethnocentric distortion." Cohen's call for a "China-centered" Chinese history—one that begins in China, asks questions of the past rooted in China, and more deeply explores China's agency in that past—has increasingly been the key jumping-off point for those interested in China's modern period. Among the trends developing from the 1980s on have been studies of economics, social structures, and politics on the micro level—of villages, prefectures, regions, etc.—and those at the macro level transcending national and imperial borders; macroregions of trade; and work that attempts to fit China's history into a broad global context.

The 1990s and early 2000s saw influential studies by R. Bin Wong, Kenneth Pomeranz, and the world historian, Andre Gunder-Frank, among others, that challenged the assumptions of world-systems theorists, especially about the early economic hegemony of the European states in Asia. For example, the long-standing assumption that China's economy was "closed" and that silver paid to Chinese merchants for luxury items stayed within the empire was disputed by studies showing that China and India were the engines that drove much of the Eurasian and Indian Ocean economies until well into the nineteenth century. Similarly, what one might call the economic center of gravity of Eurasia did not shift in favor of the Europeans until the Industrial Revolution was well advanced.

Important recent work also includes more localized studies of book distribution and printing, which showed that even at the village level China's preindustrial rates of literacy were among of the highest in the world. Work in Qing legal studies has substantially altered the view of China under Confucianism as lacking a firm legal structure in civil law as well as criminal law. Along with this came comparative studies in the 1990s by William T. Rowe and commentary by Frederick Wakeman on the nature of civil society in Europe and China.

In the case of demographics, we have a more nuanced understanding of regional Chinese per capita consumption levels, which now appear to be far higher for far longer than earlier scholarship suggested. Moreover, the agricultural sector, despite the enormous dislocations of the mid-nineteenth-century rebellions, appears in recent studies to have been far more resilient and expansive in terms of keeping up with the demands of the population than had been previously supposed. The famous "high-level equilibrium trap" (see later), to the extent it was in operation at all, was a much later phenomenon than earlier studies suggested. As in history in general, there has been a large upsurge in work done on family and gender, particularly in expanding our understanding of women's agency regionally and ethnically, as well as among Manchus and Han Chinese. As we noted in the previous chapter, the work of Dorothy Ko is particularly noteworthy in this regard. Finally, as we also saw in the previous chapter and as the vignette opening this chapter suggests, there was a decisive qualitative shift in the approach to rule and empire by the Qing that recent studies have brought to light. For example, although sinification of the Manchus did take place in terms of acceptance of Neo-Confucian doctrine—indeed, on one level the urge to intellectual and administrative consistency and orthodoxy had never been stronger—the drive to maintain Manchu ethnic identity in the face of the pressures of assimilation actually increased as the century progressed. More directly for our opening account of Zuo's expedition, the Manchu goal of rulership, particularly from Qianlong's time onward, was posited less on the idea of a renewal of the Mandate of Heaven and more on creating a superempire in which all minorities had a stake. Indeed, although the Qing were increasingly belabored by maritime intruders, their main efforts continued to be adding territories and protectorates in Mongolia, Xinjiang, and Tibet. Thus, one of the enduring ironies of the period is that in many ways Qing agency was at its height in expanding imperial China to its greatest size, while at the same time facing the outside threat that would ultimately accelerate the demise not only of the dynasty but also of imperial China itself.

THE LONG NINETEENTH CENTURY I: INNER POLITICS AND CONFLICTS

The century and a half from 1750 to 1900 marked the structural, cultural, and economic decline of the world's great agrarian empires. As we have noted previously, however, in the case of the Qing, this decline would not be visible to even the experienced observer until well into the nineteenth century. Even then, such a perception would most likely be associated with the great rebellions, the Taiping and Nian, that tore at the vitals of the empire. One noteworthy development in this regard was that the reign of the Tongzhi emperor, from 1861 to 1875, was later officially designated as a "restoration" (*zhongxing*), coming as it did in the midst of the anti-Taiping campaigns and in the wake of the return of the imperial family to Beijing after the Anglo-French force had driven it from the Forbidden City and burned the Summer Palace during the Second Opium War. Yet in the middle of a

Tongzhi Emperor. The Tongzhi Emperor acceded the throne as a young boy in 1861 at a particularly tumultuous time in Qing history: The Taiping and Nian movements were still raging fiercely, England and France had just forced more concessions from the Chinese government, and the first efforts toward "self-strengthening" had just begun. Although only achieving his majority shortly before he died, his reign was seen at the time as a vital period of Restoration, as China emerged from its traumas and had made considerable progress in its self-strengthening programs by the time of his death in 1875.

classic situation of " disorder within, disaster without," the dynasty made peace with the foreign intruders, suppressed both rebellions, and began the process of rebuilding. Moreover, as we will see in the following chapter, the 1860s marked a period of cooperation between the Qing and the Western maritime powers and the 1870s saw the empire's expansion to its greatest size in history. By the late 1860s and early 1870s, high officials were attaching the raised honorific characters for restoration to their memorials to the throne. For many, therefore, it seemed that, far from sliding toward collapse, the empire had been rejuvenated.

The theory of history dominated by the dynastic cycle (see Chapter 1) did allow for this kind of reprieve, although it was always seen as temporary. Thus, the Tongzhi period was seen in context as one of the four great restorations of Chinese history, the most famous of which was the reconstitution of the Han after the Wang Mang interregnum (9–23 CE). Since the fortunes of a dynasty and how long it could stave off disaster were regarded by Chinese historians as contingent on the ability of the empire's officials, there was unanimity of opinion that *rencai* (human talent) was what was most urgently needed. Some commentators even pointed to historical precedents of dynastic cooperation with "barbarian" peoples in past restorations as a rationale for taking advantage of Western technologies and overtures. Yet, true to the character of restoration as ephemeral according to the dynastic cycle, by 1900, China's treasury was bankrupt; its export trade outstripped by European and Japanese competitors; its domestic markets turning increasingly to factory-produced foreign commodities; and its land, squeezed by the world's largest population, once again spawned the problems of tenancy and landlordism that had played such a central role in the overthrow of past dynasties.

The Structures of Late Qing Government

As we saw in the preceding chapter, the Qing made few alterations in the Ming emperor-centered structure of government. The uppermost levels were occupied by the emperor and imperial family. Because of the pivotal role of the emperor in the system, even the least dynamic rulers were of necessity busy men. In addition to presiding over and participating in a full calendar of ceremonial events and leading hunts during the imperial summer encampment to keep alive Manchu–Jurchen nomadic traditions, emperors kept up a daunting daily schedule of audiences and especially poring over official correspondence. The memorial system begun by Kangxi had now grown to the point that it made up the bulk of the most important bureaucratic paperwork. Since even the most humble magistrate technically had the right to send a memorial to the emperor, he often spent the hours from before dawn to late in the evening vetting and signing off on correspondence circulated to him. In theory, at least, this allowed the emperor to have a comprehensive idea of the state of the empire at any given time, but it was also true that memorialists tended to shade their reports with what we would call today considerable "spin." Moreover, much, if not most of this correspondence passed through the hands of senior officials, board members, and those sitting on the Grand Secretariat and Grand Council, all of whom appended their comments.

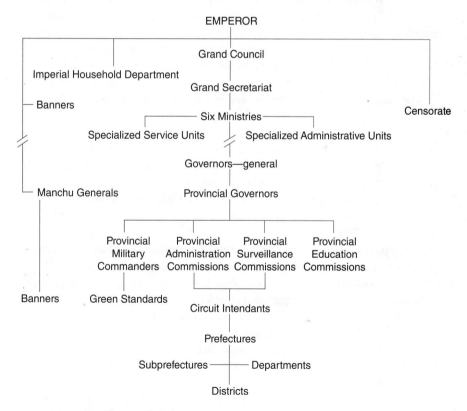

Diagram of Qing Government Structure.
Source: Charles Hucker, *A Dictionary of Official Titles in Imperial China*, (Palo Alto: Stanford University Press, 1985), p. 83.

Given the "strong emperor" structure and the considerable workload at the top, the capabilities and ambitions of Qing emperors varied widely. As we saw in the previous chapter, the late seventeenth and nearly all of the eighteenth century saw an extraordinary run of dynamic and capable emperors: Kangxi, Yongzheng, and Qianlong. The nineteenth and early twentieth centuries were less fortunate. The Jiaqing Emperor (r. 1796--1820), although his forces quelled the White Lotus uprising and disturbances in Xinjiang, escaped two assassination attempts and labored under the slow decline of Qing finances increasingly eroded by the opium trade. His successor for the next 30 years was the Daoguang emperor (r. 1820–1850). Generally characterized as not particularly capable, more recent studies have suggested that he had flashes of surprising innovation. The most noteworthy of these was in saving money by transporting bulk tribute grain by ship along the coast rather than sending it up the Grand Canal. As a prince, he had even helped defend the Forbidden City from a last-gasp White Lotus attack in 1813, shooting two of the rebels himself. Daoguang, however, had the bad fortune to reign during the acceleration of the opium trade culminating in the First Opium War with Britain and the first of the "unequal" treaties. Upon his death, China was just beginning to recover from disastrous earthquakes and floods, which took more than 15 million lives. The Taiping movement was in its formative stages, Chinese strategists were contemplating how to deal with the ever-increasing demands for concessions by foreign maritime powers, and yet another rebellion in Xinjiang had for the moment been arrested. His heir, Xianfeng (r. 1850–1861), young, dissolute, and ineffectual, faced the multiple challenges of the Taiping, Nian, and the British and French during the Second Opium War. The Tongzhi (1861–1875) and Guangxu (1875–1908) emperors had barely achieved their majority before their reigns ended. Tongzhi died at 18; Guangxu was the victim of a coup by his aunt, the Empress Dowager Cixi, after reigning in her shadow for 10 years. Finally, the boy Xuantong emperor, Henry Puyi, reigned only 4 years before the dynasty fell in 1912. He later became the Japanese puppet emperor of "Manchukuo" in 1931 and ultimately a victim of the Maoist Cultural Revolution in 1966.

Imperial eunuchs as court chamberlains exercised considerable informal power within the emperor's household and were crucial in maintaining his appointments and balancing inner factions. It was also not unusual for the imperial household to intersect with the uppermost levels of the bureaucracy. In 1860 and 1861, for example, Yixin, Prince Gong, the son of the Dao Guang emperor, half-brother of the Xianfeng emperor, and regent of the infant Tongzhi emperor, was tasked with supervising the negotiations with the British and French to end the Second Opium War. As a result, he was selected to head the newly formed *Zongli Yamen*, or foreign office, from 1861 to 1884.

As before, the positions in the civil service were drawn from successful examination candidates, although by the late Qing it was increasingly easy for the wealthy to buy degrees and for those who rendered special service to the state to be rewarded with an official position. Each position was required to be drawn equally from Han and Manchu candidates, and some positions also had Mongol quotas. The uppermost levels of the bureaucracy included the staff of the six imperial boards: War, Rites, Punishments, Works, Revenue, and Civil Appointments. There were nine ranks of civil and military officials, each rank being further divided into upper and lower divisions. Below the boards were the governors-general and governors of the empire's 18 provinces, under whom presided *daotai* (intendents of circuit), who acted as liaisons between the prefects and provincial government. The *daotai* were followed by prefects, subprefects, and district magistrates. In addition to the Zongli Yamen, the Qing had earlier added an inner Grand Council to supplement the Grand Secretariat and because of the new emphasis on the multiethnic and multicultural nature of their empire, a *Lifan Yuan*, or "colonial office," to supervise Mongolia, Tibet, and recognized minorities.

Qing Government Official. Liu Kunyi (1830–1902), Governor of Jiangxi province from 1865–1874. Along with Li Hongzhang and Zeng Guofan, Li led troops in fighting the Taipings, occupied a prominent place as a *yangwu* (foreign affairs) official during the self-strengthening period, and was one of the officials to push for reform of Qing institutions in the wake of the Boxer Rebellion.

"Father and Mother to the People"

The key point of intersection between the people and the government throughout the Qing remained the district magistrate. Although magistrates occupied the lowest official rung of the bureaucracy, they wielded considerable power at the local level and constituted the entry-level position for the majority of those called to service. Some experience at the magistrate's level was considered essential for ambitious officials, and the wide-ranging skills developed during one's district tenure often proved indispensable for advancement to the higher levels of the bureaucracy.

The position brought with it enormous responsibility, which had expanded considerably under the Qing. Although the population had more than doubled by the nineteenth century, the size of the government had remained virtually unchanged. Thus, with so many more potential candidates taking the exams, the pass rate went from around 1 in 30 to 1 in 95 to 100. Even in rural areas, the magistrate might have charge of 100,000 people—and in urban areas, perhaps 250,000. Assisted by a small group of clerks and secretaries, messengers, and constables, he supervised all aspects of local government: collecting taxes, policing and security, investigating and prosecuting crimes, settling legal disputes, sentencing and overseeing punishments—including executions—presiding over all official ceremonies, conducting the local Confucian examinations, and setting an exemplary moral example for his constituents.

He was constantly on the move, traveling around his district discharging his duties. When disaster struck, it was the magistrate who had charge of organizing local relief efforts. If floods, disturbances, or famines were the result of negligence, it was he who would be punished—in especially serious cases, by death or banishment. The magistrate's responsibilities and powers were so all-encompassing that he was referred to as "father and mother to the people."

With so much responsibility vested in such a low position in the civil service, a number of safeguards were built into the system to prevent abuses. Magistrates were required to write extensive reports on all activities of any consequence. Their personnel were encouraged to report any improprieties to the magistrate's immediate superiors. The Qing continued the "rule of avoidance" instituted under the Ming, which prevented officials from serving in their home districts and required them to be reassigned every three years to discourage corruption and influence peddling.

Yet despite the hectic schedule of the magistrate, he remained a remote figure for the vast majority of the people in the district. "Heaven is high and the emperor far away" was a Chinese proverb that seems to have been equally applicable to the local officials. For most people, the main figures of authority, as we saw in the previous chapter, remained the scholar-gentry, other leading families of the village, their own clan leaders, and the headmen in the *lijia* and *baojia* systems of village organization.

The Demographic Surge

It is commonly observed that although the Qianlong period of the eighteenth century was the high-water mark of China's wealth and power, like the *yin* and *yang* symbol with the dot of the opposite color in each field, it also contained within it the seeds of decline. The dynastic cycle of historical change posited that following the years of a dynasty's ascendency, expansion, and innovation, there always came a "golden age" in which the new order ripens and coasts on its mature institutions. Although Qianlong was still involved in territorial expansion through much of his reign, a considerable number of his initiatives were also aimed at peaceful development and consolidation, with a conservative approach to culture that put a premium on cataloging and preservation rather than innovation. As with his (in)famous literary inquisition, he sought tight control and orthodoxy of ideas. Somewhat ominously, according to this theory of history, golden ages are invariably followed by decline and, ultimately, collapse.

If a drive for cultural orthodoxy marked one aspect of Qing rule during this era, in terms of demographics and economics, vast changes were taking place. China's population, as we have seen, was generally the highest in the world for much of its history. Han China had perhaps 60 million people; by the opening of the Yuan period, the population had increased to about 100 million, keeping approximate pace with rates of increase in other parts of Eurasia. The Black Death and its aftermath, as it had in Europe, carried away more than a third of China's population, bringing it back down to around 60 million by the opening of the Ming. By mid-Ming the 100 million mark had again been achieved and by the beginning of the eighteenth century, the numbers had advanced to about 150 million.

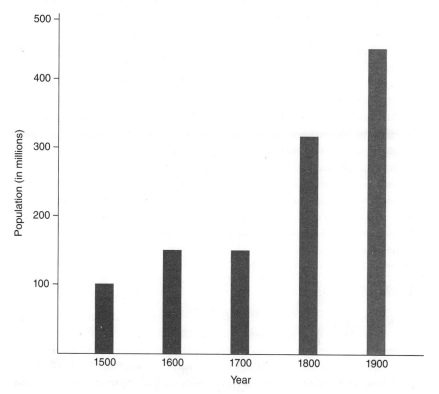

Population of China Proper from 1500 to 1900. The data here does not include population levels for Mongolia, Tibet, Manchuria, Taiwan, and Xinjiang.

The big jumps, however, were just over the horizon. By 1790, China's population had doubled to about 300 million. By 1900 it had advanced to perhaps 450 million. How can we account for such rapid increases? What effect did they have on Chinese society? How did they affect different regions? Qing territorial acquisitions tell only part of the story. Mongolia, Tibet, parts of Central Asia, and Manchuria were sparsely populated and so account for only a fraction of the gains. Two factors demographers often point to are increases in the variety and amount of food available and the drive to bring marginal lands into cultivation.

As we saw in earlier chapters, Southeast Asia had long been a source of new rice strains. Improved fast-growing wet and dry varieties were introduced in the eighteenth century that allowed raised-dike double cropping in cooler areas and dry rice cultivation in more marginal zones. Perhaps even more important was the widespread cultivation of crops introduced during the late Ming from the Americas through the Spanish and Portuguese. Here, as we noted previously as well, corn [maize], potatoes, sweet potatoes, and peanuts were among the most important, both as human staples and as livestock feed. Sugar, tobacco, indigo, and cotton also began to be produced as cash crops. Although sweet potatoes and yams need warm environments to prosper, they can be grown in a wide variety of topographical environments, as can corn and potatoes, which can survive on even more marginal land and cooler temperatures. By the nineteenth century, maize accounted for perhaps 10 percent of China's grain production, whereas the sweet potato's ability to be grown on mountainsides made it China's third largest crop, after rice and wheat.

Farm productivity dramatically increased, allowing—and in many cases requiring—larger families for the additional labor, particularly in intensively cultivated rice-growing regions. Moreover, peasants were encouraged to settle in thinly populated areas and bring them under cultivation, particularly in the northwest and in previously uncultivated uplands. At the same time, in the south settlers pushed into the mountainous regions of Guangxi and Yunnan. It was out of this matrix that one of the most stubborn struggles of the Qing era developed and exposed a problem that would plague the empire through all of the following century.

The White Lotus Movement

In the frontier area stretching across the meeting of Hubei, Shaanxi, and Sichuan provinces, a new version of an older Buddhist cult took root. Many of its adherents were recent arrivals and the reach of government and administration in the region was minimal. The emigrants had tried rice cultivation in these uplands, but the results were poor. When local officials attempted to collect taxes from them, they rose in rebellion in 1794. Sporadic outbreaks continued for the next decade. The term "White Lotus" given to the uprising dates back at least to the Buddhist school that was home to the founder of the Ming dynasty, the fighting monk Zhu Yuanzhang. There seems to be little evidence, however, that the loosely affiliated rebel groups identified themselves as such; they were called White Lotus by the Qing as a term of derision. Their resistance to the local officials was accompanied by the familiar cry of *fanqing fuming*—"Oppose the Qing, restore the Ming!"

The decentralized White Lotus militias routinely frustrated the Banner forces and Green Standard units arrayed against them. As with Mao Zedong's forces, more than a century later, theirs was a classic guerrilla strategy of hit and run, eroding the enemy's morale, and forcing them into bloody reprisals that drive the beleaguered population to your side. For their part, the Qing forces at first played into this strategy by indiscriminate destruction of suspected White Lotus strongholds as the enemy proved increasingly elusive. Qing commanders routinely complained of their inability to tell the guerrillas from ordinary civilians. Finally, after bringing in more troops, they conducted a program similar to the "strategic hamlet" strategy that the United States would later attempt in Vietnam: organize loyal militia, relocate the populace to fortified villages, and isolate the rebels to reduce their advantage of mobility.

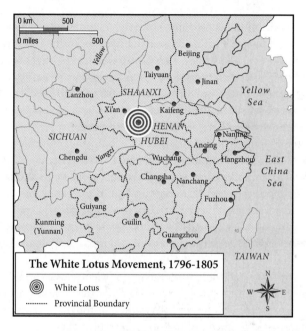

MAP 4.1
The White Lotus Movement, 1796–1805

Although the rebellion was effectively suppressed by 1805, it smoldered on for another decade and there were several results of the conflict that would plague the Qing in later years. One was that the Banner forces, which had proven their fighting ability in earlier campaigns, performed poorly in this struggle, and their lack of military effectiveness was a key factor in prolonging the revolt. The Chinese Armies of the Green Standard were only marginally better. With their aura of invincibility dissipated—and virtually eliminated by their performance later in the Opium War and the initial stages of the Taiping conflict—their powers of intimidation to prevent rebellion had largely dissolved. Even more troubling for the long term was that the local militias on both sides proved far more effective as combat forces than their professional counterparts. This, of course, could be seen as an encouragement to rebellion. In addition, however, although there was a long precedent of officials organizing local militias, their potential for contributing to government decentralization was considerable. This would become disturbingly evident later during the Taiping years when Qing officials like Zeng

Guofan and Li Hongzhang organized their own armies in their home provinces and acquired considerable regional power because of them. Indeed, Zeng himself studied the use of militias in suppressing the White Lotus movement when forming his own units to fight the Taiping and the Nian.

The Great Dying: The Taiping and Nian Eras

Although the details of the campaigns and foreign connections involved in the Taiping and Nian conflicts will be more extensively examined in the following chapter, the crisis provoked by these wars is also worth exploring here on several levels. Economics, ideology, perceptions of ethnicity and minority status, class warfare, religion, and famine and flood disaster and relief all had a role to play, as did what might be termed the "Confucian counteroffensive" and the attempts at rebuilding regions that had been so thoroughly ravaged.

Although the Taiping hybrid Christian/pre-Confucian/ millenarian theology was certainly influenced by Protestant missionaries arriving in the early nineteenth century, there were a number of critical underlying reasons for its stunningly rapid spread. The region itself played an important role in the connections among the participants and in the early leadership. As the only officially sanctioned port opened for maritime trade until 1842, Guangzhou (Canton) and its adjacent districts in Guangdong province was arguably the most cosmopolitan region in the Qing empire. The area's economy was the linchpin of China's international commerce. Along with overland trade from Russia and Central Asia and the activities of Chinese merchants in Manila and Indonesia it was the node at which China interacted with the world's global trading networks. For roughly a century and a half it had also marked the terminus of the routes by which export goods arrived for shipment, and imports and silver made their way into the interior. The region's economic vibrancy supported and was supported by the large service industry—hostels, money lenders, *huiguan* guildhalls (see later), shops, restaurants, and so forth—that had grown up along the routes leading to Canton. The region was thus a vital trade network, its role akin to that of the Silk Road or the Grand Canal.

The hinterlands to the west, however, were still part of a frontier in the process of being settled by migrants attempting to open the uplands and forests of Guangxi and Yunnan to cultivation. In some respects, the conditions were like those leading to the White Lotus uprising, with difficult harvests and minimal government attention. There were political and ethnic tensions as well. The southern regions had a long history of defiance toward dynasties centered in the north. Even before the Qin united China into an empire, the state called "Yue," which encompassed much of the two Guang provinces and Yunnan, was considered on the fringes of civilization by the northern members of the Zhou system. For a thousand years after the Qin unification, Chinese rulers attempted to incorporate northern Vietnam into their empires and that region often included parts of what ultimately remained south China. Moreover, the south routinely resisted the rule of new dynasties. This was especially true of the "barbarian"

Manchu Qing invaders. Even in linguistic terms, the southern dialects and sub-dialects are distinct from those of other regions, a difference stubbornly maintained even today in the face of government policies mandating Mandarin as the official "national" language.

Another factor scholars routinely cite is quasi-ethnic conflict. Although participants in the Taiping movement included a considerable number of South China's Zhuang and Dai minorities, the founder of the movement, Hong Xiuquan (1813–1864), and most of his early converts were *Hakkas* (*pinyin: kejia*—"guest families"), although even today some prefer appending the more polite ending *ren* ("people") to the term. Their ancestors had migrated from the north around Henan and Shandong in several waves precipitated by dynastic turnover accompanying the collapse of the Northern Song in the twelfth century, the Mongol ascension in the thirteenth, and the Qing consolidation in the seventeenth. There would also be something of a southern internal migration of Hakkas into Hunan and Sichuan during the 1860s and 1870s in the wake of the Taiping collapse.

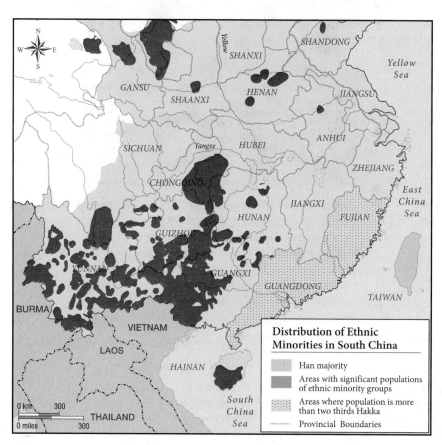

MAP 4.2

Distribution of Ethnic Minorities in South China

Hakka Fortified Villages. Ongoing tensions between Hakkas (pinyin *kejia*) and *bendi* ("locals" or "natives") led to frequent attacks and the need for the Hakkas to protect themselves. The complexes in these photos represent typical defensive structures for Hakkas in different regions. **(A)** Above is a rectangular walled village in Chonglin in the southern province of Guangdong. **(B)** The photo below shows the distinctive "roundhouse" style of a walled village in Yongding, Fujian province, with the living quarters facing in toward a central courtyard.

The newcomers of this diaspora were ethnically Han Chinese who spoke Mandarin, did not bind the feet of women, and resisted the discrimination of their neighbors. These "neighbors" were designated as *bendi* ("locals"; "natives"), who spoke local dialects, bound women's feet, and considered the Hakkas a despised minority group. Having moved into a number of thinly settled and agriculturally marginal areas in Fujian, Jiangxi, and Guangdong, the Hakkas were often impoverished, socially isolated from the *bendi*, and subject to frequent attacks by their neighbors. Their villages typically featured protective walls and fortified inner compounds. In the wake of the Taiping movement there would be years of warfare and struggle over land claims in some areas between Hakkas and *bendi*. By some estimates, perhaps a million people perished in these local fights. Small wonder that they would produce a disproportionate number of rebels and revolutionaries over the years including, it is believed, Sun Yat-sen, and many prominent Nationalist and Communist leaders.

In addition to the agricultural difficulties of the Hakkas, they shared in a more general economic downturn that marked the opening of the initial Treaty Ports and Hong Kong after 1842. As we will see in more detail in the following chapter, with the number of open ports increasing from one to five and the British in possession of Hong Kong, centuries-old trade routes abruptly and dramatically shifted. This was particularly true of the silk and tea trades, which now were more oriented toward the Yangzi Basin and Shanghai.

Not surprisingly, incidents of brigandage and piracy proliferated in the region through the 1840s. In the interior there was a rise in the number of secret society members in such organizations as the Triads. On the coast and in the rivers marking opium delivery routes, ships and small craft carrying the drug or the silver paid or received for it made attractive targets, although these carriers were often heavily armed. Thus, Hong's group of "God Worshippers," as they came to be called, was able to gain adherents from all of these groups as much as from local Hakkas. Bc of isolation from other inhabitants in the area.

The Taiping movement is one of the most heavily studied phenomena in modern Chinese history and one around which a number of debates swirl. One concerns the nature of the rebellion. Was it a peasant rebellion like many past revolts against the kinds of historically familiar rural problems like landlordism, high taxes, lack of famine and flood relief, and so forth? Many scholars, especially Marxists, have presented it as fundamentally a feudal class struggle between the peasant majority and a generally oppressive structure of scholar-gentry dominance backed up by the Confucian bureaucracy. Yet there are also a number of factors that point to a qualitative difference from past uprisings. Certainly the vast majority of participants were indeed peasants—as any mass movement in an agrarian society must be. But the ideology of the movement was certainly not peasant derived and the leadership was drawn from a wide social spectrum.

A candidate for the local Confucian examinations, Hong Xiuquan, a native of Hua County in Guangdong Province, had come upon some Christian missionary tracts passed on by a Chinese convert named Liang A-fa (also given as Liang Fa). Not long after this, in 1836, Hong failed the *xiucai*, or first-level Confucian examination, for the third time and lapsed into a nervous breakdown. When he eventually recovered, Hong gradually came to believe that the

Christian God had taken him up to heaven and informed him that he was in fact Christ's younger brother. Hong told his startled listeners that it had been revealed to him that he must now work to eliminate the "demons" possessing the country and thus bring about the Heavenly Kingdom of Great Peace (*taiping tianguo*) on earth.

Hounded from their community, Hong and his group moved into a mountain stronghold in neighboring Guangxi Province and began to gather followers from the disillusioned and unemployed, anti-Manchu elements, religious dissidents, secret societies, and fellow members of the Hakka minority. Hong had also sought the sanction of Western missionaries and approached the American Baptist preacher Issachar Jacox Roberts (1802–1871) for instruction and baptism, although he was refused the latter. By 1851, Hong's group had created a society based on Protestant Christian theology, Chinese pre-Confucian traditions, and a vision of equality in which all goods were held in common. Women worked, fought, and prayed alongside men. Foot-binding, opium smoking, and gambling were forbidden. As a sign that they were no longer loyal to the Qing, the men cut their queues and let the hair grow in on their foreheads, prompting the Qing to refer to them as "the long-haired rebels." As they represented a threat to the Confucian order of society and that society responded with harassment and persecution, Hong began to see Confucius and the *ru* (Confucian scholar-gentry and officials), along with the Manchus, as the chief demons he was to eradicate. The rebels therefore targeted the scholar-gentry in particular in their land seizures and executions (see "Patterns Up Close").

Because of the movement's radical and in many ways foreign ideology, some scholars have taken recently to calling it a revolution. Unlike past peasant revolts that sought to recover existing rights or pass the Mandate of Heaven on to a new candidate, the Taiping movement aimed at a fundamental restructuring of society. Although Hong and the movement's highest leaders styled themselves as *wang* ("king"), an otherwise radical egalitarianism initially prevailed across old class and, most startling of all, gender lines. All the elements of Confucian society were systematically broken down: the hierarchical relationships of rulers, family, and friends; the veneration of the Classics, and the separation of mental and manual work. Men and women, married and unmarried, lived in separate barracks but were considered equal, even as soldiers on the battlefield. Private property was eliminated: all wealth and materiel captured was to be put into a common treasury.

Like modern revolutions as well, class and religious enemies who refused to convert or were deemed unuseful were to be dealt with ruthlessly, as were the ruling "demon"Manchus. Scholar-gentry or officials were summarily executed. Anyone with uncalloused hands or the telltale long fingernails of a student faced possible execution as well. Confucian, Buddhist, and Daoist temples were looted and destroyed or turned into houses of Taiping Christian worship. Indeed, Taiping behavior in the scope of their destruction of

Confucian society comes close to modern definitions of genocide. For example, the subject of the vignette in the next chapter, Li Gui, was captured along with his brother by the rebels in 1860. Forty members of his extended family were slaughtered in the process and the only way the boys stayed alive was to convince a Taiping headman that their ability to read and write could be useful. As the fighting became more widespread, even peasants were not necessarily exempt. Those who insisted on staying together with family were often killed. Leaders performed a kind of triage with new captives and conscripts: those who could fight would be soldiers; those strong enough to carry supplies would be porters; the rest would die. For their part, Qing troops and militia, even from the most disciplined units, looted, burned and killed on a stupendous scale as well.

PATTERNS UP CLOSE

The Culture Wars Of The Taiping Era

The Taiping "Rebellion," "Revolution," or, as some scholars have begun to call it, "Civil War," has been one of the most intensely studied conflicts in modern Chinese history and, in many respects, remains among the most ideologically contested. Qing officials as a matter of course denounced it as an utterly illegitimate attempt to seize Heaven's Mandate, made even more heinous by using foreign religion to delude the people. Chinese and Western contemporaries also tended to use the term rebellion most frequently and tended to place it within the larger historical context of Chinese antidynastic revolts. Yet its sense of religious mission and its millenarian and apocalyptic overtones signaled that its aims were not simply to replace one emperor with another. Moreover, the laws and practices of the insurgents and their drive to eradicate Confucian society and all of China's "false" religions contained a number of features prompting some contemporaries to see it in revolutionary terms.

Twentieth-century insurgent leaders frequently placed themselves in the Taiping revolutionary tradition. Sun Yat-sen, who did so much to create the Revolutionary Alliance that ultimately ousted the Qing and created a republic in China, was regaled with tales of Taiping derring-do as a boy in Guangdong and even welcomed some aged Taiping veterans to his movement. Mao Zedong and many Communist and Nationalist leaders also at various times identified themselves with Hong and the Taipings. This was particularly true in the PRC, where the official term for the movement is "Taiping peasant revolutionary movement." A number of the most important histories of the movement outside the PRC also put it squarely in the category of a revolution—at least one

continued

claiming that modern Chinese history should properly begin with the Taipings. Recently, historians seeking to find less politically charged terminology have come to use "Taiping Era," "Taiping War," or, as the subtitle of a recent work puts it, *Civil War in 19th Century China*.[1]

[1]Tobie Meyer-Fong, *What Remains: Coming to Terms with Civil War in 19th Century China*. Stanford, CA: Stanford University Press, 2013.

The many different ways of interpreting the conflict even today prompt the question: How did the Taiping and the Qing present themselves to the people they sought to persuade to join them? What values did they bring to bear in the cultural war in which they engaged? One way of approaching the question is to explore the propaganda literature, posters, and broadsides and so forth that both sides produced.

In many ways the Taiping appear to have had the more difficult task in that Christianity of any denomination had never enjoyed widespread popularity in China. A recent study argues that the Taiping attempted to place their version of Christianity as "God-worshipers" in the pre-imperial context of the worship of Di/Shangdi. They thus claimed that emperors, in reserving to themselves the right to worship God/Di, had blasphemously turned China away from its "true" religious tradition. It was the role of the Taiping, therefore, to eliminate the entire imperial and Confucian edifice, return China to its true religious roots, and realize the linkage those roots shared with other Christian sects. Early Taiping edicts and proclamations, for example, play down the "foreign" origins of Christianity in favor of references from the *The Book of History/Documents* and the *Rites of Zhou* that depict people other than kings as worshiping God or Heaven. Moreover, early Taiping propaganda frequently extols Confucian virtues and even mentions Confucius and Mencius as worthy models—although these disappear as the theology of the movement evolves.

Perhaps the perfect expression of the religious message propagated by the Taiping may be found on their seals (see page 172). Here the characters are arranged in a cross, and the message they convey shows the hierarchy of belief (see illustration): the largest and boldest characters, "*shangdi*" (God), appear where the vertical and horizontal members of the cross intersect. They are flanked by the words *tai* and *ping* (Great Peace). Above *shangdi* are the words "Heavenly Father" (*tian fu*); below *shangdi* in equal parallel columns are the words "Heavenly Elder Brother Jesus" and Heavenly King Hong (Xiuquan)."

Not surprisingly, the most effective message broadcast by the Taiping was the patriotic one of ousting the Manchu Qing, as in this 1853 proclamation in the form of a poem by an unknown author:

A proclamation to comfort the people:
Do not tremble or let your heart be troubled;

Only because the realm of the great Ming
Was usurped by the Tartars (i.e. Manchus)
I intend to raise the Han and destroy the Manchus,
Leaving no corrupt officials.[2]

[2]J. C. Cheng, *Chinese Sources for the Taiping Rebellion 1850–1864.*
Hong Kong: Hong Kong University Press, 1963, p. 63.

Qing counterpropaganda concentrated on several major weaknesses in the Taiping social order, which itself never had a chance to develop a peacetime administrative footing (see illustration). Taiping communalism was attacked on several fronts, as confiscatory of land and goods, whereas gender segregation was stigmatized as antifamily. Condemnation of Confucianism, Buddhism, and Daoism was portrayed as uprooting China's deepest traditions and replacing them with "barbarian" religion. But the most potent arguments were centered on preservation of the family-based social order and, in a mirror image of Taiping appeals, to patriotism. As an 1854 proclamation by Zeng Guofan put it,

> Now, the Yue [i.e., Guangdong] bandits (Taipings) steal some (cultural) dregs of foreign barbarians and adhere to the religion of God; from their fake king and fake ministers down to the soldiers and menial servants they address one another as brothers. . . . In short, the moral system, ethical human relations, cultural inheritance, and social institutions and statutes of the past thousands of years in China are at once swept away. . . . How can all those who study books and know the characters sit comfortably with hands in sleeves [as bystanders] without thinking of doing something about it?[3]

[3]Jen Yu-wen, *The Taiping Revolutionary Movement.*
New Haven, CT, and London: Yale University Press, p. 231.

In the end, of course, Zeng played a major role both in subduing the movement militarily and ideologically. Like Buddhism for more than a thousand years, Taiping religion carried the stigma of foreignness about it, the more so since in most places it was imposed by force. Like so many other revolutions—indeed, like the regime of the first emperor of the Qin—the complete refashioning of the social order sparked a powerful resistance. When the war was over, that resistance proved resilient enough to carry some of its core ideas down to the present. The Taiping ideology—except for mounting distaste for and distrust of Manchu rule—died with Hong and his inner circle.

continued

Taiping Seal. This Taiping seal, perhaps dating from 1860 or 1861 is wonderfully furnished with religious and political symbolism. On the outside borders we have a double phoenix and facing dragons on right and left: both imperial symbols appropriated by Hong Xiuquan. The two largest characters, top left and top right, say "Imperial Seal." The arrangement of the other bolded characters along with the two smaller vertical columns in the center form a cross. The large central bold characters say "God the Heavenly Father"; the two small characters flanking these are taiping, or "great peace." Next to them are the characters "gracious harmony" (right) and "convivial peace" (left). The two columns under Heavenly Father say "Heavenly Elder Brother Jesus" (left) and Heavenly King Hong (Xiuquan) "the sun." Starting on the extreme right and working toward the center the columns read: "Eternally maintaining Heaven and Earth; exalted for myriad years; the savior of the world and young monarch." Reading in from the left, we have: "Eternally granting Heaven's favor; the true king Guifu (lit. "Honor and Blessedness"); ruling over the bountiful earth." Jonathan Spence cites the Chinese scholar Wang Qingcheng, who suggests that the script is a kind of acrostic and should be read:

> *Of God the Father, the Heavenly Elder Brother Christ*
> *The Heavenly King Hong, the sun, the ruler of the*
> *bountiful earth,*
> *The savior and young Monarch, the true king Guifu,*
> *Exalted for myriad years, eternally granting Heaven's*
> *favor,*
> *Eternally maintaining Heaven and Earth in gracious*
> *harmony and convivial peace.*
> (Spence, *God's Chinese Son*, p.xxviii)

Another rich area of scholarly exploration has been the nature of Taiping religion. Again, the alien nature of many of its core beliefs and the relatively short time of its existence ensured that it never struck deep roots in terms of ideological vitality. Hong's claim of being Jesus's younger brother sent on a mission from the Christian God the Father to eliminate the "demons" of rival beliefs and bring about the millennial Heavenly Kingdom of Great Peace was simply too "other" for the great majority of those in the new Kingdom. Thus, one of the most effective weapons in the Qing arsenal was pro-Confucian propaganda.

Probably no one was more effective at this ideological counterattack than the powerful official Zeng Guofan (1811–1872). Zeng and his protégé, Li Hongzhang (1823–1901), are probably better known for their efforts at self-strengthening. But both received their start putting together militia in their home provinces to fight the Taiping. Zeng was particularly renowned for his dedication to Confucian ideals and was thus an ideal choice to attempt to restore Confucian society in recaptured areas and to rekindle loyalty to deeply ingrained traditions. As illustrated in this chapter's "Patterns Up Close," both sides used posters, broadsides, storytellers, and ceremonies to make their respective points, although the Qing appeal to family and clan loyalty and regional solidarity against the invaders from the south was particularly effective.

Famine and Frustration, the Nian Rebellion, 1853–1868

As the Taiping movement was gathering momentum in the south, a more diffuse uprising was taking shape in the north. In addition to the mass bloodletting of the Taipings, the period from 1849 through the 1850s saw an extraordinary series of natural disasters in the empire. In 1849 alone, earthquakes, floods, and an outbreak of plague in Zhili (the metropolitan province surrounding Beijing), Hubei, and Zhejiang, and a drought in arid Gansu claimed perhaps 15 million lives. This was followed by two record floods of the Yellow River in 1851 and 1855. With the government in desperate need of money for disaster relief, but deprived of the tax revenues from the rich areas worst hit by these disasters and the capture of large swaths of territory by the Taiping, relief was slow and sporadic.

Gathering in some remnants of the White Lotus sect and propelled by the lack of flood and famine relief, the Nian rebels—named for the northern Chinese dialect many spoke—rose up in 1851 largely from frustration at the inability of the Qing to either help them or resist foreign demands for treaty revision. Some students of Chinese demography have also suggested that the unusually large number of single men in the region—the result of high rates of female infanticide—may also have been a contributing factor.

The movement achieved its greatest power under Zhang Lexing (1810–1863), a landlord and wealthy salt trader/smuggler, who organized the movement along the lines of the Qing banner system and claimed the imperial mantle. Following the epic 1855 Yellow River floods, which shunted the river mouth hundreds of miles away from its former position and caused tens of thousands of deaths, the movement gained further strength because of the inability of the Qing to relieve the victims while fighting the Taiping further south.

The Nian movement, unlike the Taiping, never developed a coherent ideology other than anger and frustration with what they perceived as Qing misrule. They never seriously pursued an alliance with the Taipings, which might have produced different results for both sides. In fact, when on occasion Taiping *wangs* sent instructions to Nian leaders, they were pointedly ignored. In the end, Qing forces were able to crush them piecemeal, particularly after the capture and execution of Zhang in 1863. The movement smoldered on for a few more years until its final collapse and suppression in 1868. Like the Taiping movement, it left the economy of the region in ruins, devastated large areas through the use of scorched earth tactics on both sides, and left appalling casualties—in this case anywhere from 100,000 to a quarter million dead.

Rebuilding and Reform

Although the collapse of the Taiping movement did not occur immediately with the fall of Nanjing in July 1864, only a few remnants remained to escape to remote areas. One such unit, the Black Flags, ultimately ended up in Vietnam, where they stubbornly fought the French into the 1880s. Nanjing itself saw the suicide or slaughter of perhaps 100,000 Taiping adherents and a devastating fire. With so much of China's most productive land repeatedly fought over and its elaborate infrastructure of bridges, canals, irrigation ditches, paddies, raised beds, and so forth severely damaged—to say nothing of the other rebellions still being fought—the task of reconstruction facing the Qing was one of the largest in human history to that point.

The financial cost alone was more than the government would be able to handle for the remainder of the nineteenth century. Writing more than a decade after the war in 1877, Li Gui would note that vast stretches of once-productive farmland were still lying uncultivated from the conflict. Among other problems, the government was hamstrung by low tariffs on foreign goods mandated by the various treaties with the United States and European countries. Customs collections in a number of places had been replaced by a temporary system, soon made permanent, run by Chinese and foreigners called the Imperial Maritime Customs Service. Another temporary expedient turned permanent was the tax system called *lijin* (**likin**). Unable to raise the tariff rates beyond the 5 percent mandated by treaty, the Qing established internal transit taxes on foreign goods to pay for the war effort and subsequent reconstruction. Both systems would survive long into the twentieth century. In addition, rebuilding efforts competed for funds with the costs of self-strengthening programs and the wars, rebellions, and indemnities faced by the Qing during the remainder of the century.

Despite these difficulties, all of the largest and a majority of the smaller of the 600 or so cities destroyed in the rebellion were rebuilt, notably Hangzhou and Nanjing. In the case of Nanjing, the repopulating and reconstruction was carried out by Zeng Guofan, whose armies had done so much of the damage to it in their repeated attempts to capture the rebel capital. Along the way, Zeng and officials in other areas took pains to rebuild and construct new temples, shrines, and public buildings, and encourage the wealthy to organize and contribute to the effort. In many cases, stuck without funds from the imperial government, the monies were raised locally, sometimes with the area's officials leading the way.

The increased reliance on local funding and initiative in reconstruction, along with the enhanced power of regional officials commanding large militia armies in their home provinces, is often cited by scholars as leading to a drain of power from the central government to the provinces. By the end of the century, regional competition among officials such as Li Hongzhang and Zhang Zhidong would play a large role in preventing cooperation between their forces during the Sino-Japanese and Boxer wars.

Another scholarly question that has received considerable recent study is that of the development of "civil society" in China. This concept, explored by the pioneering sociologist Max Weber (1864–1920), looks at the degree of informal, or nonstate, control exercised by clubs, societies, guilds, artisan associations, chambers of commerce, and even local political parties in maintaining the day-to-day activities of subjects or citizens of a state. These are also seen as alternate spaces for political discussion and activities, a kind of informal counterbalance to state policies and ideology. As such, social scientists have tended to see them as seedbeds of movement toward representative government and democracy. But was this the case in Qing China?

On one level, one could make the argument that this is another instance of imposing the structures that were historically important in Europe on Chinese history in a way that stretches the facts uncomfortably to fit the theory. It suggests that if a civil society existed in that Chinese social space beyond the magistrate's purview, why did it not evolve into representative institutions? Thus, like the question of why China had no industrial revolution, it assumes that the presence of the one suggests a deficit of some sort in the other. Certainly China did not lack associations, societies, artisan leagues, guilds, and so forth, but did they constitute the kind of counterbalance to the state that Weber and others had in mind, or were they essentially reinforcing the governing institutions and ideology?

This raises yet another point. Although protest movements and revolts of various scales were endemic to Chinese history, there really were not political parties as such with coherent programs in opposition to Confucian ideology.

Among the educated—and China, along with Japan and Korea, boasted some of the world's highest nonindustrial levels of literacy—there were different schools of Neo-Confucianism, but not really any in direct opposition to government orthodoxy. As the century wore on, the capital and major cities saw patriotic demonstrations and even riots—for example, after the Sino-Japanese War in 1895—however, the opposition was not to the imperial system as such but to those holding the throne (and as Manchus) who were seen as incapable of defending the country and hence as undeserving of Heaven's Mandate. The Taipings certainly mounted a sweeping and systematic critique of the established order, but even with a radically different ideology and social structure still retained an imperial system. Thus, if a prime requirement was pluralism and relative independence of a civil sector, even the independent organizations relied on funding from the scholar-gentry and support of officials to maintain themselves. Moreover, although the scholar gentry often opposed the *actions* of local officials, they were in their positions of prestige because of the Confucian system and their own success or that of family members in the exams. Beyond this, the *baojia* system of social control that bypassed the scholar-gentry and included all villagers within its network of decimal responsibility was directly tied to the Confucian bureaucracy.

One area that has sometimes been cited as resembling the discourse of civil society is the phenomenon of *qingyi* or "pure discussion." As we will see again in the following chapter, *qingyi* arose in the period after the Taiping Rebellion and centered largely on discussion of strategies and tactics involved in self-strengthening and more broadly in what the government should emphasize in terms of reform for defense of the empire and for re-establishing China's rightful place in the emerging world order. As with other elements of the memorial system, any official could comment on these issues. Yet even here amid debates that pitted those advocating various degrees of borrowing Western technologies and institutional concepts against those who believed the answer was bringing in "human talent" and a more strict and austere Confucianism, the questions revolved far less around ends than means. Moreover, given the torturous political path that the Empress Dowager and her inner circle pursued, *qingyi* was used at least as much for political intrigue and score settling as it was to bring fresh ideas to the fore. Hence, its place within the government itself and its overall deference to political orthodoxy disqualifies it from being "civil society" in the Weberian sense.

The Height of Nineteenth-Century Qing Expansion

Despite the Qing Dynasty encompassing China's greatest period of wealth, power, and territory, there was hardly a period within it when a rebellion of some sort was not in progress. As we have seen, some of them grew from inadequate government responses to natural disasters or famine; some to attempts at tax collection; and some, like the great Taiping movement, a revolt against foreign minority rule, economic distress, religious conflict, and ethnic rivalries.

Elements of all of these could be found within the various Muslim uprisings of the era, especially in the extreme western areas subdued during Qianlong's reign, but ruled by the "loose rein" method of dealing with border peoples. Closer to home, revolts by Hui (Han Chinese) Muslims still loyal to the Ming had marked the mid-1600s. By the late eighteenth and through nearly all of the nineteenth century, however, Yunnan and Xinjiang marked the sites of protracted struggles. In the process of subduing these, however, Qing agency during the "Restoration" period reached its height.

In the 1820s a series of Turkic invaders moved into Kashgaria led or co-led by the Ismaili Khojas from Kokand. In the case of these invaders, both ethnicity and religion played a role in the sense that Muslim Hui traders resisted the invaders and fought against them alongside Qing forces. A cycle of invasion and resistance then prevailed over the next 20 years until the Qing drove the last of the Khojas, the brutal Wali Khan, back to Kokand in 1857. Upon the Qing withdrawal from the area, however, this region of "Kashgaria" came under the purview of Yaqub Beg, whom we met in the opening vignette of this chapter.

unrest

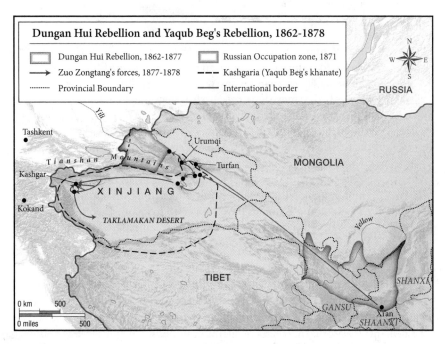

MAP 4.3
Dungan Hui Rebellion and Yaqub Beg's Rebellion, 1862–1878

Hui People: Three Mulahs, CA. 1890. Islam was introduced to Yunnan in 1253 when Kublai Khan, the fifth emperor of the Yuan Dynasty, pacified Dali. In 1273, Sayyid Ali Omer Shams al-Din was appointed Prime Minister (now called governor) of Yunnan. During his reign, he established 12 mosques in Kunming. Islam has since spread all over Yunnan Province, mainly in Kunming, Yuxi, Honghe, Wenshan, Dali, Baoshan, Zhaotong, Chuxiong, Simao, and Qujing prefectures and municipalities. Many ethnic Hui, some Dais, Bais, Tibetans and Zhuangs have converted to Islam. There were an estimated 500,000 Muslims in Yunnan in May 1996, and some 717 mosques in service.

While Yaqub Beg was establishing his proto-state of Kashgaria, two revolts by Hui people and local minorities in southwestern Yunnan and in the vast Northwest from Shaanxi to Xinjiang capitalized further on local disputes, which expanded into generalized rebellion against the Qing. The catalyst for the first revolt, in 1855, called by the Burmese name Panthay for the Shan minority involved with it, was a clash between Hui and (non-Muslim) Han tin miners. There had also been long-smoldering resentment toward the Qing for an earlier massacre of Hui. The situation became extremely complex as conflicts also arose between Sunni and Sufi Muslims and a number of Yunnan minorities, all of whom shifted loyalties several times over the next eighteen years amid the more general anti-Qing disturbance. When the revolt finally was suppressed, many of the rebels fled to Burma. The second revolt, by the Dungan Hui of the Northwest, lasted from 1862 till Zuo Zongtang's expedition in 1877. As the rebels scattered after their defeat by the Qing, they fled west to Russia.

It was this revolt that had brought Zuo to the eastern part of the region. Although he was ruthless toward rebels of any sect, he also made infrastructural improvements to the region and launched a successful program to grow grain to help supply his army. But the expeditions were expensive, the land largely uninhabitable and thus difficult to forage on, the people marked by internecine conflicts and shifting loyalties, and the new weapons from foreign countries costly and their operators largely untried. Moreover, the distances were unimaginably vast and so far beyond the pale of Chinese civilization as to be in another, and disturbingly alien, world.

The new opponent, Yaqub Beg, with a coalition of Turkic Muslims from Kokand, had initially resisted the encroachment of Hui Muslims retreating from Zuo Zongtang's armies. Seeing their attempts in the west as an invasion, he declared *jihad* on the Hui and their non-Muslim Han allies and drove them from Urumqi in 1870. In the midst of this confused situation, Russia, Great Britain, and the Ottoman Empire all claimed a stake. All three empires had been engaged in attempting to exert direct or proxy control over the region of Central Asia north of Afghanistan, involved in a decades-long series of border intrigues originally called **The Great Game** by East India Company intelligence officers and later popularized in a story of that name by Rudyard Kipling. For all three of these empires, as we saw in the opening vignette, Yaqub Beg's Kashgaria made a highly useful buffer state. Thus, all three extended tacit recognition to it. For Zuo and his partisans, however, it marked a vital part of China that the Qing could ill afford to lose.

Zuo ran into intense *qingyi* opposition from China's leading self-strengthener, Li Hongzhang. A rapidly strengthening Japan had occupied Taiwan in 1874 and the various foreign powers had more than doubled their treaty ports in 1860. To Li, Xinjiang was too remote, costly, and unproductive to make it a priority. Moreover, its inhabitants were barely touched by Confucian civilization. A far better use of the available resources, Li argued, would be to employ them to improve coastal defenses against the Western maritime powers and Japan. In the end, Zuo's argument won the day and, as we saw in the vignette, his 1877–1878 campaign was successful beyond all expectations except perhaps his own. His army outmaneuvered, outgunned, and overpowered Yaqub Beg's forces.

His victories had a stunning effect on the players of the Great Game; one claimed it was the most startling victory in Asia in the past 50 years. All were in agreement that China's armed forces seemed not only rejuvenated, but also a match for any European or Ottoman troops seeking to oppose them. For his part,

Zuo followed Qing policy in killing resistors and promising leniency to those who defected to him. He established Han, Manchu, and Mongolian settlers in the area after driving many of the Turkic peoples out. As for Yaqub Beg, some sources say he was poisoned; others claim that he committed suicide. His son and grandsons were captured, castrated, and put to work in the Forbidden City as imperial eunuchs.

For all the spectacular gains the Qing armies had made, their diplomats almost bargained some key ones away. Having given the Russians back much of Yili in the Treaty of Livadia in 1879, the Chinese negotiator Chong Hou faced angry demands at home that he face execution for his efforts. Zuo stood ready with his army to take on the Russians and drive them from the territory. Negotiations resumed under the son of Zeng Guofan, Zeng Jize, and the Russians agreed to return the territory in the Treaty of St. Petersburg in 1881.

THE LONG NINETEENTH CENTURY II: ECONOMICS AND SOCIETY

One of the long-term problems of modern Chinese economic and social history, as we noted in the section on historiography in this chapter, is that of the sustainability of Chinese agriculture in the nineteenth century. That is, did the population reach a point at which it exceeded the capacity of the land to sustain it, and if so, when? Were there tools or machines or other technologies that might have increased productivity sufficiently to hold the problem at bay? What bearing did this have on government and society? How did it affect the quality of life?

Demographics and the Land: Population and Sustainability

One factor that must be kept in mind is that in the period from 1700 to 1900, the empire's population tripled, whereas its land usage only doubled. This increase came despite the enormous death toll of the Taiping, Nian, and Muslim rebellions, which may have carried off as many as 30 million people, or roughly 8 to 9 percent of the population at the time. Only about 10 percent of China's land is arable and perhaps 80 to 85 percent of the people lived in rural areas. Even today, with China's population more than three times what it was a century ago, there are still vast territories that are underpopulated or even totally uninhabited. Resource-rich Manchuria would only be seen as an area for settlement in the late nineteenth century—and then at least in part as a hedge against Russian and Japanese intrusion. Thus, the fertile areas around rivers and by the coasts are densely populated, whereas large areas of Xinjiang are completely devoid of people.

Another difficulty in terms of land usage and sustainability revolves around inheritance laws and customs. As we noted in previous chapters, land tenure has always been a problem, even to the present time. We will take a closer look at village life later in this chapter, but it is useful to observe here that the average land holding in the fertile areas of central China at this time was slightly less than three acres. The land was held in strips, sometimes in noncontiguous sections, around a central group of village houses, much like the configuration of feudal holdings in medieval Western Europe. China, however, did not practice primogeniture—leaving the family holdings to the firstborn male—so each son got a piece of the land. Some families, especially those counting a member of the scholar-gentry in their number, amassed considerable holdings over time and were able to sustain themselves on this system fairly well. Smaller holders, however, squeezed by their inability to feed themselves on their ever-diminishing tracts, sold them off and joined the labor pool, or migrated to towns and cities to try their luck there. In many cases they engaged in handicrafts of various sorts and so added to the vibrancy of the empire's commercial sector. The majority, however, rented land as tenants, hoping eventually to make enough to acquire property again. Thus, the rise in tenancy was accompanied by a rise in landlordism, particularly in those areas ravaged by the mid-nineteenth century rebellions.

As the century wore on, and despite the reputation of towns and cities as repositories of the vices against which virtuous Confucians stood, many landlords ended up with houses in the city and thus became absentee landlords. At times when the countryside was rocked by instability, the foreign treaty ports also served as refuges. It was also the case that toward the end of the century, the increasing number of merchants sought to take advantage of the government's chronic need for revenue and bought degrees. Some sought to buy their way into scholar-gentry respectability in this way, acquiring rural holdings but keeping their compounds in the cities.

Given these factors, scholars have long debated the varying trajectories of China and the industrializing countries of Europe and, later, the United States. Such comparisons often presuppose that industrialism is an inevitable evolutionary stage for societies and that the West in this regard represents the advanced model for all to follow. The question is often posed in the following terms: given China's huge population, giant internal economy, abundant resources, and technological leadership, why did it not experience its own industrial revolution? Some argue that since so much of China's leadership in technology and material culture had been established as early as the Song period, China should have gone through an industrial revolution then. Instead, they argue a variation of what we identified in a previous chapter as "the Needham Question": that from roughly 1500 on, China's rate of innovation slowed considerably, although the population increased. Farming techniques showed little technological advance, but local, regional, and even national commercial networks grew markedly.

A "High-Level Equilibrium Trap"?

Theories growing from these observations have centered on the work of Mark Elvin, who hypothesized that China had long been caught in a situation called a *high-level equilibrium trap.* That is, comprehensive and sustained innovation like that of an industrial revolution tends to take place when a society is in a state of imbalance or disequilibrium. Eighteenth-century England in this view had severe problems of high wages, surplus capital, poor transportation, legal disabilities imposed on religious dissenters, and restrictive laws on imports of cotton goods that prompted investment in technologies and working arrangements to improve efficiency.

China, however, it was argued, had been able to keep agricultural pace with its population growth but had essentially run out of new lands to open up. Having more children in peasant families meant that up to a point their additional labor allowed the farming to be done more intensely. The growing labor supply, however, consumed what commodity surplus there was and did not allow any particular class to acquire a deep pool of capital that could be invested in new enterprises—except to buy more land. Improving labor efficiency seemed unnecessary—even disruptive—because labor was so cheap and abundant. Even in an area in which greater efficiencies might have been advantageous—communications and transportation—there seemed to be no pressing need to make infrastructural improvements.

China had good internal east–west transportation on its rivers and north and south by the Grand Canal and the coasting trade. Although foreign firms after the mid-nineteenth century dominated the river steamer trade and one of China's government-sponsored merchant-run self-strengthening enterprises tried to recapture that trade, the majority of river traffic was carried by innumerable small craft. Even bulk cargoes such as tea were transported along footpaths by porters carrying it in packages lashed to huge pack frames. Officials routinely objected to creating steamboat lines or railroads because they viewed them as taking away employment opportunities. Thus, by the late nineteenth century these economic factors were in equilibrium but incapable of breaking out of this "trap."

The figures supporting this theory were backed up by anecdotal evidence as well. When Chinese officials first visited the United States in the 1860s and 1870s, one of the things they found most striking was the relatively small population farming a vast amount of land, which was only feasible by the use of a variety of machines as a substitute for human labor. At a time when, in the face of the incipient threat of rebellion, officials were especially careful not to upset the people, the disruptions of creating an industrial base in this labor-rich environment were often deemed too dangerous to pursue.

A number of critiques have since been offered of this hypothesis. As we noted earlier, Marxists inside and outside of the PRC have tended to invoke class conflict, imperialism, and incorporation into the capitalist world system as the primary causes of China's "failure" to industrialize. Others have invoked a variation on the idea of "China-centeredness." World historians, for example, have criticized the assumption of the European historical trajectory as the proper model. That is, the question should not be, "Why didn't China have an industrial revolution?"—which implies negative exceptionalism, but rather what factors coalesced in Britain that allowed it to happen there? Others have noted that the fact that even into the twentieth century China's population continued to grow without suffering mass famine suggests that there was still plenty of "stretch" in the system.

Still others mount a cultural critique of Confucianism's emphasis on the moral primacy of peasant production over commerce as a root cause of the lack of capital aimed at innovation. The success of Japan, with its pervasive Neo-Confucian influences—and the robust industrialization of the "Confucian-capitalist" societies of Taiwan, Singapore, South Korea, and now the PRC itself—suggests difficulties with this contention. Moreover, recent work on Qing commercial networks suggests that despite orthodox Confucian distaste for commerce as an unproductive necessary evil, China had undergone a commercial revolution in the late eighteenth century and trade was an indispensable and growing element of the economy.

Although there is no strong consensus at this point about definitive circumstances in studying China's agricultural sustainability or possibilities for indigenous industrialism, it seems safe to conclude that

> there existed a convergent and self-regulating "trinary structure" of agricultural dominance, the landholding peasantry, and physiocratic government. This structure created an overall equilibrium and allowed long-term growth of a particular type. In this system, the peasantry, not the state, played a central role in determining China's path. (Deng, Kent. *A Critical Survey of Recent Research in Chinese Economic History (online).* London: LSE Research Online, 2006. P. 24)

Commerce and Commodities

As we saw in the previous chapter, China's international trade had long been an important part of the economy—if not one deemed essential in the Confucian hierarchy of values. The luxury trade in such goods as silk, porcelain, lacquerware, and especially tea had vastly expanded in the eighteenth and early nineteenth centuries. So much of these commodities was being exported that the Western maritime trading nations became increasingly concerned with what they perceived as a drain on their silver reserves, much of which was drawn from the Americas. It would be in large part to address this perceived imbalance that Western traders would try a wide variety of commodities to export to China until opium came to predominate by the 1830's. Later, machine-made textiles and other industrial products also made their way into the empire in increasing numbers.

Although the role of the empire as a whole was passive in the sense that it was expected that buyers would come to approved ports to trade, it should also be noted that there had traditionally been, and despite Qing official prohibitions would continue to be, hundreds of thousands of Chinese merchants, craftspeople, and laborers living abroad. For hundreds of years they had mostly been concentrated in Japan, Korea, Southeast Asia, and Indonesia. By the mid-nineteenth century, however, thousands were arriving in Cuba and South America as "contract laborers"—part of the infamous **coolie trade.** Thousands more were initially bound for the gold fields of California as free emigrants, and their successors soon came by the tens of thousands to work on railroads and infrastructure throughout the American west. In North America and, after the coolie trade was abolished, in Cuba and Peru, many of those who stayed went into business. By the turn of the nineteenth century there was scarcely a major country in the world that did not have a Chinese community in it.

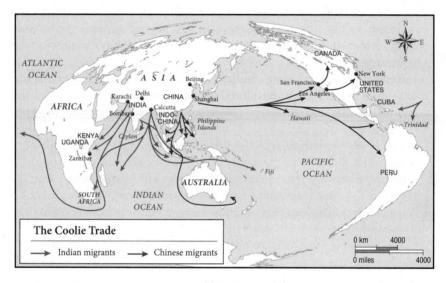

MAP 4.4
The Coolie Trade

The vibrancy of Chinese expatriate commerce was paralleled at home. The immense size of the empire and its highly varied regional differences make it difficult to generalize about commerce as a whole. One thing that does seem evident, however, is that sometime during the later eighteenth century the number of merchants greatly expanded. This may be related to the expansion of the luxury trades in central China; it may also bear on the increased amount of labor and the demand for various kinds of handicrafts.

In any case, one piece of evidence we have for a growth in trade is the increase in *huiguan*, the translation of which is usually given as "guildhall," although this does not quite convey all of its functions. *Huiguan* were originally hostels in Beijing for officials from Guangdong and other southern provinces when they needed lodging in the capital. By the eighteenth and early nineteenth centuries, they had grown into a large network of places to stay for officials and, increasingly, merchants from the same region. A *hui-guan* allowed its guests to register in the district, often provided them with room and board, gave them entrée into local associations, helped them with official paperwork, and generally smoothed their way in doing business in an area with which they might not be familiar. At the same time, they kept the home town or district connection alive through understanding one's native dialect and perhaps even knowing friends or relatives. These institutions followed Chinese emigrants abroad as well: in San Francisco they were known as "the Six Companies," with each representing a different district in Guangdong.

The proliferation of these institutions is seen as an indicator of large numbers of merchants of various goods circulating around the empire, often selling regional specialties like silk and tea from around Hangzhou or wine from Shaoxing. Closer to home, regional and local commerce was carried on in market towns and villages dotting the provinces, prefectures, and districts of the empire. As a number of scholars have pointed out, these networks more often than not crossed provincial boundaries, making the study of the economics of a particular province problematic, if not in some cases meaningless.

The standard model, although not without its critics, of the placement, marketing, and social structure is the one developed by G. William Skinner. In most cases, the main town in the *xian*, or district—more or less the equivalent of a county in the United States—was the seat of local government and the base of the district magistrate. Because it was the center of local government there would be an extensive staff attending his *yamen*, or office. If the district was a large one, the staff might include the *mufu*, or the informal group of "friends, guests, and colleagues" an official tended to acquire as his career was becoming established. There would also be a number of influential scholar-gentry with homes in the town so as to be in closer touch with authority. There was a degree of protection as well, since nearly all district capitals were surrounded by a defensive wall. Numerous merchant concerns would also be located near the seat of power.

The district capital and the large and intermediate-size market towns were generally surrounded by marketing villages arranged around the core town in a kind of hexagon. For the convenience of the local customers who would be walking to market, different marketing villages opened their shops on different days during the traditional Chinese 10-day week. In most cases the distances were fairly small, around three miles or so. Thus, the market towns were the pivots around which local and regional—even national—business revolved. Traveling merchants and wholesalers purchased and sold to small retailers in the lesser market towns where peasants brought their surpluses and handicrafts for sale. This was also true for those dealing in cash crops like tea, cotton, or tobacco and commodities such as silk, which often had local reputations within the larger areas known for them, such as *longjing cha*, the famous "Dragon Well Tea" of the districts near Hangzhou.

Village and Family Life

Although changes were certainly noticeable in the family, among the genders, and in the confidence Chinese displayed in the Confucian system—particularly among urban Chinese—the durability of long-standing traditions is probably far more striking. As we have seen throughout, the family remained the central Chinese institution. Within it, the father continued to be the most powerful figure, and the Confucian ideal of hierarchical relationships between husband and wife, father and son, and elder brother and younger brother remained in force. Daughters, although most often treated with affection, were also considered a net drain on family resources because they would marry outside the family. Thus, the education they received was generally aimed at fostering the skills the family of their husbands-to-be would consider valuable—cooking, sewing, running a household, and perhaps singing and poetry. Enough literacy was also desirable to read such classics as "Admonitions for Women," the "Classic of Filial Piety," and other guides to proper behavior. Although it was often repeated that "women hold up half the sky," the proverbial wisdom remained that "a woman with talent is without virtue." Yet, as we have seen in other chapters, underneath the veneer of Confucian model behavior there was often considerable flexibility in women's opportunities and agency. This was most marked among many of China's minorities, but to a surprising degree applied to Han women as well.

As we will see in more detail in the following chapter, the disruptions of the nineteenth century began to have some effect on this situation of women's subordination.

Although there had been a slow trickle of foreign influence into China, particularly in the treaty ports and their adjacent regions, the decade following the Sino-Japanese War (1894–1895) saw an upsurge in it, particularly as the Qing moved belatedly toward reform and underground revolutionary movements began to gain adherents. As we will see later, feminism along Western lines began to make itself felt in Chinese intellectual circles, as embodied by the woman revolutionary, Qiu Jin. Women in Taiping areas had had a brief taste of equality in the mid-nineteenth century, although it had been undermined by Taiping excesses and the Confucian revival afterward. With wealthier Chinese beginning to send daughters abroad to be educated, the impressions they returned with began to erode some Chinese customs, although the full impact of this would not be felt until the 1920s and 1930s. Meanwhile, such customs as the selling of young girls and female infanticide continued to be common, particularly in economically hard-pressed areas.

The Domestic Economy. The growth of the export trade in the eighteenth and nineteenth centuries encouraged further development and specialization of long-standing Chinese domestic industries. **(A)** Moneychangers known as *schroffs* test the quality of the silver taken from foreign concerns in exchange for Chinese goods. **(B)** A worker and overseer demonstrate the operation of a silk reeling machine. **(C)** Women sort tea—the chests for packing the tea are stacked behind them.

CONCLUSION

Although about 80 to 85 percent of China's population remained rural, the old structures of the empire's peasant-based society were slowly beginning to crumble. As we saw during White Lotus, Taiping, Nian, and the eras of the Muslim rebellions, tensions among peasants, village headmen, scholar-gentry, and local officials were never far from the surface. Landlordism, and especially the growing instance of absentee landlordism, tended to stretch these tensions further. China's "physiocratic" approach to economics and its relationship to demographics and sustainability also played a prominent role. As some controversial studies of rural Qing society have suggested, even with the most advanced intensive farming techniques available and the introduction of better crops like corn, peanuts, and potatoes for marginal areas, the land was approaching the limits of its ability to support the population without the widespread introduction of power-driven machinery.

Others, however, detect a somewhat greater ability to sustain a growing population by traditional methods even into the twentieth century. Living on the edge of poverty in many areas, with old trade routes and handicrafts disrupted, many peasants saw in the Taipings, the Nian, and other local rebellions a desperate way to change their situations. But in the end, the radical ideologies and ruthlessness of the rebels disillusioned them, and in many places their poverty increased because of the immense destruction and the flight of many wealthy scholar-gentry to the cities. As a result, by the beginning of the twentieth century, absentee landlordism had become an increasingly acute problem. As some scholars have noted, the land problems of China—and its parallels in India and the Ottoman Empire—were an important impediment to an effective response to the scientific-industrial challenge of Europe and America.

Yet for all of these corrosive circumstances wearing down the Qing body politic and society, the empire actually expanded right into the final quarter of the nineteenth century. As we saw in the opening vignette and with the ideology of restoration in the 1860s and 1870s, there was a distinct sense of Qing agency, of control of the direction of events, among many officials. To no one was this more true than Zuo Zongtang. Moreover, Zuo's expedition also represents the high point of the fruits of self-strengthening, the borrowing of foreign technology and institutions to preserve the Confucian state. Part of the success of Zuo's army was because of the Gatling guns, Remington rifles, and Krupp artillery his men employed that were purchased from American and German manufacturers. For many, as we will see in more detail in the following chapter, the melding of such Chinese and Western things was genuine cause for optimism about the fate of the dynasty.

The economic policies of late imperial China, however, were increasingly at odds with those of the industrializing and commercially expanding West. For Chinese thinkers, this was considered sound both in ideological and in economic terms. Confucianism held that agriculture was China's primary concern, that rootedness in the land was the seedbed of the values of humanity, loyalty, and filial piety, and that the values of the merchant—particularly the drive for profit—were in direct opposition to these. As the nineteenth century advanced, nothing would provide more concrete evidence of the moral correctness of this position than the opium trade.

FURTHER READING

Cheng, J. C. *Chinese Sources for the Taiping Rebellion 1850–1864.* Hong Kong: Hong Kong University Press, 1963. For students interested in the documentation generated by both sides in the conflict, with sound introductory and explanatory material.

Cohen, Paul. *Discovering History in China: American Historical Writing on the Recent Chinese Past.* New York: Columbia University Press, 1984. Pioneering study and critique of American historiography on China advocating a more "China-centered" approach to Chinese history.

Deng, Gang. *The Premodern Chinese Economy: Structural Equilibrium and Capitalist Sterility.* London and New York: Routledge, 1999. Highly ambitious and sweeping economic history stretching from pre-imperial times to late imperial ones, Deng argues for the "triune" equilibrium of a free peasantry, agriculture, and physiocratic government as staples and as impediments to capitalist development.

Elvin, Mark. *The Pattern of the Chinese Past.* Palo Alto, CA: Stanford University Press, 1973. Classic study, subject to intense debate even today that looks at three large questions: Why did China stay together as an empire when others fell? Why did China lead the world in technology during the medieval period? Why did that leadership fall off? Introduces the theory of the high-level equilibrium trap.

Meyer-Fong, Tobie. *What Remains: Coming to Terms with Civil War in 19th Century China.* Stanford, CA: Stanford University Press, 2013. How did ordinary people experience the Taiping Rebellion or, as she puts it, "civil war?" Extensive excerpts of individual experiences of the war and reconstruction.

Pomeranz, Kenneth. *The Great Divergence: China, Europe, and the Making of the Modern World Economy.* Princeton: Princeton University Press, 2000. Perhaps the most influential recent work on the comparative economics of Eurasia. If Northwestern Europe and Asia as a whole, and China in particular, were comparable in so many ways as late as 1750, what factors were crucial in creating and sustaining an industrial revolution in Europe rather than Asia? Pomeranz locates part of the answer in the huge growth in the use of coal and the creation of energy based industries, and the far flung empires and trade connections of the Europeans in securing the materials they needed, rather than in the increasingly intensive use of labor and limited resources available from the Asian periphery.

Rhoads, Edward J. *Manchus and Han: Ethnic Relations and Political Power in Late Qing and Early Republican China.* Seattle: University of Washington Press, 2000. Takes up many of the questions raised by the competing models of Qing rule and extends them into relations with the Han Chinese into the nineteenth and early twentieth centuries. Sees them evolving from military caste to ethnic group over time.

Teng Ssu-yu and John King Fairbank. *China's Response to the West: A Documentary Survey, 1839–1923.* Cambridge, MA: Harvard University Press, 1954. Despite the scholarly consensus that the impact–response school is hopelessly out of date as a theoretical construct, the documents in this classic volume are expertly translated and still highly useful for students of the period.

Wakeman, Frederick E. *Telling Chinese History: A Selection of Essays.* Los Angeles and Berkeley: University of California Press, 2009. Wide-ranging volume of essays through the career of a leading scholar. Especially relevant here are essays on the early Qing and one on the problem of civil society development in Qing China.

Wakeman, Frederick E. *Strangers at the Gate: Social Disorder in South China, 1839–1861.* Los Angeles and Berkeley: University of California Press, 1966. Classic study of the intense interplay of the volatile ethnic, political, ideological and foreign elements in Guangdong from the Opium War to the Taiping Rebellion.

Wang, Wensheng. *White Lotus Rebels and South China Pirates: Crisis and Reform in the Qing Empire.* Cambridge, MA: Harvard University Press, 2014. Set against the backdrop of the White Lotus years and the rising tide of maritime lawlessness centered around the opium trade, Wang argues that the Jianqing reign was not one of slippage from the high point of the Qianlong era, but one of reform and consolidation.

CHAPTER 5

THE LAST EMPIRE
IN TRANSITION II:
IMPERIALISM AND
RESISTANCE, REFORM,
AND REACTION,
1795–1900

Every day the visitors from the different countries numbered in the tens of thousands and were evenly divided between men and women. Jammed shoulder to shoulder, following hard on each other's heels, they crowded together bustling with life. Apart from the Chinese, only the Turks appeared to dress in a distinctive fashion, the attire of the rest being generally uniform in style. Wandering among them was like entering the bazaars of five great capitals, with tens of thousands of treasures on display, and I found myself in a state of utter amazement—and not a little apprehension. In addition, the handful of Chinese seen by the foreigners here had all been in work clothes, so one dressed more elegantly had the crowds continually closing in on him to catch a glimpse of yet another novel sight. I met with no one who did not exchange a kind word or, effusive in his admiration, offer me additional good wishes. Nonetheless, everyone pressing in on me at every turn was like being surrounded with no means of escape. I had hoped to capture the particulars of this time and place with special care, but they simply defied description.

—From Charles Desnoyers, *A Journey to the East:*
Li Gui's "A New Account of a Trip Around the Globe".
Ann Arbor: University of Michigan Press, 2004, pp. 96–7

Such was the awestruck reaction of the young Chinese visitor, Li Gui (1842–1903)—shared by nearly 10 million others from dozens of countries around the world—to the riches of the American Centennial Exposition in Philadelphia in 1876. Following the lead of the British 25 years earlier in celebrating their new status as "Workshop of the World" in the Great Exhibition of 1851, the United States sought to showcase its successful recovery from civil war and its burgeoning industrial power by mounting its own world's fair to celebrate 100 years of nationhood. For Li Gui and the Chinese readers of the account of his trip around the world, *Huan you diqiu xin lu* (*A New Account of a Trip around the Globe*), however, his visit to the exhibition was rich with significance of a different kind.

Born in the year of China's defeat in the First Opium War (1839–1842) and imposition of the humiliating Treaty of Nanjing by the British, Li's life spanned the age of Western imperial expansion in China. Moreover, his activities intersected in many important ways with major aspects of China's troubled efforts at resistance, reform, and reaction. At 18, his Confucian studies were abruptly halted when the Taiping rebels moved into his region, leaving his parents and dozens of family members dead and imprisoning Li Gui and his brother, Li Ying, for two years. Upon his escape in 1862 he worked briefly for the Sino-foreign "Ever-Victorious Army," supporting the Qing against the Taipings. But he found longer-lasting and, ultimately, more significant employment with the Imperial Maritime Customs Service—officially a Qing government agency but one staffed by Chinese and foreign personnel (see Chapter 4). It was here, in one of the rare institutions built on Chinese and foreign cooperation, that he formed the official and informal connections that led to his visit to the American Centennial.

During the period of relative calm following the Second Opium War (1856–1860) and the crushing of the Taipings in the mid-1860s, a group of leading Chinese officials had begun programs aimed at self-strengthening—selectively borrowing foreign technologies and institutions to bolster the Confucian state and society against the military, ideological, and cultural threat represented by the rising industrial powers of the West. By 1876, a number of initiatives were already underway—the first Chinese diplomatic representatives were being dispatched, hundreds of Chinese students were studying abroad, the first modern industrial plants and arsenals had been started, and a Chinese river steamer company had even begun operation. But for self-strengthening (*ziqiang*; or commonly, *yangwu* ["foreign matters"]) proponents like the young Li Gui and his sponsor, Li Hongzhang, the Centennial represented an opportunity to see the greatest collection of the world's technology and ingenuity ever assembled displayed on a few square miles of fairground. And so Li Gui found himself amid the tens of thousands of spectators daily at the fair—with a good many of them gawking at him in his official robes as part of the spectacle.

As had Li Gui, however, his readers would now require a major adjustment in their views of China's current place in this new commercial and industrial world:

> Considering that the intent of countries in holding expositions is primarily to display friendship and extend human talent, particular emphasis is placed on the four words "expand and strengthen commerce." For the most part, though, we Chinese have not seen this as advantageous nor, since so few of us have gone abroad, have we fully grasped its implications. . . . We Chinese alone seem capable of thinking that the intent of the Westerners in undertaking these

exhibitions rests on principles against which we should guard at any cost. Yet as a means of enriching the country on the one hand, and benefiting the people on the other, how could attendance at this exposition be considered wasteful?

(Ibid., p. 100)

Nowhere were the maturing fruits of the commercial and industrial revolutions enriching other countries on more dramatic display than in the exhibition's Machinery Hall, where the colossal, futuristic Corliss steam engine silently powered the majority of the hall's seemingly infinite variety of devices. For Li, it was a powerful corrective to the objections of many Chinese to the suitability of using foreign technology and the possible cultural consequences it entailed:

The display of machinery was immense, with machines for digging coal, pumping water, forging and smelting, land cultivation . . . so many that it was impossible to count. . . . To this one must now proclaim the state of the cosmos to be that of one vast machine. . . . As for the proper use of machines, we must not speak of citing the ancients' well sweeps [as in Daoist cautions about the evils of "ingenuity"] and generalize about the use of such devices as inappropriate, but instead, buy all those without exception that might benefit the people.

(Ibid., pp. 118–19)

More alarmingly, Li had already seen many of the ideas advocated by Chinese self-strengtheners being implemented in Japan, whose exhibition area at the Centennial was directly across the aisle from China's—and three times as large:

I find this country [Japan] to be carefully studying Western institutions, technology, and manufacturing, determined to unlock their deepest secrets. For example, opening mines for the five metals and coal helps the country, while strengthening the military through administrative reform and building machine shops, mints, and offices for telegraphs, posts, steamships, and railroads benefit the nation and people even more. Hence, among the four classes of people, all those who closely follow foreign affairs or can speak or write foreign languages are gathered together, overlooking no one, so that their services may be obtained and encouraged in the future. . . . In selecting candidates for these positions, their official responsibilities will, in all cases, require them to be excellent with the brush, bold and generous, discerning and skilled, and unwilling to drift complacently along in old ways of thinking.

(Ibid., p. 102)

For the remainder of Li's life, however, the political and cultural concerns of those willing to "drift complacently along in old ways of thinking" would work to frustrate the efforts of the self-strengtheners, whereas China's spiraling weakness tempted foreign powers toward ever-increasing aggressiveness. The political winds of court politics, dominated increasingly by the Empress Dowager Cixi's efforts to preserve the Manchu hegemony of the Qing, played their part as well, as self-strengthening officials were alternately favored and shunned over decades of factional infighting. The last years of Li's life marked perhaps China's lowest point in the modern era: in the most dramatic and humiliating role reversal of the past 1,500 years, Japan, after barely a generation of exposure to Euro-American influence, had eclipsed China as a military power and humiliated the empire in war in 1894–1895. Now it threatened to extend its sway throughout the region. In the wake of this disaster, the European powers sought to establish "spheres of influence" in a China on the verge of collapse. Finally, after an abortive attempt at reform in 1898, the last organized attempt at anti–foreign resistance, the Boxer War, collapsed in the face of multinational invasion and the imposition of the most crippling foreign treaties yet. Within a decade, the Qing and imperial China itself would melt away in the face of revolution.

Centennial Exposition: Chinese Exhibit and Corliss Engine. (A) The *pailou*, or ceremonial entry gate, to the Chinese exhibit at the American Centennial Exposition. The large characters proclaim "The Country of the Great Qing" (*Da Qing Guo*). If one looks very closely one can also see the chrysanthemum banners and wall hangings of the Japanese exhibit directly across the aisle. **(B)** The literal center, as well as the center of attention, in the Centennial's Machinery Hall was the enormous Corliss steam engine, rated variously at 1400 to 1500 horsepower. The steam was piped to it from remote boilers and its 30-foot flywheel was attached by means of shafts, belts, and gears running under the floor to nearly all of the hundreds of devices in the building—except those of the British, who insisted on using their own engines to power their machines.

CHINA CONFRONTS THE AGE OF IMPERIALISM

As we saw in Chapter 3, the Qianlong era (r. 1736–1795) marked both the greatest influence and power of imperial China and the period in which the first hints began to appear of trouble to come. Some of the problems facing the Qing began to emerge within a year after Qianlong stepped down from the throne in 1795. As we saw in the previous chapter, a Buddhist sect with secret-society connections called the White Lotus sparked a smoldering rebellion, which took years to suppress, at the same time highlighting the limitations of the Manchu Bannermen and Chinese Green Standard armies as a military force.

More subtle, but perhaps more ominous for the agrarian-based imperial order as a whole, were the new conceptions of the role of economics and trade developing outside the tightly regulated systems of China, Japan, and Korea. China was being steadily drawn into the emerging European global commercial system. As their closed mercantilist economies, which resembled China's in many ways, were being steadily eroded by Britain's growing push for free trade in the opening decades of the new century, however, China's long-standing systems of exchange control proved an increasingly troublesome fit. Thus, China's efforts to retain a tight rein over its export trade in tea, porcelain, silk, and other luxury goods, coupled with a new assertiveness to eradicate the growing, lucrative, and illegal opium trade, created a crisis with Great Britain in the summer of 1839, which led to the First Opium War, China's initial military encounter with the industrializing West.

Trade and Diplomacy

As we have seen, the technical excellence, high level of craftsmanship, and delicate beauty of such Chinese export goods as lacquerware, porcelain, silks, intricately carved and appointed wooden furniture, and even wicker and rattan pieces increasingly tempted international tastes. By the mid-eighteenth century, there was a pronounced trend among the well-to-do in Europe and their colonies abroad toward what the French called *chinoiserie*, real or fake Chinese-style items.

As we have also seen, nowhere was the taste for things Chinese more pronounced than in the increasing demand for porcelain. The English imported 7 million porcelain pieces in 1721 alone, whereas the Dutch and other Europeans imported as much as 70 million during the seventeenth and eighteenth centuries. Tea, however, remained the most lucrative export of all. A variety of export teas, including the fermented *oolong* that stood up exceptionally well during long ocean voyages, had become the European beverages of choice by the end of the eighteenth century. It had supplanted or at least supplemented coffee in most European countries, which had enjoyed its own fad when the Ottomans left large stocks of it behind in Austria after the siege of Vienna in 1683. With Japan and Korea closed to European maritime commerce, except for the Dutch, China remained the sole source of tea until later in the nineteenth century. By then Japan began to vie for the trade and the British began to grow tea plants in the uplands of Assam in India. It was not until the mid-1870s, however, that China's share of the trade began to appreciably diminish.

Tea Trade. By the end of the 18th century, tea had become the largest and most lucrative export item for China's *cohong* merchants and their partners in the various East Indian companies of the European maritime powers. Here, tea chests are loaded on to a sampan lighter to be ferried out to the merchant ships riding at anchor in the harbor at Canton in front of the foreign factories and "godowns," or warehouses.

Thus, by the end of the eighteenth century, the *cohong* merchants and their counterparts in the East India companies of the British, French, and Dutch—and now merchants from the new United States—were able to keep trade lucrative and tightly controlled. But the mode and level of this commerce held different significance for the maritime powers of the West than for China. Whereas Canton/Guangzhou and its adjacent coastal littoral were tied to maritime trade, the other cities of the empire relied on China's enormous internal economy or, in the case of the centers on the Silk Road or the caravan routes to Russia, on the lucrative but limited trade carried out along those avenues. As it had been for millennia, the chief concern of the Qing was the health of the agrarian economy in which the vast majority of the population was engaged. As we have seen, the Ming emperors in the mid-fifteenth century had been able to simply end China's overseas merchant enterprises and voyages by fiat, with no discernable damage to the overall health of the empire's economy. The resulting system of passive trade by which merchants came to China to purchase items had been seen not only as symbolic of China's central place in the political and cultural universe. It was also one by which China and the emperor voluntarily dispensed the fruits of China's wealth to an eager and needy outside world. As such, its regulation was seen as a highly useful political tool by which the less civilized peoples of the periphery could be controlled and acculturated to Chinese norms, while keeping potentially harmful influences at bay.

For the European maritime countries, however, particularly Great Britain, power came from control of increasingly far-flung markets and colonial empires. Thus, maritime trade routes and ports were the sinew and muscle of British

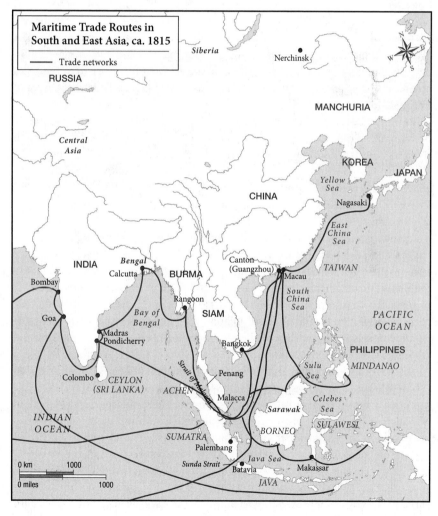

MAP 5.1

Maritime Trade Routes in South and East Asia, ca. 1815

economic influence. By the 1790s, with the China trade at record levels and the wars accompanying the French Revolution making European trade increasingly problematic, the British decided to attempt to open diplomatic relations with the Qing. As much as anything else, their hope was to begin the process of placing trade in what the British considered more appropriate channels. Moreover, British merchants also realized that with more Chinese ports open, China had virtually unlimited commercial and consumer potential.

In the summer of 1793, therefore, they dispatched Lord George Macartney (1737–1806), an experienced diplomat and colonial governor, to Beijing with a large retinue and substantial numbers of presents thought to represent the best of British goods and manufactured products. Significantly, the presents included fine telescopes and astronomical instruments, a planetarium, watches and chronometers, and some of Britain's first machine-made textiles, as well as mechanical toys and automata and other items intended to make a splendid display. His mission was to persuade the Qianlong emperor to allow the stationing of diplomatic personnel in the Chinese capital and the creation of a system for the separate handling of ordinary commercial matters and diplomacy along the lines of European practices.

As we have seen previously, the Qing had allowed the Russians to maintain a mission in Beijing. This, however, was not considered a precedent for the British requests because Beijing was a terminus of the caravan routes from Siberia and Central Asia. The Russian mission, sanctioned by the Treaty of Nerchinsk in 1689, was treated as a commercial enterprise with regulations governing the Russian personnel much like those enforced among the Canton factories. In fact, the Russians posted there were forbidden to return home.

Qianlong therefore rebuffed Macartney's attempts to establish a British embassy. The translations made by the British of the flowery and stilted phraseology used by the court for dealing with outlying nations no doubt irritated readers in the British government, as did the tone of condescension implicit in the emperor's refusal. In addition to observing that China really had "no need of your country's ingenious manufactures," Qianlong stated frankly that permanent foreign embassies were contrary to the intention of the current system and would "most definitely not be permitted."

A second British mission in 1816 under the direction of Lord William Amherst (1773–1857) met with even more complete rejection. Although Macartney had managed a modified genuflection in response to the Chinese court protocol of the *ketou* or "kowtow"—prostrating oneself three times and knocking one's head on the floor three times per prostration—Amherst refused unless a Chinese official of comparable rank performed the rite before him as the envoy of George III. He was thus refused entry to the empire and, to add disaster to failure, was shipwrecked on his return trip. After being rescued, interestingly enough, the voyage home led him to St. Helena in 1817, where he had several interviews with the newly exiled Napoleon Bonaparte.

Macartney Mission. The Macartney Embassy, also called the Macartney Mission, was a British embassy to China in 1793. The goal of the embassy was to convince Emperor Qianlong of China to ease restrictions on trade between Great Britain and China by allowing Great Britain to have a permanent embassy in Beijing, possession of 'a small unfortified island near Chusan for the residence of British traders, storage of goods, and outfitting of ships', and reduced tariffs on traders in Guangzhou.

Contrasting Views of Commercial Relations

One overriding reason that Europeans and Americans were pushing to bring the Chinese into their diplomatic and commercial system was the widespread perception that China was benefiting from a huge trade imbalance. As large as the tea trade had been through the eighteenth century, it exploded in the final decades after the British cut tea duties in 1784. Tea imports alone dwarfed what the British earned from their export goods to China. Thus, the remaining imports had to be paid for in silver. Although, as we saw previously, recent scholarship has shown that China's economy actually supported much of the interconnected Eurasian commercial system, contemporary merchants and political economists were convinced that China's control of trade functioned in the same way as did European mercantilism. That is, they believed that the hard currency paid to Chinese merchants essentially stayed within the allegedly closed economy of the Qing Empire, draining the West of its stocks of silver. However, as Qianlong's reply to Macartney noted, Western merchants offered little that the Chinese needed or wanted.

As the new century dawned, therefore, European and American commercial interests were becoming increasingly anxious to find trade goods acceptable to the Chinese. Some of the items to which they resorted seemed at first glance to be quite promising. Some, however, were whimsical in a way that suggested an almost comical misunderstanding of Chinese culture and tastes. One group of enterprising American merchants, for example, experimented with gathering ginseng root from woodlands in the northeastern United States. Ginseng, of course, had been used medicinally for millennia all over East Asia and was a favorite additive to food and tea. They discovered, however, that their potential customers preferred Korean ginseng and thus sold little of the American variety to the *cohong* merchants. Attracted by questionable rumors that chiming clocks and mechanical toys would sell as novelty items, some merchants attempted to try cargoes of these. Although some sales were made, the Chinese cultural bias against giving timepieces as gifts because they were considered bad-luck signs of approaching death tended to curtail their popularity. Thus, by the beginning of the nineteenth century, a growing number of merchants were clandestinely turning in desperation to a lucrative new commodity, with tragic consequences.

Smugglers and Missionaries

When tobacco was introduced into China from the Americas via the Philippines, the fad of smoking quickly spread. In southwestern China, tribesmen living in remote mountain villages began combining small quantities of opium resin with tobacco. The Dutch, who briefly maintained bases on Taiwan in the mid-1600s before being expelled by Koxinga, introduced the practice of smoking opium by itself there from Java, from which it spread gradually to the maritime provinces of south China. Disturbed by the growing use of opium beyond normal medicinal practice in the area and even more alarmed that some at court had experimented with the drug, the Yongzheng emperor banned the smoking of the substance as early as 1729. For the rest of the century, opium use remained a strictly localized problem in China's south and southwest.

As a consequence of the victories of the British East India Company's forces over the French and their allies in India during the Seven Years' War (1756–1763), the Company's territory had been extended from Calcutta to include the area around Patna, historically a center of medicinal opium production. Although company traders were prohibited from carrying opium to China as contraband, an increasing number of non-Company merchants and those Company men trading on the side willing to take the risk discovered that they could circumvent Chinese regulations and sell small quantities of the drug for a tidy profit. Their customers at first were the wealthy of Canton society, and the exotic *yangtu* ("foreign mud"), as opium was nicknamed, soon became a favorite local fad. Success

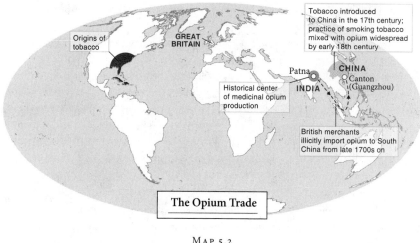

Origins of tobacco

GREAT BRITAIN

Tobacco introduced to China in the 17th century; practice of smoking tobacco mixed with opium widespread by early 18th century

Patna

CHINA

Canton (Guangzhou)

Historical center of medicinal opium production

INDIA

British merchants illicitly import opium to South China from late 1700s on

The Opium Trade

MAP 5.2
The Opium Trade

increased demand, and, like the twentieth-century smuggling of cocaine and marijuana from Latin America to the United States, by the early decades of the nineteenth century, an elaborate illicit system of delivery had been set up along the south China coast. Heavily armed opium clippers offloaded their chests of tarry opium balls onto sparsely inhabited offshore islands, from which Chinese wholesalers picked up the drug and made their rounds up the labyrinth of small creeks and rivulets snaking through the South Chinese coast. The soaring profits from this illegal enterprise fueled piracy and lawlessness along the coast, and the opium trade soon became the most divisive issue in relations between China and the West.

The relationship that the British East India Company and the *cohong* had thus assiduously developed over the previous century was now swiftly eroded by the new commodity. For the British, the mode of the trade collapsed the barriers between commerce in legitimate goods and that in opium. The Company oversaw export production of the drug in India and collected taxes on it. It then auctioned lots to independent merchants to whom it extended credits payable in silver when the drug was sold in China. Company men often received their credit payments at the Canton factories to furnish a ready supply of silver for the purchase of legal Chinese commodities, such as tea or silk. The Company thus circumvented both its own regulations and the Chinese prohibitions, but allowed the taint of corruption to permeate its actions. This in turn led to payoffs not only to its own officials who connived at this practice, but also, even more, to the *cohong* and local Chinese officials, especially those in customs and the local Board of Revenue (*hubu*). The East India Company itself was now fatally compromised because an estimated one quarter of its revenues in India were directly tied to opium production by the 1830s.

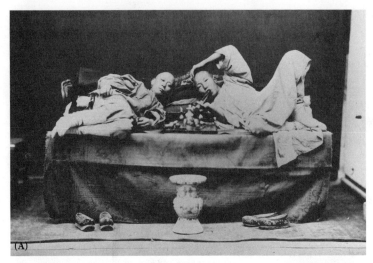

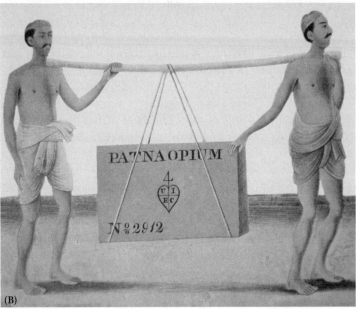

Opium Trade. Perhaps nothing was so ruinous over the long term—and the precipitant in part of two wars—as the importation of opium into China. **(A)** Here, two smokers relax with their pipe and lamp in a photograph from the early 1870s. The opium was heated in the brass bowl of the pipe held over the lamp until it began to smoke, and the users then inhaled. **(B)** The semi-clandestine opium trade had reached such proportions that it was estimated that a quarter of the revenue of British India was derived from the drug by the mid-1830s. In this picture, two porters transport an opium chest hung from a two-man carrying pole.

Moreover, the political climate in England unwittingly opened the doors wider for the opium trade. As part of the general reform movement that widened the political franchise in 1832, growing free trade agitation in England put an end to the East India Company's privileged position in China in 1833. With the monopoly lifted, the number of entrepreneurs seeking quick riches in the opium trade exploded. With wealth came power, and in the foreign trading factories in Canton, newcomers like Jardine, Matheson & Company, Lancelot Dent, and David Sassoon engaged in the opium trade vied for prestige with older firms involved in legitimate goods.

The push for legitimacy among the opium merchants coincided with an aggressive attempt by Westerners to force China to open additional trading ports for legal items. Chinese authorities, however, viewed this Western assertiveness as driven primarily by opium and Christian evangelism, pushed by Protestant missionary societies galvanized by reform at home and the prospect of conversions abroad. Indeed, the connection seemed blatant when enterprising missionaries like Karl Gutzlaff (1803–1851) literally found themselves handing out bibles on one end of a ship while opium traffickers offloaded their cargoes on the other.

Far worse than the corruption on both sides of the exchange, or the undermining of the missionary effort, however, were the effects of the trade on the ordinary inhabitants of South China. The huge rise in availability and consequent plunge in prices increased opium usage to catastrophic levels. Indeed, the progress of the trade in many ways resembles the impact of "crack" cocaine in the twentieth-century United States. The power of opium to suppress pain and hunger made it attractive to the poor engaged in physical labor, although the dreamlike state it induced often made it dangerous to work under its influence. Its addictive properties led people to seek it even at the expense of food, thus creating a health crisis for tens of thousands, made infinitely worse by the drug's notoriously difficult withdrawal symptoms.

Moreover, lax and capricious enforcement of the imperial edicts prohibiting the smoking of the drug coupled with the high local levels of corruption reduced respect for local officials further in a region already smoldering with latent anti-Qing sentiment.

Commissioner Lin Zexu and the Opium Trade

The collision came in the spring of 1839. It would soon grow into the opening event of China's century of *guochi*—"national humiliation." The Daoguang emperor sent Lin Zexu (1785–1850), a scholarly, uncompromising official with a reputation for courage and honesty, to Canton as an imperial commissioner. Lin's daunting task was to cut off the opium trade at its source, and he was given wide-ranging powers to deal with both Chinese and foreign traffickers. Both idealistic and pragmatic, he sent a letter to Britain's new queen, Victoria (r. 1837–1901), lecturing her on the immorality of the trade, while at the same time setting up facilities for the recovery of addicts. As for the proximate cause of the problem, he demanded that all foreign merchants surrender their warehoused opium and sign a bond that they would not, under penalty of death, deal in the drug anymore. The Canton foreign community, seeing this as perhaps the first unwelcome step toward a major policy shift, stood pat and refused. Lin blockaded the port and withdrew all Chinese personnel from Western firms. His determined stance finally cracked the stalemate, and the dealers eventually surrendered 20,000 chests of opium, with most also signing the pledge. Lin then publicly disposed of the opium by mixing it with slaked lime and flushing the resulting slurry into the sea, accompanied by prayers asking forgiveness of the sea gods for polluting their realm with this noxious poison. Following his actions, however, the dealers appealed to the British government for compensation.

Commissioner Lin Destroys the Opium. This drawing depicts Lin Zexu "burning" 20,000 chests of opium surrendered by foreign merchants. In fact, however, he did not actually burn the drug, but mixed it with water, salt, and lime, and flushed it through sluiceways out to the sea. The mixture created clouds of fumes, which misled some onlookers into believing it had been burned.

The combative British foreign secretary, Lord Palmerston (1784–1865), seized on the claims to settle the long-standing diplomatic impasse with the Qing over foreign representation and open ports. However, there were other difficulties. Although the precepts of Chinese law and its relationship to personal morality and group responsibility had been part of the bedrock of Confucianism for two millennia, the British felt the Chinese judicial system, with its emphasis on group responsibility balancing that of the individual, was unreliable and capricious. Moreover, the Chinese use of torture to extract confessions was considered "medieval" in post-Enlightenment Britain, and with more and more British nationals doing business in China, the number of judicial complaints was bound to multiply. There had already been cases in which foreign sailors involved in the deaths of Chinese subjects had been publicly put to death by Chinese authorities as part of the principle of group responsibility, although their personal culpability was doubtful or absent.

In a show of force, therefore, the British sent a fleet of warships to Canton to demand reparations for the confiscated opium, pressure the Qing to establish diplomatic relations, and open more ports. Four centuries had now passed since China had commanded the seas as the world's premier naval power under Zheng He. The lack of real naval competitors for so long had resulted in a near total absence of Chinese warships. The only vessels available were modestly armed with seventeenth-century cannon and used for customs collection. What now rode before them in the waters adjacent to the factories were leading examples of the evolution of two centuries of refinement in sail-powered warship design and the beginning of the new age of steam and armor in fighting craft. When negotiations broke down, a small Chinese squadron sailed out to confront the British men-o'-war. With contemptuous ease, the British force sank several and scattered the rest. Although scholars have debated its ultimate significance ever since and little changed immediately in the way the Chinese themselves viewed their foreign relations, the incident inaugurated the use of force by the industrializing maritime powers in their dealings with China and East Asia as a whole. It was a threshold they would cross repeatedly as the century wore on.

THE ERA OF "UNEQUAL TREATIES"

The (First) Opium War (1839–1842), as it came to be called, contributed mightily to a dramatic shift in perceptions of China in Europe and the United States. As we have seen, among the cosmopolitan *philosophes* of the Enlightenment, China's apparent power, efficient bureaucracy, Confucian conceptions of government, and its land-centered agrarian policies were generally highly regarded. Indeed, China was often held up as a model of humane and tolerant government against which to compare the shortcomings of European despotisms. This image, however, had already begun to fray somewhat with the reports of the Macartney and Amherst missions.

Shifting Views of China in the West

Now the struggle beginning in the fall of 1839 between China and Great Britain would lay bare for the first time in world history the gap between the military capabilities of industrializing countries and those, like China, whose armed forces had fallen into disuse. The military had never been a particularly honored profession in imperial China, and now the old saying "good iron is not made into nails; good men are not made into soldiers" seemed tragically apt. The consequences of maintaining scattered Manchu banner garrisons to thwart anti-Qing activity, discouraging militia recruiting, and underfunding the Armies of the Green Standard were immediately put on painful display. The massive, oaken, three-deck English ships-of-the-line, mounting as many as 128 guns, moved with impunity among the small Chinese fleets of coastal vessels frantically sent to oppose them. The armored steam gunboat *Nemesis*, whose heavy pivot gun allowed it to dominate riverside batteries, put ashore British and Indian troops virtually at will.

The changes in perception on both sides wrought by this mismatch altered the way Westerners tended to view China for the next century, whereas for the Chinese it triggered a long and painful search to capture the fruits of modernity while not sacrificing their cultural distinctiveness. For Westerners, the political revolutions embodying Enlightenment ideals advanced the idea of progress—material, political, moral—as a primary goal. The Industrial Revolution made this notion concrete in terms of technological advancement and satisfying human wants. Thus, in

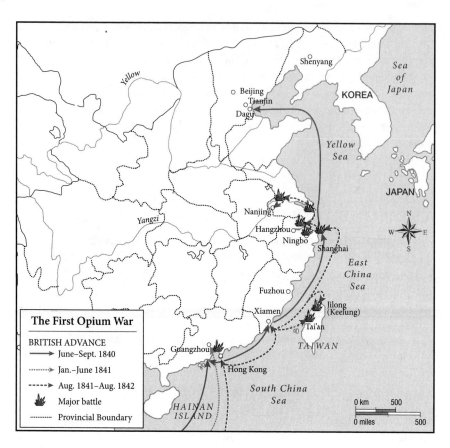

MAP 5.3
The First Opium War

the space of a generation or two, China, which seemed to so many in the eighteenth century a model of sound, stable government and humane values, was now portrayed as "a living fossil." The world's largest exporter of technology for so many centuries, China was to now be characterized as hopelessly "backward." And perhaps most painful of all for an empire that had seen itself as the center of world civilization for so long, it would be stigmatized as barbaric or semicivilized as its failure to modernize along Western lines became more acute, while modernization itself was becoming the primary yardstick of civilization.

Over the next two years, with a brief truce called in 1841, the British methodically attacked and occupied ports along the Chinese coast from Canton to Shanghai at the mouth of the Yangzi River, for the most part without serious opposition. As the British planned to move north to put pressure on Beijing, Chinese officials opened negotiations in August 1842. The resulting Treaty of Nanjing (Nanking) marked the first of the century's "unequal treaties" that would be imposed throughout East Asia by European powers.

Steam Power Comes to China. The East India Company's steamer *Nemesis* destroys a Chinese war junk in Anson's Bay, January 7, 1841. The technologies of the Industrial Revolution were on full display when hostilities between Britain and China broke out in 1839. The *Nemesis* featured an armored hull assembled with detachable sections, and a shallow draft and a steam-powered paddle wheel for river propulsion. A large pivot gun could rake shore batteries with fire. The versatility and power of the *Nemesis* convinced Lin Zexu and other Qing officials that China needed, at the very least, the same kinds of "strong ships and effective cannon" if it were to defend itr coasts and rivers. By the 1860s, the first attempts at building such craft were finally under way.

Open Ports, Consuls, and Most-Favored Nations

Although, ironically, the treaty ending the war did not specifically mention opium— its legalization as an import would come in a later agreement—the Nanjing accord favored the British position in every important particular. The Qing ceded the British the island of Hong Kong, which, because of its sparse population and deep-water harbor, was already in use as an important opium transshipment point. The Chinese agreed to open the ports of Shanghai, Ningbo, Fuzhou, and Xiamen (Amoy), in addition to Guangzhou (Canton), and the British imposed an indemnity on the Chinese to pay the costs of the war and repay the value of the opium confiscated by Lin Zexu.

The prospect of opening markets in China for British manufactured goods prompted the British to also write the concept of *nontariff autonomy* into the treaty: China could now charge no more than a 5 percent tariff on British goods. By way of comparison, the United States, anxious to protect its infant industries from British competition, sometimes charged as much as 100 percent on some imported items. As for protecting its subjects from the vagaries of Chinese law, the British took their lead from arrangements European countries had made in the Ottoman Empire. There, foreigners were the responsibility of their respective consuls. Thus, a consular system was now set up in the open Chinese ports and a policy of *extraterritoriality* was mandated: British subjects who violated Chinese laws would now be tried and punished by British consuls and consular courts.

Following the British lead, France and the United States signed similar treaties with the Qing over the next several years. Qing officials, desperate to find some kind of leverage against the British, now resorted to "using barbarians to check barbarians" in their negotiations with Western countries. In this case, they hoped to capitalize on the animosities between, for example, the United States and Great Britain or Britain and France, to keep them from forming a united front. For their part, the Americans in the negotiations for the Treaty of Wangxia (1844) not too subtly suggested to the Chinese that the United States might aid them in future disputes with the British—and drove home the idea with a parting gift for the Chinese negotiators: a matched set of newly invented Colt revolvers.

Chinese hopes for this carrot-and-stick approach came swiftly apart, however, as the later treaties routinely included a *most-favored nation* clause: any new concessions granted to one country automatically reverted to those who by treaty were "most-favored nations." Thus, granting special privileges to some countries at the expense of others would no longer be possible once nearly all treaty powers were most-favored nations. The barbarians could no longer be relied on to check themselves.

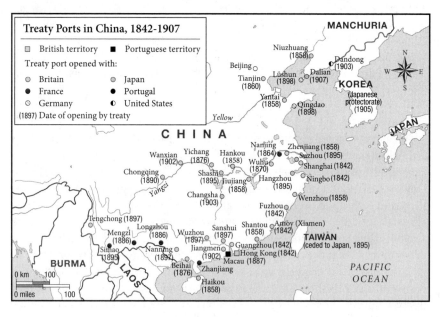

Map 5.4
Treaty Ports in China, 1842–1907

RESISTANCE—THE TAIPING MOVEMENT AND THE SECOND OPIUM WAR

In addition to the spread of the opium trade to the newly opened ports, long-established trade routes for more legitimate items swiftly shifted from Guangzhou to more convenient outlets. The growth of Shanghai was especially important in this regard because it served the Yangzi River, the greatest highway through China's heartland. Shanghai grew in population from around 50,000 in 1845 to more than a million by the end of the century. Coastal trade increased at a similar pace, whereas Hong Kong grew as the primary point of opium transfer to small smuggling vessels. As we saw in the previous chapter, the swiftness of all of these changes and their accompanying economic dislocation, along with smoldering discontent at the inability of the Qing government to resist foreign demands, made south China particularly volatile. In 1851 the region exploded in a rebellion that became the largest civil war in history.

The Opening of the Taiping Movement

As we saw in the preceding chapter examining the internal circumstances leading to the Taiping movement, the precipitating factors were in many ways symbolic of the diverse cultural influences penetrating South China. One aspect of this diversity that has fueled considerable debate revolves around the nature and degree of Western influence in the region. As indicated in Chapter 4, the kind of Western influence that bears most directly on the ideology of the Taiping movement is Christianity. Although Christian missionary work had been banned by an edict from the Yongzheng emperor in 1724, proselytizing was now protected in the newly opened foreign enclaves. Even before this, however, foreign missionaries circumvented Qing prohibitions on preaching in the interior by sending *colporteurs*—Chinese converts acting as missionary assistants—into the countryside with newly translated Bibles and other materials. Thus, Christian literature, often indifferently translated and not well written by the standards of the literati, was available to men like Hong Xiuquan. As a rule, however, such pieces were seen more as curiosities than as compelling moral instruction.

With the opening of the treaty ports and the acquisition of Hong Kong, however, missionary schools were swiftly set up and became avenues for a number of boys with aspirations to work in international trade to learn foreign languages and gain useful skills. While small, this development also added to the pool of Christian and quasi-Christian individuals on which Hong's group could draw. As we saw in the previous chapter, however, Hong and his followers when faced with persecution, fled to the mountains for defense. By late 1851, his movement had gathered enough strength to stand against local government forces and began an advance to the north. By 1853 they had captured the city of Nanjing and made it their capital, renaming it *Tianjing* (the heavenly capital). That winter they were barely prevented from driving the Qing from Beijing by a snowstorm and determined attacks by the Xianfeng emperor's (r. 1851–1862) elite Mongolian cavalry. For the next decade they would remain in control of the Chinese heartland, and the long, bloody contest to subdue them would leave thousands of towns and villages devastated for decades to come.

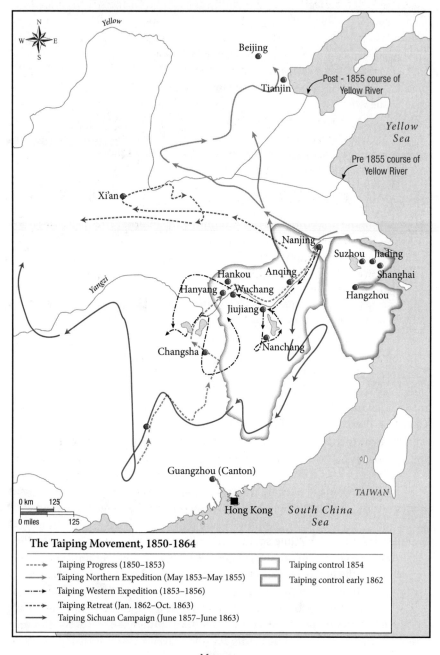

MAP 5.5
The Taiping Movement, 1850–1864

Foreign Mercenaries in the Taiping Rebellion. Frederick Townsend Ward, born in Salem, Massachusetts in 1831, had led an adventurous life as a soldier of fortune and "filibuster" before coming to China. Finding work as a mercenary for Qing forces fighting the Taipings, he commanded the famous Ever Victorious Army until his death in battle near Ningbo in 1862. His successor, Charles George Gordon went on to fame as EVA commander and even greater notoriety when he died in the battle for Khartoum, in the Sudan, in 1885. Note the artist's fanciful depiction of the Taiping wearing queues.

For the missionaries in China, the prospect of a Christian movement taking power made it appear as though the will of God was finally rewarding their efforts. As time went on, however, missionaries and diplomats became less sure of where the movement was heading. Roberts himself and a handful of other missionaries visited Nanjing, and although they were impressed with the new order in many respects, they were also appalled at Hong's theological interpretations and his huge retinue of concubines. Still, Hong and his advisors, particularly his relative Hong Rengan (1822–1864), talked about instituting Western-style administrative reforms and building a modern industrial base—something Western well-wishers had continually urged on Chinese officials. At the same time, however, a powerful Taiping China might repudiate the unequal treaties and throw the new trade arrangements into disarray. Thus, by 1860, the treaty powers determined to continue recognizing the Qing as China's legitimate rulers.

The Second Opium War, 1856–1860

At the height of the Taiping fighting in 1856, a new dispute arose between the Qing and the British and French. After four years of intermittent fighting, it produced the next round of "unequal treaties" that greatly expanded foreign interests and control in the empire. Britain, France, and the United States all felt by the mid-1850s that the vastly expanded trade in China—and now beginning in Japan—called for the opening of still more ports. They also sought an end to all Qing prohibitions on missionary activity in the interior and more complete diplomatic relations along Western lines, including the right to open embassies in Beijing and for the Chinese to send diplomatic representatives of their own abroad.

The catalyst came in late 1856. A Chinese customs patrol in Canton hauled down the British flag on the *Arrow*, a Chinese vessel whose registry had been falsified to take advantage of British trading privileges. The British seized on this purported insult to their flag as an opportunity to force treaty revision. The French, who considered themselves the protectors of Catholic missionaries and their converts, saw an excellent opening to pressure China on the missionary issue and so joined the British.

The war itself was fought intermittently in a highly localized fashion. The British seized the walled city of Canton, captured the governor-general of Guangdong and Guangxi—and member of the Grand Secretariat—Ye Mingchen (1807–1859) and sent him into exile in India, where he died three years later. As the conflict moved into 1857, however, the Great Rebellion in India consumed British attention through much of the year, whereas in China negotiations dragged on intermittently and the Qing remained preoccupied with the Taipings. In 1858, a draft treaty was worked out, but the Qing court refused it. Returning in 1860 with a large expeditionary force, British and French troops fought their way to Beijing, drove the emperor from the city, and burned and looted the Summer Palace. The final treaty stipulated that a dozen ports be opened to foreign trade, that opium be recognized as a legal commodity, that extraterritoriality be expanded, and that foreign embassies be set up in the capital. A newly created Chinese board, the Zongli Yamen, was to handle Qing foreign relations, and the Chinese were invited to send their own ambassadors abroad.

REFORM THROUGH SELF-STRENGTHENING, 1860–1895

The end of the Second Opium War began a period lasting through the early 1870s, sometimes referred to by historians as the "cooperative era." There were few major disputes between the foreign powers and the Qing; indeed, in several instances, foreigners worked closely with Chinese officials to help them in assessing ways to upgrade their defenses, lay the foundations of modern industrial concerns, and start programs that signaled institutional change. The motives of these men ranged from simple altruism and missionary devotion to "enlightened self-interest": that is, the idea that a strong, modern China would be a more stable trade and diplomatic partner, although also one that might seek to alter the balance of its relationship with the treaty powers.

Defeating the Taipings and the Nian

Chinese officials were indeed desperate to roll back the foreign threat and suppress the Taipings. They were hardly in agreement, however, on how this might be accomplished. Few advocated simply fighting the foreigners with whatever means were at hand. Most, like the emperor's brother, Prince Gong (Yixin, 1833–1898), felt that over time these new peoples would be assimilated to Chinese norms, like invaders and border peoples of the past. In the meantime, however, they should be "soothed and pacified," but not unconditionally. As the prince later allegedly remarked to the British minister, Rutherford Alcock, "Take away your opium and your missionaries and you will be welcome."

To do this, however, China needed to build up a military force and supporting infrastructure strong enough to prevent further encroachments by the treaty powers. As the decade wore on, a growing number of officials began to look for answers beyond the simple demands for "strong ships and effective cannon" that had previously been emphasized. Toward this end, they advocated a policy that came to be called *ziqiang*—self-strengthening. During the 1860s, the two most

Self-Strengtheners. Zeng Guofan (left) and Li Hongzhang were two of the key figures in China's self-strengthening movement. The two men began working together during the last years of the Taiping Rebellion, both having formed and led militia armies in their home provinces of Hunan (Zeng) and Anhui (Li). Both men also pioneered the use of modern weapons by their troops. After Zeng's death in 1872, Li emerged as China's most powerful official and the most active proponent of self-strengthening.

prominent of these officials were Li Hongzhang and his senior colleague Zeng Guofan, both of whom we met briefly in Chapter 4. Both men had distinguished themselves as Confucian scholars and as leaders of militia armies in their home provinces of Anhui and Hunan during the Taiping years. In 1864, their combined forces finally captured the Taiping capital at Nanjing and forced the suicide of Hong Xiuquan, bringing the movement to an end.

Like a number of leaders during these desperate times, Li and Zeng were also distinguished by the flexibility of their thinking and, increasingly, by their growing familiarity with the new weapons and techniques brought to China by foreign forces. Both had utilized foreign mercenaries during the war. Indeed, the British, whose economy had suffered from the double blows of the squeezing off of the American cotton trade during the Civil War and the shutting down of Chinese demand for British textiles during the Taiping years, found themselves tacitly supporting such technically illegal foreign militia adventures. The most famous of these units, **the Ever-Victorious Army** (for which the subject of our opening vignette, Li Gui, had briefly worked), had been led by an American, Frederick Townsend Ward (1831–1862), and following Ward's death, by an Englishman, Charles George Gordon (1833–1885), later to win greater fame by dying in battle at Khartoum. Organized like the Sepoy forces of the British East India Company, these units were officered by foreigners but manned by Chinese troops trained in Western drill and arms. Li Hongzhang in particular had used the Ever-Victorious Army as a potent strike force in his Huai Army and developed an early appreciation for the utility and efficiency of Western arms.

Ever Victorious Army Troops. The Ever Victorious Army was a strike force unit of Qing militia armies between 1860–4. It was made up of mercenary Chinese soldiers but commanded and trained by foreign officers. It also gave Chinese officials like Li Hongzhang and Zeng Guofan an opportunity to see at close hand Western drill and weapons use. Both men used it as a vanguard unit in their forces. The Army was formed and initially commanded by the American, Frederick Townsend Ward (1831–62). Upon his death the command was assumed by Captain Charles Gordon (1833–85).

Confucian "Essence" and Western "Application"

By the end of the rebellion, therefore, these officials had begun to move toward a strategy of what a later slogan by Zhang Zhidong (1837–1909) called ***zhongxue wei ti; xixue wei yong*** (Chinese studies for the essentials; Western studies for practical application). As we have seen in past chapters, Chinese philosophical concepts tended toward the desire for correlation and the reconciliation of opposites. In this tradition, *ti* and *yong*, or "essence" and "function/application," became the two key terms in the self-strengthening formulation. It thus enabled the *yangwu* (foreign matters) proponents to accommodate the need for new foreign technologies within historically and philosophically acceptable terminology.

The two sides of the concept, however, were not equally balanced. As with many Neo-Confucian formulae, the "essence" element was considered primary and the method of implementation—"practical application"—secondary. Thus, their proponents could argue that their chief aim was the preservation of the fundamentals of Confucian society, while being flexible about the appropriate means of attaining their goals. Opponents, however, particularly the influential scholar Wo Ren (1804?–1871), argued that the formula could—and eventually would—be reversed: that "function" would eventually degrade the essence. Here, they pointed to the alleged Westernization of students sent abroad and the wearing of Western clothes in Japan as examples of the dangers of this approach.

The self-strengtheners nonetheless sponsored an impressive array of projects in the 1860s and early 1870s: a foreign language and technical school (*Tongwenguan*), the Nanjing and Jiangnan (Kiangnan) arsenals, a modern navy yard at Fuzhou, initiatives to send Chinese students to the United States and Europe, a modern shipping concern (the China Merchants' Steam Navigation Company), and the first moves toward sending representatives abroad from 1875 to 1880. The Imperial Maritime Customs Service, as we have seen, grew to be a genuine Sino-foreign enterprise, legendary for its efficiency, and survived the fall of the Qing into the Republican and Nationalist years: its last inspector-general, the American Frederick Knox Little, resigned in January 1950.

Opposition to such programs also mounted during the period and continued throughout the century. These were the people Li Gui had characterized as mouthing ancient Daoist platitudes in the vignette beginning this chapter. The debates they sparked were often fought out within the rubric of *qingyi*, as we noted in the previous chapter. Often highly placed—including, at times, the Empress Dowager Cixi (1835–1908) herself—these opponents believed the kind of change necessary to create an industrial base in China would erode the social, cultural, and economic ties that held their society together. In the end, they said, the people would cease to be Chinese in any meaningful sense and become like Europeans and Americans. As much as anything else, the lack of a clear strategy at the top and the ferocity of these debates among Chinese officials worked to frustrate the hopes of the self-strengtheners through the turn of the century.

PATTERNS UP CLOSE

The Chinese Education Mission

One of the more interesting and innovative initiatives of the self-strengthening period, roughly 1860 to 1895, was the Chinese Education Mission, which lasted from 1872 to 1881. The mission was the product of a man who, in many ways, represented the new type of individual shaped by the divergent cultural influences emerging from the treaty port system. Rong Hong, better known by the Cantonese pronunciation of his name as Yung Wing (1828–1912), had been educated in a missionary school in Hong Kong before being invited to attend prep school in the United States. On graduation from Monson Academy in Massachusetts, he attended Yale in the early 1850s, converted to Congregationalism, and became a naturalized U.S. citizen and the first Chinese to graduate from an American university in 1854. Anxious to use his new skills to aid in China's modernization, he went to Shanghai, where he established a tea business and made some visits to the Taipings, where his suggestions may have found their way into Hong Rengan's ambitious plans for China's modern renewal. In 1863, he was summoned to an interview with Zeng Guofan, who commissioned him to travel back to the United States to buy the machinery that would become the basic plant of the Jiangnan (Kiangnan) Arsenal in Shanghai.

Having completed this mission, and now with the support of Zeng and Li Hongzhang, Yung proposed an ambitious plan to send young boys to schools in New England to replicate the total immersion educational experience he had undergone. He envisioned that on completing their higher education, they would go back to China and form the nucleus of a modern, Western-style education system to train the personnel for China's modernization.

The plan was ultimately put into operation in 1872 and over the next three years 113 boys were sent to homes and schools in the Connecticut River Valley and an Education Mission headquarters established in Hartford. To keep Yung's Western bias somewhat in check, an official named Chen Lanbin (1816–1895) was placed in overall charge of the enterprise. The students learned English with their host families, attended local schools, and met periodically with their Chinese teachers for instruction in the Confucian classics. From 1872 till 1875, when the first Chinese ministers to be sent abroad were named, the Education Mission also functioned as a quasi-diplomatic endeavor. Chen was sent during this time to Cuba and Yung to Peru to investigate the oppressive conditions of Chinese laborers there and, as a result of their respective reports, China negotiated an end to the "Coolie Trade" to those areas. For their efforts, Chen and Yung were named China's first ministers to the United States, Spain (because of Cuba), and Peru, taking up their official duties in 1878.

The Education Mission itself was quite popular locally and the subject of considerable coverage in the American press. For their part, the boys proved apt pupils and some also became exceptional athletes: the Mission even had its own baseball team, "The Orientals," that posted winning seasons against local schools and clubs. Li Gui, the subject of our vignette in this chapter, met with Yung in Hartford and interviewed the boys when they visited the Centennial in August 1876. He devoted an entire chapter in his journal to his conversations with them and came away extremely impressed by their learning, self-confidence, and easy familiarity with both Chinese and Western cultural norms. As for the aims of the mission, Li was quite clear: "The Way [*dao*] and Virtue [*de*], the [Confucian] bonds and principles, constitute the *ti*, or essentials; the techniques of the West are *yong*. We must have both *ti* and *yong* so that in the future we will have a nation whose abilities are utilized and whose knowledge cannot but exceed that of the present."

Unfortunately for the sponsors of the Mission, a number of elements intruded that led to its closure a few years later. Although early fears that the boys would convert to Christianity because of Yung's leanings proved unfounded, their wearing of Western clothes, concealing their queues, and overall Americanization in manners and attitude alienated the new Mission directors on their arrival from China. In addition, hopes of getting the students enrolled in American military academies were ultimately dashed, and the cost of maintaining the Mission proved increasingly problematic to sustain. Sino-American tensions were also on the rise because of anti-Chinese activity in California and the West. By 1881, despite appeals by such prominent Americans as Mark Twain and ex-president Grant, the Qing court authorized the closing of the school and the return of the students.

Treated like cultural pariahs when they first returned, many of the boys ultimately distinguished themselves in China's modernization efforts in mining, railroads and telegraphs, a variety of technical endeavors, and the revamped military after the turn of the century. Several occupied cabinet-level positions in the early Chinese Republic. As for Yung Wing, castigated for so long by many Chinese commentators as a kind of cultural traitor, he has recently been reconstituted in a more favorable light: in 2004, China Central Television aired a multipart documentary on the Mission called *The Boy Students*. Rebroadcast several times, it became one the world's most-watched television programs.

Self-Strengthening and Economics

Many of the programs to improve China's economy and trade were set up as "government sponsored-merchant operated" enterprises. One of the most promising of these was the China Merchants Steam Navigation Company, founded in 1873. The company's purpose was to recapture the carrying trade on China's rivers from foreign operators. With key purchases of foreign steamers and dock facilities during the early and mid-1870s, the company had gone far toward reclaiming a significant percentage of China's river traffic by 1880. However, renewed foreign competition, half-hearted governmental support, and traditional avenues of graft eroded the company's position until it folded later in the decade. In many respects, the company's experience marked a crucial tension between the entrepreneurial instincts of the merchants and the expectations of officials in regulation and receiving regular payoff income. The government itself and officials critical of self-strengthening were quick to point out the high cost of such programs, their potential for corruption, and the futility of attempting to beat the Westerners at their own game.

Amid the halting attempts at government-sponsored innovation, however, there were also other economic forces at work that would have a profound effort on China's later development. The first is that in the treaty ports themselves, the economic climate created by the Western powers for their own benefit exposed much of China's urban population to aspects of modern industrial and commercial society. A substantial class of people, sometimes referred to as "compradors" or "the comprador bourgeoisie," who made a living mediating between Westerners and Chinese interests had developed by the end of the nineteenth century.

The other long-term process at work was the growing influx and popularity of European, Japanese, and American consumer goods diffused from the treaty ports to the interior. Qing efforts to safeguard domestic markets through the Canton system and internal transit taxes like *likin* had been steadily beaten down by war and by the mounting economic pressure of cheap foreign goods. By the end of the nineteenth century, foreign machine-made cotton cloth dominated the Chinese interior, John D. Rockefeller's Standard Oil Company was giving away kerosene lamps to market their fuel, the British American Tobacco Company had established its products in the empire, and even the Japanese invention of the rickshaw had become a popular mode of transport in China's cities. With the Qing finally committed to railroad and telegraph construction and mining and with China's commercial ports resembling more and more their foreign counterparts, the seeds of economic modernity had been at least fitfully planted.

FROM REFORM TO REACTION

Although China's efforts at self-strengthening seemed promising to contemporaries during the 1870s, the signs of their underlying weakness were already running just beneath the surface. The man at the center of so many of these efforts, Li Hongzhang, called "China's Bismarck" by his Western admirers, was all too aware of the political constraints he faced. The ascension of the infant Guangxu emperor in 1874 brought the regency of the Empress Dowager Cixi (1835–1908). Intelligent, ruthless, and highly attuned to the political winds at court, she had already proved adroit in seizing the premier position among imperial concubines. Desperate to preserve Manchu power, as well as her own, Cixi constantly manipulated factions at court and among the high officials to avoid concentration of power in any particular area. Such maneuverings, sometimes favoring Li's self-strengthening colleagues and as often opposing them, severely hampered the long-term health of many self-strengthening measures. In addition to the vagaries of court politics, the new programs were costly and usually required foreign experts. China's finances were continually strained by the immense costs of recovery from the rebellions, the artificially low treaty tariffs, and the obligation to pay old indemnities.

Imperialism on the Confucian Periphery

Despite the spectacular success of Zuo Zongtang's efforts in Xinjiang and the caution with which the players in the Central Asian "Great Game" now approached the Qing, the 1880s saw new foreign tensions elsewhere. France had been steadily encroaching upon Southeast Asia since the late 1850s. Smarting from its defeat in the Franco-Prussian War in 1870 and encouraged to vent its martial frustrations in colonial endeavors, it had renewed its efforts in the early 1880s. Vietnamese resistance, however, led by the Black Flags—some of whom were Chinese who had fought with the Taipings decades before—was on the verge of rolling back the French. Because of its own long history of empire and influence in the region, China had customarily placed itself in the position of suzerain and so opposed the growing French presence there.

Li Hongzhang therefore covertly supported the Black Flags, and to preempt outright Chinese intervention, the French launched a surprise attack on the modern Chinese naval facilities at Fuzhou, sinking the cream of China's steam fleet. Although Chinese forces gave a better account of themselves in other engagements, the French emerged from this conflict with control of the whole of Vietnam, which they promptly combined with Cambodia and Laos into the colony of French Indochina in 1885.

In 1885, as China was still involved with France, tensions with Japan over Korea also threatened to dislodge that kingdom as a Qing client state. As early as 1873 some advisors to Japan's new Meiji Emperor (r. 1868–1912) had argued for a Japanese expeditionary force to "open" Korea to Japan in much the same way that the United States had pressured the Tokugawa Shogunate to sign commercial treaties and allow a foreign diplomatic presence in Japanese ports from 1853 to 1855. When a consensus was reached that this was not feasible, a Japanese force was sent instead to Taiwan to punish the island's aboriginal inhabitants for killing some fisherman from Okinawa. After substantial negotiation, the Japanese withdrew their forces but the Chinese grew increasingly wary of Japan's growing power and presence. In 1879, through negotiations with China and the diplomatic good offices of the former American president, U.S. Grant, Japan purchased the disputed Ryukyu (called by the Chinese Liuqiu) Islands.

Now in Korea Japanese diplomats were exerting influence over the Korean court as it sought to deal with the Tonghak Rebellion, which had been alternately smoldering and flaring up since 1863. China, alarmed again at foreign intrusion into what it considered its own backyard, sent a team of officials to keep watch on Qing interests, and both sides quickly threatened to send troops. In the agreement between Li Hongzhang and Ito Hirobumi (1841–1909) at Tianjin (Tientsin) in 1885, both sides agreed not to take any action in the future without informing each other.

By the early 1890s, however, rising tensions surrounding the Korean court and intrigues by Japanese and Chinese agents involving various factions threatened war once again. Japan sent a force that was claimed to be diplomatic; troops of a Chinese counterforce were killed when a Japanese warship sunk their transport, the *Gaoxing*. By the fall of 1894, both sides were sending troops and naval forces to Korea and a full-scale war over the fate of Korea and northeast Asia was underway.

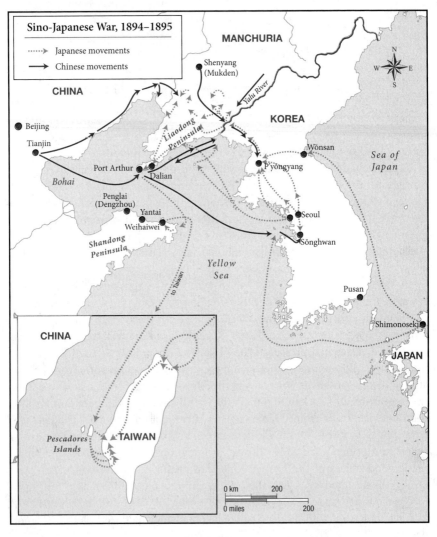

MAP 5.6
The Sino-Japanese War, 1894–1895

Ukiyo-e Prints of the Sino-Japanese War. The Sino-Japanese War of 1894–95 marked one of the most significant role reversals in world history. Japan, which for millennia had been subject to Chinese influence, had now, in the space of less than thirty years of exposure to the industrializing West, defeated Chinese forces with brutal efficiency. Japan's perception of China increasingly became one of frustration and contempt as they saw themselves as the new "natural" leaders of East Asia. These woodblock *ukiyo-e* prints, for centuries a highly popular medium in Japan, depict the new order as interpreted by Japanese artists. In the top print, traditionally garbed Qing pikemen reel before a Japanese cavalry charge; the bottom depicts the surrender of Chinese commanders at a Japanese camp early in the war in October, 1894. Note the Western uniforms, weapons, fierce postures and features of the Japanese conquerors compared to the terrorized, distorted features of the Chinese as they flee and humble themselves in abject surrender.

The Sino–Japanese War

Lasting less than a year, the war between China and Japan over control of Korea graphically exposed the problems of China's self-strengthening efforts in a way that caused a wholesale questioning not only of the modernization programs themselves but also of China's position as the Confucian "elder brother" state. Because China's programs were generally carried out by individual officials negotiating with foreign firms and advisors, there was little coordination among the forces these men controlled. Li Hongzhang, for example, arranged the purchase of so much materiel from Germany's Krupp works that it was said that Alfred Krupp kept a portrait of Li over his bed. The result was that different Chinese military units were armed with a wide variety of noninterchangeable weapons and ammunition, making it difficult for them to support each other. China's newly rebuilt steam fleet of iron-clad and steel-hulled warships, although impressive in size and armament, faced similar problems. Unlike the Japanese ships, China's vessels in many cases had their components separately built at various dockyards in Europe. In one memorable incident during the Battle of the Yellow Sea in 1894, the recoil from the mismatched, oversized guns aboard the Chinese flagship destroyed its own captain's bridge. The Chinese fleet was also accompanied by foreign advisors of assorted nationalities, who squabbled among themselves as to tactics and exercised the right of independent withdrawal from the engagement. Worse still, Chinese gunners found to their dismay that many of the shells they were firing were filled with sand rather than explosive—the result, it was said, of the Empress Dowager's diversion of naval funds to rebuild the Summer Palace destroyed in 1860. In one of the most poignantly ironic twists of this incident, part of the naval funding was rumored to have paid for a marble pleasure boat, with side paddlewheels, standing permanently in the Palace's artificial lake.

Marble Boat and Summer Palace. The burning and looting of the Summer Palace by the Anglo-French expeditionary force in 1860 had been traumatic for the fleeing Qing court and it was of considerable significance to rebuild it as a sign of the ongoing dynastic "restoration." It was said that the Empress Dowager Cixi had appropriated funds for the repair of the palace that had been earmarked for naval development. One of the most visible, and for many, ironic, features of the rebuilt Summer Palace was therefore the stationary marble paddle-wheel boat built to replace a wooden pleasure craft lost in the fire of 1860.

Although many of the land battles were hotly contested, superior Japanese organization and morale enabled them to drive steadily through Korea. A second force landed in southern Manchuria to secure the territory around the approaches to Beijing, and Japanese naval forces reduced the fortress across from it at Weihaiwei. By the spring of 1895, after some preliminary negotiations, Li Hongzhang made a humiliating trip to the Japanese town of Shimonoseki to meet his old Japanese counterpart Ito, who was now revered as the architect of Japan's constitution of 1889. To further add to his humiliation and misery, Li was shot in the face during an assassination attempt, although he recovered shortly and saw the negotiations through. In the conversation with his old diplomatic opponent, one can feel Li's weariness and frustration:

> **Li**: In Asia, our two countries, China and Japan, are the closest neighbors, and moreover have the same [written] language. How could we be enemies? Now for the time being we are fighting each other, but eventually we should work for permanent friendship . . . so that our Asiatic yellow race will not be encroached upon by the white race of Europe.
>
> **Ito**: Ten years ago when I was at Tientsin (Tianjin), I talked about reform with [you]. . . . Why is it that up to now not a single thing has been changed or reformed? This I deeply regret.
>
> **Li**: At that time when I heard you . . . I was overcome with admiration . . . [at] your having vigorously changed your customs in Japan so as to reach the present stage. Affairs in my country have been so confined by tradition that I could not accomplish what I desired. . . . I am ashamed of having excessive wishes and lacking the power to fulfill them.
>
> (From Ssu-Yu Teng and John K. Fairbank,
> *China's Response to the West.* Cambridge,
> MA: Harvard University Press, 1954, p. 126)

The severity of the treaty provisions, however, served notice that Japan had now moved from the camp of the victims of imperialism to that of the imperial powers themselves. In addition to the annexation of Taiwan and the adjacent Pescadore Islands, the control of Korea, and, temporarily at least, the seizure of the South Manchurian Liaodong Penninsula, China was forced to agree to the largest indemnity yet, 200 million silver *taels* (around 150 million gold dollars). The only bright spot for China was that France, Germany, and Russia, all of whom had interests in the area, were worried that Japan was growing too powerful and so forced the Japanese to return Liaodong to China in what became known as the Triple Intervention. In 1896, China leased the peninsula to Russia who soon enhanced it with a fortress at Port Arthur and set the stage for the Russo-Japanese War in 1904–1905.

The Treaty of Shimonoseki signaled to the Western powers in East Asia that China was now weak enough to have massive economic and territorial demands forced on it. Thus, a "race for concessions" began in which France demanded economic and territorial rights in south China adjacent to Indochina; Great Britain did the same in the Yangzi River valley; Russia and Japan made demands in the north for rights in Manchuria; and a newcomer, Germany, demanded naval bases and rights at Qingdao (Tsingtao) on the Shandong Peninsula. China's total dismemberment was avoided in 1899 when John Hay, the U.S. secretary of state, circulated a note with British backing suggesting that all powers refrain from securing exclusive concessions and instead maintain an "open door" for all to trade in China.

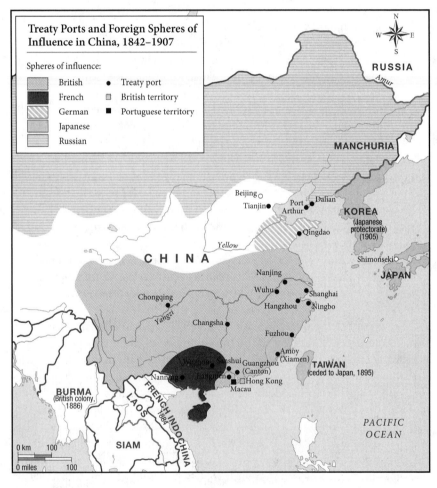

MAP 5.7

Treaty Ports and Foreign Spheres of Influence in China, 1842–1907

Slicing the Pie. A pie represents 'Chine' (French for China) and is being divided among caricatures of Queen Victoria of the United Kingdom, William II of Germany (who is squabbling with Queen Victoria over a borderland piece, whilst thrusting a knife into the pie to signify aggressive German intentions), Nicholas II of Russia, who is eyeing a particular piece, the French Marianne (who is diplomatically shown as not participating in the carving, and is depicted as close to Nicholas II, as a reminder of the Franco-Russian Alliance), and the Meiji Emperor of Japan, carefully contemplating which pieces to take.

Reform: The Hundred Days

Amid these growing foreign tensions, the aftermath of the war produced a domestic crisis as well. The terms of the Shimonoseki treaty had prompted patriotic demonstrations in Beijing and raised levels of discussion about reform to new levels of urgency. A group of younger officials headed by Kang Youwei (1858–1927) petitioned Emperor Guangxu, now ruling in his own right, to implement a list of widespread reforms, many modeled on those recently enacted in Japan. Kang had established a reputation for himself as an advocate of the idea of Confucius as a reformer in his *Kongzi gaizhi kao* (*A Study of Confucius as Reformer*), arguing that late versions of Confucian texts in which the sage was presented as conservative or reactionary were forgeries. Guangxu issued a flurry of edicts from

June through September 1898, attempting to completely revamp China's government and many of its leading institutions. Resistance to this "hundred days'
reform" program, however, was extensive, and much of it was centered on the
emperor's aunt, the Empress Dowager. With support from her inner circle at
court, she had the young emperor placed under house arrest and rounded up and
executed those of Kang's supporters who could be found. Kang and his junior
colleague, the writer and political theorist Liang Qichao (1873–1929), managed
to escape to the treaty ports. For the next decade they traveled to overseas Chinese
communities attempting to gather support for their Constitutional Monarchy
(sometimes given as Preserve the Emperor) Party (*Baohuanghui*).

(A)

(B)

Kang Youwei and Liang Qichao. (A) Kang Youwei (1858–1927), was a Chinese
scholar noted initially for his role in popularizing the role of Confucius as reformer. After the Sino-Japanese War he dedicated himself to institutional
reform. Meeting with the young emperor Guangxu to put forth his ideas, the
emperor issued a number of edicts based on Kang's suggestions in the summer
of 1898 that became known as the Hundred Days of Reform. Following the
Empress Dowager's coup against the emperor, Kang and his colleague, Liang
Qichao, went into exile where he continued to promote his advocacy of
constitutional monarchy until the revolution of 1911–12. **(B)** Liang Qichao
(1873–1929), Chinese scholar, journalist, philosopher and reformer, took part
in the Hundred Days with Kang Youwei, and barely escaped with his life after
the Empress Dowager's coup. Like Kang, he traveled extensively, visiting the
many Chinese communities around the world seeking support for the Constitutional Monarchy Party (*Baohuanghui*; literally, "preserve the emperor party/
association"). One of China's most prominent pioneering journalists he had a
hand in founding a number of newspapers, and was instrumental in popularizing Western philosophical and scientific works among Chinese intellectuals.

Reaction—The Boxer Rebellion and War

The turmoil set off by the "race for concessions" among the imperial powers was particularly intense in north China, where the ambitions of Russia, Japan, and Germany clashed. The course of extraterritoriality in treaty provisions during the century had now reached a point where essentially all foreigners enjoyed immunity from Chinese laws. These privileges had also been extended to Chinese Christian converts under the protection of missionaries. Conversions by "rice Christians" to take advantage of these immunities had become increasingly common and hotly resented by the local populace. Thus, with the stepped-up activity of German missionaries on the Shandong Peninsula came a new wave of anti–foreign sentiment, increasingly emanating from a group called the Society (later "Militia") of the Harmonious Fists (*Yihetuan*). Initially anti-Qing as well as antiforeign, the members' ritual exercises and name prompted the foreign community to refer to them as the **Boxers**. By late 1899 the Boxers were regularly provoking the foreign and Christian communities with the aim of pushing their governments to pressure the Qing to suppress the movement, by which they hoped to stir up rebellion against the dynasty.

In the spring of 1900 matters came to a head. Boxers assassinated the German ambassador, Baron Klemens von Ketteler (1853–1900), and the Germans demanded that the Qing crush the movement once and for all, pay a huge indemnity, and erect a statue to their ambassador as a public apology. In the midst of this crisis, the Empress Dowager, who had been negotiating in secret with the Boxers, declared war on all the foreign powers in China and openly threw the court's support behind the movement. The result was civil war across northern China as Boxer units hunted down missionaries and Chinese Christians. Many Chinese army units aided the Boxers in attacking foreigners, and the foreign diplomatic quarter in Beijing was besieged from June until August.

The foreign governments quickly put together a multinational relief force led by the Germans and British and largely manned by the Japanese but including units of nearly all the countries with interests in China. By August they had fought their way to the capital and chased the imperial court nearly to Xi'an. Amid considerable carnage in the mopping up of alleged Boxer sympathizers, Li Hongzhang, in his last official duty before his death, was commissioned to negotiate the end of the conflict for the court. With Qing power utterly routed, the foreign governments were able to impose the most severe "unequal treaty" yet: they extracted the right to post troops in major Chinese cities, they demanded the total suppression of any antiforeign movements, and they received such a huge indemnity—450 million silver taels, or $335 million—that China had to borrow money from foreign banks to service the interest on the payments. The only bright point in the Boxer Protocols of 1901 was that the United States agreed to return its share of the indemnity money to China on the condition that it would be used to send Chinese students to study in American institutions. Some of it also supported the founding of Tsinghua University in Beijing.

Company of Boxers, Tien-Tsin, China.

Boxers on the March, 1900. The complex politics and cultural clashes surrounding the Boxer (*Yihetuan*) movement paralyzed northern China and left it open to the final foreign invasion of the 19th century. The anti-foreign secret society, at first opposed to the Qing as well, had by 1900 joined with the Empress Dowager in declaring war on all the foreign powers in China. Boxers and Qing army units surrounded the foreign diplomatic compounds in Beijing for most of the summer of 1900 until a multinational force fought its way to the capital and began a bloody campaign of pacifying the region. Here, Boxer fighters march in the port city of Tianjin.

CULTURE, ARTS, AND SCIENCE

Although the late Qing period is often seen by scholars as one more concerned with cataloging and preserving older literary works than with innovation, there was nevertheless considerable invigoration as a result of foreign influences toward the end of the dynasty. Reversing the trend of thousands of years, the most significant Chinese developments in science and technology were those arriving from the West as products of the Industrial Revolution and the new kind of society emerging there.

Poetry, Travel Accounts, and Newspapers

Although the form of the interlocking "three excellences"—painting, poetry, and calligraphy—remained largely unchanged, their content increasingly contained subjects related to China's new position in the age of imperialism. Although sometimes confining himself to more traditional fare, Huang Zunxian (1848–1905), for example, wrote many poems base on his experience as a diplomat in Japan and the United States.

China's increasing need to understand the nature of the threat confronting it prompted an increasing number of atlases, gazetteers of foreign lands, and, by the 1860s, the first eyewitness travel accounts. Many of the early attempts at compiling information of foreign countries were copies of Western works whose sophistication gradually increased as the century wore on. The most significant of these were Wei Yuan's (1794–1856) *Illustrated Gazetteer of the Maritime Countries* of 1844 and Xu Jiyu's (1795–1873) *Record of the World* of 1848. These accounts, especially Xu's, formed the backbone of what Chinese officials new about the outside world until the first eyewitness accounts of travelers and diplomats began to arrive in the late 1860s.

Although hundreds of thousands of Chinese had emigrated to various parts of the world by the mid-1860s, it was only in 1866 that the first authorized officials began to visit foreign countries and not until 1876 that diplomats began to take up their posts in foreign capitals and ports. All of these men, however, were required to keep journals of their experiences, and by the later part of the century China began to acquire a far more complete sense of what the outside world was like. The diaries of the diplomats Zhang Deyi and Guo Songtao were particularly significant in this regard.

A new popular medium also emerged in the treaty ports and eventually in most Chinese cities as well—the newspaper. For centuries newsletters tracking official doings at the capital had been circulated among the elites. However, the 1860s saw the first popular Chinese language papers, the most prominent of which was *Shenbao*. By the turn of the century, Liang Qichao (mentioned previously) had emerged as China's most influential journalist and scholar, having started and edited five newspapers, each heavily influenced by his views on reform. Such publications and the growing numbers of journals and popular magazines, many started by missionaries anxious to use science and Western material culture as a vehicle for their work, were vitally important in the transfer of ideas between Chinese and foreigners.

Science and Technology

As we have seen, the most pressing need for China during the early nineteenth century was considered military technology. During the period between the Opium Wars, Chinese officials attempted with some success to purchase guns and cannon from European and American manufacturers to bolster their coastal defenses. It was quickly apparent to the self-strengtheners, however, that China must begin to understand the basic principles behind these revolutionary weapons and begin to manufacture them on their own. Moreover, this would be impossible to do unless the infrastructure was in place and such supporting industries as mining, railroads, and telegraphy were also set up. One early move in this regard was the founding of the All-Languages Institute (*Tongwen Guan*) in 1861. Founded to provide interpreters for the newly arriving diplomats in Beijing, the foreign experts employed soon allowed the school to become a kind of all-purpose science and technology academy as well. With the founding of arsenals and dockyards and their supporting infrastructures, the need for technical knowledge accelerated. Here the Chinese Education Mission to the United States, as well as later student missions to England and Germany, was meant to create a nucleus of trained personnel to modernize Chinese industry and defense.

Ironically—because of the general animosity directed against them by Chinese officials—missionaries were key players in science and technology transfers. Unlike the Jesuit missionaries of the seventeenth century, Protestant missionaries in the nineteenth century directed their efforts at ordinary Chinese, but often did so by attracting them with the new advantages of science. Central to their efforts was the role of medical missionaries in setting up clinics and using their presence in the community to foster conversion. The missionary community was also active in popularizing developments in Western science and technology through journals like *The Globe Magazine*.

By the latter part of the century, increasing numbers of Chinese scholars were becoming involved in the study of foreign subjects, going abroad for education, and involved in translation of Western works into Chinese. The Chinese mathematician Li Shanlan (1810–1882), for example, collaborated with Shanghai missionaries in translating works on algebra, calculus, and analytical geometry. Later, Liang Qichao and Yan Fu (1854–1921) studied and translated a wide range of foreign scientific and social science works by John Stuart Mill, Thomas Huxley, Herbert Spencer, and Charles Darwin, as well as such Enlightenment authors as Hobbes, Locke, Hume, Rousseau, and Bentham.

Thus, although China had not yet completed its move to the new scientific-industrial society, the momentum had already begun among the empire's intellectual leaders. Even so, nearly all agreed that the future would not lie in slavish imitation of the West. In the meantime, however, the example of Japan confronted them only a short distance away.

CONCLUSION

In many respects, the long nineteenth century, spanning as it did the spiral down from China's apex of power to near dismemberment, was perhaps modern China's most disastrous period. With the failure—or at best only partial success—of reform, the mass bloodletting of the Taiping and Nian period, and the apparent futility of the Boxer War, revolution now seemed the only viable solution. But the revolution itself would be strung out over decades of weak central control, feuding warlord enclaves, civil war, and world war before the ultimate victory of the Communist Party and the founding of the PRC in 1949.

The way we see history and its significance, however, is always formed in retrospect. As the German philosopher Hegel put it, the owl of Minerva (the goddess of wisdom) only flies at sunset—we cannot know the significance of an age until it has passed. Moreover, history does not often divide itself neatly into well-defined periods or ages: these are the invention of historians. Thus, as we have noted, sometimes directly, sometimes by implication, the interpretation of historical events is constantly in flux. So it is with what we have termed the "last empire in transition." In looking at this crucial period of China's imperial history we have seen immense changes in the way scholars have judged its overall direction, how they have evaluated the significance of certain events, and how they have come at the material from different theoretical perspectives. In these two chapters we have tried to strike a balance in how the material is presented by exploring the historiography and approaches of prominent writers in the field and to be somewhat more "China centered" by looking at internal matters in the Qing empire first before exploring the phenomenon of imperialism. In this respect, we have emphasized the story of Zuo Zongtang's expedition in Central Asia because it reveals some important aspects about how contemporaries saw events unfolding and the times when there seemed to be genuine optimism about the success and the definitions of success of Qing efforts.

Scholars taking the long view of the late Qing will perhaps in the near future see it as the beginning of China's (re)ascendancy, rather than—or as well as—the end of an age. Despite the immense trauma to come in what is often called China's "century of revolution," by the latter decades of the twentieth century the spirit of what reformers were calling "using foreign things to help China" was yet again on the rise. By the first decade of the twenty-first century, China had become an economic giant, second only to the United States. And, perhaps fittingly, its Shanghai Expo of 2010 took its cue as China's "coming-out party" in many ways from that of the United States in its Centennial Exposition that so amazed Li Gui in 1876. The story of China's reemergence as a premier world power is the subject to which we now turn, and in this story the owl of Minerva has not even begun to flap its wings.

FURTHER READING

Chu, Samuel, and Kwang-ching Liu, eds. *Li Hung-chang and China's Early Modernization*. Armonk, NY: Sharpe, 1994. Collaborative volume of essays by leading writers on late Qing China offering the most complete treatment and assessment of Li Hongzhang.

Desnoyers, Charles. *A Journey to the East: Li Gui's "A New Account of a Trip around the Globe."* Ann Arbor: University of Michigan Press, 2004. Translation with introduction of Li's extensive visit to Philadelphia and other U.S. cities in 1876 and his voyages to London, Paris, Suez, India, Singapore, and Hong Kong before arriving back in Shanghai.

Hevia, James. *Cherishing Men from Afar: Qing Guest Ritual and the Macartney Embassy of 1793*. Durham. NC: Duke University Press, 1995. Award winning examination of the role of symbolic behavior and causes and resolution of conflict within the context of the first British embassy to the Qing.

Judge, Joan. *Print and Politics: "Shibao" and the Culture of Reform in Late Qing China*. Stanford, CA: Stanford University Press, 1996. Important study of emergent journalistic culture and its impact on the spread of reform and self-strengthening ideas in the newspaper, *Shibao*.

Levenson, Joseph. *Confucian China and Its Modern Fate: A Trilogy*. Los Angeles and Berkeley: University of California Press, 1968. Although dated in many respects in light of current scholarly trends, the far-reaching scope, elegance of style, and value of the work as a milepost in American history writing on China makes it worth exploring.

Perry, Elizabeth J. *Rebels and Revolutionaries in North China, 1845–1945*. Stanford, CA: Stanford University Press, 1980. Although it deals with a century-long time span, this is a particularly good study of the Nian and the conditions from which they sprang.

Platt, Stephen R. *Autumn in the Heavenly Kingdom: China, the West, and the Epic Story of the Taiping Civil War*. New York: Knopf, 2012. New perspective on the Taiping era and its interconnections with the global economy and informal Western intervention in the 1860s.

Polachek, James. *The Inner Opium War*. Cambridge, MA: Harvard University Press, 1992. Although dealing with the controversial topic of the Opium War, this work is a good example of a more "China-centered" approach to the documentation of the Chinese policy debates concerning the conflict.

Rhoads, Edward J. M. *Stepping Forth into the World: The Chinese Educational Mission to the United States, 1872–81*. Hong Kong: Hong Kong University Press, 2011. Most complete treatment of Yung Wing's Education Mission and a meticulous tracing of the lives and careers of the students.

Spence, Jonathan. *God's Chinese Son: The Taiping Heavenly Kingdom of Hong Xiuquan*. New York: Norton, 1996. Using newly discovered documents and exchanges between Hong and missionaries, Spence attempts to recreate the inner world of Hong.

CHAPTER 6

FROM EMPIRE
TO PEOPLE'S
REPUBLIC, 1901–1949

> *Grieving over my native land,*
> *Hurts my heart. So tell me:*
> *How can I spend these days here?*
> *A guest enjoying your spring winds?*

—"On Request for a Poem," Qiu Jin

For Qiu Jin (1875?–1907), the daughter of a secretary in the Qing bureaucracy—and by her early twenties the wife of a minor Beijing official and mother of two children—her self-imposed exile described in the verse above would prove both melancholy and instructive. A witness to the carnage of the Boxer War and the Allied counterattack and punitive expedition of 1900–1901, she and her husband, Wang Tingjun, had barely escaped the capital with their lives. Now, as for so many Chinese, the humiliation of the preceding 60 years had reached a point where the air was desperately alive with talk of radical reform and, increasingly, revolution. Qiu Jin would choose the latter.

Like so many Han Chinese, she increasingly came to see the Manchu rulers of the Qing Dynasty as the chief impediment to meaningful change in the empire. Like many of those opposed to the Manchus, she decided to go to Japan to study and search out like-minded Chinese radicals, leaving her husband and children behind. Japan at the turn of the century occupied an anomalous position in the minds and emotions of many Chinese intellectuals. China's humiliating defeat at the hands of the Japanese in 1895 had set in motion a surge of patriotic protest, the abortive Hundred Days of Reform in 1898, the "race for concessions" on the part of the treaty powers, and, indirectly, the Boxer uprising. Moreover, the 20,000 Japanese troops of the Eight Nations Alliance sent to raise the Boxer's siege of the foreign legations in Beijing were by far the most numerous of that expeditionary force. There was also, however, a grudging admiration for Japan's success in making itself into a modern imperial power. Thus, it had become a preferred model for Chinese reformers and revolutionaries who traveled there to observe Japanese modernity and make connections in its expatriate Chinese communities.

For Qiu, arriving in Japan in 1904, being a witness to that growing empire's success against Russia in 1904–1905 was even more compelling proof of the efficacy of its approach and the weakness of China's present state. Soon she had made contact with several Chinese revolutionary groups and joined one that became part of the coalition put together by Dr. Sun Yat-sen, the Revolutionary Alliance, or *Tongmeng hui*, in 1905. Her radicalization continued in other ways as well. She cut her hair short and adopted a variety of nontraditional dress, even wearing men's suits. Her actions as a full-time revolutionary separated from her family also displayed increasingly insistent feminist themes. A skilled calligrapher and respected poet, much of her work reveals her views of the role women must play in the revolution:

> *Do not tell me women*
> *Are not the stuff of heroes,*
> *I alone rode over the East Sea's winds*
> *For ten thousand leagues . . .*

And even more directly:

> *Shame and failure!*
> *I am already twenty-seven*
> *Yet have no glory to my name*
> *I only worry for my country*
> *And do not know how to expel these invaders.*
> *I am glad my ambitions will not rot and waste away,*
> *Not when I hear the roar of war drums.*

Qiu returned to China in 1906 to begin her revolutionary work. She taught briefly in a girl's school in Zhejiang and founded *Zhongguo Nübao* (*China Women's Newspaper*) in nearby Shanghai. The following year she moved to Shaoxing as headmistress of a girls' school and joined the staff of a nearby academy being used as a front for revolutionary activity. Qiu and the headmaster of that academy, Xu Xilin, developed a complex and ambitious plan to start an uprising in Anhui and Zhejiang provinces, but trouble plagued the enterprise almost from the beginning. Local revolutionaries were to draw Qing troops away from Hangzhou, while Qiu's forces would occupy that city and Xu's would take Anqing. Instead of the coordinated attacks called for by the plan, however, Xu launched his assault prematurely and, although he succeeded in killing the provincial governor, En Ming, he was promptly captured and executed. The Qing then began rounding up suspected revolutionaries and Qiu, although lacking support, improvised a plan to take Shaoxing. Several days before the attack, however, a Qing unit surprised and surrounded her and eight of her comrades

[handwritten marginal note: education important to revolutionaries]

as she was leaving her school. After a brief skirmish they were captured. Among the incriminating evidence discovered were her diaries, assorted documents, and a substantial cache of guns and ammunition.

Two days later, on July 15, 1907, having written a pro forma confession of her activities, she was forced to kneel in the public square of her home village, Shanyin, her arms pinioned behind her back, while an executioner claimed her head at the stroke of his broadsword. Although the provincial authorities had foiled this revolutionary plot, their beheading of Qiu Jin caused widespread revulsion and deepened animosity toward the Qing. Her martyrdom resulted in the transfer of the governor who ordered her execution and the suicide of the magistrate who supervised it. Her grave swiftly became a revolutionary shrine and her heroism made her a model of resistance and feminist icon over the next century to Republicans, Nationalists, and Communists alike.

The saga of Qiu Jin is symbolic in many ways of the complex and turbulent patterns of Chinese history during the first half of the twentieth century. Despite belated efforts on the part of the Qing to finally create a constitutional monarchy in the last years of their rule, it would be Qiu's organization, Sun Yat-sen's Revolutionary Alliance, that would shortly overthrow more than two and a half centuries of Manchu rule. Sun's new Chinese Republic, however, soon gave way to factional infighting and barely survived the death of its president, Yuan Shikai—who in his last days attempted to restore the monarchy. A decade of feeble rival governments whipsawed by warlord satrapies ultimately gave way to Sun's reconstituted Nationalist Party, which, under Chiang Kai-shek, united most of the country but swiftly entered into a prolonged civil war with Mao Zedong's Communists. In the midst of this, Japan would annex Manchuria and invade China, only to suffer complete defeat in World War II. With the civil war renewed in 1946, it would be Mao's party that would ultimately create the present People's Republic of China in 1949.

Like Qiu Jin herself, the period was one in which many conflicting social forces and intellectual trends came to the fore. Among China's intelligentsia, interaction and adaptation of Western values and political ideas were already making themselves felt in the final

Qiu Jin. As they were in many areas of the world, the ideas of modern feminism were among the mix of radical influences entering China at the turn of the 20th century. For Qiu Jin, wearing men's attire gave her a degree of notoriety as well as enhancing her view that women too would power the revolution, and the revolution itself would empower women. In the event, however, suffrage for women would not come with the revolution of 1911, and Qiu Jin, executed by the Qing in 1907 for her revolutionary activities would be among the movement's most prominent martyrs. This undated photo shows Qiu Jin in male Chinese dress.

years of the nineteenth century. By the time of World War I, writers were calling for science and democracy, vernacular literature, and emancipation of women. In the 1920s and 1930s China's largest cities, notably Shanghai, were becoming recognizable as modern metropolises, as the gap between rich and poor grew more and more dramatic. The World War II years saw the Nationalist's Republic of China elevated to Allied status with the United States and Great Britain, along with massive American aid, and the expectation by the victors that China would emerge from the war as the great power of East Asia. It would take decades more, however, for that idea to be realized; and it would take place under a very different—and for much of that time, antagonistic—regime.

THE REPUBLICAN REVOLUTION

As we saw in the preceding chapter, Qing efforts at both technological and institutional reform failed to develop a sustained, comprehensive program to meet the Western challenge during the nineteenth century. Following belated attempts at institutional reform in the wake of the Boxer uprising in 1900, a variety of radical groups, aided by the growing numbers of overseas Chinese, began to work for the overthrow of the Qing.

Late Qing Efforts at Reform

With the return of the imperial court to Beijing in 1901 and the presence of substantial numbers of foreign troops stationed in the capital, the Qing finally turned to institutional reform. The new approach was symbolized in part by the grudging accommodation made by the Empress Dowager in holding audiences with foreign diplomats and their wives, even allowing herself to be photographed with them. The first decade of the new century, however, also brought with it more substantive changes.

During the flight of the imperial family from the capital, Cixi had found the retreat humiliating and arduous. Thus it was said by some that her newfound support for many of the reforms she had resisted in 1898 was born of determination to avoid such treatment in the future. This feeling was shared by two of the empire's leading proponents of self-strengthening, Li Hongzhang and Zhang Zhidong. Li, as we have seen, was at the forefront of the reform effort since the early 1860s, only to see it shattered in the war against Japan and the peace talks at Shimonoseki, where he shouldered the burden of negotiating for the Qing. His last official act had been to conduct the talks to end the Boxer conflict with the Eight Nations' representatives. For Zhang, an advocate of education reform and popularizer of the self-strengthening motto, *Zhong xue wei ti, Xi xue wei yong*, the Boxer catastrophe showed clearly the need for the kinds of reforms that had made the Eight Nations Alliance so powerful. Other officials, noting that many of their colleagues—including Li and Zhang—had ignored orders from the imperial court to attack the foreigners during the Boxer uprising, feared the breakdown of the government's ability to rule and the growing regional power of local officials.

大清國當今慈禧端佑康頤昭豫莊誠壽恭欽獻崇熙聖母皇太后

Empress Dowager Cixi. The real power behind the throne from 1861 until her death in 1908, the Empress Dowager Cixi (1835–1908) of the Manchu Yehenara clan was the mother of the Tongzhi emperor and the aunt of emperor Guangxu. She had started as an imperial concubine of the Xianfeng Emperor and was elevated to Empress Dowager when her son by Xianfeng, Zaichun, was installed as emperor in 1861. Reigning as co-dowager empress with Xianfeng's wife, Ci'an until Ci'an's death in 1881, Cixi consolidated her power in the court over the young Guangxu emperor. Guangxu's attempts at reform in 1898 under the influence of Kang Youwei convinced Cixi of a conspiracy aimed at restricting her power and she and court officials and eunuchs loyal to her launched a coup, placed the emperor under house arrest, and executed some reformers and drove others to exile. After the defeat of the Boxers and the court's humiliating flight to Xi'an, she ultimately threw her support behind the reform efforts and held audiences for foreign diplomats, as well as posing for official photographs. In this picture she is posed surrounded by motifs of Daoist longevity. The legend above the photograph gives her titles closing with "Saintly Mother and Empress Dowager."

Now finally in the majority, therefore, the reformers put together a systematic program to attempt the reinvigoration of Qing rule. At the end of January 1901, an imperial edict was issued announcing the new direction:

> We have now received Her Majesty's decree to devote ourselves fully to China's revitalization, to suppress vigorously the use of the terms "new" and "old," and to blend together the best of what is Chinese and what is foreign. (http://afe. easia.columbia.edu/ps/cup/qing_reform_edict_1901.pdf/)

While reiterating the need to find and employ talented people, the decree went on to note that the "root" of China's problems lay in the huge number of sinecures with their entrenched, inefficient bureaucratic posts, rigid practices of seniority, and endemic corruption. With regard to Western learning it was argued that it had been limited to superficial study of technology and military matters. An entirely new approach must now be undertaken to understand the deeper wellsprings of Western wealth and power.

Already, in 1901, several important changes had been put into operation. The old format of eight-legged essays was abolished for the military, local, and provincial exams. The new examination material was to be oriented more toward technical expertise and practical affairs. The old Zongli Yamen, in place since 1861 to deal with foreign affairs, was now reorganized as the Ministry of Foreign Affairs and placed above the existing Six Boards in terms of protocol status. The old Imperial Academy had been replaced during the Hundred Days' Reform in 1898 by the newly created Imperial University. Now other universities on the new model were swiftly set up. In 1904, a complete overhaul of the educational structure of the country was undertaken. The old Confucian academies were closed and a graded primary and secondary school system based on the Japanese model—itself based largely on the American model—was introduced.

Over the next two years, the remaining Confucian exams were finally abolished and new tests designed around more practical elements of statecraft were introduced. The old Armies of the Green Standard and Manchu Banner units were disbanded and two large armies, Northern and Southern (Beiyang and Nanyang), were set up. The colorful but anachronistic uniforms of the old armies were abandoned in favor of the modern khaki and olive drab coming into use in foreign forces. A more efficient quartermaster division was instituted and up-to-date artillery, machine guns, and rifles of uniform calibers and ammunition types were phased in. Perhaps most dramatically, the government itself was to be restructured more or less along the lines envisioned by Kang Youwei and Emperor Guangxu—who still languished under house arrest.

In 1905, an imperial commission was sent abroad to study the constitutional systems of the great powers, and on its return a plan to turn the Qing into a constitutional monarchy over the next decade was created. In 1908 the court accepted a draft constitution based on elements of several European models, although most heavily influenced by Japan's. The court announced that these reforms would be phased in over the next nine years, after which the constitution would go into effect. The first element, the creation of provincial assemblies, was begun in 1909. The following year, a National Assembly was convened, with half of its makeup members of the provincial assemblies and half composed of those who had connections to the court—roughly equivalent to the Commons and Lords in the English Parliament. After repeated petitions from various quarters to convene the new parliament, the court agreed to open it in 1913, several years ahead of schedule.

Toward Revolution

While Qing reform efforts were proceeding apace, however, the plans of revolutionaries were moving even more rapidly. The central figure in this regard was Dr. Sun Yat-sen (1866–1925) a man, like Yung Wing (Rong Hong), the subject of our "Patterns Up Close" in the previous chapter, in many ways emblematic of the changes in China during the nineteenth century. Born near Canton, Sun received the fundamentals of a classical education but then undertook Western medical training in Hong Kong and developed a thriving practice in Canton. As with growing numbers of Chinese seeking their fortunes outside of China, Sun lived for a while with his brother in Hawai'i and traveled extensively throughout the worldwide Chinese diaspora. Since growing numbers of Chinese who opposed the government had moved to the relatively safe Chinese communities abroad or within the treaty ports, Sun gained exposure to a wide spectrum of dissent. A student of European and American history, his political ideas were already germinating by the time of the Sino–Japanese War. One story claims that he sent a letter suggesting certain reforms to Li Hongzhang during the war, although no reply from Li has ever been discovered. Like many of his countrymen, Sun was caught up in the great wave of patriotic anger that prompted demonstrations in Beijing and other Chinese cities in the wake of the war. Although many, like reformers Kang Youwei and Liang Qichao, saw China's salvation in following the Japanese model of constitutional monarchy, the war convinced Sun that the feeble and increasingly corrupt Manchu government was itself the biggest obstacle to China's regeneration. Thus, during his time in Hawai'i in 1895, Sun formed his first revolutionary organization, the *Xingzhong hui* (Revive/Resurrect China Society).

Within a few months of the war's end in 1895, Sun had embarked on a course of insurrection. Unfortunately, it took a great deal of time, failure, and compromise for his efforts to ultimately create a viable revolutionary movement. His initial attempt was nearly his last: convinced that the Qing were on the verge of collapse and required only a local uprising to start a sweeping general movement to overthrow the dynasty, he smuggled a few men and guns into Guangdong from Canton and attempted to draw the local villagers to his colors. His first revolutionary battle was a disaster and most of his small band were killed or captured. Sun barely escaped with his life. It did nothing to diminish his

Sun Yat-sen and Family in Hawai'i.
Sun Yat-sen (1866–1925) was in many ways emblematic of the "new" Chinese men and women growing up in the late 19th century in the age of treaty ports, foreign influences, and growing unrest with the apparent shortcomings of Qing rule. By the 1890s, there was an extensive network of overseas Chinese communities throughout Asia and increasingly in Europe and the Americas. Sun's brother, Sun Mei, had emigrated to Hawai'i, at the time an independent kingdom, and became a successful merchant and farmer. Sun Yat-sen spent a total of seven years in Hawai'i, living with his brother, founding his first revolutionary organization, the *Xingzhonghui* (Revive/Resurrect China Society), there in 1895, and lived there with his family at the turn of the century. At one point, anxious to come to the United States and even apply for citizenship, he obtained a Hawaiian birth certificate in an attempt to show his residence in what had become American territory. In the photo above he is shown with his family members in 1903.

determination, however: over the next 16 years his groups would make a dozen more attempts before finally succeeding.

From this point Sun, like Qiu Jin, spent most of his time in the treaty ports and among Chinese expatriates looking for financial support, recruits, and connections to other dissident groups. Not surprisingly, he was shadowed by Qing authorities from the outset. In the summer of 1896, for example, the Zongli Yamen instructed its legation in Washington to report on his activities in the United States. Visiting London that October, the Chinese legation there took more direct action: trailed by Qing informers, he was secretly kidnapped and held in the Chinese diplomatic compound pending trial and execution. Sun, however, was able to smuggle a letter out to an old Hong Kong mentor and colleague, James Cantlie, who alerted British authorities to negotiate his release. From an obscure amateurish revolutionary on the dissident fringe of Chinese politics, Sun was transformed into an international celebrity as newspapers all over the world picked up the story. The prestige gained gave him increasing entrée to like-minded groups and became an invaluable funding and recruitment tool.

With the collapse of the reform movement in 1898, Sun's efforts faced competition from an unexpected quarter. Now Kang Youwei and Liang Qichao were moving among the same expatriate circles trying to expand and fund their *Baohuang hui* (Preserve the Emperor Society). The rivalry was bitter between the two groups, with each side trying to undermine the others' efforts. For Sun and his allies, however, coalition building continued apace. One of the most significant events in this regard was the founding in Tokyo on August 20, 1905, of the *Tongmeng hui* (Revolutionary Alliance or Chinese United League), with Sun as its first president.

While in Japan, Sun had taken the Japanese alias of "Nakayama," the Central Mountain. From this point he was popularly known as Sun Zhongshan, the Chinese rendering of that name and the one most commonly used today in the PRC. His home town of Xiangshan (Fragrant Mountain) was renamed Zhongshan soon after his death in 1925. Seventy representatives from 17 of China's 18 provinces were present at the founding of the Revolutionary Alliance. Their affiliations ranged from old anti-Qing secret societies to radical revolutionary movements of the kind to which Qiu Jin belonged. In the first issue of its official publication that November, *Minbao* (the *People's Tribune*), Sun promulgated for the first time his most famous doctrinal statement: **The Three People's Principles** (*San min zhuyi*).

San Min Zhuyi

Originally titled *San da zhuyi* (the *Three Great Principles*), Sun's core ideas were relatively straightforward, although the third, *minsheng*, was never fully explicated by him before his death. Thus, it has been subject to rival interpretations by Communists and Nationalists ever since. Sun once credited his time in the United States and study of American history—particularly the phrase "of the

Cutting Ties to the Past. Following in the tradition of other anti-Qing movements, the men during and after the Xinhai Revolution of 1911–1912 cut their queues in solidarity with the revolution.

people, by the people, for the people" in Lincoln's Gettysburg Address—with inspiring the Three Principles. They are as follows:

- *Minzu* (Nationalism): Expulsion of the Manchus and all imperial interests and complete control of national sovereignty. The first part of this concept was distilled into the phrase *qu chu Da lu*—"drive out the Manchus." Unlike the ethnolinguistic-based nationalisms of other regions, however, Sun insisted that China's diversity required a constitutionally based nationalism more along the lines of that of the United States, in which unity was achieved by agreement on broad principles of civic rights and duties.
- *Minquan* (Democracy): Representative institutions based on a constitution. The voices of the people must be heard and the structure of government must be responsive to those voices and efficient in carrying out the people's will. Thus, the new government was to have legislative, executive, and judicial branches as well as a "Control Yuan" and an "Examination Yuan" as revitalized carryovers from the imperial administrative apparatus. Sun recognized too that historically the Chinese had no real experience with representative institutions of the type he envisioned. Hence, he foresaw a period of one-party tutelage until the people grew used to the new forms of democratic institutions.

- *Minsheng* (The People's Livelihood): The idea that the government is responsible for the welfare of the people and for ensuring the prosperity of all classes runs deep into pre-Confucian times. The concept of the people's livelihood was also central to Mencius's philosophy of proper government and was an article of faith in China's imperial ideology. Sun himself felt that nationalization of certain key industries would be necessary and felt that *minsheng* with respect to China's dominant industry, agriculture, revolved around an equitable system of land distribution and usage. This, of course, had been one of the great concerns of every preceding dynasty. Sun, however, felt that the key to the problem lay in the ideas of the American economist, Henry George. For Sun, all land would be assessed at a base value and then taxed according to that value and that of any later improvements or speculative increases. The government also reserved the right to buy back the land at the assessed value for redistribution as a hedge against underreporting the value of each plot. Thus, Socialists claim Sun's program as their own because of the public ownership of the land and the use of the taxes for all, as well as his later connections with Bolshevik Russia. Free marketers note that Adam Smith applauded the idea of such a tax and point out that the "single tax" system helped discourage landlordism, while also encouraging productivity.

As the first decade of the twentieth century entered its second half, Sun's coalition gained strength, although its repeated attempts at fomenting uprisings continued to fizzle. Yet the steady growth of the influence of the movement and the pervasive sense that the Qing were less on the verge of reform than on the verge of collapse allowed Sun's groups to penetrate nearly all levels of society. Recent scholarship has also suggested that many of the old scholar gentry felt threatened by the Qing reforms and the new system of assemblies as the proposed locus of power. Moreover, as the assemblies were formed many of their members became increasingly resistant to Qing efforts at increased centralization. In addition, by the end of the decade, the influence of Sun's coalition was growing rapidly in the overhauled and newly organized Qing army.

On October 10, 1911, celebrated ever after as "Double Ten," an accidental explosion in a Wuchang barracks signaled a premature takeover of the base by the revolutionary faction. In the confusion, the revolutionaries, lacking a commander, gave the base commandant, Li Yuanhong (1864–1928), the choice of leading the insurrection or being executed. "I am your leader!" he is reported to have replied. He went on to twice be the president of the Chinese Republic. The military revolt quickly spread to other bases and the Qing collapse so long expected by Sun and his allies appeared to be immanent.

Ironically, at the onset of the insurrection Sun was fundraising among the Chinese community in Denver, Colorado, which, only a few decades before, had been the site of some of the worst American anti-Chinese violence of the nineteenth century. The *Xinhai geming*—the **Xinhai Revolution**, so named for the year 1911 in the old Chinese calendar—had spread by November to many provincial capitals where the New Army factions made common cause with anti-Qing scholar-gentry and other nationalists. There were some pitched battles, notably a victory by Qing forces under Yuan Shikai at Hanyang in November, and, more tellingly, a crucial win by the revolutionaries the following month at Nanjing. On the whole, however, it consisted primarily of uprisings in provincial cities whose new governments seceded from Qing rule piecemeal.

It was here that the role of the Qing commander, the durable Yuan Shikai, proved crucial. Yuan had been selected by the Qing to quash the revolution but Yuan stalled for time and tried to get a sense of the drift of events before committing himself. He then agreed to command the imperial forces on condition that he be made premier in the new constitutional monarchy. Meanwhile, he had attempted to open negotiations with the revolutionaries, who initially rebuffed him. Following the Nanjing victory, however, he struck a deal with the insurgents whereby his forces would come over to them in return for his selection as president of the new republic, formed upon the abdication of the Qing on February 12, 1912. Thus, after serving less than three months as president, , Sun Yat-sen was elbowed aside by the revolution he had done so much to begin.

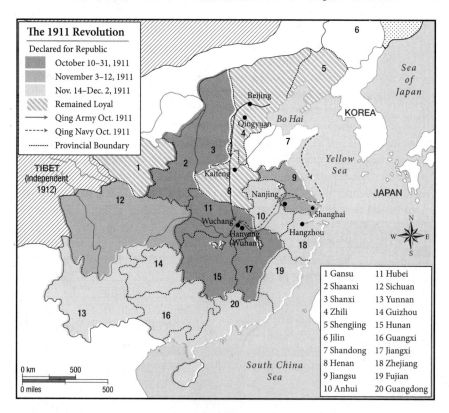

MAP 6.1

The 1911 Revolution

Descent From Republic

The new Republic of China was freighted with difficulties right from the beginning. Pro-Sun factions within the government lobbied for his return. The Revolutionary Alliance became a political party, the **Guomindang** (GMD) (*Kuomintang*) or Nationalist Party, which won a plurality in the initial elections. Its leader, Song Jiaoren, however, was assassinated before he could form a government. In addition, because so much of the revolution had consisted of provincial revolts, the vast majority of which were not led by Revolutionary Alliance groups, the country was left regionalized and fragmented and ruled in many places by military strongmen. Anxious to suppress dissent and complete the changeover from Qing institutions, Yuan suppressed the GMD, which responded with a revolt sometimes called "the second revolution." Yuan crushed the revolt by the summer of 1913 and drove Sun out of the country.

With the coming of World War I, things unraveled further. Japan, allied with Britain, quickly acted on this relationship to seize the German colonies in Shandong and the Pacific. Capitalizing on the preoccupation of the imperial powers with the war in Europe, Japanese strategic planners moved swiftly to further their aims of a united East Asia under Japanese aegis. Encouraged by China's difficulties in creating a viable government, the Japanese issued the Chinese a document in January 1915 that became known as the Twenty-One Demands, although because the demands were divided into five groups the Japanese insisted on calling it the Five Requests.

Japan's war with Russia had yielded effective hegemony in Manchuria. Although Manchuria was formally still a part of China, the Japanese had eliminated Russian competition for concessions and resources there and acquired control over the Chinese Eastern Railway and South Manchurian Railway. Japan had also extracted mining and development rights in the region and increasingly saw Manchuria as a destination for Japanese immigration as its home islands became more crowded. Over the long term, Japan viewed Manchuria as a client territory and buffer zone against Russian expansion into China or Korea. Thus, the Demands addressed a number of issues designed to reinforce this state of affairs. Japanese planners sought to unite a weak China with a strong Japan to create an "Asia for the Asiatics" to resist further imperial encroachment by the European powers.

The first group of demands was therefore aimed at confirming and consolidating Japanese control over the former German concessions in Shandong. The second group demanded an extended sphere of influence in Manchuria including extraterritoriality, rights of settlement, control over the administrative and financial sectors, and access to raw materials in adjacent Inner Mongolia. Group Three would give Japan control over the heavily indebted Hanyeping mining and manufacturing complex. China was forbidden to grant additional coastal or island concessions to any other power but Japan in Group Four. The most contested set of conditions came with Group Five. Japan reserved the right to hire or approve all financial and law enforcement officials in China. Japan would receive railroad concessions in China and acquire effective control of Fujian Province, directly across the Strait from Japanese-annexed Taiwan.

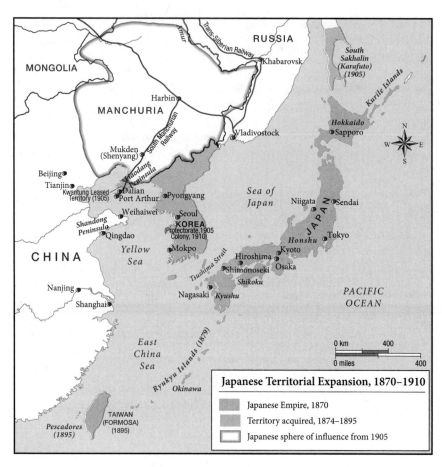

MAP 6.2

Japanese Territorial Expansion, 1870–1910

As discontent with his regime was swiftly mounting, Yuan felt he could not take on Japan. He managed, however, to leak the contents of the Demands, which Japan had insisted be kept secret, to the Americans and Europeans and stalled for time. In a sharply worded note sent by the American secretary of state (and three-time presidential candidate) William Jennings Bryan, Japan was warned that the Demands constituted a serious breach of the Open Door policy. Great Britain, for its part, retreated from its alliance with Japan. Realizing the international furor the Demands had generated, the Japanese dropped the last set of provisions and sent an ultimatum to Yuan demanding a quick reply. Yuan agreed to the revised Demands on May 9 and the treaties were signed later that month. For the next 34 years, May 9 was commemorated in Republican and Nationalist China as National Humiliation Day.

As discontent with the provisions of the appeasement policy grew and with an anti-Japanese boycott barely suppressed, Yuan decided that the country would be more manageable if the monarchy were restored. In September 1915 he announced plans to inaugurate a new dynasty. He called together a Convention of Citizen's Representatives, which dutifully voted unanimously to restore the monarchy. On December 31, Yuan announced that the coming year would be the first of the new Hongxian reign in the reconstituted imperial era. Predictably, the forcing through of the new order encouraged rebellion rather than stabilization. Within a few months, Yunnan, Guizhou, Sichuan, Shandong, and several other provinces had declared their independence of Yuan, vowing to protect the Republic. Yuan belatedly backed away from the restoration, which, in any case, effectively ceased with his death on June 6, 1916.

The Decade of the Dujuns

With Yuan's death, his successor, the former Wuchang commander and now president, Li Yuanhong, declared China a republic again. If anything, however, the government's control continued to erode in favor of rival cliques in the north centered on the remnant of the Republic in Beijing and the governors and military leaders of the south based in Canton. By summer 1917, Germany's resumption of unrestricted submarine warfare, which in April had pushed the United States to declare war, now prompted both claimants to the Republican mantle in China to do so as well. Although China sent no troops to the Western Front, the British and French recruited 140,000 Chinese laborers to free their own soldiers for combat duty.

Disagreements about China's role in the war, factionalism among the emerging class of *dujun*—military governors—and different interpretations of the functions of the Republic led to what was in effect a civil war. The government in Beijing, dominated by the "Anfu Clique"—a group of officials largely from Anhui province who had created a club called *Anfu* (literally "peace and happiness/good fortune")—loosely controlled the north, whereas a floating coalition of southern *dujun* and civilian provincial governors held sway in much of the rest of the country. In the middle of this highly confused and shifting situation, Sun Yat-sen's GMD set up its own Republic of China in Guangdong Province.

For the next decade, a chaotic pattern of more or less continuous fighting by warlords, expropriation of land, and exorbitant taxes levied by rival *dujuns* wore down the remnants of post-Qing society, impoverished countless millions, and left the country so disunited that many foreign and Chinese observers despaired of it ever having a functional government. The warlords themselves were, as disordered times often produce, a highly eclectic group. Some were disappointed political aspirants; some were former provincial governors; some military adventurers; some bandit chieftains. Along with them were a handful of idealists genuinely groping for social and political revival. Some warlords were arguably psychopathic in their behavior; others were simply out to enrich themselves and live lives of gilded debauchery.

There was Zhang Zuolin, the warlord of Manchuria, who spent his days on a political razor's edge balancing his own aspirations, those of the Japanese who sought to use him, and those of assorted Chinese governments. Ruthless and politically adroit, he wore a giant ruby on his skullcap and traveled about in his own private train. The Japanese attempted to blow that train up in 1917. They would be more successful in 1928. By doing so they drove his son, Zhang Xueliang, into the Nationalist camp, where he took part in one of the strangest dramas of the era: the Xi'an Incident (see later).

There was Zhang Zongchang, named by *Time* magazine "China's basest warlord," whose nicknames included "The Dog-Meat General" (after a gambling game he enjoyed), "72 Cannon Zhang," and, purportedly, "Old Eighty-Six Cash" because his sexual organ was said to be the size of a stack of that many coins. It was also said that he had the body of an elephant and the brain of a pig. Cruel, canny, and dissolute, his personal train was reputed to be stocked with prostitutes representing a fair portion of the world's ethnicities. During the Russian Civil War, he employed thousands of former Tsarist troops and proved innovative in the use of armored trains. Although callous as a commander, he also kept a large unit of Russian nurses on hand for treating casualties. Showing a considerable knack for colorful behavior, he once promised on the eve of battle to triumph or come back in a coffin. Having lost the battle, he had his men carry him through a nearby town sitting in a coffin enjoying a cigar.

On the other side of the behavioral fence was Yan Xishan, "the Model Governor of Shanxi." Yan fought with the Revolutionary Alliance forces and ultimately established a power base in Shanxi Province that lasted with minor interruptions until he fled with the Nationalists to Taiwan in 1949. Although continually buffeted by competing warlords, he created a surprisingly stable regime. Eclectic in his political ideas, he developed an approach to development, "Yan Xishan Thought," that borrowed from nearly every major ideology of the early twentieth century. Progressive in his efforts to improve the lives of the rural inhabitants, he built roads, encouraged industry, and supported women's education while outlawing foot-binding, gambling, and opium smoking.

Tending somewhat more toward the bizarre was Feng Yuxiang, "the Christian General," who in the service of his Methodist faith taught his men assorted prayers and, it was said, drew them up in serried ranks and baptized them with a fire hose. Yet his Christianity and that of his troops helped ensure a modicum of discipline that enhanced his reputation as a commander. He took part in the Nationalist's Northern Expedition in 1926 and held several high positions in the new government in the late 1920s before breaking for a time with Chiang Kai-shek over resisting Japan's incursions into Manchuria and northern China. After

(A)   (B)   (C)   (D)

Warlords. (A) Yuan Shikai (1859–1916). Yuan's career as an official and military man had been varied under the Qing and he was among the first of the reformers to push for the new Beiyang and Nanyang Armies. Sent by the Qing to quash the revolution, he ultimately made propositions to both sides, threw in his lot with the revolutionaries, and as part of his bargain elbowed Sun aside to become president of the Republic of China from 1912 until 1916. Factionalism, resistance to his rule by Sun's newly formed Guomindang (Kuomintang), and imposition of the Twenty-One Demands by Japan ultimately pushed him to attempt to create a new imperial dynasty, which quickly dissolved with his death. **(B)** Marshal Feng Yuxiang in 1924 as he appeared at the head of his troops entering Beijing , when his soldiers seized the Forbidden City and drove the young emperor Henry Puyi from the palace. Feng was known as the Christian General and later fought with Chiang Kai-shek's Nationalist forces. Turning more leftward after World War II, he broke with Chiang and died as the Civil War was going badly for the Nationalists in 1948. His widow, Li Dequan, served as the new People's Republic of China's first Health Minister. **(C)** Yan Xishan, 1883–1960) was a Chinese warlord who served in the government of the Republic of China. Yan effectively controlled the province of Shanxi from the 1911 Xinhai Revolution to the 1949 Communist victory in the Chinese Civil War. As the leader of a relatively small, poor, remote province, Yan Xishan survived the machinations of Yuan Shikai, other warlords, the Japanese invasion of China, and the subsequent civil war, being forced from office only when the Nationalist armies with which he was aligned had completely lost control of the Chinese mainland. His ideas were progressive in many respects, outlawing opium and supporting women's education. **(D)** Zhang Zuolin (1873–1928), One of the most notorious—and politically precarious—warlords, Zhang controlled much of Manchuria, though always with a wary eye on neighboring commanders and especially on the Japanese Kwantung Army. Surviving one assassination attempt by the Japanese in 1917, they succeeded in 1928. Ultimately the Kwantung Army secured Manchuria for Japan and it became the puppet state of Manzhouguo (Manchukuo).

World War II he drifted more leftward in his politics until his death in 1948. In 1953 he was recognized by the People's Republic as one of the few "good warlords." His widow, Li Dequan (1896–1972), served as the PRC's Minister of Health in from 1949 to 1965.

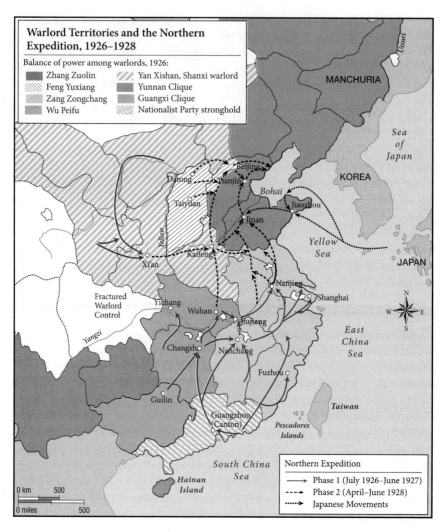

MAP 6.3

Warlord Territories and the Northern Expedition, 1926–1928

The Reemergence of Nationalism

Although some warlords arguably had the desire to help the country, none of them had a political program solid or appealing enough to garner widespread support. In addition, none of them commanded sufficient power to subdue the others or their coalitions. Even Sun Yat-sen at this point, although he had a political program, controlled only a small area around Canton. With the republic in shambles and China hijacked by the warlords, Sun remained a profoundly inspirational figure for Chinese nationalists, mostly through his numerous publications issued from exile in the treaty port of Canton. In fact, one of the most galling ironies of the period is that the treaty ports, the most visible signs of China's humiliation at the hands of Western imperialism, were now the chief refuges for those fleeing the chaos of the interior and those engaged in reform or revolution. Indeed, Canton and Shanghai were to be the seedbeds of the movements that would carry China into the twenty-first century.

For the moment, however, the impetus toward a new nationalism would come from a different quarter. With the armistice ending the Great War in November 1918 and the opening of the peace conference at Versailles in 1919, the victorious Allies faced a myriad of daunting issues. In addition to dismantling the Ottoman, Austro-Hungarian, and German empires and dealing with the new Bolshevik regime in Russia, there were a number of problems directly affecting the political configuration of Asia. The American president, Woodrow Wilson, in his famous Fourteen Points, which not only had become America's war aims, but also were widely understood as the Allied war aims, had advocated "self-determination" for all peoples. Throughout the colonies and territories held by both the Allies and the Central Powers, many interpreted this as a hopeful sign of increased colonial autonomy or even independence. Indeed, in the Covenant of the proposed new international body, the League of Nations, a "mandate" system was created in which existing Allied colonial powers would act "in trust" for territories not yet able to govern themselves. Those territories deemed capable of forming states were to be given independence immediately or within an agreed upon time.

The yawning gap between promise and performance with regard to the aspirations of those in the colonies, however, had already shown itself in tragic relief. In April 1919, anxious about growing agitation for Indian independence, British Gurkha troops mowed down civilian demonstrators at Amritsar, prompting worldwide condemnation and the court-martial (and acquittal) of the British commander. In China, expectations were high that because China had been accepted as a member of the Allied and Associated Powers and because of the contributions of China's Labor Corps, there might be movement on some of the provisions of the unequal treaties. Most observers expected that there would be some settlement of the status of the German concessions Japan had seized and held under the Twenty-One Demands. For its part, Japan wanted a racial equality clause inserted into the League Covenant. Failing that, the Japanese wanted to retain the concessions in Shandong.

For Wilson and the British, it was feared such a clause would prevent ratification of the treaty. In the United States, senators from the Jim Crow south would certainly vote it down, as would senators from the Pacific Coast, the source of opposition to Asian immigration. The British Empire, too, had internal and external immigration restrictions on Asians. Negotiations with the Japanese continued for weeks but in the end it was decided that it would be better to have Japan sign the League Covenant and try to settle the Shandong dispute separately.

The decision announced on May 4, 1919, by the Allies at Versailles to allow Japan to keep the German concessions in China set off mass demonstrations and a boycott of Japanese, and in short order, other foreign concerns. The decision was especially dispiriting because feelings were already running high in anticipation of National Humiliation Day. This **May Fourth Movement**, as it came to be called, is often cited as the modern beginning of Chinese nationalism. Combined with the intellectual and cultural ferment of the New Culture Movement (see later), a new political assertiveness increasingly made itself felt. Shortly thereafter, for example, inspired by the Bolshevik Revolution in Russia, a Chinese Communist Party was founded in 1921. Among the few dozen charter members was an obscure assistant librarian at Peking (Beijing) University named Mao Zedong. Two years later, despairing of assistance from the democracies of the West, Sun Yat-sen availed himself of aid offered by the Third Communist International—Comintern—and began to recast the GMD along Bolshevik lines. It would be the uncertain union of these two parties in a united front from 1924 to 1927 that would finally effect a degree of unification on China. It would also create the preconditions for a devastating civil war that would not be decided until 1949.

May 4 Demonstrations. The keen sense of betrayal by the victorious Allies at the Versailles Conference felt by Chinese who had believed that China's contribution to the Allied war effort merited rolling back the unequal treaties and restraint on the part of Japan erupted into protests beginning May 4, 1919 at Beijing (Peking) University. Here protesters demonstrate outside the Gate of Heavenly Peace (Tiananmen) marking the entrance to the old Forbidden City.

From "A Heap of Loose Sand" to a United Front

The intellectual and cultural ferment of the late 1890s and early 1900s had resulted in a flurry of new ideas with which Chinese intellectuals now had to contend. In addition to an entire spectrum of Western political theory from monarchism to anarchism arriving in translation, the ideas of Western classical economy, Marxism and socialism, Darwin and Spencer all came to the fore along with new interpretations of Confucian classics and a wide range of Meiji-era Japanese scholarship. The new education system and universities, particularly Peking University, became hubs for these ideas to circulate among China's new intellectuals, many of whom had only a partial Confucian education.

The years after the founding of the republic were particularly fertile in this regard, so much so that the champions of the new ideas began to talk of a **New Culture Movement** and a Literary Revolution. Seeing the relative power of the West and the current weakness of China, the legacy of Confucius was roundly attacked and Neo-Confucian values stood on their head: value the new, instead of the old; youth instead of venerable age; science, not tradition; democracy, not monarchy. Since new ideas required new language, the era also spawned a vernacular language movement, whose advocates urged the abandonment of the literary language of the classics in favor of the way contemporary people actually spoke. The movement resulted in a flurry of vernacular language journals, the most famous of which adopted the French title *La Jeunesse*, or **New Youth**. They were the laboratories in which some of China's most famous twentieth-century writers like Li Dazhao, Chen Duxiu, Hu Shi, and Lu Xun worked out their initial literary experiments.

Among the most insistent and influential were Li and Chen. Li (1888–1927), a professor and librarian at Peking University, was an early contributor to *New Youth*, of which Chen was the editor. They posited imaginary figures of "Mr. Science" and "Mr. Democracy" to take on what they considered the false premises of "Mr. Confucius." In November 1918, Li published an article signaling a new direction. Having dabbled somewhat in Marxism, his "The Victory of Bolshevism" celebrated the end of World War I not as an Allied victory over the Central Powers, but rather as a victory for the masses over militarism. In short order he started a Marxist study group that came to include the young Mao Zedong (1893–1976). In July 1921, 13 delegates from various provinces representing a little more than 50 members—and 2 Comintern representatives—met in Shanghai to form the **Chinese Communist Party** (CCP). Chen Duxiu was appointed to its Central Committee and Mao became secretary of the branch in his home province of Hunan.

From the outset the new party faced several problems that appeared far more intractable than those faced initially by the Bolsheviks. Marxist-Leninist theory insisted that the proletariat of industrial wage workers would be the vanguard of a socialist revolution. Lenin's theoretical and practical activities further insisted that in the case of Russia, the Communist Party should be a vanguard of the vanguard, a select group of professional revolutionaries who would seize political control at its center and then proceed to remake society from the top down. Peasants were considered a problem in this schema because they were essentially conservative, tied to the results of their production—rather than being "alienated" from it as were industrial workers—and thus lacked the revolutionary spirit that would inspire them to risk all for sweeping societal change. From the beginning, Bolshevik cadres

(A) (B) (C)

Founders of the Chinese Communist Party. (A) Chen Duxiu (1879–1942) played a prominent role in a number of pivotal arenas in early 20th century China. He participated in the Xinhai Revolution, was a proponent of the New Culture Movement and founder of its signature journal *New Youth*, and took an active role in the May Fourth Movement Along with Li Dazhao. Chen was a co-founder of the Chinese Communist Party in 1921 and its first General Secretary. (B) Like Chen, Li Dazhao (1888–1927) had championed the New Culture Movement and the idea of making science and democracy central to the new Chinese society struggling to develop. He was also an early champion of the Russian Revolution, writing "The Victory of Bolshevism" in *New Youth* in 1918. (C) Mao Zedong (1893–1976) would emerge as the best known and most influential of the founders of the CCP, becoming the Party's chief theoretician, military leader, Party Chairman, and head of state of the People's Republic from 1949, with a brief interruption from 1959 to 1966, until his death in 1976. Even today, the core ideology of the CCP and the People's Republic is still given as "Marxism-Leninism-Mao Zedong Thought."

faced difficulty and often fierce resistance from Russian peasants, especially as the party engaged in forced requisitioning of supplies in rural areas.

Although both countries were similar in their relative poverty, China differed from Russia in several important respects. Russia's industrial sector was small by Western standards, but it was fairly modern and concentrated in large urban factory complexes, making it somewhat easier to organize workers. China's modern industrial sector was far smaller and more diffuse. Even more than Russia, China's population was made up overwhelmingly of peasants—the "problem" population. Moreover, without a working central government in China, it would be next to impossible to seize power and remake society from the top down.

Hence, the CCP, whose members at this point were mostly urban, and their Comintern advisors came to the conclusion that a Communist revolution in China would have to await the country's national unification and its evolution into some form of constitutional capitalist state before the structures would be in place to seize control. In this connection, Sun's Nationalist Party seemed like the best candidate to effect such a transformation. Sun had picked up considerable support in the wake of the May Fourth movement. Indeed, he became increasingly strident in campaigning for a more unified Chinese national spirit, noting that the Chinese people were currently like "a heap of loose sand" (often rendered as "a sheet of loose sand") in their lack of national cohesion. On December 31, 1923, in a speech to the Canton YMCA, Sun declared that "We no longer look to the Western Powers. Our faces are turned toward Russia."

Help from that quarter was not long in coming. Comintern agents approached Sun with money, weapons, and training in revolutionary organization and tactics. The Whampoa Military Academy in Canton became a center for GMD training, with officers going to Moscow for further study. Among those who made the trip but came away distrustful of his new allies was Chiang Kai-shek (*pinyin:* Jiang Jieshi; 1887–1975). That distrust would play a central role during China's next five decades. For now, however, the new resources and training and

Sun Yat-sen and the Reorganized Guomindang. On the heels of Sun's disappointment with the lack of Western aid for his Nationalist (*Guomindang*) Party's efforts to create a united China, he turned to the new Soviet Union and its Third International (Comintern) agents for help. In return for agreeing to allow members of the newly formed Chinese Communist Party to join with Sun's party in a united front, Comintern sent organizers, weapons, money and provided training to key personnel. **(A)** Sun (seated) and the young Chiang Kai-shek in 1924 at the Whampoa Military Academy in Canton, the center of Guomindang training and political organization, of which Chiang was president. **(B)** Comintern members from different countries attending the organization's 7th Congress in the summer of 1935. From left to right: George Dimitrov (Bulgaria); Palmiro Jogletti (Italy); Wilhelm Florin (Germany); Chen-Shao-Zo (China). Rear: Otto Ruusinen (Finland); Klement Gottiwald (Czechoslovakia); Wilhelm Preck (Germany); Dimitri Manuilsky (Stalin's personal deputy).

the reorganization of the party into a more efficient revolutionary configuration yielded dividends. The price that Comintern extracted from Sun was the creation in 1924 of the First United Front: CCP members were to be allowed to join the GMD as individuals, and all would work toward eliminating the warlord territories and unifying the country.

Sun's death from cancer in 1925 temporarily halted the plans for the Northern Expedition to reunite the country. The pressure to begin the offensive increased considerably, however, in the wake of the May 30 Movement. Following the shooting in Shanghai by a Japanese factory guard of a Chinese worker accused of sabotage, on May 30, 1925, British police opened fire on Chinese gathered in front of the police station to protest the affair. The killing of 11 of the demonstrators set off nationwide strikes and protests.

Already, members of both parties had been sent ahead to propagandize the people in the rural areas. Mao in particular proved adept at this and was already beginning to part with the Marxist-Leninist notion that the peasants lacked revolutionary potential. In fact, in his later *Report on the Hunan Peasant Movement*, he waxed rhapsodically about their zeal and organizational acumen. With United Front organizing being carried out in multiple provinces and GMD leadership

Northern Expedition. Guomindang troops of the Northern Expedition's National Revolutionary Army assembled for an address by their commanders following the capture of Hankou, Wuhan in August, 1926. As one of China's few industrial areas as well as an important river port, the capture of Wuhan was pivotal in driving the unification of China forward and in gaining diplomatic recognition for the nascent regime. Within a few months of securing the city the Nationalist regime made it the seat of the new government as it moved north and east down the Yangzi.

assumed by Chiang Kai-shek, who had been Sun's military chief, the Northern Expedition was launched in July 1926. The GMD organized a National Revolutionary Army in the south and the CCP fomented Communist-inspired strikes in the industrial cities of the Yangtze Delta, including Shanghai. From the beginning, support for the movement was overwhelming: Hunan's capital, Changsha, fell in less than two weeks and most of the southern warlords fought only briefly before coming over to the movement. By November, the GMD/CCP forces had secured most of the Yangzi Valley and were moving into position to strike north. Here the going would be harder as the warlord forces attempted to form an opposition alliance. Moreover, for the treaty powers, the situation was troubling since a stated goal of the GMD was complete Chinese sovereignty, although neither side wanted to expand the campaign into an international conflict. Foreign diplomats still in Beijing talked about recognizing the new government and the British had already turned some of their concessions in central China over to the GMD.

As 1927 moved through its early months, however, the bonds between the GMD and CCP ruptured. The CCP and the left wing of the GMD had taken the important industrial centers of Wuhan and Shanghai (excluding the foreign concessions), setting the stage for a showdown with the right wing. The growth of the CCP through the campaign and its key role in fomenting strikes in cities yet to be taken made Chiang increasingly mistrustful of their intensions as well as those of the Comintern and the left wing of his own party. In April, therefore, he launched a preemptive purge of Communists in Nationalist-held areas. Caught between Comintern's insistence on maintaining the United Front and the situation on the ground confronting them, the Communists hesitated and then mounted a series of hopelessly ineffective coup attempts in various cities. Much of the old CCP leadership was lost. Li Dazhao, for example, was seized from the Soviet embassy and executed. Chen Duxiu was condemned by his own party as a "right-wing opportunist." Although much of the leftist opposition was now eliminated, a remnant that included Mao Zedong fled to the remote province of Jiangxi to regroup and create its own socialist Jiangxi Soviet. Here, and later in the caves of Yan'an in the north, Mao would put into practice his ideas of peasant revolution and their power to build socialism.

PATTERNS UP CLOSE

Chinese Patterns of Revolution?

One of the more enduring questions for historians and social scientists is that of the nature of revolution. What is a reliable definition of it? What differentiates revolution from other kinds of social upheavals? Is it a modern phenomenon, or has it been present throughout history? Do

continued

revolutions have recognizable patterns to them? Are these similar across temporal, spatial, and cultural lines?

Given the topics we touched on in Chapter Four, looking at revolution in the context of Chinese history makes all of these questions more complex and elusive. On the one hand, if one uses "revolution" in the broadest possible sense, for example, in talking of a Neolithic Revolution or one giving rise to civilization, then we can say with certainty that China underwent such transformations. Comparative study of the causes, progress, and effects of modern revolutions, however, raises some perspectival problems in looking for definitions and patterns. All states face political and social upheavals at one time or another. China, like many other countries, faced numerous peasant revolts and, of course, dynastic changes. When do these, however, become revolutionary?

Comparative study becomes more difficult if we consider that definitions and patterns of what we have come to associate with revolution come largely from the American and French revolutions, although students of such upheavals have thrown in the English Civil War and Glorious Revolution on occasion. The French Revolution, for example, the central model for exploring revolutionary patterns, is specifically the product of European Enlightenment theories that sought to completely recast society by means of "reason" rather than tradition. Indeed, the idea that society *can* be changed not only politically but also by creating new institutions and social norms has occupied the central place of most definitions of revolution ever since. The politics, ideologies, goals, and outcomes of these upheavals are thus culture bound to the extent that they sprang from the Western European experience and its North American offshoots. Moreover, they became models for subsequent revolutions more broadly in the world through the increasing intellectual hegemony of Europeans and Americans in their empires and enclaves. Even what may be considered the prime model of ideological opposition to expanding capitalist, imperialist society—Marxism—is derived from assumptions of the universality of the Western historical, economic, and political experience.

The applicability of transferring these ideas to a different cultural and political context is thus a prime difficulty. How does one seek, as Paul Cohen (see Chapter Four) put it, to pursue a China-centered Chinese history in this regard, when so much of the rationale and ideology of revolution has arrived from abroad? We may argue, for example, that although every dynastic change in Chinese history has involved some political and institutional modification, the fundamentals of the system have been remarkably consistent since they were created during the revolutionary changes of the First Emperor of the Qin and the adoption of Confucianism by the Han. If we utilize the "standard" way of looking at revolution as not simply a political change of personnel, but an attempt to radically alter the structures of a particular society, then the Taiping movement certainly stands out, although practical considerations of fighting for survival forced it to abandon a good deal of its most radical ideology along the way. It also raises another interesting question: the revolutions in the West and Russia saw themselves in part as emancipating people from the strictures of religion. The Taiping "Revolution," however, imposed a far more brutally orthodox form of religion on its subjects. In this respect it shows parallels with another non-Western movement: the Islamic Revolution of Iran in 1979.

And what of the Boxers? Here too, their spiritual world—with its magical assumptions of invulnerability—would prompt many to see it as a reactionary movement. Assessments of its meaning and significance have varied from "protonationalist" to "reactionary nativist" over the last century—often in relation to China's political situation, which itself was highly influenced by foreign revolutionary ideologies and goals. Certainly Sun Yat-sen's Nationalist Party and Mao Zedong's Chinese Communist Party borrowed heavily from the Enlightenment legacy of the West as worked out in the American and French revolutions and subsequent political and economic ideas of Europe and the United States. Significantly, much of the practical training for Sun's and Mao's revolutionary parties also came by way of another foreign adaptation of the Enlightenment legacy and Marxism—this time by the Bolsheviks in Russia.

Finally, in looking at patterns of revolution and their relationship to modern Chinese history, it is worth noting that in many respects it is part of a larger pattern in which a new kind of society—a *scientific-industrial society*—has been displacing the older agrarian societies for the past two centuries. The kinds of revolutions taking place in Russia and China became worldwide phenomena during the course of the twentieth century, aided by the World Wars. The world historian Theodore Von Laue called it "the world revolution of westernization," and it posed a question that all countries in various stages of this transition find themselves asking: "How do we become 'modern' without becoming 'Western?'" It is the question implied by the self-strengthening formula attempting to balance "Chinese studies" and "Western studies." As some scholars of the Chinese century of revolution have noted, the Nationalists would ultimately fail because they placed too much faith in the urban, "modern" sector of Chinese society at too early a stage of development. The Communists, forced by concrete "Chinese" circumstances, were able to make their ideological adaptations more successful by ignoring significant aspects of Marxist theory—and even Russian practice.

Even as China today becomes an economic superpower, how well the leadership will be able to square an evolving vision of "modernity" with a constantly reinterpreted remembrance of "Chineseness" will be the ultimate test of how viable this pattern of revolution will turn out to be.

CIVIL WAR TO WORLD WAR

The collapse of the First United Front and the retreat of CCP forces appeared at first to mark a decisive victory for Chiang and the right-wing GMD. As had so many other groups in China's history, however, the CCP's sojourn into the remote highlands of Jinggang in Jiangxi put them out of reach of the Nationalists and allowed them to regroup and attract new followers. As it had for the theology of the early Taiping adherents, this pattern also allowed Mao to buy the time to work out his crucial variant of rural communism, which Marx and Lenin found impossible to envisage.

The Nationalist Republic of China

Believing the Communist threat to be effectively eliminated, Chiang resumed his Northern Expedition in 1928, submitting Beijing to his control but failing to eliminate the strongest northern warlords. Nevertheless, China was now at least nominally unified, with the capital in Nanjing. The GMD party congress now functioned as a parliament with Chiang as president. Chiang made substantial progress with railroad and road construction, as well as cotton and silk textile exports, even during the economic downturn of the 1930s. Thanks to the silver standard adopted by the new government, rather than the fatal gold standard of most other countries, the financial consequences of the market crash and Great Depression remained relatively mild in China. Chiang made little headway, however, with land reform. Furthermore, the volatile relations with the remaining warlords made the government vulnerable to bribes. Hovering above all after 1931 was the Japanese annexation of Manchuria and creeping encroachment on northern China.

Although never as successful as Sun in attracting favorable international attention, Chiang did at least attempt to act the part of a modern "generalissimo," the title by which he was commonly known in the West. Sun's education had been culturally eclectic in the sense that he did not have a solid classical base on which to graft the foreign ideas he encountered. Like the last generation of Chinese reformers before the revolution, Chiang had remained fundamentally Confucian in his understanding of China's moral legacy and his ideas in this regard would be on bold display in his New Life campaign for China's moral regeneration. Confucian morality was coupled with a powerful sense of military discipline and his actions as GMD and Republic leader tended to reflect the hierarchical nature of both. He knew some English, although he was never fluent. He was married in a Christian ceremony and positioned himself as a full partner of Roosevelt and Churchill during the war with Japan.

His greatest asset in the international arena, however, was his wife, born Soong (*pinyin* Song) Meiling. The daughter of the influential Shanghai banker "Charlie" Soong, Meiling (1898–2003) and her sisters, Qingling and Ailing, were, with the exception of Mao's wife, Jiang Qing, the most powerful women in twentieth-century China. Qingling (1893–1981) was now the widow of Sun Yat-sen and would one day be a member of the CCP Politburo. Ailing (1888–1973) married the Nationalist finance minister, H. H. Kung. Of the three, it was said that one loved power (Meiling), one loved money (Ailing), and one loved China (Qingling). A graduate of American schools, Methodist congregant, and speaker of mellifluous English, Madame Chiang Kai-shek would become the ablest war-time propagandist of a Nationalist China presented as standing alone for democracy against Japan before 1941 and as a valiant ally of the United States and Great Britain for the remainder of World War II.

Soong Sisters. China's most powerful women in the first half of the 20th century, the three Soong (Song) sisters are shown here attending a ceremony in China's wartime capital of Chongqing in 1942. From left to right: Soong Meiling, Madame Chiang Kai-shek; Madame H.H. Kung, Soong Ailing, center; and Madame Sun Yat-sen, Soong Qingling, on the right.

People's War

By the early 1930s, however, despite Nationalist China's apparently promising start, the signs were already there to give its leaders pause. The Communists had not been destroyed as previously believed but had begun to build a viable state in the form of their Jiangxi Soviet. Mao's experiences in Hunan had led him to a theory and practice of seeing landlords as the equivalent of bourgeois capitalists in the countryside and thus the class enemy of the peasants, who now assumed the role of the proletariat. The promise of land reform by means of overthrowing the landlords as a class stimulated the revolutionary fervor of the peasants to change the governmental and social structure to ensure the new order. Moreover, the peasants would be the leading participants in Mao's concept of "People's War"—a three-stage conflict involving the entire populace and borrowing from sources as diverse as Sun Zi's *Art of War* and American tactics against the British in the War for Independence. The first stage was guerrilla warfare to wear down a more powerful enemy's strength and morale. The second phase comes with the armies in rough parity, allowing more conventional tactics and wider flexibility while retaining momentum. The third phase is signaled when the insurgents are more powerful than their opponents and can finish them off and mop up any remnants.

In this conception, "the guerillas are the fish and the people are the sea" in an initial stage of what is called today "asymmetrical warfare." That is, the fighters are indistinguishable from ordinary people, move among them and are supported by them, and strike at enemy targets of opportunity. All elements of society have a role to play: the young and strong as fighters; children as couriers, spies, and logistical support; the elderly as home guards in the base areas. In the words of one popular song, "the people are the army and the army is the people." Thus, unlike the warlord armies or even Chiang's forces, which foraged freely, bullied the local people, and conscripted men and boys wherever they found them, the **People's Liberation Army** worked with the peasants, paid and bartered its own way, and even set up schools and medical stations to win "hearts and minds." Along the way it socialized the populace to the basic elements of Marxism-Leninism and, now, the first elements of what would become **Mao Zedong Thought**.

Mao's ideas were aided by the efforts of such able commanders as Lin Biao, Peng Dehuai, and especially Zhu De (1886–1976). Receiving his military training in late Qing military academies and in the Beiyang Army, Zhu had fought the Qing in the 1911 revolution, spent time as a warlord and opium addict, studied in Germany—where he met Zhou Enlai—and fought for the GMD in the Northern Expedition. Ordered to march against Zhou during the collapse of the United Front, he instead joined the CCP forces, bringing with him 10,000 men. His close association with Mao and successful generalship prompted the local peasants to regard them as one person, whom they nicknamed "Zhu-Mao."

By late 1930, although aware that Kwantung Army maneuvers in Manchuria were becoming increasingly aggressive, Chiang was increasingly anxious to completely eliminate his internal enemies. Although Japan had generally pursued its goals on the Asian mainland through diplomacy in the 1920s—for example, selling the former German territories back to China as part of a general treaty in 1922—the late 1920s increasingly saw Japan's Kwantung Army in Manchuria pursue its own policy of expansion. Anticipating that the Manchurian warlord Zhang Zuolin—who had escaped a Japanese assassination attempt in 1917—might throw his loyalty behind Chiang Kai-shek, the Kwantung Army succeeded this time in blowing his train up in 1928. As we saw earlier, one effect of this killing was that Zhang's son, "The Young Marshal," Zhang Xueliang, now made common cause with the Nationalists. Another, however, was that the Kwantung Army now became the effective rulers of Manchuria.

As the depression took hold, international trade fell off dramatically as countries raised tariff barriers to protect their domestic industries. Japan, which relied heavily on exports, was hit particularly hard. It now sought to create a self-sufficient economy within its empire—what economists call *autarky*. Manchuria was seen as a vital economic link in this system. Politically, however, there was division in the Japanese government about what the status of Manchuria should be. Sensing opportunity in the uncertainty following Zhang Zuolin's assassination and the Nationalists' movements in northern China, the Kwantung Army's adventurous General Ishiwara Kanji (1889–1949) and his subordinate, Colonel Itagaki Seishiro (1885–1948) plotted to seize control for Japan. Without permission from either Tokyo or the Kwantung Army leadership, Ishiwara and his men manufactured an incident near the Manchurian city of Mukden (modern Shenyang) on September 18, 1931, that they used as a pretext to occupy the city and take over the region. His move was supported by ultranationalist junior officers and, presented with a successful fait accompli, the Japanese government acquiesced. They placed the last emperor of the Qing, Aisingioro Henry Puyi (1906–1967), now a grown man, on the throne of an allegedly independent state called "Manchukuo" (pinyin: *Manzhouguo*), "the country of the Manchus." The Kwantung Army also briefly encroached on territory near Beiping ("Northern Peace," the name given to Beijing after the Nationalist capital was moved to Nanjing) and occupied Shanghai. The incident became the first real test of the League of Nations' resolve. The League's Lytton Report the following year condemned Japan for its actions and revealed Manchukuo as a plain case of annexation. The Japanese response was to resign from the League.

Mao Fei and Jiang Fei

While events were unfolding in Manchuria, Chiang, despite the advice of many of his generals, elected to pursue a more conservative course. Following the proverbial advice of "disorder within, disaster without," he noted that "the Japanese are a disease of the skin, while the communists are a disease of the heart." Starting in November 1930, therefore, he mounted increasingly massive "Total Encirclement" and "Bandit Extermination" campaigns over the next four years aimed at eliminating the CCP's expanding Jiangxi Soviet. Each one, however, was defeated by the superior mobility, local loyalty, and guerilla tactics of Mao's growing "People's Liberation Army." As the Jiangxi Soviet forces grew in confidence and power, each side denounced the other as "bandits" (*fei*): for Chiang they were *Mao fei* (Mao's Bandits) or, more commonly, *gongfei* (Communist Bandits) ; for Mao they were *Jiang fei* (Chiang's Bandits).

Because the earlier attempts at encirclement did not work, Chiang adapted his strategy with the help of German advisors. Under the new approach marking this Fifth Encirclement campaign, Chiang turned to bordering the CCP areas with a ring of trenches and blockhouses to eliminate the mobility of his opponents. As

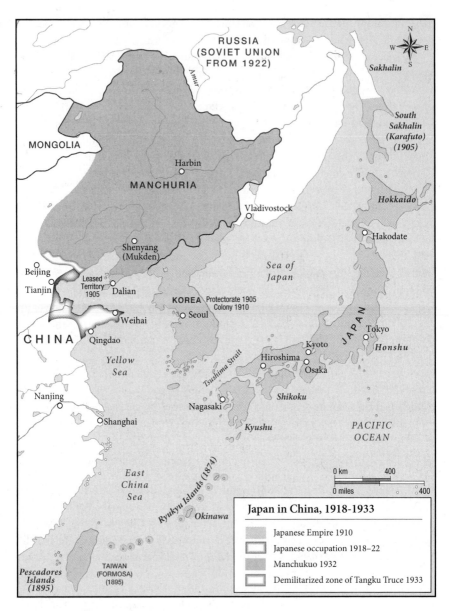

MAP 6.4
Japan in China, 1918–1933

each ring was secured, the army then advanced further inward and dug in again, thus slowly robbing Mao's army of its greatest asset. Although urged by his Comintern advisors to fight a positional battle, Mao broke out of the contracting Jiangxi Soviet area with perhaps 100,000 troops in an attempt to find a secure base from which to continue the fight.

The Long March and Xi'an Incident

Once free, the majority of the Red Army embarked on its epic **Long March** of 6,000 miles, inscribing a semicircle from the south through the far west and then northeast toward Beijing. Along the way, harassment by Nationalist troops, warlords, and local people as well as hunger, famine, heat, swamps, bridgeless rivers, and desertion decimated the bedraggled marchers. Some were also left behind to organize peasants in areas that looked promising. About 30,000 eventually straggled into the small enclave of Yan'an (Yenan) in 1935, for the moment out of Chiang's reach. In later years Long March veterans would occupy a hallowed place in CCP history, not unlike the survivors of Washington's stay at Valley Forge during the American War for Independence. Living in caves cut into the loess soil, they set up communes and concentrated on agricultural production and reconstituting their forces.

Long March; Mao Zedong. Having broken out of the Nationalist encirclement of the Jiangxi Soviet, Mao's forces embarked on an epic and torturous year-long journey from 1934 to 1935 before the remnant of the army arrived in remote, cave ridden Yan'an. In this often reproduced photo of Mao and his troops on the March, Mao occupies the center on horseback with his third wife, He Zizhen (1910–1984) riding in back of him.

The Communists had seized on Japanese aggression as a valuable propaganda tool and declared war on Japan as early as 1932. Within the GMD, however, Chiang's continuing obsession with eliminating his internal enemies increasingly subjected him to the charge of appeasing Japan. Nonetheless, he went ahead with plans to launch a sixth campaign to destroy Mao's forces and, in early December 1936, arrived in the ancient capital of Xi'an to set up his headquarters. While staying at the famous Huaqing Hot Springs outside the city, he was roused from his sleep on the night of December 12 by troops of the Young Marshal and his allies. Leaving his false teeth in a glass by his bed, Chiang jumped out a window in his nightshirt and bare feet and tried to clamber up the stony hills nearby. Convinced he would be executed on capture, he was instead presented with eight demands by his kidnappers, the most important of which was to end the civil war and form a second united front to resist Japan. Mao sent Zhou Enlai, his ablest diplomat, and negotiations proceeded for the next two weeks. Finally, on Christmas Day, Chiang was released, unity was proclaimed, and Chiang and Zhang Xueliang went back to Nanjing. Zhang was court-martialed and sentenced to 10 years in military prison. Instead, he spent 40 years under house arrest in Nanjing and Taiwan until Chiang's death in 1975. He then moved to Hawai'i, where he died in 2001 at the age of 100. Huaqing Hot Springs was celebrated for decades in the PRC as "Capturing Chiang Kai-shek Spring."

Japanese encroachment into North China and Inner Mongolia had steadily continued through the mid-1930s. By early 1937, Japanese and Nationalist encampments faced each other in the Beiping suburbs separated by an uneasy truce. For the Japanese, the prospect of a United Front against them added urgency to their situation. Seeing their chances for additional unchallenged acquisition quickly fading, the Japanese accused the Chinese of capturing a Japanese soldier near the Lugou (Marco Polo) Bridge and on July 7 demanded his return. Although the soldier later came back to his unit, the Japanese seized on the so-called "Marco Polo Bridge Incident" and launched an all-out assault on China. The War of Resistance Against Japan, and in many respects, the opening of World War II, had finally come.

A NEW SOCIETY AND CULTURE

Although Chinese society was beginning to change through the reforms during the last days of the Qing, the more dramatic transition began after the death of Yuan Shikai in 1916. As we saw earlier in this chapter, the intellectual ferment of the New Culture Movement, the vernacular language trend in literature, the nationalist and Marxist agitation in the wake of the May Fourth and May Thirtieth movements, as well as a developing feminism and a drive for female emancipation effectively drove Confucianism from the intellectual mainstream. This movement would continue in the 1920s and 1930s and encompass a wide spectrum of ideas that drew increasingly from current international trends. Along the way it would produce a number of China's most influential modern writers and theorists.

To some extent, the modernization of the Chinese intellectual and cultural world was paralleled by a pattern of modernization of economic and social conditions. That is, even during the most chaotic years of the Warlord Period, China's industrial indices rose, in some cases dramatically, but always more or less on a par with rates of growth in more economically advanced countries. Yet as impressive as these rates appear, it must be remembered that the base from which they are measured is quite low. China built thousands of miles of paved road and two major trunk railroads and even began air service between some cities by the beginning of the war with Japan in 1937. But its overall industrial production was below that of Belgium. Even so, the country's halting steps toward unification and infrastructure building disproportionally affected the cities. There, one had electrical service, cinema, automobiles, and streetcars. The people increasingly dressed in the international standard of suits for men and dresses for women. In the rural areas, however, grinding poverty remained the order of the day, providing fertile ground for Mao's theories of peasant revolutionary potential.

	USA	China	Japan	Korea
Total GDP (in mil US $)	65,400	9522	4445	651
Population (thousand persons)	127,250	528,000	69,254	22,899
GDP per capita (in US $)	514	18	64	28

Table of Comparative Industrialization for 1935: China's Gross Domestic Production in 1935 Compared to Selected Countries.
Source: For total GDP, industrial composition of GDP and population, Chinese data are from, Yeh (1977, p. 97, Table 1) and Luo (2000, p. 27, Table 2), Korea data are from Kim (2008, pp. 392–393, Tables 1–1 and 1–2). Japanese data are from Ohkawa et al. (1974, p. 202), and the US data are from US Department of Commerce, Bureau of the Census (1976, part I, p. 224).

Toward a New Culture?

As we noted earlier, the last decade of the Qing had been marked by a growing tide of translations of such seminal Western thinkers as Darwin, Spencer, Huxley, Mill, Marx, Malthus, the British political economists, and an ever-expanding group of Enlightenment and Romantic writers. At the center of this movement was the interpreter and translator Yan Fu (1853–1921), although Liang Qichao and others also availed themselves of the trend. The large number of Chinese expatriates in Japan immersed themselves in the literary and intellectual scene there, where some, like the writer Lu Xun, were also exposed to Russian literature. Perhaps even more significantly, developing ideas of feminism coupled with the growing movement toward systematic education of women were on their way to changing the structure and dynamics of family and gender.

The rise of China's university system, with Peking University under its progressive president, Cai Yuanpei (1868–1948), as the most vital center of philosophy, politics, and literature, opened up the intellectual scene to a growing number of people who had passed through the new primary school system instead of having a Confucian education. Many, as we saw earlier, felt that China's new status as a republic required not only political change but also radical social change if China was to occupy its proper place in the modern world. Some, having imbibed the Social Darwinist idea of survival of the fittest among races and peoples, felt that only deep social change could save China. For them, the first order of business was to break out of old ways of thinking.

By the time that *New Youth* was being published, the writers and thinkers it attracted were calling for a wide variety of cultural and social change and experimenting with ideas and literary forms that their contemporaries in the West and Japan were using. Literary realism, pragmatism, positivism, materialism, socialism, and even anarchism and anarchist-feminism were among the hallmarks of this trend. Scholars have perceived a number of phases within what was coalescing into the New Culture Movement. Since the Manchus and Confucianism were seen as root causes of China's troubles, not surprisingly some of the first essays dealt with calls to abandon the Sage's philosophy. As we noted earlier, such writers as Chen Duxiu argued that one needed to be scientific, not philosophical, value youth, not age, value democracy, not monarchy—even value women equally with men, not hierarchically.

The next phase, the **Literary Revolution**, was largely initiated by Hu Shi (1891–1962), who had studied at Cornell and Columbia universities and was a student of the philosopher John Dewey. In keeping with Dewey's idea of pragmatism, Hu strongly advocated a new vernacular literature that would avoid the old classical forms in favor of straightforward substance and feeling. Vernacular language was an aid to nationalism and China was badly in need of a unifying nationalism, advocates reasoned. In addition, it would be an aid to mass literacy, a vital element of modern nationhood.

Another phase dealt with a proper philosophy of life and the role of science. Some argued that metaphysics was necessarily prior to science; others like Ding Wenjiang (1887–1936), a geologist, argued for the primacy of science as a universal analytical tool. The science side of this debate attracted the materialists and Marxists like Chen and Li Dazhao as well. The period also saw the "doubting antiquity movement" and a number of debates on Chinese versus Western values. The vitality of China's intellectual scene through the early 1920s and the connections that many of the advanced students and faculty had to Western institutions also attracted high-profile visitors like Dewey, Bertrand Russell, George Bernard Shaw, and Albert Einstein. As we saw earlier as well, the New Culture Movement meshed effectively with the nationalism to which the May Fourth Movement gave rise.

Other key figures associated with or influenced by the movement include Lu Xun (1881–1936), Lao She (1899–1966), and Ding Ling (1904–1986). Lu Xun, the pen name of Zhou Shuren, whose years in Japan in the early twentieth century made him turn away from his medical studies and toward social criticism, is widely regarded as China's greatest twentieth-century writer. His earliest work appeared in *New Youth* toward the end of World War I. He had spent time immersing himself in Russian literature and borrowed Nicolai Gogol's title for his pivotal short story, "Diary of a Madman." In perhaps his most famous piece, "The True Story of Ah Q," as in all of Lu's work, there is a heavy sense of the social and cultural entropy of a China unable to move forward toward modernity and mired in its most destructive traditions. Indeed, in "Diary," the narrator's madness revolved around a vision of China as a nation of cannibals consuming each other and devouring their young. The final entry made by the Madman still haunts today: "Save the children!"

Lao She (1899–1966), the pen name of Shu Qingchun, was a writer and playwright of Manchu descent. His father, a Bannerman, died during the Boxer Rebellion and Shu supported himself and his mother as a teacher. He continued his studies in London, where he was influenced by the work of Charles Dickens, and much of his work bears both the bite of social commentary and the sly humor of his model. Later he worked as a commentator and propagandist during the war with Japan. Lao She's most important novel was *Luotuo Xiangzi*, literally "Camel Xiangzi," but often translated as "Rickshaw Boy" or simply "Rickshaw." The book traces the gradual wearing down and death of a Beijing rickshaw puller. His later three-act play, "Teahouse," traces the tumultuous history of China from 1898 to 1949 through the lives of those who meet in a Beijing teahouse.

Ding Ling (1904–1986), born Jiang Bingzhi, was China's most widely known woman writer and in many ways epitomized the trends toward women's emancipation and feminism. She fled the prospect of an arranged marriage for the progressive environment of Shanghai. Her most influential early work was "Miss Sophia's Diary," in which she traces the trials of a young woman's coming of age in the repressive atmosphere she understood so well. By the early 1930s she had become an activist and joined the Communist Party following the Nationalist's execution of her husband, the poet He Yepin. Ding Ling herself was put under house arrest and brutally interrogated by the GMD before escaping and joining Mao's forces in Yan'an. There, however, her satirical writings on Party hypocrisy toward women made her unpopular with Mao and the party leadership, a condition that hounded her during the Anti-Rightist campaign of the late 1950s and the Cultural Revolution of the 1960s.

The New Feminism

By the time Ding Ling was establishing her reputation as a writer, there had been a considerable amount of intellectual ferment, much of it radical even by international standards, on feminism and the role of women in China. In some respects this may be the most far-reaching cultural trend of all.

As we have seen throughout this narrative, it has been deceptively difficult to generalize about the lives of women in Chinese history. Source material written by women themselves has been comparatively scarce and most of it has

The New Culture Movement. (A) Cai Yuanpei (1868–1940) was a Chinese educator and the president of Peking University (*Beijing Daxue*) at a time when it was the intellectual center of China's modern intellectual life. **(B)** Lu Xun (or Lu Hsun) was the pen name of Zhou Shuren (1881–1936.) One of the major Chinese writers of the 20th century. Considered by many to be the founder of modern Chinese literature, he wrote in the vernacular as well as classical Chinese. Lu Xun was a short story writer, editor, translator, critic, essayist and poet. His best known works such as "The True Story of Ah-Q," and "Diary of A Madman," savagely depict the entropy and collapse of the old social order in the warlord period. In the 1930s he became the titular head of the Chinese League of the Left-Wing Writers in Shanghai. **(C)** Lao She (1899–1966) was another highly versatile writer, noted particularly for his novel *Camel Xiangzi* (sometimes given as *Rickshaw Boy*) tracing the gradual descent and death of a rickshaw puller. His play *Teahouse* traces the history of the first half of the 20th century through a group of friends who gather regularly at a Beijing teahouse. Here he tends his home garden in 1964, two years before his death during the Cultural Revolution. **(D)** Perhaps China's most famous woman writer of the mid-twentieth century, Ding Ling (1904–1986). Writing women's lives at a time when feminism was increasingly rooted in progressive Chinese intellectual circles, her most influential early work, "Miss Sophia's Diary," traces the coming of age of a young woman in a brutally repressive family environment. Joining the Communist Party, she periodically ran afoul of its leadership for her outspoken critique of Party actions toward women.

been written through the lens of Confucian values emphasizing familial and societal hierarchy. Yet the perception of extreme oppression of women through the centuries has also been tempered by scholarship in which women exert considerable agency on a number of fronts. Women in Shang and early Zhou times led armies and held high office, though by late Zhou times a new male political exclusiveness had also manifested itself. As we saw, however, there had been a loosening of such restraints during the Tang—including a powerful woman ruler—and scope for a small number of women to achieve literary fame even during the Song. Among China's many rural peoples and minorities, women spirit mediums and shamans held a revered place in local folk religions. Some scholars have also suggested that it is misleading to interpret the division between the inner (home) sphere dominated by women and the outer sphere dominated by men as hierarchical. Both men and women, the argument goes, recognized the primacy of the home and family in relation to the outside world.

Thus it can be argued that the roles of men and women in imperial China viewed through a more culturally "China-centered" lens were far more complementary than previously supposed by outside scholars. Nonetheless, as the nineteenth century wore on, the exposure of increasing numbers of overseas Chinese and official travelers to Western ideas and social norms suggested that the drive for social and political emancipation of women in the West was a source of strength to be examined and perhaps emulated. Li Gui, for example, in his examination of the American Centennial, wrote a highly favorable essay on the Women's Pavilion there and strongly advocated educating Chinese girls and cultivating their skills for self-strengthening. He even expressed qualified support for women's suffrage and office holding.

Support for women's education in the service of political and social reform was also taken up by Kang Youwei and Liang Qichao in the 1890's. Moreover, the turn of the century education reforms dismantling the old Confucian academies resulted in a push for women's education and the founding of girls' schools and academies. Indeed, entire new fields in education and journalism opened up for Chinese women in the first decades of the century. As we saw at the beginning of this chapter, this was the world in which young Qiu Jin was absorbing radical politics and, on returning from Japan, fomenting revolution as headmistress of a girls' school. The question of the purpose of women's education and emancipation, however, increasingly moved to the fore. For the male advocates of feminism, especially Kang and Liang, and the poet Jin Tianhe (1873–1947), who saw in European suffrage movements appropriate models, women's emancipation was part of the larger drive for modern nationhood. Even Qiu Jin, immersed in feminism and revolution, saw women as leading the struggle for national regeneration, rather than for the sake of their own emancipation and self-recovery.

More far reaching in her radical thought was the anarchist-feminist He (Yin) Zhen, 1874–1947. Influenced by the growing force of labor struggles both world-wide and in China's small industrializing sector, He-Yin Zhen was among the first to locate the phenomenon of a gendered work force in pre-capitalist and pre-industrial China. In essays such as "On the Question of Women's Liberation" and "On the Question of Women's Labor" she asserts that the fundamental issue is not class but the more basic one of "the problem of livelihood". In this respect she uses the philosophical dualism of male/female (*nannü*) as her mode of analysis. Similarly, in critiquing her male counterparts like Liang Qichao, she situates the oppression of women not as a symptom of social inequality but as its underlying cause. Thus, revolution and suffragism may be worthy goals but they will be at best only a partial liberation. In later works her anarchism emerges more prominently as she calls for anti-militarism and the disbanding of armies.

Social Change in City and Country

The frustration of He Yin-Zhen, Lu Xun and others with what they saw as China's glacial pace of social change notwithstanding, China's urban areas were undergoing a profound transformation in their architecture, material culture, and amenities. This in turn had a marked effect on the pace of social and cultural change in the major cities. Although traditional social mores were still very much in evidence, China's major urban centers began to look more and more like their Western and, especially, Japanese counterparts.

Nowhere was this more in evidence than in Shanghai, "the Paris of the Orient." Although the most modern sections of the city were to be found in foreign enclaves such as the International Settlement and the French Concession, most of the city had electrical service, modern advertising media such as billboards and neon signs, electric streetcar lines and busses, high-rise buildings with elevators, and department stores. Shanghai's port facilities and the Bund, which thoroughly resembled a European port rather than an East Asian one, were among the most modern in the world. Although China's other major cities were somewhat behind Shanghai in these areas, Tianjin, Guangzhou (Canton), Beijing, and Nanjing were all in the process of installing these amenities.

Much had changed culturally in the cities as well. As both Qiu Jin's and Ding Ling's experiences had shown, the treaty port cities were the places that provided not only refuge from China's confused politics, but also the most modern social, political, and cultural trends. Although plenty of traditional practices—concubinage, arranged marriage, informal bond servitude, private vendettas, and so forth—could still be found there, they were also the hotbeds of radical politics and bohemian lifestyles. Bars, nightclubs, dance halls, cinemas, and posh modern and traditional restaurants could all be found as well. Like Ding Ling, many women of the new generation born after 1900, caught between the glimpses of modernity they had in newspapers, magazines, and movies, and the insistence of their extended families

The Modern City: Scenes of Shanghai Life. Shanghai in the 1920's and 1930's had grown into the booming "Paris of the Orient," and its modern conveniences and amenities set the pace for urban development for all of China's large cities. In the three photographs here, we see **(A)** the notable European style architecture marking the Huangpu waterfront of one of its main thoroughfares along the Bund; **(B)** the mixed traffic of street cars, automobiles, and pedestrians on a typical street; and **(C)** the contemporary fashions of young urban women with unbound feet wearing heels and some sporting the Chinese contribution to modern elegant dress, the *qipao.*

on Confucian morality, fled to the transforming cities seeking the freedom they promised.

Fashion tended to reflect this as well. The political act of cutting off one's queue after 1911 completely changed men's hairstyles for the remainder of the century. Men increasingly abandoned the traditional gowns and adopted Western style shirts and trousers, suits, and leather shoes. Even more striking were women's fashions. Stylish urban women were bobbing their hair in the 1920s like their foreign counterparts; some adopted the short dress of "flappers." Others adapted the more traditional women's gowns by shortening them and putting slits in the side to reveal the leg, creating the famous *qipao*. Many also began to wear foreign-style heels—especially as bound feet were rapidly going out of fashion. Women and men both avidly took up smoking cigarettes and it was considered the height of chic behavior to enjoy the latest cocktail with a cigarette in a nightclub and dance, even with strangers.

Although these practices helped mark in even bolder relief the divide between urban and rural life, there was also something of a reaction against it even in the cities. The most visible element of this came from Chiang Kaishek's abortive **New Life Movement**. Many Chinese commentators noted that with the collapse of Confucianism, there was nothing to provide a unifying philosophy of life for the nation. It is worth noting that the same critique is often made about today's China as making money has supplanted ideology as societal motivation. Chiang's solution was to promulgate a code of behavior and vision of the world that borrowed from European fascist nationalism, military discipline, and Confucian ethics. The aim was to forge a philosophy embodying what he considered the best of the Western and Chinese traditions. In addition to dedication to the nation, the New Life Movement emphasized the small things that would in time lead to a more ordered and efficient society: good personal and dental hygiene; sobriety; no spitting or urinating in the street; keeping fights and loud arguments to a minimum. Guidelines were even given for the proper lengths for women's dresses and the size of the side slits in them. A set of loosely affiliated groups advocating this conservative and nationalist approach was ultimately knit together by the GMD in its semiofficial arm called the Blue Shirts—not unlike Hitler's S. A. Brown Shirts or Mussolini's Fascist Party Black Shirts. Indeed, the comprehensive control that Chiang enjoyed as president, commander in chief of the armed forces, and head of the GMD was in many ways comparable to that held by those other leaders. Moreover, he expressed his support for fascist practices on a number of occasions.

For China's vast majority of rural peasants, however, relatively little changed. Despite the verbal support consistently given to the idea of land reform as a key element of the Three People's Principles and a number of promising ventures involving model farms and cooperatives, the GMD government remained constrained by a lack of finances and the pressures of civil war, encroachment by Japan, and suppressing or winning over the surviving warlords. Chiang's primary base of support, moreover, was the urban bourgeoisie, whom he continually squeezed for revenue. Thus, the land reforms of Mao's Jiangxi Soviet stood in marked contrast to the bootless efforts of the Nationalists. Nonetheless, the period saw a number of demographic and sociological studies of rural life, most notably by Fei Xiaotong and the one-time husband of the novelist Pearl S. Buck, John Lossing Buck. What the studies revealed, however, was the utter destitution of large areas of the country punctuated by small isolated regions of relative prosperity. Absentee landlordism grew markedly, migration to cities increased, and the people, preyed upon by warlords and revolving-door kleptocratic governments during the decade from 1916 to 1926, found only pockets of respite during the "Nanjing Decade" from 1927 to 1937.

WAR OF RESISTANCE, COALITION, AND RENEWED CIVIL WAR

Japanese troops moved on Beiping and attacked Shanghai in the summer of 1937 followed soon by methodical attacks on most of the Chinese ports. Chinese resistance was stiff in the opening months, particularly at Shanghai. The Japanese, however, were able to use the big guns of their fleet, as well as their superior mobility and air power, to flank the Chinese forces and force them to retreat toward the capital at Nanjing. Knowing that the capital required a determined stand, Chinese forces dug in, but also took the precaution of moving the government far west to Chongqing (Chungking), where it would remain for the duration of the war. After a week-long siege, Nanjing surrendered. Realizing the need to defeat China as quickly as possible to avoid a war of attrition, the Japanese subjected the capital to the first major atrocity of World War II: the Rape of Nanking.

The Rape of Nanking and the Great Retreat

Although scholars are still debating the exact number of casualties, it is estimated that between 200,000 and 300,000 people were systematically slaughtered in Nanking (Nanjing) often in deliberately gruesome ways: being hacked to death, burned alive, buried alive, used for bayonet practice, and beheaded. Rape was used as a strategic weapon to further terrorize and humiliate the populace. There were instances of officers engaging in beheading contests, the running totals of which were followed in the sports pages of Japanese newspapers. In at least one case, an officer challenged a colleague to cut a man in half lengthwise with one stroke of his sword.

Like the deliberate bombing of civilians by both Axis and Allied air forces later in the war, however, the killing in Nanjing resulted in the exact opposite of its intended effect. Instead of crushing Chinese morale, the orchestrated slaughter galvanized Chinese resistance. Continually harassed as they retreated from Nanjing, the Chinese, like the Soviets a few years later in the face of Nazi invasion, pursued a scorched-earth policy of trading space for time to regroup. In an epic mass migration, Chinese soldiers and civilians stripped the land of every usable article—including the invaluable contents of the Palace Museum—and moved it ultimately to the remote region around Chongqing. While there were

The Rape of Nanking. The mass, orchestrated slaughter of hundreds of thousands of men, women, and children following the Nationalist surrender of the capital at Nanking (Nanjing) to the Japanese expeditionary force in December, 1937, was the first major atrocity of World War II. Called by some today "the forgotten Holocaust," it was, however, widely reported at the time with extensive photographic and newsreel footage. Japanese commanders urged their men on to brutal torture and execution, using rape in particular as a means of spreading mass terror. In the grisly photo above, a group of severed heads marks the spot of one such execution. Beheading contests between Japanese officers were routinely organized and even followed in the Japanese press.

several large hard-fought battles with the Japanese involving Nationalist and Communist armies over the next couple of years, the Chinese forces for the most part used the vast interior for hit-and-run tactics, effectively limiting the Japanese to the northeast and coastal urban centers. To slow the pace of the Japanese advance from the north, Chinese forces blew up strategic Yellow River dikes, flooding vast amounts of land along the North China Plain. Increasingly, however, the Nationalist forces faced resupply problems that prevented them from mounting large, sustained offensives.

For their part, the Japanese, aware of the dangers of a long war with China, made several peace overtures. Since these insisted on recognition of Manchukuo and Chinese cooperation under Japanese leadership, however, Chiang Kai-shek refused them. In 1938, the Nationalist official Wang Jingwei (1883–1944) broke with Chiang and urged acceptance of the Japanese proposals. In 1940, Wang emerged as the head of the collaborationist "Reorganized National Government of the Republic of China," under the slogan, "Peace, Anti-Communism, National Construction." The new government claimed to represent those areas under

Japanese occupation outside of Manchuria and lasted until a few days after the Japanese surrender in September, 1945.

Japan faced international condemnation for its invasion and nowhere was this more true than in the United States. The day before Nanjing surrendered, Japanese planes sunk an American gunboat, the U.S.S. *Panay*, despite the large American flags painted on its decks, while it was evacuating foreign civilians from the war zone. Although the Japanese apologized, it ratcheted American anti-Japanese feeling up considerably. The United States, Britain, and France repeatedly demanded that Japan stop the war over the next several years, but by 1939, both sides had settled into a stalemate. With the coming of World War II in Europe and the Rome, Berlin, Tokyo Axis in 1940, Japan acquired powerful allies, and with the defeat of the Netherlands and France that year, the position of those countries' Pacific colonial empires now became imperiled.

The war in China severely drained Japan of material and human resources. Many of those resources—oil, tin, rubber, rice—were in ample supply in French Indochina and the Dutch East Indies. The Japanese swiftly acquired air and naval bases in Indochina from the French Vichy occupation government as a first step toward domination of the region. American protests and sanctions put mounting pressure on Japan to find a way to finish the war. Their solution was to cripple American air and naval power in the Pacific by the attack on Pearl Harbor and the Philippines of December 7–8, 1941, and launch an all-out offensive to capture the resources of the region over the next six months.

The Pacific War

As one wry observer in Chongqing put it, "Pearl Harbor Day in America was VJ (Victory over Japan) Day in China." At one stroke, China's allies now included two of the world's most powerful military and industrial powers, Britain and the United States. The War of Resistance Against Japan now expanded to include the Pacific War. Assured of ultimate victory and with a small but growing supply of Lend–Lease equipment coming by air into "Free China," Chiang could bide his time, not overly risk his forces, and consolidate his hold to resume the civil war when Japan had been defeated. Meanwhile, the tiny but effective fighter squadrons of the American Volunteer Group—the famous "Flying Tigers"—were soon vastly supplanted as the U.S. Fourteenth Air Force. In addition, under the direction of General Joseph "Vinegar Joe" Stillwell, Chinese troops were being trained by U.S. forces in the latest weaponry and tactics. With the coming of the new B-29 long-range bomber, the first systematic American raids on Japan would fly from Chinese airfields in June 1944. Japan's response was a major offensive to take the airfields. Not long after, however, American planes would subject Japan to massive incendiary raids from bases in the Marianna Islands.

Flying Tigers; Chinese Forces Training with U.S. Instructors. (A) The official name of the "Flying Tigers" was the American Volunteer Group. Formed in the fall of 1941 before American entry into the war, the group was put together by Claire Chennault (1893–1958), who was retired from the U.S. Army Air Corps and hired by Chiang Kai-shek to rebuild a Chinese air force that had been decimated by the Japanese. Scraping together a force of mercenary pilots flying obsolescent early model Curtiss P-40 fighters, the Flying Tigers developed highly effective tactics against the far more maneuverable Japanese fighters. Adopting the tiger as their symbol, they also painted fierce shark faces on the noses of their planes. After the American entry into the war, the group was absorbed into the U.S. Army Air Forces, and was outfitted with newer, faster, better armed models of the P-40, but retained its distinctive nose art. Here, Chinese armourers of 74th Fighter Squadron inspect a P-40 at the Flying Tigers' base in Kumming on February 1st 1943. **(B)** Both Allied war planners and Chiang Kai-shek had hoped that China would be a central part of the offensive against the Japanese once Britain and the U.S. entered the war. However, the logistical difficulties of supplying Chinese forces and the American strategy of approaching Japan through "island hopping" militated against a massive U.S. presence on the Asian mainland. Nonetheless, a concerted effort to train Chinese soldiers in modern weaponry and tactics was launched by the Americans under the command of General Joseph Stillwell, nicknamed "Vinegar Joe" for his directness and acerbic sense of humor. Though Stillwell spoke Chinese and had spent time in China, he and Chiang disliked each other intensely, so much so that Chiang eventually had him replaced. Here, in a lighter moment, Stillwell shares a laugh with Chiang and Madame Chiang, with Madame diplomatically linked arm in arm with both men.

If the Nationalist strategy against Japan tended to be defensive and conservative, the Communist forces had no alternative but to be more aggressive. In many important respects, Japanese strategy played remarkably into Mao's hands. In fact, some scholars have asserted that it was the war with Japan that really saved the Communist movement in China. The Japanese pursued a "points-and-lines" occupation strategy of northern China, preferring to take towns and cities along major road and railroad lines. This left vast swaths of territory potentially in the hands of the mobile guerilla bands of the CCP's Eighth-Route and Fourteenth-Route Armies. Moreover, to cow the populace, the Japanese favored the "Three-All Policy": kill all, burn all, loot all. The few survivors of these attacks were purposely left to tell their neighbors the horrors they could expect if they resisted the Japanese. More often than not, as with atrocities in Nanjing, they induced local people to join the CCP resistance instead. By the time of Japan's surrender in September 1945, the CCP's control extended over most of northern China and about 100 million people.

U S S R
MONGOLIA
MANCHURIA (MANCHUKUO)
REHE
KOREA
JAPAN
Sea of Japan
Yellow Sea
CHINA
PACIFIC OCEAN
South China Sea
INDIA
BURMA
SIAM (THAILAND)
FRENCH INDOCHINA
PHILIPPINES
Bay of Bengal
Hainan
Taiwan
Hami
Baotou
Beijing
Tianjin
Taiyuan
Lanzhou
Yan'an
Xi'an
Nanjing
Shanghai
Hankou
Chongqing
Fuzhou
Amoy
Kunming
Ledo
Dacca
Lashio
Guangzhou
Nanning
Hanoi
Hong Kong (British)
Vladivostok
Tokyo
N
W
E
S
0 km 500
0 miles 500
Japan in China, 1931–45
Japanese Empire up to Sept. 1931
Japanese protectorate from 1932 (Rehe 1933)
Area occupied by Japan by Dec. 1941
Area occupied by Japan Jan. 1942–Aug. 1945
Direction of Japanese advance
Shaanxi-Gansu-Ningxia border region under Communist control
Communist offensive against Japanese 1940
Main supply routes from Allies
Jiangxi Soviet
Long March (April 1934–Oct. 1935)

MAP 6.5
Japan in China, 1931–1945

To the Gate of Heavenly Peace

Chiang Kai-shek and Madame Chiang Kai-shek had become international celebrities by 1943 as well as symbols of a free, modernizing, and democratizing China. Chiang was *Time* magazine's "Man of the Year" a number of times during the 1940s and Madame Chiang had brought a joint session of Congress to its feet with her pleas for increased aid to China. More important for the course of the war and immediately afterward, Chiang's position as an ally of equal standing with Winston Churchill of Britain and Franklin Roosevelt was validated at the Cairo Conference in November 1943. As part of the understanding that emerged among the three leaders, Nationalist China would get both Manchuria and Taiwan back from Japan, Korea would be made independent, and China would be recognized as the new dominant power of East Asia. Of enormous practical and symbolic importance was that just over a hundred years after the Treaty of Nanjing, the United States and Britain abrogated all unequal treaties—including the Boxer Protocols—and abandoned the principle of extraterritoriality for their citizens in China. Shortly thereafter, the United States also loosened its restrictions somewhat on Chinese immigration.

Although the China–Burma–India theater was a vital one to the Allied war effort, for the Americans it remained secondary to their drive through the Pacific to move on Japan. American, British, Indian, and Chinese troops fought the Japanese in Burma to reopen the Burma Road to supply China. Moreover, the war in China tied down perhaps 2.5 million Japanese troops and so made the opposition in the Pacific that much thinner. But the hopes of many planners for a much more decisive Allied effort in China were frustrated by logistical and political difficulties that nearly proved insurmountable. For most of the war, only the barest trickle of American supplies could be flown into China over "the Hump," the 20,000-plus-foot barrier of the Himalayas. Given China's immense materiel needs, one commentator likened it to "feeding an elephant with an eye-dropper."

The political dimension was less straightforward and in many ways more difficult. Given China's history with foreign encroachment, Chiang was understandably worried about a large American presence in China. Stillwell, for his part, detested the generalissimo, a sentiment echoed by Chiang toward his American counterpart. Ultimately, Chiang succeeded in having Vinegar Joe replaced. The ongoing need for effective intelligence on the actual situation in China, however, and the ways in which a more effective Sino-American strategy might be pursued resulted in several high-value observers being sent to report on the situation.

Three important events in 1944 set the stage for both countries' approach to the final year of the war and toward coalition building. In June, Roosevelt sent his vice president, Henry Wallace, to Chongqing to confer with Chiang in hopes of developing a more coordinated war strategy and to discuss the postwar world. At the same time, a team of U.S. military observers code named "Dixie Mission" was detached to Yan'an to observe Mao's forces and discuss supply and strategic matters with them. A few months later, brigadier general Patrick Hurley met with both Chiang in Chongqing and Mao in Yan'an to begin the cooperative end game against

Japan. Hurley came away with an agreement from Mao of continued cooperation with Chiang and the United States to work for Japan's defeat. It was believed at the time that this might be the basis for a coalition government at war's end.

When the end came in August–September 1945, the situation in China was enormously confused. The Soviets had, per the Yalta Agreement in February 1945, come into the war against Japan three months after Germany surrendered, which coincidentally was two days after the first atomic bomb was dropped on Hiroshima. They immediately drove deep into Manchuria. Mao's forces moved swiftly to take Japan's surrender there, and Chiang prevailed on the United States to airlift his forces there as well. On arriving, the Chinese found that the Soviets had stripped nearly all the industrial equipment from the region and carried it back to the USSR. Both sides adopted a wary truce over the next several months. The Americans, anxious that a united China dominate the region in the postwar order, sent the secretary of state, (General) George C. Marshall, to China in an attempt to work out a compromise between the antagonists. In January 1946, both sides agreed to a set of preliminary steps toward creating a coalition government, and a People's Consultative Conference promulgated plans to recognize all political parties and nationalize all the armed forces. By the end of the year, however, both sides had broken on when to call a National Assembly to put together a new constitution. The Nationalists called it for the end of December, and when the CCP boycotted the proceedings, the Nationalists pushed through their own constitution.

Fighting between the two groups, which had continued sporadically during the negotiations, now began again in earnest. Marshall frantically tried to embargo U.S. aid to either side, but the State Department, despite many of its representatives favoring the CCP's position, ultimately tilted toward Chiang. By 1947, with the tensions of the developing Cold War rapidly increasing and the United States pursuing a policy of "containment," aid to Chiang was increasingly seen as part of a world strategy to reign in the expansion of the Soviet Union and Communism more generally.

Mao and Chiang Toasting Coalition Government. The Second United Front of Nationalist and Communist forces had remained shaky all through the war and had already begun to unravel by the final days of the conflict. In a desperate attempt to mediate, the American Secretary of State, General George C. Marshall attempted to steer both sides toward a coalition government. In this ironic photograph from September, 1945, Mao and Chiang toast each other in the euphoria of victory over Japan. They would shortly be at war again for the final time.

Mao's conception of "people's war," as noted earlier, had three distinct stages. Although Mao's forces had considerable success with the guerrilla phase against Chiang's repeated encirclement campaigns the 1930s, the fact that the Japanese were extraordinarily cruel foreign invaders had made it even more effective. Thus, as the civil war resumed in 1946, the CCP had made huge gains during the war and were moving into the next phase of people's war: equality of forces. At this stage, where both sides are roughly equal in strength, the former guerrilla forces feel freer to attack their enemy in more conventional fashion, even engaging them in positional battles when the odds are favorable. As we saw above, the advantages growing from this situation are a much wider set of available military choices, a larger and more secure base area for supplies and support, and the realization on the part of both sides that the momentum has shifted, and with it the morale of both sides as well.

Despite the material superiority of the Nationalists and their still potent but withering American resupply efforts, the PLA had moved into its strongest position by mid-1947. Mao's forces increasingly dominated the rural areas, where its land reform efforts stimulated the revolutionary zeal of the peasants. For their part, the Nationalists, who had tended to see the cities and towns as their strongholds, retreated to these base areas and left increasingly large expanses of countryside in the hands of the CCP.

By ceding these areas, however, the Nationalists, already having created bad blood in a number of places including Taiwan, where they quashed an independence movement after the Japanese surrender, allowed themselves to be economically strangled. Through 1947 and 1948, the CCP-held areas launched an embargo of goods to urban areas, causing immense inflation on a par with the German hyperinflation of the early 1920s and sowing panic among the populace, now swollen with refugees. The United States, seeing that there was now no hope of salvaging the Nationalist position, cut off aid amid bitter recriminations that would continue on a low boil through the 1950s over "who lost China."

In January 1949, PLA forces occupied Beiping. Chiang Kai-shek resigned the Republic of China's presidency. Through the next several months the large cities fell and the Nationalist forces scattered, some changing sides, some simply surrendering, and others going home. Toward the end of the year, several large units moved down into remote Yunnan and northern Burma and Thailand. Already many were being evacuated to Taiwan, where, with renewed American aid, they would build a Nationalist redoubt and Chiang would spend his final years in the frustrated hope of going back to retake the mainland.

For his part, Mao would mount the enormous Gate of Heavenly Peace, the great portal through which one must pass to enter the old Forbidden City, and announce the founding of the new PRC on October 1, 1949. And although the Nationalists are no longer the only political party on Taiwan and those who once represented mainland Republic of China districts in the Legislative Yuan in Taipei are long gone, the two rival claimants for the "real" China still face each other in mutual competition across the narrow strait separating them. Their ultimate disposition awaits resolution sometime in an uncertain future.

PLA Forces Entering Beijing. Despite the large amounts of modern American equipment and control of China's major cities, the Nationalist forces were outmaneuvered and strangled by CCP control of the countryside. Here, victorious Communist troops enter Beijing on May 2, 1949. On their banner are pictures of Mao Zedong in the center, flanked by his generals Lin Biao (left) and Zhu De (right).

CONCLUSION

The period from 1900 to 1949 was perhaps the most politically convulsive and culturally diverse era of modern China. It began with the Boxer War, China's last attempt under the Qing to forcibly resist foreign encroachment, and each passing decade of the first half of the twentieth century saw a major conflict: the Xinhai Revolution, the Warlord Era, the Northern Expedition, the Nationalist/Communist civil war, the war with Japan, and the reprise of the civil war. The pattern of incomplete revolution begun with the founding of the Republic in 1912 continued throughout the period against a backdrop of continuous warfare. The GMD unification was never stable enough, nor were its finances, to ensure uniform development of all sectors of the polity and economy. Perpetually in debt, Chiang Kai-shek's government, increasingly reliant on a cobbled-together ideology of fascist discipline and Confucian morality, could point to few comprehensive accomplishments before the Second United Front and war with Japan.

World War II, however, put Chiang's China, however flawed, into the position of a major power and, with the end of the war and the beginning of the Cold War, a key recipient of American support. Even after Chiang's defeat and flight to Taiwan, that support continued although in progressively reduced form. Although both Chiang and Mao Zedong claimed the mantle of Sun Yat-sen, it would be Mao's PRC that would ultimately emerge as the major power.

FURTHER READING

Buck, John Lossing. *Land Utilization in China*. Chicago: University of Chicago Press, 1938. A classic of sociology and demography, Buck's study encompassing tens of thousands of rural farms in 22 Chinese provinces gives us the most complete snapshot of China's rural conditions before land reform under the People's Republic.

Esherick, Joseph. *Reform and Revolution in China: The 1911 Revolution in Hunan and Hubei*. Berkeley: University of California Press, 1976. The 1911 Revolution has been comparatively underexamined and this volume represents a pioneering effort.

Levine, Marilyn A. *The Found Generation: Chinese Communists in Europe during the Twenties*. Seattle: University of Washington Press, 1993. Interesting account of the little-known experiences of young Chinese radicals studying in Europe, many of whom had served in the Labor Corps during World War I.

Liu, Lydia H., Karl, Rebecca E., and Ko, Dorothy, eds. *The Birth of Chinese Feminism: Essential Texts in Transnational Theory*. New York: Columbia University Press, 2013. Seeks the radical, transnational roots of Chinese feminism in the writings of He-Yin Zhen. The authors include an authoritative introduction and explication of the intellectual climate in turn of the century China and translations of He-Yin's works with a comparative analysis of essays by Liang Qichao and Jin Tianhe.

McCord, Edward A. *The Power of the Gun: The Emergence of Modern Chinese Warlordism*. Berkeley: University of California Press, 1993. The most thorough monographic treatment of the individuals and the period. Examines military and political motivations of the major actors. Sees the pattern of warlordism as a symptom and failed attempt at a solution of federalism to the collapse of the Republic.

Salisbury, Harrison E. *The Long March: The Untold Story*. New York: Macmillan, 1985. Solid, well-written account of the Long March by a veteran New York *Times* reporter who retraced the route and interviewed veterans and locals along the way. Reflective of interactions between Western reporters and party members during the early days of the Four Modernizations as well.

Shoppa, R. Keith. *Chinese Elites and Political Change*. Cambridge, MA: Harvard University Press, 1982. An early work in which the author uses a microregional approach in a study of Zhejiang Province. The regional zone and analysis of identity is used as well in his text, *Revolution and Its Past*.

Taylor, Jay. *The Generalissimo: Chiang Kai-shek and the Struggle for Modern China*. Cambridge, MA: Harvard University Press, 2009. Magisterial biography of Chiang by a former State Department official and author of a biography of Chiang Kai-shek's son, Chiang Ching-kuo. Sees Chiang as a far more complex and important figure than he is generally portrayed as.

Tuchman, Barbara. *Stillwell and the American Experience in China, 1911–45*. New York: Macmillan, 1971; Grove Press, 2001. Pulitzer Prize–winning work of popular history. Traces Stillwell's career as a military "China hand" in the years before World War II and his especially stormy relationship with Chiang Kai-shek.

Waldron, Arthur. *From War to Nationalism: China's Turning Point.* Cambridge, U.K.: Cambridge University Press, 1995. Looks at the critical events of 1924–1925, especially the May Thirtieth Movement, the death of Sun, and the introduction of increasingly radical nationalism as precipitating factors.

Xu Guoqi. *Chinese and Americans: A Shared History.* Cambridge, MA: Harvard University Press, 2014. Examines a number of case studies of Chinese in America and Americans in China. Particularly good in looking at the influence of Frank Goodnow on Yuan Shikai's efforts to revive the monarchy and the influence of John Dewey on the New Culture Movement.

CHAPTER 7

THE PEOPLE'S REPUBLIC: THE MAOIST ERA, 1949–1976

While Mrs. Yang went off to the Neighborhood Committee to listen to documents about the proletarian dictatorship over class enemies, her husband stayed at home to nurse a bad cold and listen to the radio. When she came back, she found him sitting at the table, white faced and sweating, clutching the radio. "It's over," he told her with a look of terror. "Oh my God in heaven, it's all over for us now." Ever in frail health, that night her husband became horribly ill, delirious with fever. He was finished by sunrise. Before the storm hit he was literally frightened to death. . . . Mrs. Yang sighed. "He was lucky of course."

She went on to describe the fate of her daughter, who was now badgered incessantly in school to condemn her parents:

At first I tried to soothe her but that only made her angry; she would denounce me in her sleep. . . . Then one evening I awoke suddenly. The room was strangely still. I sat up very quietly to see. Her bed was empty . . . the floor was covered by all her crumpled papers, her confessions from the evening. The window was opened. And on the desk was an empty bottle of liquid pesticide. . . . Her body washed up against a factory sewage pipe the next day.

—from Liang Heng and Judith Shapiro, *After the Nightmare.*
New York: Macmillan; Collier Edition, 1987, pp. 106–7

The story of Mrs. Yang was repeated hundreds of thousands of times during China's Great Proletarian Cultural Revolution, which officially lasted from 1966 to 1969, although its aftermath continued until the death of Mao Zedong in 1976. It was conceived by Mao and a small group of his supporters as a way to purge the CCP and the country at large of alleged "bourgeois" traits and Soviet-style "bureaucratism" that had manifested themselves during the leadership of Liu Shaoqi (1898–1969) in the early 1960s. After carefully cultivating PLA chief Lin Biao, who made the famous "little red book," *Quotations from Chairman Mao Zedong*, required reading, Mao launched a political assault on his party opposition accompanied by appeals to the "masses" and pushed the PRC to the brink of civil war.

In swift order millions of school-age Red Guards attacked their teachers under Mao's call for "permanent revolution." Soon all authority was under siege by Peoples' Neighborhood Committees and local ad hoc tribunals. Those with any foreign contacts or supposed bourgeois tendencies were required to write endless self-criticisms, often suffering continual physical abuse and public humiliation during "struggle meetings" in which their erstwhile neighbors and colleagues accused them of a wide variety of ideological crimes. Many died in the process or, like Mrs Yang's husband, succumbed from sheer terror in anticipation of what was to come. Some, like Mrs. Yang's daughter, committed suicide; others, like future Chinese leader Deng Xiaoping, were "sent down" to the countryside to "learn from the peasants" by doing hard manual labor. By 1969, with pro- and anti-Maoist army units fighting each other in some areas and the country on the verge of collapse, Mao declared the Cultural Revolution completed. Two years later, Lin Biao died in a plane crash—possibly shot down—attempting to flee the country.

The Cultural Revolution represents both the climax and the finale of the pattern of Mao's rule by mass mobilization. The years from 1949 to 1976 saw constant government campaigns to enlist the citizens of the People's Republic in everything from volunteering to fight the United States in Korea, to eliminating vermin, to land reform and collectivizing agriculture, critiquing party performance—and suppressing those who spoke up. As we saw in the opening vignette of this chapter, the pattern included repeated attempts to completely eliminate the last vestiges of "feudal" and "bourgeois" thinking while catapulting China directly into complete socialism. The rationale for such programs sprang from several related sources: Mao's belief in the "mass line": suggestions and reports on conditions were to be collected and assessed by party cadres, who passed them up to the party leadership, where they would be analyzed and made into policy—"from the masses, to the masses." Mao's vision of China as "poor and blank" was also an important factor: China may be impoverished, he said, but in a way this is an advantage in building a new society: like a blank sheet of paper, the possibilities are open-ended to write the most beautiful characters on it.

Finally, what really mattered in building New China, Mao asserted, was the proper attitude rather than immediate technical expertise. If one believed and acted as a good Communist—that is if one were properly "red" rather than merely "expert"—then the technological problems would ultimately be solved by the wisdom and talents of people properly led. Thus, with a different ideology, the argument follows the earlier pattern of the nineteenth-century debates between the self-strengtheners and the Confucian fundamentalists (see Chapter 5). One could even say that this pattern's interactions and adaptations have continued to this day: during the Mao years the slogan was "politics takes command" and the reds had the upper hand, whereas during the brief Liu Shaoqi period the experts gained ground. The Cultural Revolution again

Images of the Cultural Revolution. The Great Proletarian Cultural Revolution, lasting from 1966 till 1969—though continuing many of its programs until 1976—was perhaps the most disruptive ideological campaign of the Maoist era. In the poster on the top left (**A**), we see a typical idealization of Mao and his writings as the sun that lights the way to socialism for workers and peasants carrying the "little red book," *Quotations of Chairman Mao Zedong*. The poster, from May, 1969, bears the slogan "Long Live Mao Zedong Thought!" In photographs (**B**) and (**C**) ideological victims are paraded through the streets in the bed of a truck and displayed on a platform before jeering mobs denouncing them for the crimes of "rightism" and "following the capitalist road" proclaimed by the signs they wear around their necks. (**D**) In the last photograph, the cult of Mao and his appeal to the youth of the country to foment "continuous revolution" is depicted in his meeting a crowd of the Communist Party's youth group, the Young Pioneers. Mao has donned the neckerchief of the Pioneers for the occasion.

sought to make "political correctness" (the original meaning of the term) the guiding force. Then, after 1978, the momentum once more shifted toward expertise during Deng Xiaoping's Four Modernizations. Even now the struggle to balance proper ideology with keeping China's economy surging and building technological prowess remains the chief preoccupation of the party leadership.

"FROM THE MASSES"—CREATING THE PEOPLES' REPUBLIC, 1949–1961

As we saw in the previous chapter, Japan, having encroached on China since the Sino-Japanese War of 1894–1895 and annexed Manchuria in 1931, launched a major invasion of China in July 1937. Occupying the major coastal areas and interior cities in a thin "points-and-lines" configuration, they maintained a short but brutal colonial regime from 1937 to 1945. Japan's defeat in World War II by the Allies shortly led, despite two American attempts at creating a coalition government, to the resumption of the Civil War between the GMD and the *Gongchandang*, the CCP. In 1949 the Communists finally prevailed after four more years of fighting.

"We Have Stood Up"

On October 1, 1949, Mao Zedong addressed a crowd from atop the Gate of Heavenly Peace that guarded the old imperial Forbidden City in Beijing and announced the founding of the People's Republic—a date that ever since has been celebrated in the PRC as "National Foundation Day." To this day as well has persisted the assertion that he uttered that day the most famous statement of the end of China's "century of humiliation." In fact, however, it was a little more than a week before, on September 21, during the People's Political Consultative Conference, that he said "Ours will no longer be a nation subject to insult and humiliation. We have stood up."

Within days, the Soviet Union and nearly all of the Communist Bloc countries had recognized the new government. Within a year, most of the Western European countries—including Great Britain—and India and Pakistan had also extended their recognition. The United States, however, refused and insisted on maintaining diplomatic relations with the Nationalist's Republic of China as the legitimate Chinese government. Despite repeated requests from the PRC's new foreign minister, Zhou Enlai, the United Nations, under American pressure, refused to seat the PRC representatives and retained those of Chiang Kai-shek's regime. Chiang himself fled the mainland city of Chengdu on December 2 for Taipei (*pinyin*, Taibei), Taiwan, to regroup and attempt to continue the fight from there. He would never set foot on the mainland again.

MAP 7.1

The People's Republic of China and the Republic of China, 1950

The task of rebuilding the country that now fell to the new government was a formidable one. As Mao went on to say in his Consultative Conference speech, "Our revolutionary work is not completed." The civil war had further exhausted the national resources from their already minimal levels at the end of World War II. Even more than Russia at the time of the Bolshevik Revolution, China was still fundamentally a peasant-based country with perhaps 80 percent of the population involved in agriculture. What industry existed was concentrated in or near the major cities, especially Shanghai. Hong Kong and Macau remained European colonies. Much of the industry developed by the Japanese in Manchuria had been stripped and carried away by the Soviets in the last days of World War II.

As we have seen, the interaction of Marxism-Leninism and the reality of Chinese economic conditions had resulted in the key adaptation of Mao's theories of revolution putting peasants instead of industrial workers at the forefront of the movement toward socialism. Although this appeared to work as a strategy for revolution in a peasant-based society, it was still an open question as to whether it would work in rebuilding the infrastructure and economy of the country as a whole. Would it be possible, for example, to leapfrog from agrarian feudalism, with only a nascent bourgeoisie, directly to socialism? Would it be necessary to create a degree of bourgeois capitalism first to have enough industry to "socialize?"

Mao therefore decided that now that the party controlled urban and industrial areas, the government would, much like Lenin's New Economic Policy for Bolshevik Russia in the early 1920s, encourage a degree of capitalist flexibility among the "patriotic bourgeoisie." The official policy was thus labelled New Democracy: ". . . a dictatorship of the united front of all the revolutionary classes under the leadership of the proletariat," whose initial task was "to complete China's bourgeois-democratic revolution." Only then would conditions be ripe for the transition to socialism. Against this backdrop the Korean War and the drive to complete land reform on a national scale inaugurated the party's mass line politics.

The Opening of the "Mass Line": Resist America—Aid Korea

During the 1950s, a central aspect of Mao's theories was the idea that the Chinese people were really the only reliable resource the country possessed. Lacking a workable industrial and transportation base, China's early Maoist years thus were marked by a pattern of repeated mass mobilization campaigns. Among the initial ones were the "Resist America–Aid Korea" campaign in support of Chinese intervention in Korea; the Three-Anti and Five-Anti campaigns against corruption, bureaucratism, and economic crimes; and the national effort at land reform.

Emboldened by American statements suggesting that the northeast Asian mainland was outside the U.S. "defense perimeter," the Democratic People's Republic of Korea (North Korea) launched an invasion of the Republic of Korea (South Korea) in June 1950 in an attempt to unify the peninsula. The Democratic People's Republic of Korea forces initially seemed on the verge of victory, quickly taking Seoul and pushing the Republic of Korea and U.S. forces into a small perimeter around the southern port of Pusan. Under General Douglas Macarthur, still directing the Allied occupation of Japan, a daring amphibious assault was launched at Seoul's port city of Inchon and the North Korean forces were routed. The struggle became an early test of the UN Security Council, which, with the Soviet Union boycotting the vote in protest, branded North Korea an aggressor and sanctioned international intervention in what was termed a "police action."

The People's Republic, however, became alarmed as the UN forces were driving deep into North Korea and approaching the Yalu River border with China. Moreover, Macarthur was quoted as desirous of attacking the PRC, and the U.S. Navy had sent its Seventh Fleet into the Taiwan Strait in an effort to shore up the ROC. In October 1950, a massive Chinese force of "People's Volunteers" crossed the border and attacked the UN forces in North Korea. By November the Chinese forces under the able commander Peng Dehuai (1898–1974) were pushing the UN forces back into South Korea. As part of the seesaw fighting over the next three years, UN troops pushed the Sino-Korean army out of Seoul in March 1951 and the fighting stalemated around the 38th Parallel dividing north from south. Seoul itself would change hands yet again before the armistice was signed.

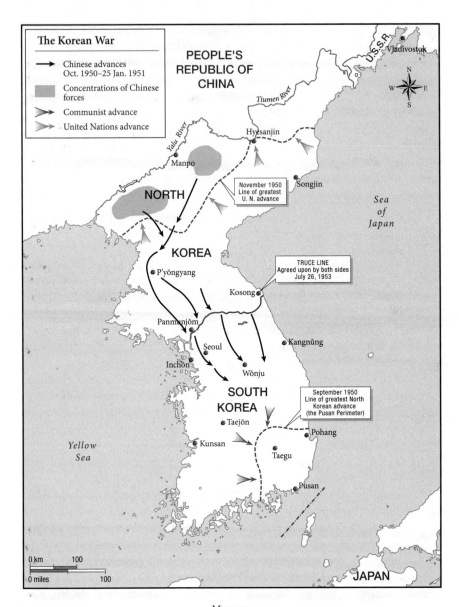

MAP 7.2
The Korean War

In support of the Chinese effort in Korea, the People's Republic mounted the **Resist America–Aid Korea** mobilization campaign. The campaign's aims were to break down latent friendly feelings toward the United States because of past ties of business, immigration, and the World War II alliance against Japan, as well as any remaining pro-GMD sentiment. Party workers carried out propaganda initiatives insisting on solidarity with Korea and all socialist states, called

全力支持抗美援朝志顾军部队

Chinese Troops in Korea. The drive of U.N. forces in Korea toward the Chinese border prompted a counteroffensive by PRC forces called the People's Volunteer Army, and a mass campaign called "Resist America, Aid Korea." This poster done in the Socialist Realist style, pictures a PVA infantryman outlined against a rising sun and bears the slogan, "Support the Resistance to the USA with All Your Strength and Aid the Volunteer Army!"

for volunteers for the army, and encouraged citizens to ferret out those with American ties or suspicious activities or ideas. Several alleged spy rings were broken up and their members executed, and the program merged with a more general effort to eliminate "counterrevolutionaries." Yet it was also the case that the success of the Chinese against the modern, well-equipped U.S./U.N. forces gave a thrill of pride to Chinese people even outside the PRC. Moreover, it generated considerable initial support for the other mass campaigns of the 1950's. For many it was the most convincing sign yet that China had indeed "stood up."

San Fan/Wu Fan: The Three-Anti and Five-Anti Campaigns

The **Three-Anti and Five-Anti campaigns** were aimed at consolidating party supremacy in government and the economic sector. As we have seen, the party had initially encouraged patriotic bourgeoisie to reopen factories and industrial enterprises and was willing to tolerate a certain degree of capitalism to stimulate the economy, restore a degree of urban normality, and reassure overseas Chinese and foreign investors as to the new regime's intentions. The war in Korea and the hardening of Cold War positions, however, cut this short.

Toward the end of 1951 the party announced the "Three-Anti" (*san fan*) campaign: Anticorruption; antiwaste; anti-"bureaucratism." The number of officials had ballooned as the party moved into all areas of the country and took over each level of administration. In addition, there were officeholders who were not party members and a considerable number—90 percent in some cities—who had been in the GMD and changed sides during the final years of the civil war. This campaign therefore aimed to purge nonparty members, test the loyalty and reliability of party officials, and eliminate real and potential GMD sympathizers. In much the same way as the Resist America campaign, citizens were pushed to denounce bureaucrats for assorted crimes. They would be "struggled," humiliated, imprisoned, fined, and, in some cases, executed.

Within months, in January 1952, the party launched the Five-Anti (*wu fan*) campaign. The economics of the New Democracy had never been subject to a consistent program or approach. Policy tended to be ad hoc and reflected the Party's conflicted approach toward market economies, priorities in developing different sectors of the economy, and the persistence of bourgeois values. In a pattern that Maoist-era Chinese painfully learned to anticipate, therefore, the Five-Anti movement targeted capitalists and patriotic bourgeoisie that it had previously encouraged. The items to be opposed in this campaign were bribery, theft of state property, tax evasion, cheating on government contracts, and stealing state economic information. Party cadres and volunteers went door to door to interrogate business owners and encouraged employees to write letters outlining their bosses' offenses. As Mao ominously put it, "We must probably execute ten thousand to several tens of thousands of embezzlers nationwide before we can solve the problem." Indeed, by 1953 the government had effectively reined in the business community and had begun the process of nationalizing most of its assets. Despite the disruptions of the campaign, however, China's industrial production increased markedly during the first half of the 1950's.

Toward Collectivization I: Land Reform

The largest campaign by virtue of the vast number of peasants in agrarian China was land reform. How best to divide and utilize farmland had been a problem faced by every Chinese dynasty, often with excessive landlordism seen as a primary culprit in its unfair distribution. As we saw in the previous chapter, Sun Yat-sen had designated "the people's livelihood" as one of his "Three People's Principles" and championed a reform scheme based on the ideas of the American economist Henry George. Mao's idea, which had been pursued previously in the areas controlled by the party, was much more direct: expropriation of landlord holdings and distribution of that land directly to tenants and the landless.

In June 1950, the new government enacted the **Agrarian Reform Law**, under which "the system of peasant land ownership shall be introduced." Not only was the land of landlords to be confiscated, but also that of monasteries and religious institutions was to be taken over and distributed to the poor and landless. Party cadres moved into the remaining untouched rural areas and proceeded to expropriate land and divide it among the local peasants. "Patriotic landlords" who voluntarily submitted to the process were for the moment accorded relatively lenient treatment. Those who resisted, or were disliked by their tenants, like the targets of other campaigns, were struggled. They were commonly trussed up and made to kneel while cadres urged their tenants to verbally and physically abuse them. They were then often summarily executed by the cadres or lynched by their former tenants. By some estimates, land reform took as many as 2 million lives.

Land Reform with a Vengeance. In this photograph from 1952, a farmer kneels at gunpoint before a Communist court enforcing land redistribution policies. Like thousands of others, the landowner was convicted of being a "class enemy" and was executed.

Peasant land ownership, however, caused agricultural productivity to increase markedly. By 1952, the government announced that land reform had been completed and that the national budget was balanced and commodity prices were stabilized. Since so much of the livelihood of the country and the revenues to fund industrialization hinged on agriculture, land reform was seen as the first step toward collectivization, which, it was believed, would result in far greater efficiency and yields. Indeed, one encouraging sign of the success of the program thus far was a contract to export 100,000 tons of rice to India.

First Five-Year Plan and Soviet Aid

Meanwhile, with land reform accomplished, China's first five-year plan went into effect in 1953. The Five-Year Plan was part of a "general line" initiated by the party to "basically . . . accomplish the country's industrialization and the socialist transformation of agriculture, handicrafts and capitalist industry and commerce over a fairly long period of time."[1] As with the Soviet model in the 1930s, the immediate goal was the ratcheting up of heavy industry with a secondary emphasis on light industry and consumer goods. The Soviet presence in China was unprecedented in its size and scope. China sent nearly 40,000 people to the USSR for training, while more than 11,000 Soviet technical advisors came to China during the decade. During the First Five Year Plan, Soviet advisors worked on 156 separate development projects in China. China received a loan from the Soviet Union for the construction of power stations and began operations at its first open-pit coal mine. A Joint Commission for Cooperation in Science and Technology was set up in 1954 and oversaw research on over a hundred different projects, including those related to nuclear technology. In all, between 1950 and 1959 China received approximately 1.4 billion dollars in aid from the Soviets.

Toward Collectivization II: From Producers Cooperatives to the Great Leap Forward

With the first steps in place to put the general line into operation, party leaders decided it was time to move ahead toward the "socialist transformation of agriculture." The party leadership felt that by going slowly and consolidating their gains at each step they could greatly ease the transition. Thus, in 1953 peasants were encouraged to form "agricultural producers cooperatives" in which villages would form units to share scarce tools and machinery. Those who joined were given incentives in the form of better prices and tax breaks. By 1956, agricultural production had recovered to pre–World War II levels and was registering impressive gains.

China's agricultural progress notwithstanding, Mao and his inner circle were growing impatient with the pace of collectivization. If production could be ramped up sufficiently, the surplus agricultural funds from taxes and exports could then be used to fund a more ambitious Second Five-Year Plan. Moreover, the Chinese had been borrowing heavily from the USSR through the 1950s and had availed themselves of Soviet technicians and engineers. All of the progress of the decade might be radically slowed or halted if agricultural revenues could not keep pace. Finally, with agricultural and industrial production keeping pace with each other, bottlenecks in agricultural raw materials for things like textiles had developed.

---

[1] From Colin Mackerras and Robert Chan, *Modern China: A Chronology from 1842 to the Present*, San Francisco: Freeman, 1982, p. 455.

Mao therefore prodded the party into its most colossal mass mobilization project yet: **the Great Leap Forward**, which was in effect the Second Five-Year Plan, slated to start January 1, 1958. The entire population of the country was to be pushed into a campaign to communalize agriculture into self-sustaining units that would function like factories in the fields. Men and women would work in shifts and live in barracks on enormous collective farms. In Mao's view the campaign would not only vault China into socialism but also go far toward eliminating "contradictions among the people" that were key impediments to such a transition: among them the contradiction between urban and rural, between industrial and agricultural, and between mental and manual labor. A more diffuse contradiction it might also eliminate was that between ideology and economic development, since the two would be combined in one movement. In addition, creating an industrial infrastructure in rural areas would reduce the amount of investment diverted from industry to agricultural development.

By way of bringing the industrial to the agricultural, peasants were to surrender all their iron and steel tools and utensils to be melted down and recycled into steel to build the new infrastructure of the communes. A stated goal of the campaign, in fact, was to surpass the steel production of Great Britain within 15 years. The most recognizable symbol of the campaign was the backyard steel furnace, which commune members were to build and run for their own needs. In keeping with the Red approach to the program, technical problems were to be solved by the "wisdom of the masses." The entire country would therefore modernize its rural areas and infrastructure in one grand campaign. Moreover, with industry decoupled from the urban areas, the communes would begin to generate the amenities of city life on their own, thus reducing and ultimately eliminating the rural/urban contradiction. Similarly, with the entire country yoked to the program, the intellectuals as a class would be thrust into the world of manual labor as they "learn from the peasants," and their expertise would help drive the program and aid in the educational needs of the countryside and so eliminate the mental/manual divide.

Predictably, the Great Leap was the most catastrophic policy failure in the history of the PRC. Knowledgeable critics of its utopian features had been cowed into silence by the Anti-Rightist campaign (see later), and the initial wave of enthusiasm that greeted the mobilization swiftly ground to a halt as peasants began to actively resist the seizure of their land and implements. The quality of almost all of the steel produced was virtually worthless, and the effort used a considerable amount of precious coal. Moreover, in sacrificing scarce tools and kitchen utensils, millions of peasants now had few or none to use in farming or everyday chores. So many were forced into building the communal structures and making useless steel that by 1959 agricultural production in China had plummeted and the country experienced its worst famine in modern times over the next several years. Among the other factors involved in this disaster were an extraordinary interval of bad weather; over-reporting of grain production—encouraging the government to

Eliminating Contradictions: The Great Leap Forward. The Great Leap Forward was an economic and social campaign of the Communist Party, reflected in planning decisions from 1958 to 1961, which aimed to use China's vast population to rapidly transform the country from an agrarian economy into a modern communist society through the process of rapid industrialization, and collectivization. **(A)** Employees of the Shin Chiao Hotel in Beijing build small, rudimentary steel smelting furnaces in October 1958. **(B)** In this photo from April 1958, villagers welcome the arrival of tractors to their cooperative. **(C)** Workers labor on the huge Sanmenxia Dam project on the Yellow River. The Great Leap Forward did not work as planned. By 1962, famine cost China some 30 million lives.

requisition larger amounts than could be sustained—and excessive requisitioning from the most accessible areas. By 1962 an estimated 30 million people may have died in the wake of the GLF.

Blooming and Contending: The Hundred Flowers and Anti-Rightist Campaigns

In May 1956, long before the disaster of the Great Leap and with the progress of land reform and the agricultural producers cooperatives cause for optimism, Mao felt the time was opportune to take the temperature of the nation's intellectuals, industrial leaders, and opinion makers. Many had initially been enthusiastic about the general direction of the party and socialism in general, but Mao was not sure whether they were really behind the programs or simply being circumspect. Some were disappointed with the pace of development promised by the "socialist transformation of industry in commerce," and the effects of increased state ownership of industry. The experience of earlier mass mobilizations had made many anxious about being designated as class enemies as per the party's inclinations. The international scene, including the revolt in Hungary against the Soviet-backed regime there and de-Stalinization under Khrushchev all caused a degree of anxiety in the Party. Moreover, Mao's attitudes toward the intelligentsia tended to be antagonistic: later, during the Cultural Revolution, he would call them "the stinking ninth category" of the "Nine Black Categories" of the people's enemies.

Nonetheless, the party proceeded to apply the "mass line" technique to the intellectuals: teachers, professors, writers, editors—opinion makers of any kind. Adopting a slogan from China's philosophically rich Late Zhou period, "Let a hundred flowers bloom, let a hundred schools of thought contend," they threw open the door to public criticism of the party's record, assuring the intellectuals that offering their critique was patriotic. By mid-1957 the trickle of criticism had become a torrent. Significantly, students at Peking University, the center of the May Fourth Movement less than four decades before, began hanging "big character posters" on what would become the first of several "democracy walls" over the coming years. Many criticized policies toward intellectuals and the politicization of education. When some critics questioned the basic foundations of socialism and suggested forming an opposition party, Mao acted swiftly. In early June, the **Hundred Flowers** campaign was terminated and the **Anti-Rightist** campaign was launched. Calls for an opposition party were denounced as the worst kind of right-wing thinking—as opposed to the correct left-wing thinking of the party. Those accused of "rightism" were rounded up and subjected to "reeducation": in addition to being imprisoned and made to endure endless "self-criticism" sessions, many were also sentenced to long stretches of "reform through labor" in remote peasant villages. Ironically, it was the "expert" Deng Xiaoping, later the architect of China's market economy, who supervised this crackdown on ideological dissent.

REACTION AND CULTURAL REVOLUTION, 1961–1976

The miscalculations of intellectual sentiment during the Hundred Flowers program and the hasty capping of it by the Anti-Rightist campaign marked the first large misstep for Mao's road to socialism. The Great Leap Forward debacle of the following year convinced even many of Mao's closest supporters that the party needed to change its path. Thus, 1959 saw a major shakeup in party and national leadership. Peng Dehuai, highly respected for his leadership during the civil war and in Korea, was especially vehement in his criticism of Mao and the Great Leap. Mao showed Peng's private letter to him to his Politburo colleagues and solicited opinions about possible courses of action. Peng was then dismissed as PLA head and replaced with Lin Biao. Mao had already announced that he would not stand for another term as PRC chairman. Liu Shaoqi, whom Mao in a few years would denounce as the "number one person taking the capitalist road," and "China's Khrushchev" now became chairman. His new state council included Madame Sun Yat-sen (Soong/Song Qingling)—whose sister, Soong/Song Meiling, ironically enough, was Madame Chiang Kai-shek—and the new army chief, Lin Biao, who would soon play a central role in Mao's comeback and the Cultural Revolution that followed.

China's "Thermidorean Reaction," 1960–1966

The new regime, ratified at the party conference at Lushan in August 1959, represented a tilt toward the expert camp and, as such, has been called by some scholars a **Thermidorean Reaction,** though others dislike the term as redolent of later Maoist and Red Guard hyperbole. Its origin lies in the French Revolution and refers to the swing away from the most radical phase, the Reign of Terror, toward the more conservative rule of the Directory in July 1794, the month of Thermidor in the French revolutionary calendar. Thus, China's first decade under Mao's brand of Communism—with its pattern of mass mobilization and proper political attitude over technical expertise—was dialed back considerably. Over the next several years, Chinese Communism would swing toward a less "red" and a more expert approach to modernization. Although disagreements with the Soviet Union would result in the Sino-Soviet split of 1960, education would recover somewhat and China would register some key technological breakthroughs—including a nuclear device. Mao, however, disillusioned with the party's new direction, would plot his political comeback, which culminated in the Cultural Revolution of 1966.

The turbulence of the first round of the Maoist years ebbed considerably under the leadership of Liu Shaoqi. The decade began, however, with the "Sino-Soviet split," in which Soviet apprehensiveness about China's radical programs and Mao's distrust of Soviet policy changes under Khrushchev led to a complete withdrawal of Soviet aid and advisors in 1960. The Chinese had earlier been taken aback by Khrushchev's denunciation of Stalin's excesses in his "secret" speech of 1956. Because the Soviets also appeared to be softening their stance toward the United States, the Chinese felt that the USSR had departed from Lenin's "correct" views on capitalism and imperialism. For their part, the Soviets, faced with the prospect of nuclear war with the United States according to the American policy of "massive retaliation," felt that Mao had been irresponsibly cavalier in his pronouncements, especially his 1957 speech "American Imperialism Is a Paper Tiger." Here Mao asserted that he was not afraid of a nuclear war even if half of China's population were killed. For Western observers accustomed to seeing the Communist world as a "monolith," it was the first real divide among ideological allies since Tito's independent stance in Yugoslavia in 1948. By the end of the decade, Chinese and Soviet forces would be exchanging fire along several disputed border crossings.

Nonetheless, the early 1960s saw a reassertion of the need for education and technical training in China under Liu, and China made several important technological advances. Chief among these was the detonation of China's first nuclear device in October 1964. This was quickly followed by the testing of a thermonuclear (hydrogen) bomb in 1966. Chinese scientists also synthesized insulin and made advances in missile technology that would yield the first Chinese satellites in the following decade. Extensive studies of China's natural resources also disclosed large coal deposits and led to the discovery of oil fields at Daqing and in the extreme west. These years were also marked by a drive for economic stability in the wake of the difficulties of the Great Leap and famine. In 1962 Liu Shaoqi and Deng Xiaoping announced a series of agricultural reforms under the guidance of Chen Yun (1905-1995) that allowed for some private ownership and encouragement of local markets. There was also more flexibility of decision-making within the larger state-owned enterprises. These policies in many respects anticipated, although in a very modest way, the reforms of Deng's later Four Modernizations. The economy did in fact stabilize considerably, despite the withdrawal of large amounts of Soviet capital and technical assistance.

Liu's regime also engaged in a more assertive policy of border rectification. Chinese forces had entered Tibet in 1959 to suppress an independence movement, resulting in the flight of the Dalai Lama to India. In securing Tibet, however, disputes arose regarding the actual border with India, aggravated by India's granting of asylum to the Dalai Lama and those who fled with him. To bolster its claims on the border area in question, the Indian Army established a number of forward bases and posts. In October, 1962, Chinese forces moved into the disputed regions and fought a month-long undeclared war until withdrawing and submitting the issue to negotiation. This kind of display of force to make a point would be seen again in Vietnam in 1979, although with far less effectiveness.

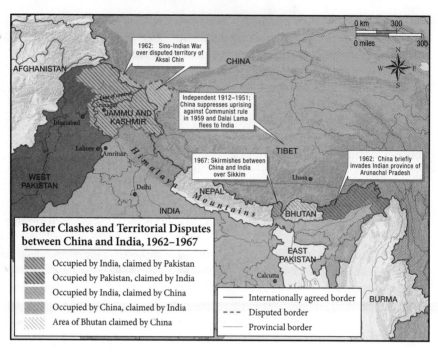

Border Clashes and Territorial Disputes between China and India, 1962–1967

- 1962: Sino-Indian War over disputed territory of Aksai Chin
- Independent 1912–1951; China suppresses uprising against Communist rule in 1959 and Dalai Lama flees to India
- 1967: Skirmishes between China and India over Sikkim
- 1962: China briefly invades Indian province of Arunachal Pradesh

Border Clashes and Territorial Disputes between China and India, 1962–1967

- Occupied by India, claimed by Pakistan
- Occupied by Pakistan, claimed by India
- Occupied by India, claimed by China
- Occupied by China, claimed by India
- Area of Bhutan claimed by China

—— Internationally agreed border
– – – Disputed border
·········· Provincial border

MAP 7.3
Border Clashes and Territorial Disputes between China and India, 1962–1967

The Cultural Revolution

As China's Communist Party and government assumed a more Soviet-style approach to running the PRC, Mao Zedong grew increasingly uneasy about the direction of policy. Though recent scholarship his emphasized the Stalinist tendencies in Mao's rule, there were aspects of the Soviet Union, especially its top-heavy bureaucracy, that Mao found especially distasteful. For Mao, the CCP was reverting to bureaucratic behavior and becoming increasingly unresponsive to the needs of advancing the revolution toward pure Communism. Mao's position of politics taking command was in direct opposition to the increasingly technocratic stance he saw in Liu Shaoqi's policies. Moreover, he was especially disturbed by Liu and Deng's back-peddling on communal agriculture and state control of the economy. Although out of power, Mao was still revered in party circles as the great revolutionary leader, the "indispensable man" who had led the movement from certain destruction in 1934, through the exodus of the Long March and the War of Resistance against Japan, to ultimate triumph in 1949. In plotting his political comeback, therefore, he played to his seemingly unassailable strengths as an exponent of selfless Communist virtues.

Mao spent the early 1960s writing widely circulated essays extolling the virtues of devoted Communists and creating a new base for himself, especially among younger party members. Two endeavors along the way were a reissue of Mao's elegiac 1939 piece, "In Memory of Norman Bethune," and 1963's injunction in *Chinese Youth* to "Learn from Comrade Lei Feng." Both were pointed examples of selfless service: Norman Bethune (1890–1939) was a Canadian doctor who worked with Mao's Communists during the period of their bleakest prospects; Lei Feng (1940–1962) was a young PLA soldier who died sacrificing himself to save others. Both were held up as models of how to "serve the people" (*wei renmin*), thus bringing to the fore the virtues of "redness" during a time when experts held sway. Lei Feng, in fact, became the model for a popular movement in the early 1960s and helped to place Mao once again at the center of party activity.

Perhaps the most important step in this regard was the publication of his famous **little red book**, *Quotations from Chairman Mao Zedong*, in 1964. His ideological ally, Lin Biao (1907–1971), as head of the PLA, made it required reading for the troops and helped Mao establish a vitally important power base in the world's largest military force. Among the more famous statements of Mao's revolutionary thinking to be found in this work are the following:

Learn from Lei Feng. In the "Learn from Comrade Lei Feng" campaign, initiated by Mao Zedong in 1963, Lei (1940–1962) became a national symbol of sacrifice. His image was one of a selfless, modest man devoted to the Party and the people, and was held up as an example for the youth of China to aspire to follow. Lei was reportedly killed in an accident while on duty when a truck he was directing backed into a telephone pole and killed him. Scholars are dubious about good deal of his legend, some questioning that he ever actually lived.

> The people of the countries in the socialist camp should unite, the people of the countries of Asia, Africa, and Latin America should unite . . . all peace-loving countries should unite, and all countries subjected to U.S. aggression . . . should unite and so form the broadest united front to oppose the U.S. imperialist policies of aggression and war and to defend world peace . . .

> Every communist must grasp the truth, "Political power grows out of the barrel of a gun."

> A revolution is not a dinner party, or writing an essay, or painting a picture, or doing embroidery; it cannot be so refined, so leisurely and gentle, so temperate, so kind, courteous, restrained and magnanimous. A revolution is an insurrection, and act of violence by which one class overthrows another.

By the spring of 1966, Mao was ready to put some of these words into action. Mao's central idea was that of "continuous revolution": that the class struggle must go on until true socialism—as opposed to the bureaucratic Soviet model—had been achieved. To do this, the people must be inculcated with "proletarian consciousness" and purged of the last vestiges of feudal, bourgeois, and revisionist thinking. Only with such an all-pervasive revolutionary proletarian consciousness could China make the final leap to complete socialism. The Party Politburo therefore announced the **Great Proletarian Cultural Revolution** and set up a Cultural Revolution Group. In a communication later known as the May Seventh Directive, Mao wrote to Lin Biao that the PLA must learn politics, military affairs, and culture: it was to be "a great school." In July, Mao made his famous swim in the Yangzi to, among other things, quash doubts about his age and health affecting his ability to lead. It marked the beginning of an enhanced cult of personality increasingly surrounding the Chairman during the campaign. Mao quickly followed this action up by resurrecting the use of big-character posters with his own titled "Bombard the Headquarters" of the party, which he felt needed to be purged of "reactionary elements" and those engaged in bourgeois thinking.

Increasingly, this meant Liu Shaoqi, Deng Xiaoping, and others in the expert category. By the beginning of August, the Politburo issued the "Sixteen Points" to guide the conduct of the Cultural Revolution, and on the 18th, a rally of more than a million was held in Tiananmen Square. The party announced the formation of the Red Guards and Mao donned the Guards' red armband as a symbol of solidarity, calling on the nation's youth to rededicate themselves to continuous revolution. They were encouraged to criticize their elders and form their own pure ideological path to socialism. Students formed themselves into squads of Red Guards and attacked their teachers and elders. Soon, Red Guard units were formed in most of the country's institutions and were given license to ferret out and struggle anyone they judged to be insufficiently supportive of the program. As we saw in the opening vignette to this chapter, those with any foreign connections or who had supported the former regime, or were perceived to be tainted by bourgeois or feudal thinking or simply lukewarm in their support for the present campaign, were singled out for public interrogation and humiliation.

Teachers were trussed up, made to wear dunce caps with their "crimes" emblazoned on placards around their necks, and splashed with ink as they were paraded through the streets. Hundreds of thousands of people from all walks of life were struggled before jeering crowds and made to confess their alleged crimes over and over. Millions were required to write constant self-confessions of their ideological misdeeds. Vast numbers of young people responded with enthusiasm to Mao's injunction to "learn from the peasants" and embarked for rural areas to work on farms. As in past campaigns, millions more of the less fortunate were sentenced to be "sent down" to work on farms or subjected to "reform through labor."

Red Guards and the Cultural Revolution. Two of the most visible symbols of the Great Proletarian Cultural Revolution of the 1960s were the omnipresent "little red book," of Mao Zedong's quotations, and the youthful, rampaging Red Guards with their distinctive armbands. (A) In this photograph from 1969, PLA soldiers do some required reading of Mao's thoughts. (B) Red Guards wave the book at a rally in Tiananmen Square in the summer of 1966, in front of the famous Gate of Heavenly Peace (Tiananmen) topped by Mao's portrait.

PATTERNS UP CLOSE

From "Socialist Realism" to "History as a Verb": The Odyssey of Hung Liu

History, as we have seen, is an elusive thing. Some might even say the idea of a "useful past"—one common definition of history—is itself an illusion. History is a moving target whose meanings can be driven by present concerns, by antiquarianism, by national and cultural priorities, by perspectives of race, class, and gender; by the desire to have at best—or worst—what the noted iconoclastic historian Carl Becker once called the "most convenient form of error" to fall back on.

As has been evident throughout this book, nowhere is the control of history more vital to understanding and regulating the present than in China. Thus, each dynasty, as well as the Nationalist and Communist governments, has customarily written the history of its immediate predecessor and seen it as a palimpsest to erase and rewrite that history in such a way as to legitimate its assumption of power. As we saw in the opening vignette to this volume, the new dynasty is invariably pictured as reforming the abuses of the last days of the one before it, thus fulfilling Heaven's Mandate. One could therefore say of the Chinese historical view what William Faulkner famously noted in his story, "Requiem for a Nun": "The past," he said, "is never dead. It's not even past."

For millions of Chinese, the traumas of the Cultural Revolution, although their pain may be numbed by the passing years, are not past either. From the great portrait of Mao that hangs from *Tiananmen*—the Gate of Heavenly Peace—to the square of the same name directly across the street that holds the chairman's mausoleum, the reminders are all around. The artistic style of the Cultural Revolution, Socialist Realism, may still be seen in paintings, posters, and even such cultural artifacts as fringed Mao portraits hanging from the mirrors of some taxicabs. They are hawked incessantly at the Great Wall and other tourist attractions. One popular recent variation is a T-shirt with a Maoist motif but with the head of U.S. president Barack Obama replacing that of the chairman. For the young these things often have a certain *kitschy* appeal; for older people they are stark reminders of the mass campaigns that caused such suffering and turmoil.

For one noted Chinese artist now working in the United States, Hung (*pinyin*, Hong) Liu, the past remains embedded in the present as well. As her husband, the art critic Jeff Kelly, points out, the Cultural Revolution is her artistic baseline. Born in 1948, her life spans that of the PRC, and before she arrived in the United States in 1984, her experience, training, and work—her entire education—like that of so many members of China's "lost generation," paralleled the violent political swings of the Maoist years.

For Hung this meant, among other things, seeing one of her teachers leap from a window after being hounded by his students. As with so many idealistic youth, Hung also responded to Mao's call to "learn from the peasants" and went to the countryside, where the realities of grinding farm work quickly set in. For her it was also the time of her initial education in the propaganda of the day, especially the stilted Socialist Realist style of Mao portraits, robust, happy peasants, brave male and female PLA soldiers combatting capitalist enemies, and "the masses" marching forth to build

Hung Liu (1948–). Hung Liu was raised in the People's Republic and underwent an art education in the Socialist Realist style of the 1950's and 1960's, and the Revolutionary Romanticism of the Cultural Revolution. Her experiences during the Revolution pushed her in a direction that ultimately led her to the United States. Her art at present seeks to recover history from early photographs of Chinese subjects that she then overlays with painting in traditional Chinese techniques to bring out the inner being of her subjects and have them become beyond time and history. Pictured above is her *Jade Lady* (2006).

continued

socialism. She also absorbed the rules of the ultrarigid Revolutionary Romantic, or Socialist Idealist, style championed by Mao's wife, Jiang Qing, at the peak of the Cultural Revolution. Even during this time Hung was working from photographs in her art and her interpretation of her experiences and reaction against the cultural dictates of this era would form in large part her philosophy and techniques down to the present.

"I am not a camera," she insists. Discovering caches of nineteenth- and early-twentieth-century photos on a return trip to the PRC after becoming established in the United States, she found herself fascinated by the lost history they encompassed. Since then, she has sought to both preserve and destroy the images—to bring the seemingly static frame of the camera into another dimension by means of classical Chinese artistic techniques: fast, spontaneous brushwork and drip techniques to create an effect of "dissolution" on the prints to add visual and emotional depth to them. She seeks to transcend the formal restraints of the old daguerreotypes and sepia-toned period photos—the older ones of which required posing for long minutes— and recover their interrupted history. This is especially true of subjects of great concern to social historians today: women, children, the elderly, laborers—ordinary people at ordinary tasks. By doing so she attempts to give them a recovered dignity and gravitas that makes them somehow extraordinary and central to the new history her brush creates.

In her own words, "I believe my work over the past 25 years bears witness to the liminal, migrating space between collective meaning and personal history." For this artist, whose life's work aims at repudiating the removal of so much Chinese history during the Cultural Revolution, it seems safe to say that she has gone far toward reducing—even closing— that liminal space: in attempting to restore the cultural balance among heaven, earth, and humanity, her use of art as an active form of restoring history has made it in her hands—and in her words—a verb.

An important component of the early stages of the Cultural Revolution was the assault on the **Four Olds**: old customs, culture, habits, and ideas. In addition to the human cost of the movement, a tragic amount of China's cultural heritage— archives, libraries, museums, temples, mosques, churches, monasteries—was lost or damaged as a result of Red Guard rampages aimed at purging the country of feudal vestiges. Confucius came in for particular abuse during this time and later as part of the "Criticize Lin Biao, criticize Confucius" campaign orchestrated in 1973–1974 by Mao's wife, Jiang Qing. The Kong family compound at Qufu in Shandong was repeatedly attacked, as were family members still there, and many priceless genealogical records were lost.

Trauma

From 1966 until 1969, when the Cultural Revolution was declared successfully completed, millions of people were hounded, tortured, killed, or driven to suicide by Red Guards and their allies. The little red book became the talisman of the movement, with people struggling to interpret it correctly to prove their ideological fitness. Study groups sprang up throughout the country because constant and correct reference to the work was mandatory in any discussion. The hermeneutics of Mao's thought became the chief preoccupation of the country. Since many of the quotations could conceivably contain multiple meanings, competitive and antagonistic groups used the work as a hammer to batter their opponents. Score settling among rivals and among neighbors became endemic to the Revolution. Guilt by association or, especially, class background, became a special concern. Those coming from peasant and proletarian backgrounds were among the most favored. Those from the "stinking ninth category"—the intellectuals—on the other hand, came in for special condemnation. This proved especially disastrous for China's educational system because the schools were essentially nonfunctional for several years, and teachers and professors were official pariahs. When things began to settle down in the mid-1970s, the educational system saw an enormous surge in students as those from China's "lost generation" tried to finish school in their twenties and attend university in their thirties and forties.

As the little red book became the central focus of people's lives and the official ideology was listed as Marxism-Leninism-Mao Zedong Thought, the cult of personality surrounding Mao, and now the book, received an enormous boost. People waved it at mass rallies and even attributed magical powers to it. Those engaged in sports read it or even kissed it before events; weight lifters hoisted the book before competing. As the world witnessed these events, with little ability to report them accurately on site, speculation ran rampant as to exactly what was unfolding. This was even true for those countries within the Soviet bloc, toward whom Mao and his new Politburo and Central Committee grew increasingly antagonistic. At one point, during their period of *détente* with the United States, the Soviets approached the Nixon administration about the possibility of a joint preemptive nuclear strike on the PRC. By 1969 armed clashes had already taken place between Chinese and Soviet units along the borders marked by the Ussuri and Amur rivers. The perception of orchestrated chaos in the PRC was captured nicely by the title of a 1967 Emmy award–winning documentary film on modern Chinese history widely used in Western academic institutions at this time: *China: The Roots of Madness*.

The End of the Maoist Era

By 1968 the country was in complete chaos as factions battled each other in several regions, most notably around the cities comprising Wuhan. It was chiefly to end this endemic civil war that the Cultural Revolution was declared over. The next two years, however, saw a vastly enhanced political position for the PLA and

Chinese and Soviet Border Clash. Tensions between China and the Soviet Union increased markedly in the late 1960s as Mao pursued his Cultural Revolution and the Soviet Union sought *détente* with the United States. In 1969, the tensions erupted in open conflict as Soviet and Chinese troops clashed along the Amur (pinyin *Heilongjiang*—"Black Dragon River") and Ussuri Rivers. Here, Chinese troops on disputed Zhenpu Island hold up Soviet helmets punctured by bullet holes on their bayonet points. The poster proclaims: "Down with the new tsars!"

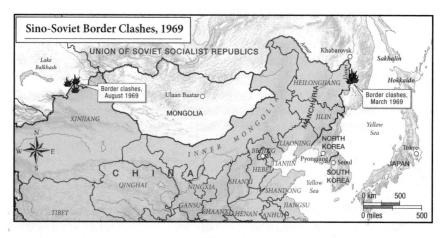

MAP 7.4
Sino-Soviet Border Clashes, 1969

Lin Biao. Despite its own factionalism, the army had played a vital role in suppressing the worst fighting and in restoring a semblance of order in the country. Its role was further enhanced by the need to defend the Soviet border. Thus, Lin Biao was named Mao's "official" successor.

Despite their outward show of unity, Mao periodically had his doubts about Lin's ultimate loyalty to him and his programs. The politicization of the army, moreover, had placed the most powerful force in the land at Lin's disposal and a split was developing between the civilian and military members of the Politburo. Although debate still continues about what happened next, it appears that members of Lin's family and an inside group of supporters planned a coup in which Mao and many of the Politburo would be killed and Lin installed as chairman. Whether Lin was actively involved in the conspiracy or played a passive role is unknown. In any event, on September 13, 1971, Lin and his wife and staff were killed in a plane crash in Mongolia while on their way to seek asylum in the Soviet Union. Fleeing at treetop level to avoid Chinese radar, the plane may have been flying too low, although there is also some evidence to suggest it was shot down.

The final years of Mao's life witnessed a number of contradictory trends, although each in its own way would deeply shape the future of China after the chairman's passing on September 9, 1976. Mao was shaken by the Lin Biao incident, the economy had been severely disrupted by the Cultural Revolution, and much of the party leadership now consisted of radicals who had replaced older members purged during the past few years. Mao's wife, Jiang Qing, along with Zhang Chunqiao, Yao Wenyuan, and Wang Hongwen—reviled shortly after as the Gang of Four (*Siren bang*)—were at the center of the radicals, although it was never clear how much their activities took place at Mao's behest or how much was on their own initiative.

Zhou Enlai, one of the few high party officials to survive every campaign during the Maoist years, brought expert Deng Xiaoping back yet again to help get the economy moving. In so doing, he opened up an ideological battle with Jiang Qing, who sought to communalize China's cities as well as the countryside. She mounted the "Criticize Lin Biao, Criticize Confucius" campaign largely as an attempt to associate Zhou with Lin and to link Zhou with the feudal ideas of Confucius. Mao now attempted to balance both factions, praising the revolutionary ardor of the Gang, while supporting Zhou and Deng's attempts at revitalizing the economy.

In the midst of these convoluted maneuverings, the Nixon administration in the United States launched an epoch-changing initiative to restore relations with the PRC. The United States and many of its allies still recognized Chiang Kaishek's Nationalist regime on Taiwan as the legitimate Chinese government and blocked any attempt to replace it in the UN and on the Security Council with the PRC. Nixon himself had been seen as an arch-anti-Communist Cold Warrior. Yet as he and his national security advisor, Henry Kissinger, realized, reaching out to the PRC might give the Americans powerful leverage (the "China Card") in their dealings with the Soviets. Moreover, a better relationship with China would also be advantageous in the negotiations going on to end U.S. involvement in Vietnam.

Rapprochement. American President Richard M. Nixon's surprise overtures to the People's Republic were quickly followed up by an unexpected visit by the U.S. Table Tennis team, already in East Asia for a match with the Japanese team (above), and a visit by Nixon and an American delegation in February, 1972. Below, the President is introduced to some of the finer points of Chinese cuisine by Premier Zhou Enlai (to the President's left).

In 1971, therefore, Kissinger met secretly in Beijing with Zhou Enlai, paving the way for the dropping of U.S. travel restrictions to the PRC; abandoning American opposition to the PRC entering the UN; arranging for a series of tournaments between the American and Chinese table-tennis teams—the so-called **Ping Pong Diplomacy**—and setting the time for a visit by Nixon the following year.

The 1972 Nixon trip to China and meeting with Mao saw most of the major diplomatic issues resolved and agreement on talks to resolve the remaining ones. In the resulting Shanghai Communique, both sides agreed to mutual diplomatic recognition, which went into effect on January 1, 1979 The issue of Taiwan was finessed by allowing the Nationalists to have a special interests office in place of their embassy in the United States. The United States, for its part, agreed to recognize the PRC as the official government of China. The United States would still provide Taiwan with weapons and defense, a provision that has remained a sticking point with the PRC. Unofficial diplomatic recognition of "the governing authorities on Taiwan" as well as commercial and other ties have been maintained under the Taiwan Relations Act of February, 1979

The deaths of Zhou Enlai in January and Mao Zedong in September 1976 thus mark a true transition in the direction China would take down to the present. As we will see in the following chapter, the last rising of Maoist radicalism would go down to defeat with the arrest and imprisonment of the Gang of Four. After a brief interregnum under the leadership of Hua Guofeng, the irrepressible Deng Xiaoping emerged to move China into a solidly expert direction: the Four Modernizations. These called for opening the country to foreign experts, aid and investment, and creating a market economy—that is, to introduce capitalism. To this day, as China moves steadily toward becoming the world's largest economy, its economic policy is officially called "Socialism with Chinese Characteristics."

SOCIETY AND CULTURE

The early years of the PRC saw some of the most far-reaching social and cultural changes in China's long history. What is equally striking, however, is the tenacity with which older traditions continued in the face of determined efforts to eliminate them. In this respect, Mao's rule was not unlike that of the First Emperor of the Qin—a comparison the Chairman himself made on occasion. The drive to create a new society, a new ideological orthodoxy, and to telescope the process by which the country could achieve "true" socialism—as opposed to what was increasingly perceived as the dead end into which the Soviet Union had stumbled—led to repeated social experiments. Undergirding it all, however, was the struggle in the party between Mao's red adherents and those of the experts, Liu Shaoqi and Deng Xiaoping.

Remaking the Countryside

The continuous fighting in many places from 1911 to 1949 had devastated large stretches of rural China. The war with Japan alone had taken some 14 to 20 million Chinese lives; 7.5 million more had died in the civil war. Although the hyperinflation of the last years of the Communist-Nationalist conflict primarily affected the cities, it did nothing to increase prosperity in the countryside. Thus, as we noted earlier, China's agricultural sector was starting from a historically low base level.

The early mass campaigns therefore had a profound effect in rural areas. The land reform campaign was initially well received. Here, the party had had decades of experience in perfecting techniques of using carrot and stick to expropriate landlord holdings and divide them among tenants. Moreover, Party cadres were skilled in steering the struggle proceedings toward their desired outcome. Cultivating peasant revolutionary spirit meant that landlords were the irrepressible class enemy, in effect rural capitalists. Thus, guilt by class association tended to trump the ethical qualities of individual landlords: even so-called Patriotic Landlords were not immune from the fury of guided tenant mobs. As in the other mass mobilization campaigns aimed at certain kinds of class enemies, long-standing grievances were brutally aired, smoldering feuds brought to reckoning, and old scores settled.

With the exception of more land going into production and the majority of the landless now having a parcel to work, daily life for peasants changed relatively little at this point. While the *danwei* (work unit) system was being set up in cities and towns, rural villages retained their former character as discrete organizational units. The Nationalists had resurrected the old Ming-Qing *baojia* system and this persisted in some areas into the early years of the new regime. Thus, family life centered on the nuclear and extended family in the village—with many villages made up of interconnected families—continued to be the norm. Over time, and with certain periods of interruption, village primary schools became common, as did the famous "barefoot doctors" providing traveling health care.

With the advent of the agricultural producers' cooperatives, the villages became more fully integrated organizational units. Still, because the village had been the traditional node of mutual support among peasants, this innovation lent itself to existing practices. The real changes came with the Great Leap Forward. The propaganda campaign for the program was pervasive and insistent and greeted with considerable initial enthusiasm. The creation of the giant communes, however, with their factorylike schedules, unfamiliar work in steel making, requisitioning of materials and land, and disruption of village and family life, soon made them highly unpopular. Even after the Leap was discontinued, the skeleton of the commune system continued and the practice of paying peasants in work-units for labor and produce would continue until the early 1980s.

Following the catastrophic famine of the early 1960s, rural life settled into a more normal routine as the party under Liu Shaoqi refrained from introducing new mass programs into the countryside. With the Cultural Revolution, however, came large-scale disruption once again. The same struggles between pro- and anti-Maoist factions in the cities played themselves out in rural villages accessible to party cadres. Adding to the confusion were the campaigns encouraging students to go learn from the peasants and the punitive exodus of those who were sent down to the countryside. Villagers often found themselves bewildered when faced with trying to use city dwellers and intellectuals to do farm chores. Many saw it as yet one more unwanted disruption in their hardscrabble existence.

"Contradictions among the People": The Cities

However difficult relations might be between the party and the peasants, it was an article of faith among both that the "rural masses" were the natural allies of the party. The situation was different in the first years of the new regime for city dwellers. China's great cities, particularly Shanghai, had been the Nationalist's primary base of support. Thus, on several levels they embodied Mao's idea of one of the chief "contradictions among the people": the urban–rural divide. The Communists could claim the support of industrial workers and the large floating population of day laborers, service personnel, carters, rickshaw pullers, and so

Re-education, Schools, and Clinics. The Cultural Revolution severely disrupted China's education system as millions of youthful Red Guards denounced and often physically attacked their instructors. The mass campaigns to Learn from the Peasants, Reform Through Labor, and Re-education shook up society even further as millions were in many cases forcibly moved to the countryside. But the political dimension of all the "re-education" also meant that schools were opened up in many areas that had formerly lacked them. Moreover, even with the mass disruptions, the work of the Party's health cadres, the famous "barefoot doctors" continued to bring basic hygiene and healthcare to remote districts. **(A)** Students of a 'May Seventh Cadre School' in Xi'an in 1974 study articles in conformance with Mao's wife, Jiang Qing's "Criticize Lin Biao, Criticize Confucius" campaign. May Seventh Cadre Schools were Chinese labor camps established during the Cultural Revolution that combined hard agricultural work with the study of Mao Zedong's writings in order to 're-educate' cadres and intellectuals in proper socialist thought. In practice, they were closer to forced labor camps. **(B)** Barefoot doctor Zhang Xianghua trains health care personnel at a medical station of Nanniwan People's Commune in May, 1974 in Yan'an, Shaanxi province, Mao's old headquarters. **(C)** A day nursery from 1973.

forth, but the factory owners, bankers, and business people had for the most part been in Chiang's camp. Wary of the ideology of the new rulers, they also considered them rude, crude, unlettered, and violent. Many city-dwellers had fled at the end of the civil war and come back in the early 1950s in response to government promises and a patriotic urge to help build "New China."

Not surprisingly, as we saw earlier in this chapter, many of the first mass mobilization efforts were directed at purging the cities of potential resistance and creating a pattern of setting one group against another to prevent the building of alliances. By the end of the decade, private ownership of property or businesses had been effectively eliminated and the state became the source and controller of employment. Although life in the cities and large towns had basic services and tended to be better than in the rural areas, the infrastructure grew only in fits and starts. Rail service and urban public transport remained at low a level while the bicycle became the favored mode of urban transport. Heat, even in large buildings, was rationed, being turned off in April and turned back on in October. Perforated cakes of pressed coal dust remained the primary fuel for heating and cooking stoves into the early twenty-first century.

Beijing Hutong. The *hutong* with its four dwellings—often occupied by different generations of the same family—surrounding a central courtyard has been the signature Beijing residential dwelling for centuries. As Beijing's phenomenally rapid growth has continued, and the furious building boom accompanying the Olympics in 2008 moved ahead, thousands of hutongs were bulldozed and replaced with high-rise apartment blocks. Many of the surviving ones are now tourist attractions. Pictured above is a view into the courtyard of a traditional hutong home.

Family life in urban areas, although often lacking the deep roots of village China, was still built around the nuclear and extended family. Living space in apartment blocks often made familial closeness problematic. The changes in traditional marriage practices begun at the beginning of the twentieth century continued: a new marriage code in 1950, amended in 1980, made divorce much easier, especially for women. The PRC was formally pledged in its constitutions to female emancipation and gender equality. In addition to having equal political rights, such debilitating practices as concubinage, foot-binding, gambling, and opium smoking had been banned from the beginning. However, it was also the case that the old practices of Confucian patriarchy and of the inner and outer domains remaining separate for men and women lingered on.

Along the way a new conception of the Chinese socialist ideal of marriage and family began to take shape and reached its highest point during the Cultural Revolution. The twentieth century in China had already seen the demise of the old ideal for the well-to-do (for men, at least) of arranged marriage and having a concubine or two in favor of romance and marriage for love as the modern model. For urban women, new personal freedoms in dress and behavior and emancipation from home seclusion and arranged marriage meant a similar kind of agency, even if full equality was not yet a reality.

But the new ideal for the socialist couple went much further. Romance was now derided as a bourgeois affectation, which those involved in building the country and serving the people must discard. Indeed, the ideal mate for a man or woman was an ideologically compatible "comrade" (*tongzhi*). Physical attractiveness, family ties, wealth, personality—all of these were now considered unimportant. Moreover, one should not choose someone from a "bad" class background, but select instead a person your comrades approve of as ideologically sound, politically correct, and imbued with the proper red attitude. Children, for their part, should be brought up to embody these attributes as well. This would be reinforced in the schools, especially when mass mobilization campaigns were underway, by the encouragement of students to observe their parents and report any ideological lapses as a higher duty to the country—as did Mrs. Yang's daughter in the opening vignette to this chapter.

The New Culture: Socialist Realism

As what Marx called an "epiphenomenon" of a given society's economic "substructure," art, literature, and other cultural products had long been considered inherently political. Mao had made this explicit in his widely recognized "Talks at the Yan'an Forum on Arts and Literature" in 1942. Thus, a prime consideration for the leaders of the new state was to articulate a theory of the arts that would make them accessible to and appropriate for ordinary people. Artists would no longer create for elites. They were now to be "culture workers" whose job was to produce revolutionary art that would represent the interests and aspirations of peasants and workers as a class. They were to depict their subjects not only accurately, but also favorably, and to understand their lives as well; hence the logic of encouraging or forcing intellectuals and artists in their role as culture workers to live with the masses and immerse themselves in their worlds so as to reveal them more faithfully. Ideally, such art should also have a kind of global appeal because of the international nature of class struggle. In fact, it should represent the best of Chinese tradition—notwithstanding its feudal and bourgeois origins—and the best of outside influences to create a new revolutionary art form.

Mao himself wrote poetry, much of it derived from incidents during his revolutionary years. The greatest influence overall, particularly on the visual arts—painting, sculpture, and cinema—however, was the Soviet import of **Socialist Realism**. One can still see the most iconic example of this form today in the great portrait of Mao that hangs over the Gate of Heavenly Peace, the portal that marks the entry to the old Forbidden City of the emperors and looks out over another monument to the style, Tiananmen Square (see "Patterns Up Close"). In the square itself, bordered by the country's most important government buildings—in Socialist Realist architectural style—one encounters their sculptural counterpart, the Monument to the People's Revolutionary Martyrs, before coming to yet another example in Mao's Mausoleum. In keeping with the idea that human beings, properly organized and motivated, can overcome any difficulties, the style features people of heroic proportions doing heroic deeds: stoic, smiling soldiers on the march with the people cheering them on; stalwart workers cheerfully laboring on mammoth construction projects; robust, well-fed peasants singing in the fields. The heroic is also brought out in otherwise ordinary themes: Mao addressing his comrades at Yan'an or party cadres teaching literacy to eager pupils in village schools. In one notable poster a PLA soldier enjoys a laugh with a child while cutting his hair as the child nonchalantly holds a toy rifle in his lap over the caption: "The Army and the People are one."

In this sense, art and propaganda become one. The men are always tall and strong; the women are always cheerful and stalwart; the children are innocently enthusiastic about the new order. The subjects are invariably marching forward and human beings are always triumphing over nature—almost the opposite of the imagery in traditional themes of Chinese landscape painting in which tiny human figures are dwarfed by the immensity of nature. The medium of the new art, oil on canvas, is also a departure from the Chinese practice of brush and ink on paper. The minimalist techniques of Chinese painting are abandoned as well in favor of stark detail and bright, even garish colors—particularly red: always an auspicious color in China and now even more so because of its association with revolution.

To be sure, some earlier forms were allowed to continue into the early 1960s. The most prominent practitioner of the old style of brush and ink landscape painting, with commentary or poetry in traditional calligraphic styles on the side, Qi Baishi (1864–1957) was active into his nineties. He, however, was also revered because he had not been one of the elite who practiced the "three excellences" of painting, poetry, and calligraphy as an avocation, but rather had been

Socialist Realist Art. Socialist Realism developed in the Soviet Union and became a dominant style in other communist countries. The style features realistic, though highly idealized subjects such as stalwart peasants smiling and singing at their work, industrial workers joyfully fine-tuning complex machinery, soldiers bravely charging into battle against imperialists, and so forth. In the poster above we see the Social Realist style typical of propaganda art during the Cultural Revolution in an exhibition in Dalian in 1976. The title is, "Cadres Lead by Example in the Building of Dazhai *Xian*," a poor commune in Shanxi Province designated by Mao Zedong in 1964 as an example of revolutionary collective agricultural development to emulate.

an ordinary carpenter whose fame was won by dint of his skill and persistence. There were also a small number of professional artists who had been trained in France and had absorbed the main twentieth-century art trends there.

During the Cultural Revolution years, however, the rules became much more narrow and stringent for acceptable forms. The mood was a highly aggressive one directed against those perceived as the enemies of the state: the Soviet Union, Taiwan (the Republic of China), the United States, and less directly against segments of the party and country in need of Proletarian Consciousness. The earlier Sino-Soviet split had discouraged artists from following the Soviet model too closely, and now the Cultural Revolution pushed a new style variously called Revolutionary Romanticism or Socialist Idealism. Thus, paintings depicted actual events such as Mao at the Red Guard rally in Beijing in June 1966 or the young Mao striding confidently across a hilltop on his way to Anyuan. One dramatically represents a rifle lesson being given to a young woman defending the border with the Soviet Union. By the late 1970s these subjects had been pared back in official circles, the cult of Mao had been brought to a close, and more traditional art forms were allowed to resurface.

In terms of literature, a similar process had been underway. History, from earliest times a preoccupation with rulers and elites, now came in for a tightly controlled Marxist and often Marxist-Leninist-Maoist perspective. Perhaps most prominent in this regard was Fan Wenlan (1893–1969), who in his last years was a member of the party's Central Committee. Fan had been associated with the "Doubting Antiquity School" of the New Culture Movement as a young man and developed his own Marxist views to compete with the modernist historical narrative of the Nationalists. In the 1950s his history writing took on more of a Maoist bent, emphasizing peasant revolution and the role of imperialism.

Like Fan, other leftist and Marxist-oriented Chinese writers from the 1920s and 1930s were in some cases still working into the early years of the People's Republic. Although he had died in 1936, Lu Xun was still highly revered, although his maverick qualities and the latitude taken in interpreting his works also left him open to criticism in official circles. Likewise, Ding Ling remained a troubling figure, and her feminist criticism of the party on women's issues brought her censure during the Anti-Rightist Campaign and Cultural Revolution. Not surprisingly, both of these campaigns cut deeply into China's literary life in terms of intimidation and coercion to follow approved lines as much as in direct punishment for violating them. In the case of Lao She, the attacks he suffered and the humiliation heaped upon him pushed him to take his own lifein1966, though at least one scholar has raised the possibility of his murder.

The most honored writer of the Maoist years, Guo Moruo (1892–1978), born Guo Kaizhen, fared somewhat better. Like most of the other writers we have considered, Guo was also part of the New Culture Movement. Like Lu Xun, he had studied medicine in Japan but gravitated toward history, archeology, and literature. In 1921, his first poetry anthology, *Goddesses*, was published and he was a cofounder of the Creation Society, an advocacy group for vernacular language. Joining the Communist Party in 1927, he spent a decade in exile in Japan before returning to China to fight the Japanese. With the founding of the PRC he remained a prolific writer in a variety of literary and social science areas and was made the first president of the Chinese Academy of Sciences, a post he held until his death in 1978. Yet he too was denounced during the Cultural Revolution, in this case by Mao himself. Like millions of others, he was forced to make abject self-confessions of his literary crimes and lapses, even to the point of suggesting that his works be burned. Two of his sons, Guo Minying and Guo Shiying, were alleged to have committed suicide while being struggled by Red Guards.

The most dominant cultural figure of the last decade of Mao's rule was his fourth wife, Jiang Qing (1914–1991). Agreeing to stay out of politics for 20 years because of party disapproval of Mao's marriage to her in 1939, the former actress became culturally active in 1963 when she campaigned to infuse proletarian themes into Peking Opera performances. Made Mao's Cultural Revolution deputy in 1966, she ruthlessly suppressed all artistic forms that were critical of the new political direction, too traditional, or insufficiently proletarian. She was most famous for championing one of the Eight Model Plays that comprised the only theater permitted during the Cultural Revolution: a ballet, *The Red Detachment of Women*. Perhaps the most famous performance of the work was the one given to the American president Richard Nixon during his 1972 visit to Beijing.

CONCLUSION

Mao Zedong is the pivotal and easily the most controversial figure in modern Chinese history. Historians are forever analyzing the role of the individual in history. Whether one adopts the so-called "Great Man" theory or the notion popularized by the German philosopher G. W. F. Hegel of the individual creating change by intuiting the *zeitgeist* of his or her age or Marxist materialism or any other more current notions, Mao emerges as an individual of, as Hegel would say, "world-historical" importance. As the philosopher Sidney Hook once noted about Lenin, Mao not only saw the direction of events and placed himself at the head of them, but also had the stubborn conviction of his own correctness to go against the apparent trends and bend them to his will. Rather than merely being an "eventful" man, he was an "event-making" one.

This tenacity of personality, however, also led to mistakes of hubris on occasion. This was especially evident in his post–civil war leadership. The skills that had served him so well as a revolutionary seem in retrospect to have frequently deserted him as head of state and to have repeatedly inflicted disaster on the early PRC. Hence, in the People's Republic today the official view on his leadership is that he was "70 percent correct": an inspired revolutionary leader but a flawed figure in government.

How then should we assess a pattern of leadership that relies on mass line politics in the service of dismantling old beliefs and structures to foment continuous revolution? What would be the end of such revolution? Would there be an end to it? The goals of the Cultural Revolution suggest at least some immediate aims: stir up the Communist Party bureaucracy, eliminate the last vestiges of feudal (i.e., Confucian) thought, push the masses past the bourgeois thinking of individual and family well-being into the realm of selflessly serving the people, and imbuing the people with the idea that a constant striving for complete redness as the only sure way to achieve China's Marxist paradise.

In these ideas are echoes of a pattern of a deeper past. Neo-Confucian debates about the primacy of thought over action versus the unity of both come to mind. Criticism by Confucian pragmatists of "superstitious" Buddhist and Daoist influences in government ideology also seem to have a degree of relevance. The heated debates about self-strengthening and the relative attention that should be paid to "Chinese learning" as opposed to "Western learning" are perhaps the most telling.

As we noted earlier as well, the course of the Chinese revolution and the Maoist years bears strong parallels to past revolutions in other places. This was particularly

true of the French Revolution, which had been the model for Marx and a key refer-
ent for revolutionary theorists ever since. During its most radical phase, and especially during the Reign of Terror in 1793–1794, France's leaders attempted a kind
of Cultural Revolution of their own. They aimed to create an entirely new society
based on reason, push the people to cooperate in the Terror, and make them com-
plicit in the bloodletting so as to have a stake in the new order. After that last desperate clash of revolution against counterrevolution, however, the millennium
would come and the perfected society would be shared by everyone. The key to it
all was that revolutionary fervor must be sustained at a fever pitch until the old
order was swept away and the new society put into place. As we saw, in China this
fervor could not be sustained any more than it could in France. In the case of
China, however, the more ideologically relaxed period following the Maoist years,
notwithstanding the ongoing presence of authoritarian government, put into
place a long-term reign of the experts. Under them, as we will see in the following
chapter, China has risen to unprecedented wealth and power.

FURTHER READING

Becker, Jasper. *Hungry Ghosts: Mao's Secret Famine.* New York: Free Press, 1996. Harrow-
ing examination of the Great Leap and its aftermath, resulting in manmade famine
of unbelievable proportions.

Chang, Jung. *Wild Swans: Three Daughters of China.* New York: Simon & Schuster, 2008.
Most current edition of the widely popular 1991 story of three generations of women
in Jung Chang's family and their trials and endurance in revolutionary and Maoist
China.

Diamant, Neil J. *Revolutionizing the Family: Politics, Love, and Divorce in Urban and
Rural China, 1949–1968.* Berkeley: University of California Press, 2000. Sophisticated monograph of comparative study of interaction between family and state both
in various regions in China and with studies of other societies in which states attempted to impose new marriage, family, and gender norms.

Dittmer, Lowell. *Liu Shaoqi and the Chinese Cultural Revolution*, revised edition. Armonk,
NY: Sharpe, 1998. A compelling analysis and attempt at rehabilitating Liu, with a
view to the conspiratorial nature of Chinese politics, of "surface" and "subsurface."
Especially informative at tracing many of Deng's reform ideas to those of Liu.

Hinton, William. *Fanshen. A Documentary of Revolution in a Chinese Village.* Berkeley
and Los Angeles: University of California Press, 1966. Classic account of the saga of
land reform in the northern Chinese village of Long Bow. Hinton was part of an investigative team there in 1948 and is generally quite favorable to the process, if not
the excesses of the process.

Li Zhisui. *The Private Life of Chairman Mao.* New York: Random House, 1994. Raw, often
disturbing insight into Mao's personal habits and health over the years by his personal physician.

Liang Heng and Judith Shapiro. *After the Nightmare*, New York: Macmillan; Collier Edition, 1987. Husband-and-wife team who went back to China to interview victims of
the Cultural Revolution to try to get a sense not only of what they endured, but also
how they coped with the continuing trauma of the aftermath of the era.

Liang Heng and Judith Shapiro. *Son of the Revolution.* New York: Vintage, 1983. Liang Heng's memoir of his young life and experiences as a Red Guard during the Cultural Revolution.

McDougall, Bonnie, ed. *Popular Chinese Literature and the Performing Arts in the People's Republic of China, 1949–1979.* Berkeley: University of California Press, 1984. Ambitious collection of 12 essays on the art and media forms of the Mao years and the beginning of the Four Modernizations and examinations of the target audiences and cultural impact of the new forms.

McFarquhar, Roderick. *The Origins of the Cultural Revolution, Vol. 3: The Coming of the Cataclysm, 1961–1966.* New York: Columbia University Press, 1997. Concluding volume of a trilogy one of the best and most compelling treatments of the events leading the tragic climax of the Maoist era. Winner of the Association for Asian Studies Joseph Levenson Prize for books on 20th century China.

Meisner, Maurice. *Mao's China and After,* 3rd ed. New York: Free Press, 1999. Masterful overview of Chinese history from the May Fourth and New Culture period to the Deng Xiaoping era. Particularly good at explain the intellectual nuances of CCP debates, economic policy, and Mao Zedong Thought.

CHAPTER 8

THE FOUR MODERNIZATIONS, 1976–1989

It is perhaps the most arresting video sequence of the late twentieth century, yet the identity of the central figure remains unknown. Indeed, relatively few of his fellow citizens have seen the footage because more than a quarter-century later the images remain forbidden in his homeland. In the world outside of the People's Republic of China, however, his bravery has been witnessed by hundreds of millions of people and his actions have been seen as emblematic of the powerful forces that have driven China's quest for wealth and power while retaining its authoritarian, one-party rule.

By the early afternoon of June 5, 1989, the Chinese government had implemented martial law in Beijing. The previous day they had moved massive numbers of troops and police into Tiananmen Square to drive out the demonstrators who, since the end of April, had been demanding more openness in government, the release of political prisoners, and political reforms to match the economic ones that had put China on the road to prosperity. Much of the carnage and confusion of the assault had been covered by international media, despite the government's attempts to censor what they would come to call the "incident." Student groups kept phone and fax lines open as long as they could to give first-person accounts of the attack in real time and later by means of video tapes smuggled out of the country. Then on the following afternoon came the unforgettable action of one man facing down the massed power of the state.

The unknown citizen, whom *Time* magazine would call one of the twentieth century's top 20 revolutionaries, alone, unarmed, and unafraid, clutching two shopping bags, placed himself in front of a line of tanks advancing on the square. The lead tank momentarily halted and with it the column. It veered left and right as the driver futilely sought to get around the man and move the tanks forward. The man matched the tank's maneuvers and incredulous onlookers witnessed what might otherwise have seemed impossible: a lone defenseless man halting an entire armored column. Then, incredibly, the man climbed up on the lead tank and began to talk to the driver. For long minutes the standoff continued as the world watched in awe. The Associated Press photographer Jeff Widener, whose still picture of the encounter became its iconic image, later compared the man to the Unknown Soldier: "He will always symbolize freedom and democracy" (Los Angeles *Times*, June 4, 2014).

Tank Man, as he came to be called, remains perhaps the world's most celebrated unknown figure. His identity appears to be obscure even to the government itself: In 1999, the Chinese president Jiang Zemin admitted that his identity was unknown, although he also revealed in English, "Not killed, I think" (ibid.). Although most people seeing his picture will forever associate him with the fortitude of the individual to "speak truth to power," he may also be seen as symbolic of the enormous changes that took place in China in the post-Mao era. The older, collectivist, mass line, red, poor and blank China had been replaced in a few short years by a society pushed forward by the arch-expert, Deng Xiaoping, into accelerating programs of market economics, openness to foreign trade, and the slogan often attributed to him with little foundation "to get rich is glorious!" Yet the cleavages in the society were growing rapidly as well. Corruption spread as entrepreneurs sought favors from party members; a gap grew between rich and poor; the government tried to curtail outside influences through campaigns against "spiritual pollution"; and the openness of the Four Modernizations that had stimulated the economy so dramatically suggested the need to many for a "Fifth Modernization": democracy. The rising expectations of the hundreds of thousands in Tiananmen Square during the spring of 1989 were ultimately distilled into the frozen moments of Tank Man's stand.

BLACK CATS AND WHITE CATS: REPAVING THE SOCIALIST ROAD

As we saw in the last chapter, the final years of Mao's tenure as party chairman saw a vitally important change in policy as well as a power struggle between the radical leftists, with the Gang of Four as the central figures and more moderate forces led by Zhou Enlai and Deng Xiaoping. The policy change was a rapprochement with the United States. Despite the 1960 Sino-Soviet split, the PRC had maintained a strong anti-American posture in its domestic and foreign policy. This was matched by American Cold War antipathy toward "Red China" as a linchpin of the Communist Bloc. By the early 1970s, however, with the Vietnam War winding down and Soviet–Chinese tensions still high, the U.S. president Richard M. Nixon made a bold visit to the PRC, which resulted in the **Shanghai Communique** of 1972. In this document, the United States and China announced plans to resume formal diplomatic and cultural relations (which went into effect in 1979), the Untied States pledged to no longer block the PRC's bid for a seat in the UN, and the United States agreed to downgrade its diplomatic relations with Taiwan (the Republic of China).

Tank Man. A Chinese man stands alone to block a line of tanks heading to secure the area around Tiananmen Square on June 5, 1989, the day after the crushing of the demonstrations. The courage of the unknown man in holding his ground in the face of the raw power of the Chinese military became the iconic image world-wide of the confrontation and killings at Tiananmen, and at sites all over the People's Republic.

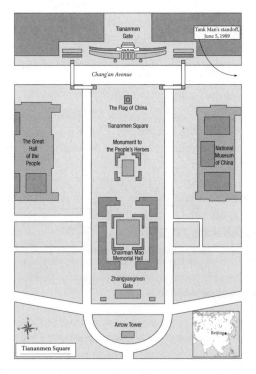

MAP 8.1
Tiananmen Square

The Hua Guofeng Interregnum

The death of Mao Zedong in September 1976 opened the way for a new "second generation" of Communist Party leaders in China. The end result was a repudiation of the Cultural Revolution and those who promoted it and an entirely different direction in strategy for building New China. In the immediate aftermath of Mao's death, the chairmanship passed within a month to the moderate Hua Guofeng (1921–2008). Although Hua claimed he had been Mao's choice to succeed him, he was less than dynamic as a leader. His initial policies were described as "The Two Whatevers": whatever policies originated with Mao were to be supported, and whatever directions Mao had given to the party were to be followed.

One policy that would change almost immediately, however, involved the **Gang of Four**. In November 1976, they were arrested and put on trial in 1980 for counterrevolution, plotting to overthrow the state and assorted other offenses. In 1981, Jiang Qing and Zhang Chunqiao were sentenced to death, with a two-year reprieve, later commuted to life imprisonment. Jiang Qing ultimately committed suicide in 1991 while undergoing treatment for throat cancer. The other two members of the Gang, Yao Wenyuan and Wang Hongwen, received 20 years and life, respectively. The six others tried with them received terms of 16 to 18 years. Those hounded and imprisoned as "rightists" during the Cultural Revolution were released. Liu Shaoqi, driven from office and the party and allowed to die from having his insulin withheld in 1969, was not only rehabilitated but also given a state funeral in 1980.

While China began to recover from the excesses of the Cultural Revolution, with even Mao coming in for criticism, the political and economic situation seemed to lack firm direction. Hua continued to pay lip service to the legacy of Mao, but looked more and more to the hardy Deng Xiaoping (1904–1997) and other experts who at this point seemed to favor a return to Soviet economic models. Deng emerged on the scene in 1978 with the title of vice premier, but in fact held the real power in the regime as Hua was increasingly criticized for his "Two Whatevers" policy. The ascendancy of the pragmatic Deng to "paramount leader" (although he kept his official title of vice premier), whose motto was, "It doesn't matter whether the cat is black or white, as long as it catches mice," swiftly led to the unveiling of the fundamental policies that remain in force in China to the present: the Four Modernizations.

Catching Mice: China's Four Modernizations

As a victim himself of the shifting political winds in the party, Deng recognized the immense damage that radical mass mobilizations could bring about. Having been long involved in economic and technical matters, he was also aware that China's communal agriculture system was rife with inefficiency and that the Cultural Revolution had, in effect, stalled the country for a decade. As we saw in the

The Gang of Four. The arrest and subsequent trial of the so-called Gang of Four, at the center of which was Mao's widow, Jiang Qing, along with several other individuals signaled a marked shift in China's policies. The members had been among the most avid proponents of the Cultural Revolution and sought to continue its most radical policies after most of the other high Party officials had backed away from them. They were charged with conspiracy and counter-revolution. Jiang Qing and Zhang Chunqiao received death sentences in 1981, though these were commuted to life in prison; the rest of the Gang received long prison terms. Jiang Qing committed suicide in 1991 while undergoing treatment for throat cancer.

previous chapter, this had resulted in a "lost generation" in the educational field. Moreover, the Chinese military and industrial sectors had long been outmoded and were falling further behind at an alarming rate. China's air force, for example, still relied on Korean War and early 1960s vintage Soviet aircraft. Coal was the chief fuel in home heating and industry, and the railroads still relied heavily on steam locomotives. In fact, throughout the 1980s China remained a favorite tourist destination for railroad buffs because it was one of the few places left in the world where coal-fired steam trains were still in widespread use.

China's isolation had prevented it from benefitting from much international trade, and consumer goods in general and the burgeoning market in electronics in particular were practically nonexistent in the PRC. What made this situation even more galling was the fact that several other Asian countries—Japan, South Korea, and even Hong Kong and Taiwan—were already key players in manufacturing and selling such goods. Indeed, although few realized it at the time, the

"Iron Rooster" Steam Train. Even as it sought to upgrade aspects of industry and technology as part of the Four Modernizations, many of China's passenger and freight trains were still powered by coal-fired steam locomotives. Because China's coal reserves were extensive this technology made sense, though critics saw it as an embarrassing symbol of China's industrial backwardness. Following travel writer Paul Theroux's widely read account of his Chinese rail journey, *Riding the Iron Rooster*, steam train enthusiasts from all over the world came in search of experiencing this old-fashioned mode of travel. The train itself was not named "iron rooster;" rather this was a sarcastic nickname given to such train travel by a Chinese man encountered by Theroux. The term itself is slang for someone or something that is cheap or miserly. Pictured here is a steam train near Zhongwei.

world was on the cusp of the computer revolution, which would soon change nearly every aspect of modern society.

Thus, the dilemma for Deng was in a way similar to that faced by Mao two decades earlier. The Cultural Revolution had, if anything, left China even more poor and blank than before. How could the leadership pursue socialism in a country with little wealth to share? Thus, Deng's strategy was bent on upgrading the quantity and quality of agriculture, industry, science and technology, and the military as quickly as possible. In a move reminiscent of that urged by the self-strengtheners of the nineteenth century, China would pursue a new policy under an old slogan, "use foreign things to help China." A key part of this endeavor to "seek truth from facts" was a new openness (*gaige kaifang*: "reform and opening") policy with regard to foreign expertise from the West. Having just restored its higher education system and reinstituted college entrance exams, China would now also allow its students to study abroad and welcomed foreign students to its universities.

Most tellingly, the plan would allow the market forces of capitalism to create incentives for innovation in all sectors of the economy. The introduction of such wholesale changes would take place in stages, tried out in regions or industries that seemed promising to work out any problems that might arise and then adopted by the nation as a whole where appropriate. As Deng put it, the new policy would be to "allow some to get rich so as to lead others to wealth." The new motto, soon emblazoned on a new kind of garment import from the West—the t-shirt—thus became "To get rich is glorious!"

Open Doors and Capitalist Roads

The most pressing need was to raise agricultural productivity. The "responsibility system," as it was called, was therefore introduced in several test areas. In many respects this was less of a radical change than at first it might appear. Many of the communes had been quietly broken up by the mid-1970s, and local markets had been informally tolerated in many areas for decades. In some cases they were vestiges of the reforms initiated by Deng and Liu Shaoqi in the early 1960's. Under the new program the communes in the experimental villages were disbanded, land was doled out to village families, and peasants were allowed to sell surplus produce and livestock at local markets after the rent and taxes were paid. The responsibility system in agriculture worked so well that by the early 1980s it was adopted countrywide. By the mid-1980s China, which had long been a byword in the West for hunger, was rapidly approaching self-sufficiency in food production. By the 1990s China would register surpluses and export a variety of food products.

In much the same way, the responsibility system was introduced into industry. A **Special Economic Zone** (SEZ) was set up in South China at Shenzhen to take advantage of capital and expertise from nearby Hong Kong. Again, the Shenzhen model proved so successful that the town itself grew into a large municipality with considerable domestic and foreign investment. Over the next several years, other SEZs were set up around the country and, cautiously at first, but then with increasing rapidity, the older state-run enterprises were turned over to private ownership. During this transition period from the mid-1980s through the mid-1990s, many young Chinese couples opted for some form of single entrepreneurship: one would hold on to his or her state job for its security and benefits while the other would attempt to start a business.

Another aid in this process was the lifting of many restrictions on mobility within China. Formerly, to keep agricultural production up and to prevent overcrowding in the towns and cities, permits were required for residency and permission to move had to be secured from one's *danwei*. As these restrictions were liberalized, people migrated to urban areas and the new industrial centers springing up. Thus, cities like Beijing and Shanghai ballooned in size and construction of housing simply could not keep up. Shanghai, for example, is today (in 2015) the world's sixth largest city, with more than 22 million people. With such extreme demand for new and expanded buildings and infrastructure, a popular joke circulating about was that the (high-rise construction) crane was China's new national bird.

Despite problems with corruption—deals were often made by means of *guanxi* ("connections") through "the back door" (*houmen*) with local Party officials—the experiments in capitalism were enormously successful, with the early SEZs expanded to the country at large once the flaws had been worked out. Through the 1980s and 1990s, China's gross domestic product (GDP)grew at an astonishing double-digit rate, and only in the past few years has it gone as low as 7 percent.

An important element of the program was the new policy of openness, sometimes called the "new Open Door" in Western media. As they had in the nineteenth and early twentieth centuries, large import–export and multinational firms turned hungry eyes toward the possibilities of a virtually untapped market encompassing nearly a fifth of the world's population. As with earlier experiences with foreign trade, however, the government and party wanted to be extremely circumspect in setting up agreements and enterprises with foreign concerns. As with the other programs of the **Four Modernizations**, such joint ventures were limited initially to the SEZs and the foreign firms saddled with complex restrictions. By the 1990s, however, as such enterprises became more common, the government steadily made doing business in China less burdensome to foreign firms. In fact, increasing numbers of Chinese firms were soon competing in international markets as well.

As China's middle class grew, so did the sophistication of ordinary consumers, and the demand for everything from cars to fast food to electronics skyrocketed. By 2010 China had by far the world's largest middle class in absolute terms, more than 500 million. As the new century began, China had, as had Japan a few decades before, a large and growing export-driven manufacturing center built on low-cost infrastructure and low wages. Many multinational companies as well as European and U.S. giants like Walmart were increasingly reliant on low-cost Chinese goods to keep their own prices competitive.

One area in which modernization in science, technology, and industry met was consumer electronics, especially computers. Japan, Taiwan, Hong Kong, Singapore, and South Korea had all profited enormously from the export of such goods, and companies like Sony in Japan and Sanyo in South Korea had become multinational giants from their manufacture. Moreover, it was widely recognized by the mid-1980s that the computer revolution was well underway, in terms of

Shanghai Skyline. Nowhere have the results of China's Four Modernizations been more evident than in Shanghai. As in the photograph above, the old architecture once dominated by the European buildings of the Bund, the International Settlement, and the French Concession; as well as the more recent Soviet style high rise apartment blocks has now been completely over-shadowed by endless lines of massive skyscrapers as Shanghai has become one of the world's largest cities. Looking down on the skyline of Puxi, the Huangpu River, and the Lujiazui Financial District, one sees the radically distinctive Pearl of the Orient TV Tower, with the large spherical "pearl" in its midsection. Other standout structures include the Shanghai World Financial Center (third tallest), the Jinmao Tower (fourth tallest), and the tallest of all, the Shanghai Tower.

both personal computers and supercomputers like the Cray line for industrial and military uses. Not surprisingly, IBM and Intel mounted early joint ventures in China. By the early twenty-first century, the Chinese Lenovo IBM "clone" line was a worldwide bestseller.

Modernizing National Defense

With Sino-Soviet relations still frosty, the PRC began to court eager Western countries for help in modernizing their military capabilities. From the American and North Atlantic Treaty Organization (NATO)viewpoints, a strong China would be an effective card to play against the Soviets. This was especially true after China invaded Soviet ally Vietnam in 1979 to punish them for their incursion into Pol Pot's Kampuchea to drive out the genocidal Khmer Rouge. Although much of the world openly or covertly supported Vietnam's action to end Pol Pot's reign of terror, their initial enthusiasm waned as the Vietnamese attempted to place their own strong man in power and dominate the region. As an ally of Pol Pot—and with a 2,000-year history of invasion and attempted suzerainty over Vietnam—the Chinese mounted a three-week incursion into the northern part of the country. Strategically, it was a show of force in the same vein as the 1962 move into India. Moreover, it also showed that the Soviets would not come to the aid of the Vietnamese, thus assuring China a degree of hegemony in the region.

As a demonstration of China's military prowess, however, it was a disaster. The PLA's weapons were obsolescent, the Chinese attacks were uncoordinated, leadership was wanting, and units even mounted the kind of human wave attacks that had proved so casualty ridden in the Korean War. Fighting almost exclusively Vietnamese Home Guard militia units, the Chinese came away with an appalling 20,000 casualties.

The military thus demonstrated conclusively that it was in dire need of modernization. Even before this, however, British military officials were meeting with their Chinese counterparts as early as 1978 to discuss defense exchanges. The official inauguration of full diplomatic relations between the PRC and the United States on January 1, 1979, was followed in a few weeks with a visit by Deng to America. The following year, the Carter administration arranged for the U.S. defense secretary Harold Brown to meet in China with officials there about establishing American listening posts to monitor Soviet activities in return for American cooperation on modern weapons.

Another, more controversial, innovation aimed at modernization was the "one-child policy." As we saw in the previous chapter, Mao felt that China's huge and growing population was an advantage because of its potential manpower for mass mobilization campaigns and as a hedge against catastrophic losses from nuclear war. But population pressures were also a powerful brake on China's development. Thus, a policy was inaugurated in 1979 mandating that families (excluding those of most minorities) were to have only one child. A second child would result in loss of subsidies for childrearing; a third pregnancy required mandatory abortion. Women of child-bearing age were required to have their monthly cycles monitored by their local *danwei*, as a check on clandestine pregnancies. Despite the many problems in enforcing such a policy and its severe cultural impact on the male-centered traditional Chinese family structure, China's population has remained remarkably stable since the 1980s, at around 1.3 to 1.5 billion. It has, however, abetted problems of selective female abortion, giving up girl babies for adoption, and, in extreme cases, female infanticide.

The "Fifth Modernization"

The heady atmosphere of the early days of these sweeping reforms brought political reformers temporarily out of hiding. There had been a foreshadowing of this a few years before, following the death of Zhou Enlai in January 1976. Despite his sometimes devious behavior in the service of survival during the confusion of the Maoist years, Zhou was an enormously popular figure. In the expectation that political reform might be in the air that spring, over the course of several days in April, more than 2 million people thronged Tiananmen Square during a memorial service for the former premier. Fearful of a mass movement developing from sentiments expressed in many of the big character posters hung up by the mourners, the government broke the gathering up. Demonstrations followed in a dozen other Chinese cities over the next several days.

Expectations were raised again in late 1978 and early 1979. Encouraged by the air of experimentation and the perception of openness surrounding the programs of the Four Modernizations, demonstrators began to call for a wide array of democratic reforms by hanging big character posters on the walls near Tiananmen Square, as they had a few years before mourning Zhou, as Mao himself had during the Cultural Revolution, and as the May Fourth demonstrators had in 1919. Although the posters ranged across a dizzying variety of subjects, an increasing number focused on demands for more open government and democracy. The most famous was also one of the first to be put up: on December 5, 1978, Wei

Wei Jingsheng. The flurry of excitement generated by the important change of policy marking the Four Modernizations in 1978 stimulated public comment on a number of issues. Following a longstanding tradition in Chinese politics, people pasted "big-character posters" (*dazi bao*) in public places calling for a variety of reforms. The most notorious critic was Wei Jingsheng (shown during his trial) who wrote an essay calling for "Democracy: The Fifth Modernization." Wei was branded a counter-revolutionary and sentenced to 15 years' imprisonment for supposedly supplying a foreign newsman with Chinese military intelligence and carrying out "counter-revolutionary agitation." Freed briefly in 1993, he was re-arrested and held until being deported to the United States in 1997.

Democracy Wall. From the end of 1978 through the "Peking Spring" of 1979, prominent walls became "Democracy Walls" as at this bus company near Xidan in Beijing. The poster in the middle is, ironically, of Premier Hua Guofeng with children.

Jingsheng's poster called for "the Fifth Modernization: democracy." The outpouring that followed in Beijing and other Chinese cities over the next several months was dubbed the "Peking Spring." Although the Beijing municipal authorities granted the growing number of demonstrators considerable leeway for some time, the demonstrations were ultimately suppressed. It has been suggested as well that Deng, like Mao during the Cultural Revolution, had allowed—even subltly encouraged the demonstrations—as a way to put pressure on political opponents of his reforms. Political agitation for a more open society, for crackdowns on corruption, and even for a multiparty system, however, continued in muted form through the decade. Wei himself has continued his agitation to the present time: imprisoned from 1979 to 1993, he was released briefly before being rearrested for talking with foreign journalists. Imprisoned again in 1994, he was deported to the United States in 1997.

TOWARD TIANANMEN SQUARE: THE NEW AUTHORITARIANISM

Since the advent of the Four Modernizations, successive Chinese leaders have wrestled with an ongoing problem that under a different guise would have been familiar to the self-strengtheners. Indeed, as we have indicated several times in this volume, it is a problem that has been faced to a greater or lesser degree by nearly every country outside the ambit of Western Europe and North America: How can a nation become modern without having to become Western? For nineteenth-century advocates like Li Hongzhang or Zhang Zhidong, the most promising approach seemed to be "Chinese studies for the essentials; Western studies for practical application." As we also saw, opponents of this approach feared that the changes introduced by the Western studies would ultimately transform Confucian China to such a degree that it might, in cultural terms, cease to be Chinese. Here they pointed to Japan, whose slavish imitation of the West, they felt, made the Japanese culturally inauthentic and exposed them to ridicule by Westerners, who saw them as inferior copies of themselves. But Japan's victories over China in 1895 and Russia in 1905 showed that in terms of Japan's newfound power, the cultural risk might well be worth taking.

For Deng and the party leadership in the 1980s, the problem was similar but more complex. China's old Confucian culture had been conclusively altered. But the new governing ideology, Marxism-Leninism-Mao Zedong Thought, was a relatively thin and young veneer superimposed on deep cultural roots that even the Cultural Revolution could not eradicate. Now the picture could potentially become even more difficult. With China opening itself again to foreign influences and with the country increasingly hungry for the new technologies being developed, the cultural baggage accompanying the material imports threatened the socialist mores fostered by the party. The problem grew steadily more acute as the PRC's citizens became increasingly consumer conscious and avidly followed foreign fashions in clothes and entertainment. By the mid-1980s China seemed to be erupting in color as the unisex blue "Mao suits," which even a few years before had been a kind of national uniform, were now vanishing. More and more people dressed in colorful, if often mismatched, foreign or faux-foreign outfits.

More disconcerting, however, were the music, rock videos, movies, and pornography now beginning to make their way into the country. American youth culture, with its call for personal freedom in everything from sexuality to politics, was fast becoming an international—even a world—phenomenon. How was the government to balance maximum material benefits from the new openness while blocking those things deemed "injurious to public morals?" As the title of one book written at the time suggested, how was China going to handle "discos and democracy?"

Spiritual Pollution

The success of the so-called "Little Dragons" or "Little Tigers" seemed to offer some possibilities. South Korea, for example, still had a tightly controlled authoritarian government. Taiwan, too, clung to one-party rule. Even Japan, with its American constitution, in many ways behaved less like a democracy and more like a family, with its interlocking interests in finance, business, and government. Indeed, the nonsocialist East Asian countries were now popularly described as "Confucian-capitalist." It was Singapore's leader, Lee Kuan Yew, however, from whom Deng borrowed most heavily. Singapore was a fabulously successful financial center but its rather free-wheeling economic sector was balanced by an authoritarian government that imposed a strict code of personal behavior and grooming on its citizens, on whom even trivial offenses brought severe punishment. Those whose hair was too long or who spit on the sidewalk were subject to fines, jail—or even caning.

In 1983, therefore, the party launched a program to fight what it called **spiritual pollution**. Characteristically, computers were welcome; pornography and rock videos by performers such as Madonna were not. Academic and popular literature was routinely screened for politically sensitive subjects like dissent or China's position in Tibet. The party developed stringent guidelines about which imports—especially literature and videos—were permitted and which ones were not. Such was the public hunger for all things foreign, however, that the guidelines proved difficult to enforce. Time and again, forbidden items seized by customs or other officials turned up in the private hands of those charged with enforcing the restrictions. The programs were, in a way, harbingers of the ways in which the government would attempt to control electronic communication by phone, fax, and, in the following decades, the Internet.

Fighting Spiritual Pollution. The opening up of China to foreign expertise, capital, and technology also saw an influx of foreign cultural influences, many of them unwelcome as "injurious to public morals." This prompted a campaign against such "spiritual pollution" as critical political literature, risqué MTV videos, and pornography, among other offensive items. Here, a box full of books, cassette tapes, movie reels, and other items seized is carried off under the careful eyes of the cameraman in the back.

PATTERNS UP CLOSE

Asian Values and Human Rights

One of the lines of defense raised by the official media in China in response to charges by Western countries about freedom of expression and the treatment of political dissidents is that there are essential "Asian values" that are fundamentally different from those of the West. Here the center of these values is Confucian, rather than Buddhist or Daoist. As we have seen, from the first Western challenge in the nineteenth century, it was taken for granted that China's—and, by extension, Confucian East Asia's—ethics were both prior to and superior to those of the West. Although the majority of China's intellectuals abandoned Neo-Confucianism by the 1920s and 1930s and the Communist era made eradicating its vestiges a major goal, its cultural and moral influence remained always just beneath the surface.

By the 1960s an intellectual, spiritual, and cultural movement revisiting the ideas of the Sage began to develop. The most influential of these "New Confucians" was the Harvard scholar Tu Wei-ming (b. 1940). Tu's approach is fundamentally geared toward self-cultivation, ethics, and, he argues, a spirituality as deeply vital as that of Christianity or Islam. The political dimension, however, was championed in its present form by Lee Kuan Yew (1923–2015), the authoritarian former prime minister (1958–1990) of Singapore. For Lee, the notion of distinct Asian values stresses, among other things, a strong hand at the top to ensure societal harmony, group values taking priority over individual rights, and a determined pursuit of market economics. In this view, the rights of individuals are seen as relative to the needs of the group, and the rampant, messy individualism characteristic of American society is to be shunned as injurious to public morals and order.

Not surprisingly, these ideas were given added force as they were picked up by Deng Xiaoping and his successors. As China's modernization proceeded and market forces came to wield increasing power in the PRC, the Communist Party sought to further anchor its rule by rehabilitating the cultural icons of the past and, in a sense, engaging in what the social historian E. J. Hobsbawm called "invented tradition." Deng and Lee met a number of times and Chinese leaders admitted frankly that Singapore's experience had much to teach them. Nowhere was this more striking than in the reinvigorating of certain Confucian values, although along strict party interpretations of what those values should entail. By the mid-1990s, the concept of a "Confucian capitalist" sphere of influence around the Pacific Rim was widely recognized, and numerous conferences—including one sponsored by Pope John Paul II at Castle Gandolfo—were held to explore the implications of these developments.

Yet it is precisely because Confucian concepts are cited in support of this assertion of Asian exceptionalism that scholars and policy makers are more than ever examining this tradition and its views on human rights. Consider the following passage from the *Analects*: "People everywhere are fundamentally the same; it is usage and custom that makes them different." In its cosmopolitan sentiments it could have come from one of the Enlightenment *philosophes*; significantly, it appears in the 1948 *United Nations Declaration on Human Rights*. Among the original signatories was Nationalist China; and it was followed later by Japan, South Korea, and even by the PRC itself. At this stage at least, none of these states appears to have let Asian values raise exceptions to the sentiments contained therein. It is also worth noting that none of the leading scholars of Confucianism today outside of the PRC—and in particular, Tu Wei-ming and the literary historian William Theodore De Bary—takes Lee's or the CCP leadership's claims of Asian exceptionalism at face value. Rather, there is fundamental agreement that just as it has become evident that there is nothing necessarily incompatible between Confucian values and rapid national development, so too is there nothing anchored deep within the philosophy, and even its historical practice, fundamentally inimical to modern, international norms of human rights. Indeed, as with the quote above, one often finds that there is much in the Confucian tradition that parallels and even anticipates these modern views, despite the Western origins of many of them. There are, however, points of emphasis and historical circumstances that have colored these traditions.

Confucius and his followers start with a view, like Aristotle, of the individual as indivisible from society. In this respect, it is not conceptually remote from Western classical and medieval ideas of corporate society—a fact with which the first Western missionaries to China were quick to draw parallels. The great philosophical divergence of the Enlightenment, in which the individual was abstracted from society and placed into an idealized state of nature—"Solitary, poor, nasty, brutish, and short" for Hobbes; "born free, yet everywhere in chains," according to Rousseau—would not be meaningful for the practical-minded Confucian.

Indeed, the social order, with its fundamental institution of the family, is for Confucians the essential model for both the world of living things and the cosmos. Just as the human nuclear family is not an arrangement of equals, so too is the radical equality of all individuals as atoms of self-interest whose aggregation makes up society a concept alien to the

continued

Confucian world iew. Instead, as we have seen, Confucius, Mencius, and their followers saw human society as the intervening, moderating layer of being between the more impersonal forces of Heaven and Earth. This layer consisted of a continuum of interlocking, hierarchical relationships bound together by filial ties of mutual affection and respect. Students of Chinese thought sometimes refer to this as the "part/whole" concept, in which each individual is in turn part of a larger whole, from the lowest life form to the cosmos itself. At every level, the relationships parallel those of the family and vary only according to size and scope. On the surface of it, therefore, it would appear that perhaps those who argue for the relative character of human rights under this system of Asian values would be on solid ground. Seen from this perspective, the Confucian concept of society would indeed appear to be unacceptably susceptible to potential abuse from the powerful. This contingency, however, and the checks and balances to mitigate it, in fact formed the bulk of the thought of Confucius and, especially, Mencius.

As we saw in Chapter 1, the *Analects* tell us that one day a disciple asked Confucius if he could sum up his philosophy in a few words. "I can do it in one word," he said. How about "reciprocity": do not do unto others what you would not have them do unto you." Hence, five centuries before Christ we have the formation of an essential Asian value nearly identical to one of the linchpins of the Judeo-Christian tradition. It is no accident that Confucius chose this concept as central to his thought because it is not only the lubricant of all social relationships in his vision of a political and moral order, but also the first and most powerful check on arbitrary behavior within it. If the family and filial piety represent the *form* of Confucian relationships, reciprocity may be said to govern their *function*.

Mencius put it more directly. Asked what he thought about the killing of a sovereign, he said he had never heard of such a thing because any ruler who was killed by the people would have long since abandoned any right to rule. Thus, 2000 years before the American Declaration of Independence, the fundamental right to alter or abolish injurious forms of government was taken as a given by Confucians. Moreover, much of Mencius is given over to systems by which rulers can insure the economic vitality of their states—the "people's livelihood"—and these reappear in various guises throughout the dynastic history of imperial China. But it is vital to note that these are never to be seen as substituting for the fundamental demands of "humaneness and righteousness."

It is in the 2,000-year history of imperial China, however, during which the Confucian system becomes the state orthodoxy and the "Han Synthesis" ensures the structures of hereditary centralized government, that one finds the most compelling evidence for the authoritarian perspective on Asian values and human rights. But even here, some scholars argue, one finds the Confucian system producing genuine heroes of human rights, carrying on a hallowed tradition of remonstrating with the powerful. On the one hand, filial piety and service to those above became state dogma and women's roles in particular became increasingly circumscribed. Yet on the other hand, during every dynasty the educated classes and state officials also, on the whole, took their duty of acting as the people's advocates quite seriously. In the normal course of governance, and especially during times of national crisis, many officials suffered humiliation, exile, or even death in the service of the people and principle—as we saw with the historian Sima Qian, who was given the choice of castration or death for offending Han emperor Wudi (see Chapter 2). He chose to be castrated so he could serve his higher duty to truth and finish his history. Chinese folklore is replete with stories of just officials who led the way in famine relief, defended the people against bandits or oppressors, brought corrupt officials to justice, became hermits living in the mountains rather than serve tainted rulers, and in a thousand other ways behaved as the conscience of the empire. And indeed, foreign visitors into the early nineteenth century uniformly remarked on how well off the people seemed, on how free they appeared to be from government interference, and how effectively they policed themselves. And it might be added that it was also the officials, scholars, and students who have prominently wrestled with the great problems of reform, reaction, and revolution from the Opium War to the present.

Thus, as the People's Republic seeks to advertise its policies as firmly within the larger Confucian tradition and avidly sets up Confucius Institutes throughout the world, what that legacy means in terms of original intent and modern practice seems likely to be contested for quite some time. For many, the Confucian constellation of Asian values encompasses the fundamental human rights of life, material and spiritual welfare, self-cultivation and emancipation, freedom to protest arbitrary behavior, and, at the most extreme, the freedom and duty to rebel and replace corrupt, incompetent, or irresponsible government with something more suitable. How well these principles will mesh with the party's efforts to create "the harmonious society" will undoubtedly loom large in the coming decades.

Another new phenomenon that required oversight was tourism. With a more liberal attitude toward religion in general (as long as it was state approved) and religious institutions and shrines from China's feudal past, as well as the loosening of restrictions on domestic and foreign travel, Chinese both inside the PRC and overseas soon crowded places of interest all over the country. For overseas Chinese, many of whom had not been "home" for decades, the curiosity about the country's present state and the lure of famous sites was a powerful incentive. In addition to the Great Wall and Forbidden City and famous places of beauty like Guilin, the discovery and development of the site of the First Emperor's tomb complex near Xi'an, with its famous terracotta warriors, discovered only in 1974, soon led it to be China's second most popular destination. The new availability of tourist visas for those from Hong Kong and, not long after, Taiwan drove the tourism market even further. Finally, with restrictions on Americans traveling to China lifted, yet another large and growing wave of visitors arrived.

All of this new activity not only strained the capacity of the government to enforce the Spiritual Pollution guidelines, but also required new accommodations and economic arrangements. Maoist-era guest houses and China's handful of hotels were woefully inadequate for modern travelers, as were their amenities. Thus, as China's building boom for housing expanded, so did that of hotels, entertainment complexes, dinner theaters, etc. Moreover, the money that tourists brought with them also proved to be a problem. The PRC's *renminbi* (RMB) or *yuan*, popularly known as a *kuai*, was not a convertible currency. Moreover, the government feared the influx of a wide variety of foreign currencies, particularly American dollars, which would surely result in a black market for money changers. They therefore created a two-tier system of currency. Only citizens of the PRC were permitted to possess and use *renminbi*. Foreigners and overseas Chinese were required to use foreign exchange certificates (FEC) redeemable only at designated sites and "Friendship Stores" set up exclusively for foreign shopping. Since the higher prices in Friendship Stores were often matched by higher-quality goods and services, local people developed a variety of stratagems to try and bypass the system. Moreover, a vigorous black market for money changing did develop despite the government's efforts. Typical of the period were the signs posted on tourist sites in Chinese, Japanese, and English giving the ascending scale of entrance prices: lowest for PRC citizens, next highest for "compatriots from Taiwan and Hong Kong," and highest for foreigners.

In keeping with the effort to hold foreign influences at bay, individual travel was restricted, required permission to enter undesignated sites, and often entailed having a minder. Most tourism at this point was therefore done in groups through tour packagers and supervised in China by the China International Travel Service. Groups were routinely tailed by local party cadres to ensure proper behavior on the part of guides and visitors, especially in dealing with requests to visit restricted or unauthorized sites. Within a decade, however, nearly all of these restrictions were radically pared back or disappeared altogether.

One Country, Two Systems

As part of the PRC's new market liberalism and its efforts to develop a way to play the "Western card" against the Soviets, Deng and the party leaders felt the time

Friendship Store. Among the difficulties facing China in the early days of carefully opening the country to foreign tourists was the lack of modern retail outlets. Moreover, China's need to control its currency and insulate it from international market forces put further restrictions on the early tourist industry. Thus, the government instituted a two-tier currency system: Chinese citizens were to use the standard *renminbi* in use since the founding of the PRC; and foreigners were to use "Foreign Exchange Certificates," which carried a nominally equivalent value to the RMB, but could be used only in approved outlets. To remedy the retail problem, Friendship Stores, which catered to the tourist trade with better quality goods and friendlier personnel, and accepted only FECs, were set up in major metropolitan areas. Pictured above is the Peking Friendship Store in 1985 with foreign tourists about to enter.

was opportune to address the remaining legacy of imperialism in the area. China still confronted colonies on her south coast in the form of Hong Kong and Macau (Macao) and so entered negotiations with Great Britain and Portugal about the eventual return of these territories. Portugal's days as a colonial power had long since passed. In the 1970s, revolutions had resulted in the independence of their last substantial holdings, Angola and Mozambique. Moreover, the quasi-fascist regime associated with Antonio Salazar, who died in 1970, had been overthrown in 1974. The successor government repudiated the colonial policies of the previous regime, withdrew its troops from Macau, and transferred its diplomatic recognition from the Republic of China on Taiwan to the PRC. Negotiations for the return of Macau began in June 1986 and resulted in an agreement to return Macau to Chinese sovereignty in 1999.

The framework for the future of Macau was in many respects constructed on a similar basis to that resulting from the negotiations with the British concerning Hong Kong. The Crown Colony had become one of the larger cities in East Asia and, after Tokyo and Singapore, the most crucial financial hub. Moreover, its position less than an hour from Shenzhen and its connections with that SEZ made it crucial to the success of the experiment there. Its acquisition by the PRC would vastly enhance China's modernization efforts. Liberal treatment of the colony's citizens would also help prevent human and capital flight on the eve of the transition. The result of the negotiations, therefore, was the Basic Law, which would govern Hong Kong's status for 50 years after the return of the colony, set for 1997, the year in which the 99-year lease on Hong Kong's New Territories would expire.

Both sides sat down to talks in 1985 and a draft was finally agreed on in 1989 and ratified in 1990. The Basic Laws for both Macau and Hong Kong stipulate

MAP 8.2

Open Cities, Special Economic Zones, and Special Administrative Regions in China, 1980–2000

that the PRC will govern them for 50 years after their return on the principle of "one country, two systems." Both would become Special Administrative Regions (SAR) overseen by Beijing, but their local governments would remain intact. Freedoms currently enjoyed in both places were guaranteed and municipal ordinances were to be honored. No restrictions were to be placed on the economic freedoms of these regions. The PRC would handle all foreign relations and defense matters in both new Special Administrative Regions.

In the case of Macau, the time since its turnover has been relatively quiet. Economically, the Special Administrative Region has gone from being an economic backwater to one of the world's prime gaming destinations. Hong Kong's history, on the other hand, has been somewhat more turbulent. Deng and his party supporters had hoped that the one country, two systems concept could be used as an inducement to the Republic of China on Taiwan to open talks ultimately leading to reunification. Until 1989, with the PRC appearing to be steadily liberalizing under the aegis of Politburo members Zhao Ziyang and Hu Yaobang (see later), there seemed to be some justification for the hope of such negotiations. After Hu's death in April, however, and Zhao's downfall in the wake of the suppression of the massive demonstrations in Tiananmen Square and elsewhere in June, such prospects appeared to vanish.

Nonetheless, the exchanges went through on schedule. In Hong Kong, however, constant friction among pro-Beijing factions and those in various degrees of opposition have made Hong Kong's politics volatile despite the region's economic vitality. One bone of contention has been over what degree of approval Beijing requires in vetting candidates for political office. In the fall of 2014, opposition to Beijing's insistence on approving the candidates for the 2017 municipal elections resulted in massive demonstrations that paralyzed the city and developed ties to the more loosely organized "Occupy" movements that had sprung up in the United States and Europe over the preceding years.

Peaceful Evolution

The economic strides made by the PRC during the early years of the Four Modernizations did not go unnoticed in the Soviet Union. Relations between the Soviets and China had been strained to the point of military action during the Cultural Revolution. The Soviet invasion of Afghanistan at the end of December 1979 prompted a swift condemnation from Deng's government and a demand for the immediate withdrawal of Russian forces. It also prompted the visit barely a week later by the U.S. secretary of defense Harold Brown to discuss the possibility of closer military ties with China. Deng told Brown, "All the world's countries should enter into an alliance" against this new aggressive Soviet posture. By the end of January, the United States announced its willingness to sell "nonoffensive" weaponry to China and the Chinese shortly announced their support of the American proposal to boycott the 1980 Moscow Olympic Games.

The Soviets were also having difficulties on the economic front. U.S.–Soviet tensions had entered a troubling period in the early 1980s, and in March 1983 the Reagan administration proposed the construction of a technologically daunting land and space-based missile defense system called the Strategic Defense Initiative (SDI). Almost immediately it was nicknamed by its opponents "Star Wars" after the hugely popular science fiction movie. For the Soviets, the challenge of overcoming such a system to keep the United States from having the advantage of both first-strike capability and a workable defense against any Soviet attack or counterattack would prove enormously costly. The war against Afghan *mujahedeen* fighters contesting the Soviet-backed Marxist government in Kabul was consuming enormous resources as well. Finally, the Soviets' belated entry into the new computer and electronic era and the increasing world economic dominance of America, Japan, and Western Europe exposed the inefficiencies of the USSR's centrally directed "command economy."

Thus, with the elevation of Mikhail Gorbachev to the office of general secretary of the Soviet Communist Party in 1985, economic reforms under the term *perestroika* ("restructuring") assumed top priority. In many ways they resembled Deng's initiatives, calling for streamlining the bureaucracy, modernizing the military and industrial sectors, and enhancing agricultural productivity. Although formally adhering to the concept of a centralized economy, some private ownership was also introduced. Perhaps more tellingly, unlike Deng's program, Gorbachev also introduced the concept of *glasnost* ("openness"), lifting a number of restrictions on freedom of expression—although this was initially a ploy to direct criticism at party members who balked at his economic reforms.

As the decade of the 1980s moved into its second half, therefore, the two most populous and powerful Communist countries were in the midst of experiments that would move them far from the Marxist ideals they still so adamantly professed. But would it be the Chinese or the Soviet approach that would prove more effective? Academics and pundits debated the relative merits of these paths, and the consensus seemed to form around the idea that, whereas Gorbachev's approach offered broad-based promise for a transition to a more open society, China's economically venturesome but politically conservative approach seemed to be the safer choice. Looking at the examples of the European historical experience, the argument went, market capitalism and wealth building would ultimately lead to a more politically open society, although the reverse—politics before economy—might be far less effective. The forces unleashed by market economics—property rights, a revamped legal system, protection of capital, etc.—would steadily drive the demand for the political rights to safeguard them. The ongoing examples of the authoritarian Little Dragons notwithstanding, the first Bush administration in the United States, without using the term directly, devoted its foreign policy vis-à-vis China to what Eisenhower's secretary of state, John Foster Dulles, had called "peaceful evolution": the idea that by encouraging trade and economic openness, the United States could subtly steer socialist countries toward evolving into a more politically open, perhaps even democratic, form over time. This notion had been repeatedly rebuked by Mao and CCP officials ever since, who saw such American strategies and aims as interference in China's domestic affairs. At the end of the decade, however, for a brief time it appeared to many both inside and outside the PRC that such openness might be achieved much sooner than predicted.

Tiananmen Square

The speed and progress of the economic reforms coupled with the waves of Western cultural influence breaking over the country led to cleavages within the party. Deng sought to balance these by including in the Politburo hard liners like Li Peng along with those associated with more liberal policies, like Zhao Ziyang and Hu Yaobang. Hu, in particular, had been regarded by students and young party members as politically progressive. In 1986, after criticism of his handling of party members suspected of "bourgeois-liberal" leanings, Hu resigned his post as party secretary. After a certain period of shuffling among the Politburo members, Zhao took over Hu's old post and Li Peng emerged as premier in 1988.

By early January 1989, a popular drive for the release of political prisoners received a significant boost with the call by China's most prominent astrophysicist, Fang Lizhi, for the release of the Fifth Modernization author Wei Jingsheng. The following month, dissidents mounted a petition drive for political amnesty. The chief catalyst of what was to follow, however, came with the death and funeral of Hu Yaobang in April. An official memorial service was held on April 22 in Tiananmen Square and an outpouring of grief and emotion comparable to that accompanying Zhou Enlai's service filled the Square with tens of thousands of students. Over the next several days the crowds grew, especially after Zhao's positive comments and suggestions for dialog with the students suggested that the party was moving in a more liberal direction. As May 4 came, the parallels between this student movement and the one 70 years before were unavoidable. At one point students even constructed a large statue they called "the Goddess of Democracy" that dominated the center of the square near the Monument to the People's Revolutionary Heroes. Meanwhile, they had mounted a hunger strike as pressure increased from intellectuals inside and outside the party—as well as from overseas Chinese and foreign governments—for comprehensive talks. The demonstrations now included people from all walks of life and there was talk of organizing a general strike. Deng sent the hardliner Li Peng to talk to the students on May 18. The students said they would end the strike and disperse if two conditions were met: that the demonstrations would be officially designated as "patriotic" and that student–party leader dialog would be broadcast live on television. Li prevaricated while noting that the "turmoil" had now spread to the nation as a whole.

Even as he was speaking, however, the decision to declare martial law and clear the Square had already been made and troops were being moved into position outside of Beijing and other major cities. In the early morning hours of

Tiananmen Square Demonstrations. As the tensions mounted through April and May, 1989, the numbers of demonstrators grew ever larger until the 97 acre Tiananmen Square was packed solid. Workers and ordinary citizens joined the students and expectations were high that some breakthrough was at hand. After meetings with Zhao Ziyang and Li Peng, however, and the realization that an impasse had been reached in the face of student demands for a nationally televised dialog and for the demonstrations to be officially designated as "patriotic," martial law was declared and the troops moved in on June 4. In these four pictures some of the drama and tragedy of the events that followed can be seen. **(A)** Tens of thousands of students confidently carry victory signs in their march for democracy on May 28. **(B)** Mere hours before the movement was crushed, jubilant demonstrators brandish rocks while standing atop an armored vehicle that they have stopped from entering the square in the early morning hours of June 4. **(C)** In this picture, taken June 3—the day before the army moved into the square in force—a company of soldiers is apparently stymied by a wall of demonstrators preventing them from advancing into the square. **(D)** Finally, the tragic aftermath confronts the camera as the dead and wounded lay atop their bicycles, which have apparently been crushed by heavy armored vehicles.

May 19, several party leaders, including Li and Zhao, visited the square to talk to the demonstrators. Zhao made an impassioned, tearful speech begging the crowd to disperse "before it's too late." Over the next several days, troops and police moved into position, some fraternizing with the demonstrators. On June 4 they began to clear the square.

The shock of the attack was perhaps even more devastating to the national psyche than the material and human destruction. The use of force against civilians was certainly not a rarity in Chinese history. The PLA, however, from its earliest days had worked ceaselessly to cultivate its image as, quite literally, the "people's" army. Its combined duties of farming, construction, and fighting during the revolutionary days had burnished the popular image further—as did its propaganda and efforts to treat the people fairly and humanely. Many of the party's most revered heroes in the cause of serving the people, such as Lei Feng, were in the army. For many, if not most, of those on the scene, it was an unshakable article of faith that "the army and the people are one!" It was unthinkable that the people's army would ever fire on "the people." Thus, even as the troops bivouacked around the square, demonstrators and locals mixed freely with them, seeking assurance that they were there as a show of force rather than to mount an attack. Although the commanders in charge of the operation were careful to bring units in from outside the city, there was still widespread feeling among the demonstrators that, after all, these were "our" sons and fathers and brothers. Even amid the lingering shock in the aftermath of the assault, many undoubtedly saw Tank Man confidently remonstrating with the lead vehicle's driver as the stubborn residue of the people's faith in the people's soldiers (see opening vignette).

To this day, the figures remain in dispute: the government put the numbers at 241 dead, mostly civilians, with 7,000 wounded, mostly soldiers and police. Reports from on the scene and later put the number of dead in the thousands. While the shooting continued, foreign reporters took large amounts of footage. Many of the demonstrators themselves used video cameras to capture the confusion and carnage and transmitted reports and photos abroad by fax in attempts to foil government censors.

Despite the international condemnation of the incident, which included sanctions by the United States, Deng announced that the reforms would continue on the basis of market economics and centralized one-party government. This marked a particularly crucial time for the party since the Berlin Wall came down that November, the Ceausescu government was overthrown in Romania, and all the old Soviet bloc governments—including the Soviet Union itself—collapsed over the next two years. Zhao Ziyang was purged from his posts within days of the massacre, and the government tilted toward the authoritarian rule of Li Peng as premier and Jiang Zemin, who moved into Zhao's former post as party secretary. After 1992 and until his death in 1997, Deng would relinquish his formal positions and act behind the scenes to effect his policies. The party would continue to condemn the policy of peaceful evolution and the Clinton administration's variant, "constructive engagement." Indeed, party leaders placed much of the blame for

Tiananmen Square on Western propaganda and even Central Intelligence Agency encouragement and involvement. Despite the continued authoritarian direction of the PRC, however, China was about to enter its period of greatest economic growth and prosperity; and the party would increasingly stake its primacy to the boom.

CONCLUSION

The pattern of Chinese history that had been followed during the Maoist years bears certain parallels with the brief interlude of the First Emperor from 221 to 208 BCE. That is, older institutions were torn up by the roots and discarded and a radical philosophy was imposed on the state and society. In the first instance, the justification had been the creation of an empire. In the case of Mao, it had been to start from scratch to end the last vestiges of imperialism and to take advantage of China's poor and blank condition to create an authentically Chinese socialism. In both cases, the will of the leader was absolute and his sway nearly complete. In both cases as well, many were sacrificed to the cause at hand.

Without pushing the parallels too far, the post-Mao period resembles the post-Qin period. There was no revolution ending Maoist rule, only the quiet departure of his death. But like the long-lived Han dynasty that followed the First Emperor, China since 1976 has left the former administrative structures largely in place, but liberalized much else, especially the economy. The Four Modernizations have unleashed the pent-up energies of China's entrepreneurs, attracted immense amounts of domestic and foreign capital, and vaulted the PRC into the upper ranks of world power. The question, however, remains as open as before, however: Will this unprecedented economic success bring with it political changes? The initial attempts at raising the possibilities of such changes were not particularly encouraging to their supporters. For many they proved disastrous. As we will see in the next chapters, the tensions inherent in tight government control and wide-open market economics would only grow more acute. The question remains: Having mounted the economic tiger, can the party ultimately dismount but stay in control?

FURTHER READING

De Bary, William Theodore. *Asian Values and Human Rights: A Confucian Communitarian Perspective.* Cambridge, MA: Harvard University Press, 1998. Stimulating discussions of the debate between those who see Confucianism as countenancing authoritarianism and those who view Confucian notions of the individual as not incompatible with world norms of human rights.

Nathan, Andrew J. *Chinese Democracy: An Investigation into the Nature and Meaning of Democracy in China Today.* New York: Knopf, 1985. The most important treatment of the Democracy Wall movement by a leading scholar of modern China. It appeared at time when the optimism for the Fifth Modernization was still fresh.

Perry, Elizabeth J., and Mark Selden. *Chinese Society: Change, Conflict, and Resistance,* 2nd ed. London: Routledge, 2003. Essay collection that explores the cleavages of modern China, especially those resulting from the rapid changes of the 1980s and 1990s. Although some barriers have been lifted, the writers argue, the government still retains its authoritarian character.

Ruan Ming. *Deng Xiaoping: Chronicle of an Empire.* Translated by Nancy Liu, Peter Rand, and Lawrence Sullivan. Boulder, CO: Westview, 1994. Account of the early years of the Four Modernizations and Deng's rise to power. Ruan Ming was a party insider and supporter of the reforms but was purged and moved to the United States.

Schell, Orville. *To Get Rich Is Glorious: China in the Eighties.* New York: Knopf, 1984. The journalist Schell was one of the first outsiders to write about the early results of Deng's reforms. The extended essay for this book originally appeared in the *New Yorker* magazine. Schell deftly explores the implications inherent in China's abrupt change of direction and the early consequences of "letting some get rich first so as to lead others to wealth."

Spence, Jonathan D. *In Search of Modern China*, 3rd ed. New York: Norton, 2012. Comprehensive history of China from the Ming Dynasty to the twenty-first century by one of the most respected China scholars working today.

Theroux, Paul. *Riding the Iron Rooster: By Train through China.* New York: Putnam's Sons, 1988. Classic account of a series of journeys by steam train through China, with a view to looking at the transitions of the Four Modernizations, by a leading—and often acerbic—travel writer. Uses the Chinese proverb "You can always fool a foreigner" as a leitmotif and personal challenge.

Tu Wei-ming. *Way, Learning, and Politics: Essays on the Confucian Intellectual.* Albany, NY: SUNY, 1993. Scholarly, yet accessible essays on historical Confucian issues, many of which revolve around self-cultivation, culminating with a personal exploration of modern themes, by the leading "New Confucian."

Zhang Liang (pseud.), compiler; Andrew J. Nathan and Perry Link, eds. *The Tiananmen Papers.* New York: Public Affairs, 2001. Translations of primary source materials by date leading up to, during, and immediately after the crushing of the demonstrations in Tiananmen Square. Especially helpful are 100 short biographies of relevant individuals in the end matter. The real identity of "Zhang Liang" is unknown.

Zhang Xinxin and Sang Ye. *Chinese Lives: An Oral History of Contemporary China.* W. J. F. Jenner and Delia Davin, eds. New York: Macmillan, 1987. One of the best of a number of accounts of how ordinary Chinese people reacted to the dizzying changes of the 1980s.

CHAPTER 9

TOWARD THE "HARMONIOUS SOCIETY": BUILDING THE FRAGILE SUPERPOWER, 1989 TO THE PRESENT

As the young American woman went about making her selections in a Beijing market, she idly turned her head to face the voices that had grabbed her attention. A large and growing group of Chinese women was studying her purchases and buying her choices themselves, regardless of their own shopping needs. As the young American heard them talking among themselves and shouting to her the repeated *putonghua* words "*jiexi, jiexi,*" she realized with a start that they were talking about her—or rather her television character, "Jessie." For Rachel DeWoskin it was a signal moment. In a flash she realized just how popular her character had become as the Chinese soap opera in which she starred, *Yang Nü Zai Beijing*—"Foreign Babes in Beijing"—established itself in the world's largest television market.

Although her father, Kenneth, was a noted economist of China, Rachel on graduation ended up in China from a sense of adventure and a job at a public relations firm. Invited to a party not long after her arrival, she was approached by a television producer to play the role of the dark-haired American temptress on *Foreign Babes*—and the foil to the blonde foreign woman who strove to be a good Chinese wife. Her account of her Chinese television career and the adventures and misadventures of cross-cultural relationships in the China of the mid-1990s emerged after her return to the United States as *Foreign Babes in Beijing: Behind the Scenes of a New China* (New York: Norton, 2005). The China revealed in her experiences is one that was changing so fast that it already would have been unrecognizable even a decade before.

Although China had undergone a brief period of international censure in the wake of Tiananmen Square, the period of the mid-1990s saw an immense acceleration in the privatizing of the economy, in international investment, in the PRC becoming the world's low-cost manufacturing powerhouse, and in a frenetic development of consumerism. All of this was accompanied by a new cultural assertiveness both inside and outside of China. It was here that the *Foreign Babes* phenomenon was at its most striking. Western film and television portrayals of East Asians had for decades maintained a certain core group of plot and character stereotypes: men were often depicted as repositories of Confucian or "Oriental" wisdom; or as "inscrutable"; or sometimes driven by diabolically fanatical hatreds, seldom completely open and often somewhat feminine in their demeanor. Women were frequently portrayed as totally subservient or outwardly submissive but internally tough and stoic; or as irresistibly exotic and seductive, particularly if they were interacting with Western men. Similar in many respects to the repertory of images of the Middle East Edward Said identified as "Orientalism," these stereotypes were deeply imbedded in the cultural residue of imperialism and China's "century of humiliation."

As if to reassert Chinese cultural agency and counter these deep-seated images, *Foreign Babes* turned them on their heads. In this dramatic series, it is the ruggedly handsome, physically powerful Wang Ling, whose stalwart character, the family man Li Tianming, is drawn by the wiles of the foreign siren "Jessie," with her individualistic, selfish, "American" ways and iron determination to have the man she wants regardless of the cost. Her blonde counterpart, Louisa, plays the new role of the "good" foreign woman, who struggles in the face of innumerable cultural and familial obstacles to be a proper, assimilated "Chinese" wife to Tianming's younger brother, Tianliang. And yet the enormous popularity of the Jessie character is also reflective of the vast and rapid cultural changes taking place in the country—despite such officially sanctioned artistic attempts to create a distinctly Chinese moral template. In the final episode, with the hard-won sanction of the Li family, true love reigns as Tianming and Jessie set out on their grand romantic adventure to America.

Foreign Babes in Beijing. Author Rachel DeWoskin poses for photographs during an interview with Reuters in New York, May 23, 2005. DeWoskin's book "Foreign Babes in Beijing" is a real-life account about living in China for five years and starring in the wildly popular series by that name. She played "Jessie," the newly developing Chinese image of the "American" woman who opts for true love with her Chinese man and ultimately goes off with him to America.

As we have noted periodically in these chapters, one of the ongoing patterns of Chinese history since the latter nineteenth century has been what the noted China historian Jonathan Spence called "The Search for Modern China." That is, how should China forge a path toward reclaiming its historic place of wealth, power, and cultural influence without losing its civilizational distinctiveness? How can it become modern without becoming Western? As with some of the issues we have examined before, the debate about "constructive engagement" and "peaceful evolution," the campaigns against "bourgeois liberalism" and "spiritual pollution," and China's leaders' growing insistence that their perspective on what constitutes "human rights" is at least as legitimate as that of the United States or the European Union may be seen as part of this overall pattern. Indeed, as China has now become the world's second largest economy and as its military, diplomatic, and "soft power" continues to grow, this assertion of historical and cultural uniqueness in modernity—as in the official designation of its economic system as socialism with Chinese characteristics—is likely to increase as well. In that respect the linkage of this pattern with a popular soap opera may not be as obscure as it would first appear.

SOCIALISM WITH CHINESE CHARACTERISTICS

Given the worldwide coverage accorded the student demonstrations in Tiananmen Square from April till early June of 1989 and the optimism the movement raised among many inside and outside of the PRC, it is not surprising that China's prestige on the world stage took a severe blow in the wake of the movement's ruthless suppression. Relations with the United States and the West in general hit a low not seen since the intense days of the Cold War. Economic sanctions were imposed and trade agreements canceled; thousands of Chinese studying abroad attempted to stay where they were rather than go home. Angry denunciations of the American belief in peaceful evolution by party leaders multiplied, and Western critics of the theory multiplied as well. The Clinton administration's renaming of the concept as constructive engagement did little to improve matters. Moreover, the years between 1989 and 1995 saw the popular triumphalist theory of Francis Fukuyama—which claimed that the fall of the Communist Bloc left Western democratic liberalism without serious competition and so represented "the end of history"—retreat in favor of Samuel Huntington's grimmer vision of the "clash of civilizations" as the dominant pattern of the world's foreseeable future. China's belated bid to reclaim some lost prestige by landing the 2000 Olympic Games for Beijing was defeated in favor of Sydney, Australia. Many claimed it was an aftershock of 1989. Much of this prestige was regained in the first decade of the new millennium, however, most dramatically with Beijing's hosting of the 2008 Olympics.

Confucian Capitalism

Even as the aftereffects of Tiananmen Square unfolded, there were also signs that, despite the apparent triumph of conservative party officials like Jiang Zemin and Li Peng, Deng Xiaoping intended to accelerate the momentum of economic reform. In 1990 China opened its first equity market, the Shanghai Stock Exchange. In 1992, like the Kangxi emperor of the Qing, Deng conducted a highly publicized tour of South China, where he took the opportunity in Shenzhen and the most economically advanced regions to urge increased market reforms and economic openness.

With China's economy recovering rapidly in the early 1990s and international capital once again entering the country, the obvious next stage would be for China to take steps to join the same financial structures and institutions as other economically powerful nations. One immediate obstacle, however, was that the *renminbi* was not a convertible currency. The Chinese government artificially supported its value and did not allow it to float on the international market as other major currencies do. This was in part because much of China's economy was still populated by state-run enterprises. In addition, wages in enterprises vying for cheap manufacturing contracts were low and the government sought to control commodity prices to check inflation and avoid large-scale impoverishment—part of the older "iron rice bowl" safety net. Moreover, the *renminbi* was not convertible because noncitizens of the PRC were supposed to use Foreign Exchange Certificates—forbidden to PRC citizens—which *were* convertible, but only within the country. Not surprisingly, a lively black market in Foreign Exchange Certificates and foreign currency, particularly dollars, had sprung up and supported a considerable underground economy. All of this deprived the government of revenues and legitimacy in international exchange. Therefore, as part of the push to expand market economics, the *renminbi* was allowed to float and become convertible in 1996 and the Foreign Exchange Certificates were discontinued. The initial steps were now in place for China to join the World Trade Organization, which it did in 2001.

The momentum of economic development in the 1990s also led to a new ideological emphasis for the party. The Communist Party's legitimacy to rule had been historically tied to its revolutionary legacy, its championing of peasants and proletarians, and, more recently, its unleashing of the people's entrepreneurial energies. To help ensure that the reforms would stay in place, Jiang Zemin announced a new set of principles in 2000 that became known as **The Three Represents** (*Sange daibiao*). Although controversial at first, the party not only adopted these principles, but also enshrined them in both the Party Constitution and the State Constitution. As the centerpiece of Jiang Zemin Theory, they have become the nexus of the CCP's claim to ongoing legitimacy. They are as follows:

> Our Party must always represent the requirements for developing China's advanced productive forces, the orientation of China's advanced culture, and the fundamental interests of the overwhelming majority of the Chinese people.

Thus, some have argued that this may be considered a move away from the ideology of the party's revolutionary roots and toward making a pact with the country to keep the economic momentum going, as this is embodied in all three of the Represents.

The acceleration of economic reforms was accompanied by a readjustment of relations between China and the West. Deng died in February 1997, and despite the tarnish of Tiananmen Square, his worldwide image as China's great reformer not only remained intact but also was further burnished by his passing. A few months later, on July 1, amid great fanfare and pageantry, Hong Kong passed back into Chinese sovereignty, under the provisions of the Basic Law and the rubric of "one country, two systems." The run-up to the handover of the Crown Colony had been accompanied by considerable anxiety on the part of many Hong Kong citizens. Many took advantage of their British passports—which allowed them to emigrate anywhere in the Commonwealth except the United Kingdom—greatly expanding the Chinese communities in Sydney, Melbourne, Toronto, and especially Vancouver. In anticipation of Hong Kong retaining its political system, the colony's last governor, Chris Patten, pushed through measures to further democratize the ruling bodies of the city as a hedge against any attempts by Beijing to rein in the autonomy of the new Hong Kong Special Administrative Region. In the end, the handover went smoothly, and despite protests by party leaders that Patten had violated the spirit of the Basic Law, things went on largely as before. Two years later, the Portuguese handed over Macao in much the same manner. Symbolic as well of the new political atmosphere was a visit by Jiang Zemin to the United States later in 1997 and one by the U.S. president Bill Clinton the following year.

Lowering the British Flag. World dignitaries and other guests to the Hong Kong handover ceremony stand and watch the Chinese flag, left, flying after the Union Jack was lowered at the Hong Kong Convention Center Tuesday, July 1, 1997. Under the agreement called the Basic Law, Hong Kong and Macau would be governed as Special Administrative Regions on the principle of "one country, two systems" for 50 years after the turnover of sovereignty.

Shattering the Iron Rice Bowl

Although Deng was gone and the party factions favoring a strong authoritarian political center were firmly in place, the economic reforms not only continued but also accelerated. By the late 1990s China was experiencing an astonishing double-digit growth in its gross domestic product (GDP), but officials were increasingly worried that if the old state-owned industries were not swiftly privatized the pace might slacken, perhaps even resulting in a recession. The Chinese economy hovered in a kind of transitional hybrid state. New enterprises appeared all the time, government controls on foreign ownership and investment were being loosened, and the rural economy was, if not booming, certainly more than keeping up with food production. The state enterprises, however, which guaranteed at least a degree of universal employment and government benefits during earlier years, were now hopelessly inefficient, burdened with outmoded technology, larded with corrupt officials and personnel, and an increasing drain on the economy with their lifetime pensions and interconnection with the welfare system.

Private High-Tech Plant. Female Chinese workers check production of photovoltaic cells for solar panels at the plant of Shanghai Shenzhou New Energy Development Co., Ltd. Lianyungang city, Jiangsu province. China accelerated its solar-energy buildout in the first quarter of 2015, adding 18% to total capacity as the government prioritized renewable-energy investment to clear up the skies and shore up economic growth.

Thus, in 1998, the new premier, Zhu Rongji, initiated a program to shut down the state-run enterprises, sell them off, and encourage more complete privatization. Although over the next several years this caused considerable disruption and created a degree of unemployment, it did provide yet another boost for the economy that would last even through the worldwide recessions of the early twenty-first century. It did, however, require vast changes in the country's social safety net and an effective end to the iron rice bowl.

During the Maoist years, excluding the Cultural Revolution, one of the party's proudest achievements was a system of free universal education and free health care. Even the most remote rural districts could expect periodic visits from "barefoot doctors," people trained in basic medical skills and the elements of hygiene, who functioned as the front line of health care in the countryside. In the 1980s after the implementation of the "one child" program, those who had a second child could lose these rights. With the economy half-privatized by the late 1990s, however, the cost of such programs, particularly health care and pensions, was becoming prohibitive. This was especially true of the many two-income families in which one member kept a state job to claim family benefits. Thus, one by one, state benefits were rolled back and fee-for-service systems put in place. Doctor and hospital visits now required fees for various procedures and medications according to a sliding scale tagged to a percentage of an average worker's income. Despite the fact that by U.S. or international standards medical costs are still comparatively low in China, the country's low per capita income means

Tutoring Center. English grammar tutor Tony Chow (left), gives a lesson to his students in a classroom of Modern Education in Hong Kong. He teaches English grammar to thousands of secondary school pupils, who attend his after-school lessons or watch video replays of them at Modern Education's 14 branches. Chow is a celebrity tutor in Hong Kong, where there are vastly expanding opportunities for offering extracurricular lessons to parents desperately seeking an edge for their children preparing for the city's intense public entrance exam for university.

that such costs occupy a substantial chunk of a worker's wages. Primary and secondary education is still free, but there has been an explosion in tutoring institutions and charter schools. As in Japan, extra tutoring is considered absolutely essential by those who can afford it because of the rigor of the three-day *gaokao*, the grueling college entrance exams. Scholarships are still available to outstanding students for university and graduate studies but tuition fees and room and board are charged to the rest. Foreign study, which used to be subsidized by the government for those who could enter higher education institutions abroad, must now be paid for out of pocket. One result of this has been that branch campuses of foreign universities in China have opened so that students can get the "experience" of overseas study more cheaply and closer to home.

One of the anchors of the old iron rice bowl had been the relative immobility of the population. Since China's main concern for so long had been agriculture, it had been vital to keep the peasants—even into the late twentieth century, 70 to 80 percent of the population—on the land producing food. As Deng's economic reforms took root and food production soared, the countryside entered into a period of prosperity. The dismantling of the state enterprises, the twin phenomena of immense opportunity and the possibility of unemployment, and the building of a vast new infrastructure of roads and railroads created a need for and a means of increased mobility. Since the

Urban Migrants. Men from rural areas seeking kitchen work hold lists of dishes they can cook in Chongqing, China in 2013. China is pushing ahead with a plan to move 250 million rural residents into newly constructed "medium" towns and cities over the next dozen years.

party, however, aimed at keeping population growth in check and worried about urban overcrowding, they were slow to undo travel and migration restrictions.

The key gatekeepers in this regard were the leaders of one's *danwei*, or work unit. They were the state's control group in urban neighborhoods, villages, and state-run enterprises. As we saw in the previous chapter, they could be so intrusive as to monitor the monthly cycles of women to ensure against unreported pregnancy. They controlled the widely disliked *hukou*, the residency permits necessary for housing and school registration. As the restrictions they controlled were rolled back, millions began to move in search of opportunity. The cities swelled in size and today are some of the largest in the world. Municipal governments were stretched to the limit to provide housing and school space to the new arrivals. Although one still needs a residency permit to have access to services, tens of millions of illegal migrants have become squatters in China's cities, attempting by various means to navigate the remains of the iron rice bowl still available and improvising substitutes for those features of it that are not.

The Beijing Olympics and Social Cleavages

As the new millennium dawned, China's role as the up-and-coming economic powerhouse continued to build. China became the largest holder of U.S. Treasury Bills and enjoyed lopsided balance-of-trade surpluses with the United States and other economic leaders. On the one hand, with giant companies such as Walmart (the largest employer in the United States) and Target acquiring more and more of their inventories from Chinese factories, prices could be held to a bare minimum, helping to keep inflation at bay in the consumer economies of China's customers. On the other hand, China itself began to mature as a consumer market, luring more and more foreign investment and stimulating the creation of such huge Chinese companies as Haier and Lenovo. In many ways China was following a similar economic pattern to Japan and, more recently, Taiwan and South Korea: In the 1950s and 1960s, "made in Japan" was a term of derision for cheap, low-quality goods. By the 1970s, however, quality control in such consumer items as cars and electronics had recast this impression; by the 1980s and 1990s Japan's preeminence in high-quality manufactured goods was firmly established. One by-product of this pattern was that wages increased as Japan became the world's second largest economy. Not only that, but other countries were now taking up the place Japan once held in terms of low-cost, low-wage manufacturing. Through the 1990s China grew into the most prominent of these. By 2015, however, China was well on the way to following the Japanese pattern of rising wages and a growing middle class and farming out low-cost manufacturing to Vietnam, India, and, most recently, African countries. This transition in the late 1990's did not come without a cost, however. Massive demonstrations rocked many of China's state-run enterprises as workers fought to keep their benefits and attempted to stop privatization, especially under suspiciously corrupt circumstances.

With this transition came what social scientists call a "revolution of rising expectations." That is, although the gap between rich and poor in China was growing, with some Chinese entrepreneurs even becoming billionaires, at the same time unemployment continued to be a chronic problem. One result was that people's optimism sometimes tended to outrun their economic reality. In 2001, China's urban middle class was estimated at 4 percent of the population, or approximately 52 million people. By the end of the first decade of the new century, China had the world's largest middle class, more than 300 million—about the size of the entire population of the United States. It is estimated that this number will more than double to 630 million by 2022. However, the expectation of achieving middle-class status and sharing the burgeoning urban amenities and consumer bounty of China and the world is increasing even faster. One milestone in this regard is that in January 2012, China's National Bureau of Statistics reported that for the first time in history, more Chinese were living in urban areas than in rural ones.

With China's rush into economic growth has come the rising expectation on the part of many for greater political liberalization. The party's position on this, as we have seen, has been to steadfastly oppose any notion that its socialism with Chinese characteristics will lead away from authoritarian one-party rule. Many have suggested, however, that as the culture becomes more materialistic and the legal system increasingly deals with matters of property rights, these will necessarily lead to redefinitions of individual human rights and a drive toward more open and representative government.

Chinese-made Appliances and Cars. (A) Customers inspect Qingdao Haier Co. Ltd. washing machines in Shanghai in 2009. Haier is China's largest manufacturer of household appliances and is developing a growing export trade. **(B)** Visitors look at a Chinese-made Dongfeng car at the Beijing Auto Show in 2006. Chinese automakers are now competing inside and outside China with global giants like GM, Honda, and Toyota. China has now become the world's second largest vehicle market.

Nowhere have these rising expectations been on more dramatic display—and led to more bitter disappointment—than in the case of minority rights. China recognizes more than 50 minority groups and, as with religion, tends to use such official recognition to accord them certain group rights and privileges. In some ways this approach follows the familiar traditional pattern of the loose rein and using barbarians to check barbarians. In the cases of Tibet and Xinjiang, the minorities are largely located within specially designated Autonomous Regions. As we saw in the chapters on the Qing, Chinese suzerainty over Tibet and Central Asia was fairly loose in imperial times and sometimes utilized political–religious interests in cementing the loyalty of different groups. As a nation-state, however, the PRC not only attempted to quell any attempts at additional autonomy or in-dependence, but also crushed incipient rebellion on several occasions, most dra-matically in Tibet in 1959. One result of this was that the Dalai Lama fled to a life of exile in India. From there he has been a catalyst for Tibetan activist move-ments agitating across the political spectrum for everything from complete in-dependence to more autonomy within the present system.

Tibetans have long charged that China has been attempting a kind of "cultural genocide" in the country by encouraging Han Chinese emigration and settlement. This accelerated considerably after 2006 with the completion of the impressive engineering feat of the Qinghai-Lhasa Railway, the world's highest. Despite some

Tibetan Protests. The exile of the Dalai Lama and Tibetan refugees since the PRC's suppression of Tibet in 1959 has resulted in a world-wide movement embracing a variety of goals ranging from greater autonomy for Tibet within the People's Republic to complete independence. Here pro-testers on a march to Tibet are stopped by Indian police in Himachal Pradesh in March, 2008 during the run-up to the Beijing Olympics.

optimism that an agreement might be reached between the PRC and the Dalai Lama on increased autonomy, anti-Chinese riots broke out in Lhasa and other Tibetan cities in March 2008. Anxious to quell the violence well in advance of the 2008 Olympics, PLA soldiers and police put the disturbances down with brutal efficiency and considerable loss of life. Worldwide support of Tibetans resulted in, among other things, disruption of the progress of the Olympic torch on its way to the Chinese capital. Over the past several years Tibetan Buddhist monks have resorted to self-immolation to bring their cause before the world media.

Even before this, however, the attacks on New York City's World Trade Center of September 11, 2001, and the subsequent "war on terror" afforded party leaders an opportunity to reinforce their military position in Muslim areas of Central Asia, ostensibly in solidarity with the United States in its wars in Afghanistan and Iraq. Taking the diplomatic initiative in a way that has become increasingly common as China's overall power expanded, the PRC signed the Shanghai Cooperation Organization Regional Anti-terrorism Structure with Russia, Tajikistan, Uzbekistan, Kazakhstan, and Kyrgyzstan. Any chance that the Muslim Uyghurs in Xinjiang thought they had to bargain for more autonomy quickly evaporated as PRC authorities began a crackdown aimed at Al Qaeda and putative Turkic separatists.

The party's insistence on clamping down on unapproved religious or ideological activity was perhaps most dramatically illustrated in April 1999, with the suppression of Falun Gong. Founded in 1992 by Li Hongzhi, a low-level civil servant, Falun Gong draws from several traditional Chinese sources, although mostly from Buddhism and the theories of *qi* (energy) that animate traditional Chinese medicine and the practice of *taiji quan*. Followers engage in exercises meant to strengthen the internal "wheel of law," or *falun*, which draws "cultivation energy" (*gong*) to the practitioner. The movement proved popular among a variety of people searching for meaning and especially among the elderly and those who had fallen through the health-care safety net. By the end of the decade Li claimed millions of followers worldwide and the group had organized itself into a kind of alternative society within China, with its own insurance and financial structure. To the party, it looked suspiciously like a dissident movement or perhaps a nascent opposition party. From 1999 to 2003, therefore, it drove Falun Gong underground, breaking up public gatherings, arresting numerous members, and launching a propaganda campaign to discredit the group. They remain active worldwide, however, and even have their own television network, "Tang Dynasty TV."

Amid the social and political–religious cleavages during the opening years of the new millennium came its first pandemic: severe acute respiratory syndrome (SARS). One observer called it the most serious crisis faced by the Chinese government since Tiananmen Square. In the fall of 2002, reports from Guangdong began to emerge of a severe pneumonialike respiratory infection, usually beginning with flu-like symptoms and quickly accelerating to the acute respiratory stage. Although investigative teams began to track and analyze the virus involved, the public health authorities withheld the news from the media and the World Health Organization for fear of causing a panic and because of possible damage to China's international

Falun Gong Demonstrations. The rise of Falun Gong in the PRC and in Chinese communities all over the world has proved worrisome to the CCP and the Chinese government who see in the religious movement the beginnings of a serious opposition party. Falun Gong supporters regularly protest at the Chinese consul-general's offices in New York and in front of other PRC offices. Here, demonstrators with the organization End the Persecution of Falun Gong Practitioners in China, protest outside the Chinese consulate in Los Angeles in 2012. The group was demonstrating against the (then) Chinese Vice-President Xi Jinping's visit to the United States.

trade and tourist industry. One serious flaw in the health system at this stage was that because the disease had not been officially analyzed and recognized, reporting it could lead to arrest for "stealing state secrets." Thus, the disease spread not only in China but also internationally until world media and the World Health Organization put pressure on PRC leaders in the spring of 2003, who launched a remarkably successful public campaign against the spread of the disease. Although thousands were infected, only a few hundred died despite the government's tardy and uncoordinated response. Again, however, China's image as a modern country rapidly moving from "developing" to "developed" took a powerful blow.

The Harmonious Society

The cleavages appearing in Chinese society as a by-product of the frenetic pace of China's unequaled economic growth had become all too evident by 2006. At a time when China was wrapping up some of the world's most ambitious construction projects like the Qinghai-Lhasa railway and the colossal Three Gorges Dam complex on the Yangzi—history's largest hydroelectric system—and China had shown its technological mettle by sending a man into space, the country was riven

Monumental Construction Projects. (A) A train travels on the *Qingzang* (Qinghai-Tibet) Railway in China's Tibet Autonomous Region, in 2014. China ultimately plans to extend a railway line linking Tibet with the rest of the country to the borders of India, Nepal, and Bhutan by 2020. China opened the railway to Lhasa, the capital city of Tibet, in 2006, which passes spectacular icy peaks on the Tibetan highlands, touching altitudes as high as 5,000 meters above sea level. The increased efficiency of travel is touted by the government as a boon to development, though many Tibetans see it as spurring Han emigration and overwhelming Tibetan society and culture. (B) Perhaps even more impressive as a technological and construction feat is the colossal Three Gorges Dam on the upper reaches of the Yangzi. The world's largest hydroelectric project, the dam was controversial from its inception because of fears of its environmental impact and the mass relocation of much of the population along the river.

by growing separations on multiple levels: Between rich and poor; between rural and urban; between low-wage workers in the exploding number of factories and mines and those comfortably in the middle class; between migrants and legal residents in the cities; between those within the tattered social safety net and those outside of it; between those with party connections and those without them; between dissident groups and minorities and the mainstream; and between those with separatist ambitions and the government security apparatus. Moreover, 7 of the world's 10 most polluted urban areas were in China, crime and divorce were on the rise, and the country appeared so caught up in making money that its moral center seemed to have vanished with nothing to replace it—a situation that various religions sought to remedy, much to the government's anxiety.

Hu Jintao, who, symbolically enough, had replaced Jiang Zemin as party chief in the PRC's first orderly and peaceful transfer of power, called on the party's Central Committee in a plenary session in October 2006 to step back from breakneck economic development for the moment to concentrate on addressing these social tensions. The result was an endorsement of Hu's concept of the **Harmonious Society** (*Hexie shehui*). Hu's vision was that economic development and reducing societal tensions resulting from rapid growth must go hand in hand. Particular attention needed to be paid to reducing the gap between rich and poor, which, if left to grow wider, would result in social disruption. Thus, he called for a model reflecting what economists call "sustainable development"—growing the GDP at a rate that will fully satisfy consumer demand without creating excessive surpluses that need to be exported. Increasing the use of technology in the service of efficiency is another aspect of the overall goal.

A third part of the approach is to increase openness and honesty in government to ensure political and public harmony. Anticorruption campaigns, of course, had been a staple of Communist Party policy since the early 1950s. As we have seen, however, one of the patterns of China's political economy since the inception of the Four Modernizations has been the disproportionate power of the single legal political party within the developing market economy. The almost universal practices of *guanxi* (connections) and *houmen* (the back door), which benefit immensely those with an entrée to the party, became further entrenched not only in the business world, but also even more in the booming real estate market. Here the chronic need for housing and development—pushed further by the new policy of building "medium" towns and cities in less developed areas to ease the rate of emigration to larger urban areas—resulted in epic corruption.

Moreover, big developers in collusion with local party officials and municipal governments routinely seized land by eminent domain, often compensating those from whom it was taken only a fraction of what was due them. As much as 6 percent of China's arable land in production in 1980 had been claimed for development by 2006. Indeed, the overwhelming majority of protests, demonstrations, strikes, and violence in the countryside had come about because of such land disputes. Finally, there was an ongoing emphasis on pursuing harmony among minorities and safeguarding their rights—although separatism,

Medium Towns. The lifting of restrictions on internal mobility in the PRC has resulted in millions of rural people moving into the cities, taxing their capacity for housing and human services. The government, therefore, has embarked on an ambitious program of building "satellite towns" as large suburbs around large cities and "medium towns" in order to absorb the emigrants as China has passed the benchmark of having more than half the population classified as urban. Above is the newly built medium town of Huaming, near the great port city of Tianjin, in 2013. Huaming was intended to be a model of the new urban planning but has suffered from poor-quality construction, lack of jobs, and the reluctance of the local villagers to give up their land to create the town.

"splittism," and terrorism would not be tolerated. Hu expanded this vision somewhat before he stepped down in 2011 to include reducing tensions between nations to work toward a "harmonious world."

Against this backdrop China staged arguably the most spectacular Olympic Games since their modern reincarnation in 1896. Past Olympics had often been used to showcase the wealth and modernity of the host country. Classic examples include Nazi Germany in 1936 and, more recently, Tokyo in 1964. In the latter case, the games took place 19 years after Japan's complete defeat in World War II and were meant to show how far the island nation had come as a peaceful member of the world community. Similarly, the Beijing Olympics, 19 years after the disaster at Tiananmen Square, were to be a symbol of China's breakneck economic progress and modernity.

The capital underwent a massive building program including a complete updating of the subway system, highways, and surface transportation. The venue itself was studded with spectacular architecture, including a high-rise building meant to suggest the Olympic torch, the "Bird's Nest" stadium, and the unique "Aquacube" natatorium. All of this, however, also included elements of the social cleavages mentioned previously: developers and the municipal authorities moved tens of thousands of people in a massive clearance of Beijing's traditional *sihe yuan hutong* residences—leaving a few neighborhoods intact as tourist attractions. As one might expect, this led to spirited protests. In anticipation of demonstrations from a number of quarters because of the intense international media coverage, the authorities designated a particular area isolated from the Olympic venues where these could be carried out under supervision.

The Olympics also showcased a high degree of grassroots nationalism, far beyond the usual attempts by the government to orchestrate it for its own purposes. Since 1984, athletes from Taiwan had competed under the title "China-Taipei" rather than Republic of China so as to avoid diplomatic difficulty with the PRC. Taiwan athletes competed in Beijing in a record number of events and the patriotic feelings of "Chineseness" tended to overcome the political differences between both regimes. Millions of PRC fans followed the daily medal count in hopes that China would surpass the United States. Red t-shirts emblazoned with the slogan "Go China!" (*jiayou Zhongguo*: literally, "More gas[olene], China!") appeared everywhere. All of this engendered a popular feeling that China was no longer a "developing nation" but one rapidly rising to economic superpower status—and accruing the prestige that rightly belongs to it. The Games showed that China had an unsurpassed capacity to stage spectacle and Chinese athletes were likewise out to make their mark as "warriors for the

The Beijing Olympics. Not having obtained the 2000 Olympic Games, Beijing's award of the 2008 games stimulated unprecedented construction in the city as well as a considerable upwelling of national pride. Many of the city's older buildings and a large number of its famous residential *hutongs* were razed to obtain the space for the assorted spectacular venues. Two of the iconic structures were the Aqua Cube swimming and diving arena (left) and the Bird's Nest outdoor stadium (right) shown here lit up at night.

nation." When the PRC's 2004 gold medalist Liu Xiang fell and scratched from the 110-meter hurdles, there was a widespread and genuine outpouring of grief for him. Some wondered whether he had been broken by the pressure of carrying the prestige of the nation on his back. Others applauded his game attempt to tough it out. The official Xinhua News Agency even saw the need to run an editorial cautioning people not to worship him as a god.

Thus, in most respects, the Olympics had the desired effect of placing China prominently back onto the world stage, as did China's first world's fair of the Communist era, the Shanghai Expo of 2010. Less successful was the aftermath of the disastrous Sichuan earthquake in May 2008, which destroyed large sections of the huge municipalities of Chengdu and Chongqing, killing upward of 70,000, injuring 37,000, and leaving 20,000 missing. The defects of the slipshod construction of so many of the new buildings were put on painful display under the extensive international media coverage. Much of it centered on the tragic collapse of an elementary school and a high school; all told, 5,335 school children are believed to have perished. The government mounted a massive rescue and relief effort but the damage was so extensive and the infrastructure so damaged that many rural areas saw no relief for weeks. One of the notable innovations of the event, however, was that for

Sichuan Earthquake. China faced a major disaster in the months leading up to the Olympics when a huge 7.8 magnitude earthquake struck Sichuan province, proving especially catastrophic in the huge city of Chongqing and the provincial capital, Chengdu. The disaster was magnified by the revelation that the previous breakneck pace of construction had resulted in a number of shoddily made buildings including, tragically, an elementary school and high school. Here, local people stand on a collapsed house in Beichuan Country in Mianyan, Sichuan Province, on May 13, a day after the main earthquake struck.

the first time Chinese reporters and television crews had a largely free hand in reporting the unfolding tragedy in real time. Although the government attempted to rein news organizations in afterward, many reporters and viewers insisted more strongly than ever on their rights to uncensored coverage.

Sustainable Growth?

In December 2007, following the rapid collapse of the market for mortgage-backed credit-default swaps and the failure of several major financial institutions in the United States, a worldwide recession took place. The U.S. government acted to prop up some of the largest companies like General Motors, but American unemployment soared and the ripple effect on international markets was in some cases catastrophic.

Although there was considerable fear that the PRC would sell off many of its holdings in American Treasury Bills, this did not happen and of all the major economic powers, China, which still exercised some artificial controls over the *renminbi*, emerged in the strongest position. Although its annual GDP growth slowed from double-digit rates to 9.6 percent from 2008 to 2011, this was still far ahead of that of the United States, which limped along at 1 to 2 percent and only began to recover after 2012. This growth, although down from China's earlier record-setting pace, was still sufficient to allow the PRC to surpass some significant benchmarks. China's export sector leaped ahead 17 percent in December 2010, signaling that it had weathered the recession quite well. Moreover, the PRC had now vaulted past Germany to become in absolute terms the world's largest exporter. The following year came another milestone: in February 2011, China passed Japan to become the world's second largest economy. Already, economists were speculating about the date on which China would surpass the United States. Estimates in 2013 put China's GDP at about 76 percent that of the United States. Although by one measure of purchasing power China's GDP came close to that of the United States in the summer of 2014, its per capita annual income of $6807 was but a fraction of the more than $53,000 for the United States.

All of this growth sustaining China's vast industrial and technological revolution requires energy, and scholars predict that China's needs will drive it to an unprecedented level of global competition for resources. During the 1990s and early 2000s China signed a series of agreements with Russia and its Central Asian neighbors for oil and gas resources. Long before this, in the 1980s, government geologists had redoubled their efforts to search out coal seams and oil and gas fields within China, particularly in the remote and sparsely populated areas of the Northeast (the former Manchuria) and far west. Exploitation of these resources was among the motives driving the encouragement of Han Chinese to these remote areas as part of the "Go West" movement. More recently, China's enormous pollution problems from its still heavy reliance on coal for electricity generation and heating have begun to be addressed by government programs aimed at "greener" sources of energy. Nearly every Chinese dwelling except those in large apartment blocks now has either a commercial or a homemade solar hot water heater, and solar panels for electricity are also becoming ubiquitous. Wind farms are being set up as well. One of the most impressive of these helps power the city of Urumqi.

"Airpocalypse." China's massive industrialization efforts, until recently based almost entirely on fossil fuels, and of those most heavily on coal, have meant that of the ten most-polluted cities on earth, seven are in China. The use of millions of coal stoves for heating and cooking have added considerably to the problems of smog and acid rain as well. In the last decade, the Party and government have begun concerted efforts to move to cleaner fuels and alternative sources of energy, but the task is enormous. In the picture above, houses and high-rise buildings are vaguely seen in heavy smog in Taizhou city, in China's Zhejiang province, in January 2015.

The PRC currently has 23 nuclear power plants in operation, with another 26 under construction and an unknown number in the planning stages. Perhaps the single biggest power source is that of the Three Gorges hydroelectric complex of the upper Yangzi River. Multipurposed to include flood control and accompanied by a widening of the river to increase navigability, the complex produces energy equivalent to 18 nuclear power plants. Critics, however, point to the vast numbers of people that were relocated, the extreme upset of the delicate ecology of the watershed, and the loss of many invaluable archaeological sites.

All of this, however, is not nearly enough to sustain the country's energy needs even for the present. Thus, Chinese geologists, capitalists, and even military personnel are canvassing the world for additional sites for resources. In the past 10 years, Africa has proven attractive in this regard. Many African countries, such as Sudan, Angola, and the Democratic Congo (formerly Zaire), are rich in a variety of resources and have seen Chinese engineers and military advisors lending aid and building infrastructure in exchange for access to oil and minerals. In 2006 China hosted a summit in Beijing with African leaders. Business agreements worth more than $2 billion were signed, and China promised billions in loans and credits for development. Some activists, however, have charged that this is the twenty-first-century version of the nineteenth century's imperialist "scramble for Africa." Closer to home, China has claimed offshore islands and regions in the seas adjacent to the PRC, Taiwan, South Korea, Japan, Vietnam, and the Philippines for oil exploration and drilling. This has been a prime focus of recent Chinese foreign policy assertiveness and an ongoing matter for concern to nearby countries and to the United States as a guardian of the regional balance (see later).

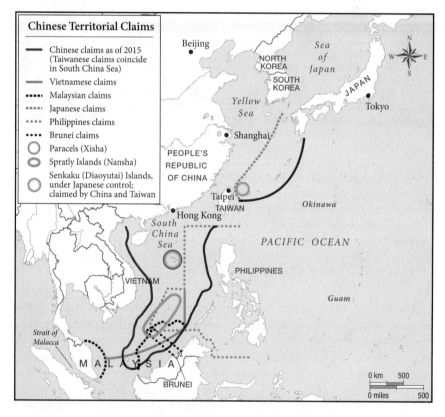

MAP 9.1
Chinese Territorial Claims

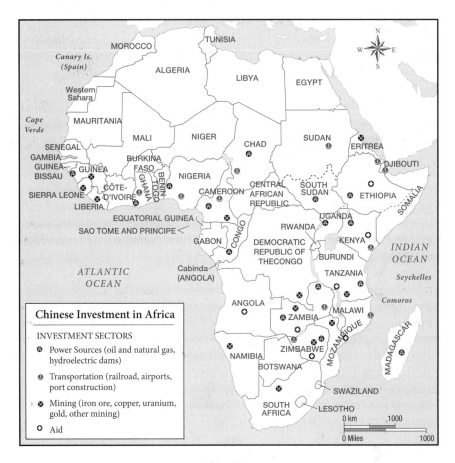

MAP 9.2
Chinese Investment in Africa

The New Assertiveness in Foreign Policy

As we have seen with the imperial era, the pattern of foreign policy in early modern China until the nineteenth century was built largely around foreigners coming to China to trade and observing the proper protocol for the government to keep them at a cultural distance—or conversely, seeking to acculturate them to Chinese norms. Within and without the empire there was an ideological conception of the civilized world as emanating from Beijing in concentric rings to the periphery of the empire itself and then beyond to lands whose degree of civilization depended on their proximity to Chinese influence. Thus, Southwest China, the western frontiers, Manchuria, and Inner Mongolia were all considered semicivilized at best; in the foreign realm, Vietnam, long occupied and influenced by Chinese culture, was seen as partly civilized, with its more Indian-influenced neighbors viewed as less so; Taiwan was considered to be in the process of cultural settlement, although its eastern mountains were dominated by aboriginal peoples; whereas the educated classes of Korea and Japan were viewed in much the same way as Anglicized "natives" of the British empire in India or Africa and their countries as cultural colonial outposts. The peoples beyond seldom entered into consideration until maritime trade and imperialism forcibly thrust them upon the empire.

The trends in historiography of China over the past several decades, as we noted in Chapter 4, have called attention to the utility of studying specific regions in China and this has its counterpart in examining recent and contemporary Chinese foreign policy. That is, as Keith Schoppa and other scholars have outlined, China's foreign relations under the PRC, although operating from a very different ideology than that of the imperial dynasties, nonetheless see the world from a similar geopolitical perspective. In this conception there are four zones, each with its own priorities and norms.

The first includes all within the present borders of the PRC, including Tibet, Xinjiang, the three Northeast provinces that make up historical Manchuria, and various minority areas within China's recognized borders. Here the government has always insisted that any activity or dissent is an internal matter not subject to outside suggestion or interference. The second, including Taiwan, Macau, and Hong Kong—and for some officials, the Chinese expatriates living abroad in East Asia—constitute what scholars sometimes call "Greater China": a zone seen as properly belonging to China but not completely unified with it politically. For Hong Kong and Macau, they are incorporated into the Chinese state under the "one country, two systems" formula. For Taiwan, there is only one China but the island for the moment is a kind of renegade autonomous province. Total independence is out of the question and the use of force to unify it with the mainland is always considered an option. The third zone is China's culturally related East Asian neighbors such as Vietnam, Korea, and Japan, those in close proximity like Indonesia, Myanmar/Burma, Laos, Cambodia, and the post–Cold War Central Asian states. Here, as China grows economically stronger and modernizes its military, it has seized the diplomatic initiative in a number of cases. Arguably, and despite the opposition of Japan and Vietnam, China has come to act in a way resembling its older assertion of Confucian elder brother suzerainty. In this case, as it does with Taiwan, it also runs into the United States as guardian of the regional status quo. Finally, the fourth zone is the rest of the world, with which China has become increasingly engaged in its quest for resources, partnerships, markets, and influence. Although space does not permit us to examine all of these aspects, three that deserve special attention are China's relations with Taiwan (see Patterns Up Close), Japan, and the United States.

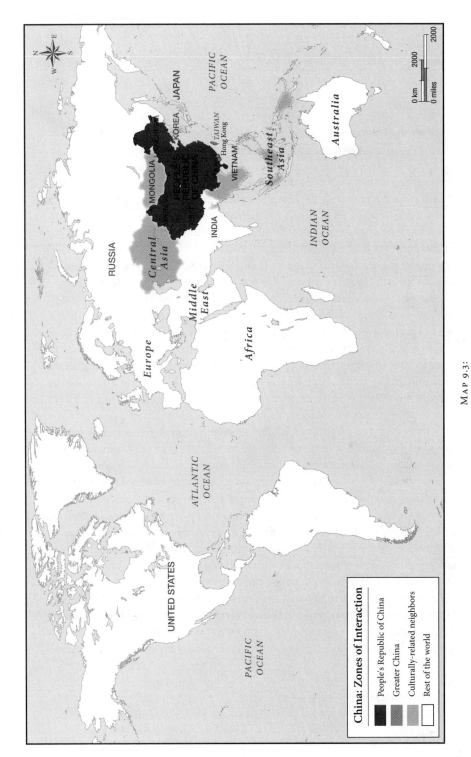

Map 9.3:
China: Zones of Interaction

China: Zones of Interaction

- People's Republic of China
- Greater China
- Culturally-related neighbors
- Rest of the world

UNITED STATES

PACIFIC
OCEAN

ATLANTIC
OCEAN

Europe

Africa

Middle
East

RUSSIA

Central
Asia

MONGOLIA

PEOPLE'S
REPUBLIC
OF CHINA

KOREA

JAPAN

TAIWAN

Hong Kong

VIETNAM

INDIA

Southeast
Asia

INDIAN
OCEAN

PACIFIC
OCEAN

Australia

0 km   2000

0 miles   2000

PATTERNS UP CLOSE

Culture Wars: Taiwan, The Peoples' Republic,
and The Struggle for Heritage

Perhaps the most persistent political goal from the inception of the PRC has been its insistence on reunion with Taiwan. With the exception of the Democratic Progressive Party's four-year interval, the governments on Taiwan have always insisted on the idea of "one China" as well. Through much of this time it was embodied by Nationalist leader Chiang Kai-shek and, after his death in 1975, by his son, Chiang Ching-kuo, who held on to dreams of retaking the mainland in the wake of an anticipated catastrophic failure of the Communist state. Since the 1950s, as we have seen, the issue has been further complicated by continued Taiwanese possession of the two island redoubts of Quemoy and Matsu (*Jinmen/Kinmen* and *Mazu* in pinyin) just off the Fujian coast, used as tripwires to involve the United States in defense of "Island China" should the PRC attempt to occupy them. Complicating things even further has been the presence of the U.S. Seventh Fleet in the Taiwan Strait as guarantor of the island's security. Moreover, decades of U.S. aid, the growth of Taiwan's economy (its GDP was ranked 21st in the world in 2013), and high-quality self-defense forces have made it prohibitive for the PRC to contemplate invasion—especially since it has until recently lacked modern naval and amphibious capability.

The pattern of the PRC's approach to incorporating Taiwan in the post-Mao era has therefore been on the one hand to use the carrot of promising a "one country, two systems" approach similar to that of Hong Kong and Macau—even with the right to retain its armed forces—while on the other threatening action if Taiwan declares independence. Hence, China engaged in war games ahead of the Taiwanese presidential elections in 1996 to discourage election of a Democratic Progressive Party candidate advocating complete separation from the mainland. In 2005, following the presidential victory of the Democrative Progressive Party's Chen Shui-bian, a law was enacted in the PRC mandating the use of force if Taiwan declares independence. On the rapprochement side, however, that same year, the leader of Taiwan's Nationalist Party (GMD/Kuomintang), Lien Chan, went to the PRC to open talks with Communist Party officials. Both parties set up offices in each other's territory from which to conduct periodic talks; both leaders have exchanged messages with each other since 2009, and direct flights have resumed between major cities on both sides of the Strait.

Yet undergirding such tensions and their relative relaxation has been the cultural struggle for the "authentic" heritage of China. When the

Nationalists fled to Taiwan in 1949 they took with them as much of China's cultural legacy as they could transport. Included in this invaluable trove were the priceless objects of the Palace Museum, the core of which had been assembled under the aegis of Qianlong, and with enormous effort had been moved to Chongqing during the Japanese invasion. The Kuomintang had for years positioned itself as carrying the true mantle not only of Sun Yat-sen's vision, but also of China's authentic cultural heritage. Under Mao, the CCP played into this strategy by making one of its foremost goals ridding the PRC of the "feudal" vestiges of the past. This, however, has faded in recent years with the renewed interest in Confucius and spreading the CCP's interpretation of his ideas and legacy on the mainland and beyond. Needless to say, the view from Taiwan on this is generally to see it as totally driven by contemporary politics rather than by a genuine desire to maintain China's cultural legacy.

One long-standing point of contention involves control of the written language. In 1956, the PRC began a comprehensive program of simplifying Chinese characters both as an aid to increasing literacy and as a sign of modernity. Although the Nationalists, too, had put together a plan for simplified characters in the 1930s, it was never put into practice. Now, however, the issue became politically heated as Taiwan officially retained the unsimplified characters, as did Hong Kong and most overseas Chinese communities. To preserve the older forms was seen as an assertion of China's cultural heritage, as a way to keep Chinese accessible to Japanese, Korean, and Vietnamese Chinese readers, and as a way to isolate the regime on the mainland. Until 2003 the use of simplified characters was banned on Taiwan; even dictionaries from the PRC were routinely confiscated during customs inspections. The separation extended into systems of Romanization as well: outside the PRC, Taiwan and Hong Kong before its turnover retained the use of the Wade–Giles system, even as the PRC's *Hanyu pinyin* gradually became the world standard. Today, although Taiwan linguists developed and popularized the use of a system called *tongyang pinyin* has also come into standard use.

Politics aside, there are sound practical arguments for the use of each form of characters. For simplified characters, ease of writing and recognition are usually cited as aids to literacy, although proponents of the older system note that in a number of cases, simplified characters are also easy to confuse. Advocates of the traditional characters note that in addition to having superior aesthetic value, the ability to use the unsimplified forms allows entrée into China's entire cultural heritage in a way that those schooled only in the new versions simply do not have. Interestingly, the

continued

renewed interest on the mainland in China's heritage has sparked a number of calls for teaching traditional characters in primary school along with the simplified versions. In 2008, 21 members of the Chinese People's Political Consultative Conference delivered such a proposal to the Ministry of Education. Significantly, it was rejected on the grounds that ongoing national policy was to promote Mandarin (*putonghua*) as the spoken language and simplified characters as the written standard. A handful of intellectuals in the PRC have even suggested that the simplified characters be phased out and traditional characters reintroduced as the standard. So far, these ideas have achieved little traction.

In 2009, Taiwan began to lobby UNESCO for an award of World Heritage status for traditional Chinese characters, which they hoped would prevent the global hegemony of the PRC's system. Already, some overseas Chinese enclaves such as Singapore have begun to use simplified characters, and

Culture Wars: Confucius Institute and Chinese Character Festival.
Since the Guomindang and Republic of China government fled to Taiwan in 1949, there has been an unremitting struggle over who represents the "real" China. One point of contention has been over the nature of the written language. The ROC insists on teaching the old unsimplified characters that prevailed in all of China before the mid-1950's, and the PRC champions the simplified characters developed during its efforts to modernize the written language at that time. Two manifestations of this cultural contest can be seen in the photographs above. **(A)** An activity sponsored by one of the dozens of Confucius Institutes around the world supported by the PRC to promulgate its interpretation of the Sage and Chinese culture more generally. The Chinese characters taught there (and in the picture) are the PRC's Modern Standard (Simplified) Characters.
(B) Children and elders participate in one of Taiwan's Chinese Character Festivals, celebrations of the older script recently sponsored by the ROC to push for international recognition of its claim to legitimacy as the heirs of China's culture.

advocates of traditional characters fear that the growing wealth and influence of the PRC will eventually allow its forms to dominate culturally as well. Hence Taiwan sent a representative to argue for support of the UNESCO bid before the PRC's National People's Congress and to reiterate the call for teaching both systems in Chinese primary schools. Although PRC officials readily concede that some difficulties with the present Modern Standard Chinese (simplified characters) exist and will undergo modification, the unofficial policy is "use simplified; know unsimplified." Significantly, the regulations governing the PRC's Confucius Institutes throughout the world stipulate that the Chinese taught in them must be *putonghua* and Modern Standard characters.

For its part, Taiwan continues the struggle for traditional characters. Taipei holds an annual "Chinese Character Festival" on New Year's Day to celebrate the beauty and utility of the old script. In 2011 the government banned the use of simplified characters in official documents—including those meant for PRC consumption. President Ma Ying-jeou has also insisted on both nationalistic and aesthetic grounds that businesses use only traditional characters on their signs. Thus, despite somewhat improved relations between Taiwan and the PRC, the culture wars smolder on.

Japan

Japan's role of aggressor on the Asian mainland is still within the living memory of many older Chinese. Japan's reluctance to admit its role in this regard—indeed, its insistence on presenting itself as a "victim" nation because of the atomic bombings of Hiroshima and Nagasaki—has on a number of occasions stirred angry patriotic responses from the Chinese. Moreover, Japan's reconstitution after the Pacific War as a democracy with an American-written constitution limiting the size of its defense forces has resulted in an ongoing American presence in the region, with troops in South Korea and Okinawa and the U.S. nuclear umbrella surmounting all. For most of this time, therefore, with Japan defeated and effectively disarmed and China viewed as an enemy or, more recently, a powerful competitor, the United States has acted as the regional policeman.

Thus, the two issues that have formed the pattern of Sino-Japanese relations from 1990 to the present have been competition and cooperation with Japanese firms in China's modernization efforts and Japan's role as a focus for Chinese nationalism. The first item has become somewhat less important as China surged ahead of Japan in GDP. In the early years of the Four Modernizations, however, Japan was at its peak as the region's financial engine. Japanese capital, engineers, and business were preeminent in developing the economies of its former colonial possessions, South Korea, Taiwan, and Indonesia. A late 1980s joke proclaimed that it was Japan that actually won the Pacific War in that it now so thoroughly dominated economically the regions it had briefly conquered militarily.

Not surprisingly, because of their proximity, shared history, cultural connections, and economic clout, Japanese companies were among the first foreign concerns to make noteworthy inroads in China. Construction firms and machinery, car companies like Honda, Toyota, and Nissan, even fast-food concerns and the mania for karaoke bars were all part of the first wave of China's new open door. But the growing success of Chinese competitors, as did that of Korean firms in South Korea, also stimulated a kind of backlash against Japanese economic concerns. Seeing the value in directing this upwelling of nationalism toward its own strategic ends, the party sought to simultaneously use it to put diplomatic pressure on Japan, while channeling it in such a way that it would become an authentic feeling among the people—without it being turned against the party.

In the spring of 2005 the perfect opportunity presented itself. Japan's Ministry of Education issued a new textbook in which Japanese atrocities such as the Rape of Nanking were glossed over, and Japan was portrayed as being forced into the Pacific War because it was surrounded by the hostile "ABCD" (America, Britain, China, the Dutch) countries. Little government encouragement was necessary for this to result in widespread protests and attempts to organize anti-Japanese boycotts. More recently, although Japan and China signed a joint agreement to share exploration and development of oil and gas fields in the East China Sea, anti-Japanese feeling has come from disputes over rival claims for offshore islands or areas of seabed containing oil reserves. In 2010 Japanese coast guard forces arrested the crew of a Chinese fishing trawler in the East China Sea in waters claimed by both countries from their earlier joint development pact. The Japanese ultimately released the crew but refused to issue a formal apology to the Chinese, which set off another round of anti-Japanese demonstrations. Both countries have claimed the uninhabited Senkaku Islands, which the Chinese call Diaoyutai, currently under formal Japanese sovereignty. The most recent dispute, and in strategic terms the most potentially dangerous point of conflict, arose in 2013, when Chinese scholars claimed China's historic rights to Okinawa and the Ryukyu (Liuqiu) Islands had been bargained away under pressure from Japan and thus should revert to the PRC. Okinawa, site of some of the bloodiest combat of World War II—including widespread use of Japanese *kamikaze* suicide planes—still has more than 20,000 American troops stationed on it as well as more than a million civilians.

Again, however, there were some attempts to iron these difficulties out. In 2007, Chinese premier Wen Jiabao visited Japan and became the first Chinese high government official to address the Japanese parliament. Although no final agreement was made about the textbook controversy, both sides agreed in principle to try to develop an acceptable shared historical narrative. Most observers feel the claims on Okinawa are an attempt by China to strengthen its bargaining position on its Senkaku claims, although Japan has thus far made no concessions.

The United States

As we saw in the preceding chapters, the pattern of China's relationship with and perception of the United States has tended to cycle from one of relative friendliness and interest—one early observer characterized it as "a barbarian paradise"—to seeing it as sinister and threatening. In the nineteenth century, the United States was generally viewed as the least aggressive of the imperial powers and until the 1880s the few Chinese works on America were generally favorable—although they tended to see many American customs as radically different from those of Chinese people. The anti-Chinese movement in the American west and the Exclusion Act of 1882, however, established an impression of America as a dark, threatening place. The Open Door, diplomatic support for China, and alliance during World War II once again made the impression a relatively friendly one. The founding of the PRC and the U.S. backing of Chiang Kai-shek then split Chinese into two camps, with the PRC fighting Americans in Korea adding to the ideological animosity of the CCP. The Cold War, Vietnam War, and the Cultural Revolution pushed the image of each side as enemy to the other to its maximum point. Then, just as quickly, Nixon's overtures and Deng's reforms went a long way to reverse the trend. Tiananmen Square once again placed the United States and the PRC leadership at odds, although much less so on the part of the citizens of both countries.

The issue of Taiwan remained a sticking point for both countries—as it does today. In addition, however, China's burgeoning economic power by the mid-1990s was increasingly being supported by its regional diplomatic influence and the streamlining and modernization of its military. Thus, issues that might otherwise have been regarded as minor threatened to blow up into potentially dangerous situations on several occasions.

In May 1999, during NATO's air war against Serbia's invasion of Kosovo, an attack on the Serbian capital, Belgrade, resulted in a missile accidentally striking the Chinese embassy. The Clinton administration had routinely been critical of China's human rights record and treatment of dissidents, and PRC officials seized on the incident to incite patriotic demonstrations against the United States, claiming that the attack had been deliberate. Although the extent of the party's hand in encouraging the protests in the PRC is unknown, the nationalist feeling that had now been whipped up pushed the demonstrators to mob the American embassy in Beijing and stone it before being dispersed.

American intelligence gathering precipitated another incident in 2001. As China became more assertive about its territorial waters and areas in which it prospected for oil and gas, it began to establish no-fly zones and extend its coastal claims hundreds of miles out to sea. An American electronic eavesdropping plane collided with a Chinese fighter during a cat-and-mouse encounter near China's Hainan Island. The American plane was damaged but landed on the island and was held by the Chinese for examination despite American protests.

Chinese Images of the United States over the Years. (A) China's relationship with the U.S. has varied over the years from alliance and vigilant friendliness to outright hostility. A few mileposts along the way include seeing the U.S. as a threatening place—as in this American illustration of the anti-Chinese Denver Riot of 1880.
(B) America as a helpful ally against Japan as with these American Army doctors.
(C) America as anti-communist during the Cold War in this Chinese cartoon of U.S. President John F. Kennedy. Kennedy is shown pontificating about America's great traditions of democracy and freedom while the Statue of Liberty's head, which he is standing on, had been cut off by the saw of the Smith Act of 1940, which had been used to convict American communists of plotting to overthrow the government. (D) Finally, America as a source of pop culture, as in this depiction of American President Barack Obama as Chairman Mao. The Chinese characters, missing the first (Mao) and last (shuai) in this picture loosely translated, say, "Chairman Mao praised me as handsome."

Again, patriotic feeling was whipped up at this instance of American violation of Chinese airspace in the service of intelligence gathering.

In addition to periodic calls on both sides for closer cooperation and some unpublicized joint activities carried out under the umbrella of the War on Terror, the United States and China still have certain issues that deeply divide the two governments, although not necessarily the two peoples. China bridles at any hint of American interference in what it considers its internal affairs, particularly with regard to Tibet and Xinjiang. As for American insistence that the PRC observe international norms in matters of individual human rights, the Chinese counter that such demands are an arrogant positing of ethno- and culturecentric Western notions (see Chapter 8, "Patterns Up Close") As we have also seen, the consistent drumbeat of opinion from American think-tanks and commentators on what appears to be the gradual loosening of China's authoritarian political grip as a product of increasing economic freedoms is dismissed by PRC spokespeople as peaceful evolution dressed up for the twenty-first century. Indeed, the administration of China's latest (as of 2015) president, Xi Jinping, has become more authoritarian, not less.

The most recent dispute between the two economic superpowers revolves around technology. Both sides are engaged in a clandestine—and sometimes open—struggle to infiltrate each other's computer networks and Internet sites in the interests of mass data mining for a variety of purposes: industrial and military espionage, checking the vulnerability of control programs for defense systems, probing for weak points in electrical grids and power plants, etc. Even as they probe American and European systems, Chinese spokespeople routinely protest Western critiques of the so-called "Bamboo Firewall," the Internet restrictions on certain categories of information in the PRC, and the pressure the party has put on American companies such as Google and Yahoo to comply. In May 2014, the United States charged five Chinese army officers with "hacking" into American defense networks, which the PRC promptly and hotly denied.

SOCIETY, FAMILY, AND GENDER

As has been evident throughout the last several chapters, China's entrance into modernity has been fraught with struggle. This has been especially true of the past 30 years during which many traditional values that had survived mass mobilization campaigns, the Great Leap Forward and the Cultural Revolution have begun to unravel not so much because of ideology but because of economics and demographics. Thus, in terms of its population growth, gender balance, and social safety net, the coming decades are likely to see changes as dramatic as those of the past 30 years.

The Reign of the Little Emperors

The **One Child Policy,** ended in the fall of 2015, had been in effect for more than a generation and its results have been as predicted in some respects, although totally unanticipated in others. The primary goal of slowing down the rate of growth of China's population appears to have been achieved, with the number of people at slightly less than 1.4 billion in 2014. It should be noted that China's achievement has been part of a worldwide trend (with the exception of Sub-Saharan Africa) that has grown out of efforts to decrease infant mortality and institute better basic health care, better education for girls, better nutrition, and a growing middle class, as well as voluntary and compulsory birth control programs. Indeed, most of the wealthiest developed countries are now hovering around the population replacement rate of 2.1 children per family; some, like Italy and Japan are actually below it.

In China's case the results of the policy have been a profound demographic shift within families, in the ratios between men and women, and in the prospects of the country being able to support an aging population. The millennia-old preference for sons has stubbornly remained. Even during the most determined efforts to eradicate the old Confucian norms, the ideas of filial piety, of the family name being carried by males from generation to generation, and of males providing for aged parents continued to hold sway. With the renewed interest in Confucianism as a model, the male-centric family received considerable cultural support. The One Child Policy has therefore been accompanied by a marked increase in the abortion of females, sex selection during pregnancy, abandoning girls for adoption, and even female infanticide. From the 1980s on there has been a lively international exchange in the adoption of Chinese children, the great majority of whom are girls. One widely publicized side effect of this has been the rise of the so-called "little emperors": boys who, as only children, are doted on excessively and grow up with an overweening sense of entitlement. To be sure, there are also "little empresses," and the most dire predictions for both have not come to pass. It is the boys, however, who have altered the gender balance. China is currently tied (with Bahrain) for the world's highest male/female ratio, 1.13 boys for every 1.00 girls.

The implications of this trend are many. As these children have moved into young adulthood and their career prospects have soared, many have postponed marriage until their late twenties or even early thirties. One of the unexpected consequences of the gender imbalance for young women has been that they have no lack of potential suitors, especially if the women are well-educated and accomplished. Although things have taken this unexpectedly favorable social turn for girls, for boys it has ratcheted up competition for the fewer potential mates available. It has also churned resentment in some areas toward foreigners dating Chinese women, thus pushing up the competition further still. Increasing numbers of young men are therefore searching for suitable foreign wives—a theme explored in *Foreign Babes in Beijing*, the TV show featured in the opening vignette of this chapter.

Senior World

If one considers the possibilities these factors present, the future may look different than the planners intended. Delayed marriage, small families, sex selection, and gender skew may dramatically force China's population below the replacement level in the coming decades. If so, the population will actually decline, as has Japan's in recent years. On the one hand, this could be viewed as part of the original goal of the architects of China's population measures and will put less pressure on the country's and the world's all-too-finite resources. Yet it is also likely to cause intergenerational problems and acute financial difficulties for the country—as it is likely to do in many countries.

With people living far longer into old age than before, the strain on those in their career years to produce enough to ensure sufficient revenues for the health of the social safety net will be high in any case. But the pressure will be enormous given the fact that there will be an unprecedented demographic bulge at the senior end of the population scale. In other words, there will be more seniors than ever before needing retirement benefits, health care, drawing government pensions, and so forth, and a far smaller percentage of people than ever before paying into the system. Hence, in 2009 the government experimented in densely populated Shanghai with loosening the One Child Policy. In 2013, it announced comprehensive plans to open the system up and encourage second children, but has been careful to keep enough control over it so as not to tax present resources unduly with a deluge of new births. As of November, 2015, China will now allow all urban couples to have a second child and lifted the remaining restrictions on those in rural areas.

Through the Maoist years there had been various suggestions for collectivist approaches to senior care and retirement. Despite this, the Chinese nuclear and extended family remained the primary institution involved in looking after the elderly. As noted above, filial piety being one of the highest virtues of Confucianism, children had a profound duty to take care of their parents in old age, and this deep cultural practice could not be eradicated even during the Cultural Revolution. In rural villages, which in some cases were actually large clans of one or more extended families, the practice had continued more or less without interruption. Even in urban areas, the arrangement of traditional dwellings, like the Beijing *hutong* with its four dwellings surrounding a central courtyard (*siheyuan*), lent itself to keeping the extended family together.

The new affluence, however, has put strains on such arrangements. Newfound mobility and migration in search of work have tended to separate families, making elder care more difficult. Lack of housing in many big cities has made it increasingly hard to keep extended families together under one roof. With the drive for personal affluence and career fulfillment has also come a desire for more privacy on the part of both the young and the middle-aged. Increasingly, independence from intrusive family relationships has been seen as a goal worth pursuing. In the new middle classes as well, many seniors seek independence from what they see as the burden of child-rearing into adulthood, as cost and career force many younger people to stay home into their thirties.

The result has been a rise in institutions to care for the elderly. Nursing homes, assisted-living facilities, and senior communities have rapidly sprung up as the generations grow more separated. Many of these institutions have a wide variety of amenities such as classes of various sorts, clubs for assorted interests, venues for social gatherings, and computer and Internet access. Although this seems to be a general trend, which is liable to expand greatly as the comparatively large cohort of the previous generation moves into its later years, it should be noted that family and rootedness are still central concerns for the vast majority of Chinese people. Indeed, *Chunjie*, Spring Festival, or Chinese New Year, is generally the busiest travel time in the world as people flock to fulfill their family obligations to come together for the holidays. Still, the famous Chinese sociologist Fei Xiaotong once characterized the United States as "a land without ghosts," meaning that Americans seemed remarkably free from family and ancestral connections. It may well be that China's headlong dash to modernity will push its people in a similar direction.

SCIENCE, TECHNOLOGY, AND CULTURE

As we saw in the previous chapter, upgrading China's scientific and technological sectors had been a high priority since the inauguration of the Four Modernizations in 1978. The disruptions of the Cultural Revolution had halted many of the promising beginnings of the early 1960s, and by 1978 China found itself hopelessly out of date in terms of military hardware, missile technology, and, perhaps most importantly, the electronics and computer revolution that was beginning to gain traction in the United States, Japan, and Western Europe. All of these areas were vastly improved in the intervening years and, as of 2015, China is one of the world leaders in computer use and technology; has an active space exploration program; and has become a world leader in a number of cutting-edge industrial technologies.

In terms of culture, the scene is more difficult to assess. China has within it all the modern media to be found elsewhere, but despite attempts by independent-minded men and women in every branch of it, the hand of the government and party are everywhere to be found, sometimes openly, sometimes all but invisibly. In keeping with the goal of the Harmonious Society and to avoid the cardinal sin of embarrassing China—and with an increasing degree of grassroots nationalism—the media often willingly engage in self-censorship, although increasingly, as in the aftermath of the 2008 earthquake, they are also taking bold stands. Those sanctioned for their efforts are said only half-humorously to have been "harmonized."

In the arts, this same uneasy balance between boldness and caution in the face of official intimidation may be found as well. Chinese painters, sculptors, and performance artists, along with writers and even landscape painters and calligraphers have demonstrated considerable boldness in art that, like contemporary art in the West and Japan, shocks traditional sensibilities and transgresses cultural forms and norms. Political arts and letters—as with movies, television, and fashion—can be cut off instantly. In the world of ideas, many of China's best known intellectuals worldwide are those who espouse dissident ideas. China's 2010 Nobel laureate, Liu Xiaobo, for example, was languishing in prison when his award was announced.

Alibaba and the Jade Rabbit

Two areas in which China has made startlingly impressive gains over the past two decades have been computer technology and space exploration. Students of the last years of the Soviet Union sometimes point to the reluctance of Communist Party planners there to invest in computer technology, especially at the business and personal levels, as a prime cause for that country's economic and political collapse. The CCP under Deng Xiaoping and his advisors made no such mistake.

IBM, for example, was a welcome foreign presence in the PRC as early as 1979 and as of 2011 had a business presence in 320 Chinese cities. It was followed by other computer manufacturers and component makers, all of whom set up manufacturing centers to take advantage of China's cheap labor and government push for advanced technology. By the 1990s Chinese clones of IBM personal computers had become pervasive, in part because of a lack of patent and copyright protection. At the same time, pirated and "bootleg" music cassettes, CDs, and DVDs—including copies of Microsoft Windows versions—had become a major underground industry.

Even as IBM and other American, European, and Japanese electronics firms were establishing themselves in the PRC, a group of a dozen engineers from China's Academy of Sciences Institute for Computer Technology started their own firm in Beijing in 1984. From doing quality checks on newly purchased foreign computers, they developed a system that could use the IBM platform to write Chinese characters. Using the name

Liu Xiaobo. A placard showing jailed Chinese dissident Liu Xiaobao is held up by a protester during a demonstration outside the China liaison offices in Hong Kong in 2010 calling for his release from prison. Liu Xiaobo, who was awarded the Nobel Peace Prize, has tearfully dedicated his award to victims of the 1989 Tiananmen Square crackdown, activists said, as his wife was held under house arrest.

"Legend" through the 1980s, the company renamed itself Lenovo in 1990 and began to manufacture its own computers. By the end of the decade it had moved into a wide variety of electronics and, like Motorola, the new technology of cellular phones. In 2005, Lenovo bought IBM's personal computer division. It is currently the largest manufacturer and marketer of PCs in the world.

The success of Lenovo is emblematic of the rapid and thorough changes that have taken place in the PRC over the past two decades. In China's cities and towns in the early 1990s road traffic consisted overwhelmingly of bicycles, both as passenger carriers and as freight haulers, sometimes in unbelievably imaginative ways. The remainder comprised small, long handle-barred tractors and pedicabs, along with an occasional passenger car or truck. On the new networks of modern turnpikes and freeways of 2015, private cars and trucks of all shapes and sizes vastly outnumber the dwindling number of human-powered vehicles. ATMs, which two decades ago were a rarity, are now ubiquitous. Saturating the country even more are cellular telephones of Chinese makes as well as Japanese and Korean models.

Perhaps even more striking are the number and quality of Internet providers and websites. Yet here is also where the intrusiveness of the government can be at its least subtle. American providers such as Yahoo and Google were among the early comers to China's Internet landscape but both ran into difficulty. Yahoo received much unfavorable publicity for caving in to government demands for access and keeping certain kinds of content, such as controversial political sites, unavailable. Google was involved in a protracted struggle with government hacking into the accounts of dissidents. Finally, in 2010 it simply decided to bypass the **Bamboo Firewall** of the censored Internet and route its customers through servers in Hong Kong. Millions of accomplished Chinese online users had long since found their own ways to use proxy servers to circumvent government restrictions. Most recently, China's largest e-commerce company, Alibaba, and Weibo, the Chinese Twitter, grew so big that they both were offering stock on American exchanges.

Equally impressive have been Chinese accomplishments in space. Although they lagged behind the United States and Soviet Union in ballistic missile systems during the Cold War, China launched its first satellite, *Dongfanghong* ("The East Is Red," a favorite Maoist hymn) atop its booster rocket *Changzheng I* ("Long March I") in April 1970. Succeeding generations of Long March boosters have put a wide variety of communications, weather, and research satellites into orbit both for China and for other countries. Since joining the commercial satellite market in 1985, China has put nearly 30 foreign satellites into orbit.

Its manned efforts and exploration vehicles have also been noteworthy. In 1999 a vehicle capable of being manned, *Shenzhou*, was launched and retrieved. Four years later, China's first astronaut, Yang Liwei, was sent into space and recovered. In 2008, a Chinese astronaut, Zhai Zhigang, made his country's first spacewalk on China's third manned mission. In 2012, China's first woman astronaut, Liu Yang, took part in the first manual docking of a Chinese spacecraft and lab module in orbit. Finally, at the end of 2013, China successfully landed its own lunar rover, *Yutu* ("Jade Rabbit"), on the moon, the first such touchdown by any country in 37 years. The military capabilities represented by these accomplishments have not been lost on other countries, particularly Japan and the United States. This was especially true when China showed it was capable of shooting down an object in orbit in 2007, in this case an aging weather satellite.

The Arts: From Raise the Red Lantern *to* Downton Abbey

The 1980s, as we noted in the previous chapter, were seen by many artists as a kind of golden age for experimentation with Chinese traditional, contemporary, and foreign ideas. One play, for example, was called *Jesus, Confucius, and John*

Lennon of the Beatles. The conservative era that set in after the suppression in Tiananmen Square muted this trend somewhat and pushed artists into covering political statements or socially controversial ideas with additional layers of subtlety. It was, however, a time when the world's focus on China allowed Chinese filmmakers like Zhang Yimou to achieve international stardom with movies like *Raise the Red Lantern, Ju Dou,* and *To Live.* Tian Zhuangzhuang revisited the Cultural Revolution in *The Blue Kite*—as did the former Red Guard, Liang Heng, in his earlier books, *Son of the Revolution* and *After the Nightmare* (with his American wife, Judith Shapiro).

The 1990s and early 2000s also saw an explosion of worldwide interest in Chinese art of all types. The market for art from the imperial era was pushed by the popularity of television shows like *Antiques Roadshow* in the United States and United Kingdom and even more by the PRC government embarking on an aggressive program of buying back Chinese art for patriotic reasons. Coupled with strict policies against removing antiques from the country, this drove prices to unprecedented heights.

It also had an effect on modern and contemporary Chinese artists. The association of modern art with protest made the work of the new generation of Chinese artists increasingly desirable. Ironically, there was also a somewhat satirical fashion for new paintings done in the old Socialist Realist style of the 1950s and 1960s, with some of the most popular subjects being copies or reimaginings of portraits of Mao Zedong. By the early 2000s there was a growing fear on the part of many successful artists that the pressure to produce and sell was undercutting the originality and creativity of contemporary Chinese art. As Li Xianting, the dean of modern Chinese art put it, "now it's as though globalization is turning into the Americanization of the whole world, which I think is really terrifying" (Duncan Hewitt, *China: Getting Rich First,* New York: Pegasus, p. 364). Since the commercialization of art is something the government can steer into acceptable channels, it also tends to be that which is most frequently exhibited in galleries and sold in shows. Still, art and dissent remain linked in both the popular mind and that of the authorities, who arrested artist Ai Weiwei in April 2011. Ai designed the iconic "Bird's Nest" stadium at the Beijing Olympics and is an outspoken critic of the government's view toward human rights. After an international campaign to free him he was released but hit with a $2.3 million fine for "economic crimes": an all-purpose charge often foisted on political opponents. In the end, his supporters came up with the money for his fine.

The media has tended to follow a similar trajectory. The government exercises control over content through official outlets like *Renmin Ribao,* the organ of the party, the *China Daily,* China Central Television, and a host of regional and local outlets. Hong Kong's press is freer, although under constant pressure to report government stories favorably. Coastal China can pick up programs from Taiwan and South Korea. Larger cities also have access to CNN, ESPN, MTV, and other foreign networks. Chinese Internet users, like their contemporaries elsewhere, are increasingly going online for news and streaming entertainment. Here again, the Bamboo Firewall is a partial deterrent, although increasingly it relies on the threat implied by not knowing how much the government is really watching and putting layers of barriers in the way of getting around its restrictions. Programming, as in many places, runs the gamut from serious documentaries and approved news features to nonsensical game shows and frothy interview programs. News reporting has become somewhat less reliant on government handouts since the days of live coverage of the Sichuan earthquake and the Olympics. Foreign programming is also immensely popular, with comedies such as the current hit in the U.S., *The Big Bang Theory* and *Friends*—which has a second life in China more than a decade after the last episode aired in America. In early 2015, the most popular series has been the wildly successful PBS production *Downton Abbey*.

Soft Power and New Citizens

As China's economic, political, and diplomatic power has increased, so has its use of what social scientists call "soft power." This is the informal influence, particularly in the cultural realm, that countries exert as they interact with each other. The United States, for example, wields enormous soft power through its movies, television, music, and fashion. There are few places in the world today where the "uniform" of young people does not include t-shirts, jeans, and baseball and flat-brim caps; and the music does not have a heavy overlay of American rock, pop, or hip-hop. This is certainly true in the PRC, where there is an enormous interest in things deemed American.

China, too, seeks to extend its soft power in a number of areas. Most recently, as we noted previously, Southeast Asia and Africa have been especially important in this regard. As early as 2004, China signed trade agreements with 10 Southeast Asian countries in an attempt to create a free trade zone in the region similar to that of the North American Free Trade Agreement in North America. China has, of course, historically seen itself as a world center and exporter of civilization. Even during the Maoist years, the PRC presented itself as the more "authentic" of the two major Communist powers and claimed a leadership role in encouraging Third World liberation. Now, having repudiated the excesses of the Cultural Revolution era, the PRC has made concerted efforts to reclaim traditional Chinese culture, particularly to contest the claim of Taiwan since 1949 to be the "real" heir of China's cultural legacy (see "Patterns Up Close").

The PRC's insistence on this authenticity has resulted in one of the more striking cultural reversals of modern times. For much of the twentieth century, modernizing Chinese regimes have sought to move beyond the legacy of Confucianism. The New Culture Movement, Sun Yat-sen's Three People's Principles, and the CCP all repudiated Confucianism. The sole exception had been Chiang K'ai-shek's New Life Movement, but even here, the thought was to blend the best of Confucian moral principles with modern norms. The insistence on a distinctly Asian philosophy of human rights, however, has now been connected to the Confucian legacy. Thus, the Sage has not only been rehabilitated but also is increasingly presented to the world as part of the "branding" of the PRC. Government-sponsored Confucius Institutes have been set up all over the world as outposts of the PRC's civilization and values, a kind of cultural missionary enterprise.

As China increasingly projects power on the world stage, the ongoing drive for the Harmonious Society and its anticorruption program both within and outside the party has produced a number of noteworthy incidents. Two of the most interesting revolve around factional struggles within the party and yet another challenge to its authority from outside of it. In November 2011, a British businessman, Neil Heywood, was found dead in his room at the ironically named Lucky Holiday Hotel near Chongqing. The Chongqing police chief, Wang Lijun, investigating the crime, suddenly sought asylum at the American consulate, and accused Chongqing's party chief, Bo Xilai, and his wife, Gu Kailai, who had business dealings with Heywood, of the murder. After considerable global attention, a convoluted police investigation, and a trial, both were convicted of poisoning him. The case revealed a deeper struggle between factions claiming the Maoist legacy of authoritarian power and a new generation of technocrats seeking to leverage their *guanxi* to create a more diffuse but, it has been charged, even more corrupt arrangement of power. Bo's tough stances on local corruption put him in the "Maoist" camp, although he too was accused of massive embezzlement and might well have been framed along with his wife for the murder by his former police chief, Wang Lijun.

The case was followed avidly in the official news outlets and especially on China's increasingly freewheeling social media by legions of bloggers, tweeters, and "netizens" of all types. As one team of commentators put it, "the crisis . . . reveals more about the scandalous state of corruption in China than any dissident or journalist could ever manage" (Pin Ho and Wenguang Huang, *A Death in the Lucky Holiday Hotel*, New York: Public Affairs, 2013, xv). Regarding corruption as a whole, the dissidents had not been idle. A new group appeared and, as had so many before it, challenged the party and government to make good on its claims to be fighting corruption. Growing out of an Open Constitution Initiative (closed down in 2009) and closely allied with the "Defending Rights Movement," the New Citizens' Movement harkened back to Sun Yat-sen's conception of building civil society by means of creating a true constitutional polity. In addition to demonstrating and petitioning the Chinese president Xi Jinping for greater transparency in the party and government, the New Citizens stand for equal education opportunities (i.e., without needing a residency permit) and vigorous defense of political and human rights and maintain a defense fund for dissidents on trial or jailed. The government sees them as subversive, especially in their implicit support for opposition parties and close parallels with American notions of peaceful evolution. In 2013 and 2014, four leaders and a number of other members were arrested and sentenced to several years in prison. In keeping with this ongoing struggle between party and dissidents, the Chinese activist

Liu Xiaobo was awarded the 2010 Nobel Peace Prize while in jail for his championing of the "Charter 08 Manifesto," which demanded greater political freedoms in China on the model of the "Charter 77" movement in the old Communist state of Czechoslovakia.

CONCLUSION

By just about any realistic measure, contemporary China has fulfilled the most important goals of the Four Modernizations. In the past 25 years it has recovered from the world opprobrium of the suppression of the demonstrations in Tiananmen Square and surged ahead of Japan to become the second largest economy in the world. It may well be the world's largest economy in absolute terms by the publication date of this text. Moreover, it has achieved most of the benchmarks that social scientists point to in assessing that elusive quality called modernity. Demographically, China is now officially an urban country with more than half of its population living in cities—signposts of industrial development achieved by Great Britain around 1850 and the United States around the turn of the twentieth century. China's cities bristle with state-of-the-art architecture, with rapidly developing infrastructural features such as international airports, superhighways, and some of the most up-to-date urban and intercity transportation systems in the world—including maglev trains capable of speeds up to 250 miles per hour. China also has the world's largest middle class, which grows larger and wealthier by the day.

Yet it is not without severe challenges. As we have seen, its population policies have, on the one hand, achieved their initial goal of slowing population growth; on the other hand, however, they have created unforeseen problems of gender imbalance and a demographic bulge at the older end of the age scale. China's pollution problems are legion, and although greater efforts are now being made, those problems and their side effects are likely to remain for some time to come. China has the world's most ravenous appetite for energy, and more and more of its political overtures and relationships are being built around supplies of resources. Similarly, its enhanced military power has become increasingly focused on the politics of energy acquisition.

The problem involving the highest stakes, however, is likely to remain the future of the Communist Party and, by extension, the form of government that will see China through the remainder of this century. Even as the party works to retain its hold on power through the promise of individual and collective wealth and the channeling of the forces guiding that wealth into the Harmonious Society—or its next incarnation—the countervailing forces in the country, in Marxist terms, its "contradictions," will in all likelihood continue to mount. It has become a cliché to observe that we live increasingly in a world that is "flat": That globalization is creating a kind of uniform system in the world, in which the exceptions such as cultural or religious fundamentalisms are the last line of resistance that proves the rule. The Communist Party in China has staked everything on its economic bargain, but will peaceful evolution or something much like it erode one-party rule? If so, what might the outcome be? Slow political change one local election at a time? A violent revolutionary impulse triggered by social media, as with the Arab Spring of a few years ago?

In many respects, then, China may be seen as one scholar has put it as a "quasi-superpower." Perhaps another way to see it is as the writer Frank Gibney once described Japan, a "fragile superpower." In a way the choices the nation faces are not unlike those portrayed in the *Foreign Babes* drama in the vignette opening this chapter: Will it follow the marriage of tradition and foreign ideas and have those foreign ideals mold themselves to China's long-term core civilizational values; or will the transgressive and disruptive power of the foreign pull the core apart?

FURTHER READING

Buruma, Ian. *Bad Elements: Chinese Rebels from Los Angeles to Beijing.* New York: Vintage, 2003. A long-time Asia watcher and critic, Buruma interviews Chinese dissidents in a trenchant and engaging style.

Chau, Adam Yuet, ed. *Religion in Contemporary China.* New York: Routledge, 2011. Sound, current material on Daoist, Confucian, and Buddhist revival and adaptation to contemporary life in China. Also explores the "gray" (unrecognized) religious movements.

DeWoskin, Rachel. *Foreign Babes in Beijing: Behind the Scenes of a New China.* New York: Norton, 2005. Highly entertaining and accessible account of the author's intercultural adventures as a soap opera star in China during the 1990s.

Dillon, Michael. *Contemporary China: An Introduction.* New York: Routledge, 2009. Well written, compact, but information rich overview of modern China's politics, economic, society and culture.

Gittings, John. *The Changing Face of China: From Mao to Market.* New York: Oxford University Press, 2005. Highly readable account of the end of the Maoist era through the 1990s and early 2000s. Well-crafted exploration and analysis of the transitions in Chinese Communism.

Hewitt, Duncan. *China: Getting Rich First.* New York, Pegasus, 2008. A colorful, sometimes heart-rending mosaic of stories of life in contemporary China by a long-time resident and correspondent for the BBC and *Newsweek* magazine.

Lam, Willy Wo-Lap, *Chinese Politics in the Era of Xi Jinping: Renaissance, Reform, or Retrogression,* New York and London, Routledge, 2015, Deeply researched biography of China's current president that explores the impact his "Maoist"- inspired policies and inclinations toward increased authoritarianism have had and will have on the contemporary PRC.

Link, Perry. *Evening Chats in Beijing.* New York: Norton, 1993. Interviews conducted by a noted scholar of contemporary China about issues of compelling interest to intellectuals on policies and conditions in China from the late 1980s through the early 1990s.

Pillsbury, Michael. *The Hundred Year Marathon: China's Secret Strategy to Replace America as the Global Superpower.* New York: Holt, 2015. Highly controversial warning that China is subtly following strategies from the Warring States period to expand its influence throughout Asia and in Africa and plans to supplant the United States as global hegemon by 2049.

Pin Ho and Wenguang Huang. *A Death in the Lucky Holiday Hotel*, New York: Public Affairs, 2013. Fascinating narrative and investigation into the death of British businessman Neil Heywood and the convoluted and corrupt path to the controversial conviction of the Communist Party chief of Chongqing, Bo Xilai, and his wife, Gu Kailai. Highly revealing about the current state of internal party politics.

Schoppa, Keith. *Revolution and Its Past: Identities in Modern Chinese History*, 3rd ed. New York: Prentice Hall, 2011. Information-rich text for introductory and intermediate students, although even advanced students can read it with profit. Approaches Chinese history from the Qianlong era to the present from the perspective of the multiple and shifting identities of China and its people—as individuals, family, and clan members, inhabitants of villages and cities, regions, empires, and nations.

Wasserstrom, Jeffrey. *China's Brave New World: And Other Tales for Global Times*. Bloomington: Indiana University Press, 2007. Powerful, accessible history, travelogue, and meditation on the vast cultural exchanges taking place within China and setting them in the context of larger trends of globalization.

CHAPTER 10

EPILOGUE: BACK
TO THE FUTURE?

What does it mean to be Chinese in the second decade of the twenty-first century? How have the dizzying changes of the past century and a half, particularly over the past 35 years, affected the identity of individuals, families, ethnic groups, the national polity—the civilization itself? As we asked at the end of the previous chapter, what changes will ultimately be assimilated over time and become recognizably Chinese? How will the direction of the PRC affect the millions of Chinese people on Taiwan and in the Chinese diaspora? What things will be tenuously grafted onto the culture and discarded over time? Will China, like India, see the old continuities of its deeper past continue to reassert themselves? Will the unfolding Chinese pattern be the new model for modernization without Westernization?

Nearly all observers and even most casual travelers visiting China come away not only with an impression of accelerating change, but also with the sense that the people have come to accept these changes and even actively embrace them. Looking over a recent English-language electronic issue of *The People's Daily* (*Renmin ribao*), for example, one finds a list of the top 10 cars sold in China for 2014. In addition to the large number of passenger vehicles sold (19.7 million; up 9.9% from 2013), all of those listed were apparent foreign makes, with the Ford Focus leading the way. This led to the following online exchange between two readers:

> The top ten most popular and sold cars are all foreign made. China cars like Geely (Volvo), BYD electric should try harder. . . . The Chinese government [has] got to make [a] proactive policy to buy Chinese made products.

The rejoinder was suggestive:

> The captions make it abundantly clear that all of these cars are made in China by Chinese firms working in partnership with so-called "foreign" companies. So not imports. You get all of the work going to local workers, none of the import costs, all of the taxes, and a cheap way to benefit from that very latest automotive technology that the rest of the world has access to, so what are you complaining about exactly? (May 3, 2015)

The article and the dialogue are instructive in several respects. First, passenger vehicles are now sold in China in numbers matching those of recent peak years in the United States. Moreover, the most popular makes of passenger cars in America are the Japanese giants Toyota and Honda. Although, as in China, the majority of these cars are made in factories in the United States, the percentage of imports is substantial as well. The dialogue between the readers resembles in many ways arguments in the United States in the 1980s about fears of foreign domination of the American automotive market. It also bears on the speed of China's transition from "developing" to "developed." Embedded in this exchange is, on the part of the second writer, a kind of easy confidence that sees the top 10 list as the proper end product of using foreign things to help China. The first writer's fears, so breezily dismissed by the respondent, in a sense seem to be anchored in an earlier time when China looked with deep suspicion on foreign joint ventures. Now, as we have seen, the PRC itself is aggressively pursuing joint ventures in developing countries. Given that the forum for the exchange, *The People's Daily*, is the official organ of the CCP, the substance of the dialogue might not be coincidental. Significantly, the link next to the one for the top 10 cars leads the reader to China's top 10 billionaires.

Regardless of the degree of editorial orchestration involved, the exchange also illustrates China's growing nationalism. Both writers agree on ends, if not means. In a somewhat jarring juxtaposition of yet more top 10 lists, one finds "Top 10 TV Drama Queens in China" hard against "Top Ten Chinese Weapons in 2014." But perhaps the greatest impact on both China and its neighbors in the immediate future will come from "the Belt and Road" initiatives. Here, a number of elements come together that boldly illustrate China's growing economic, political, diplomatic, and soft power clout. In speeches in Kazakhstan and Indonesia in 2013, China's president, Xi Jinping, outlined two plans for cooperative regional development—with the active participation of China's answer to the World Bank, the Asian Infrastructure Investment Bank(AIIB). One is called "The Silk Road Economic Belt" and aims at cooperative and coordinated resource and infra-structural development for China and the countries along the old Silk Road, in-cluding heavy freight and high-speed rail links. The other is called the "Twenty-First Century Maritime Silk Road" and seeks to involve the countries running from South China through Southeast Asia and on to India, Africa, and the Arabian Peninsula. As the PRC's official news agency, Xinhua, put it,

> The vision, once realized, will directly benefit 4.4 billion people, or 63 percent of the global population. So far, more than 60 countries along the routes and international organizations have shown interest in taking part in the two initia-tives. (March 28, 2015)

Even more ambitious, although theoretically within current technological ca-pabilities, are Russian and Chinese proposals to build a highway and/or railway under the Bering Strait to link Europe and Asia to North and South America. Proponents of these plans have routinely raised parallels to the great fifteenth-century Ming fleets of Zheng He's "Treasure Ships." The comparison is certainly geographically accurate because the Maritime Silk Road essentially follows the routes of Zheng's fleets. The plan's sponsors obviously hope too that the trade network they envision will not be subject to the same fate as Zheng's and be abruptly halted because of internal politics.

A more recent parallel and perhaps a more enduring one is that of the United States during what the publisher Henry Luce declared in 1941 to be "the American Century." Like China today in Asia, the United States had emerged from the nine-teenth century as the great power of the Americas. It flexed its economic muscles with what at the time were considered grandiose projects like the transcontinental railroad and the Panama Canal. It largely determined the political direction of the region through the Monroe Doctrine and the fruits of the Spanish–American War. It dominated the Americas economically through "dollar diplomacy." But the real thrust of Luce's editorial in *Life* magazine on the cusp of America's entry into World War II was that the time was ripe for the United States to step up into a role of global leadership to create a better world. Only the United States, he argued, was capable of such leadership by virtue of its wealth, influence, and the bloodletting that involved the other great powers at the moment. And in many respects, through World War II, the Cold War, and the collapse of the Soviet Bloc, his argument was prescient.

The present predictions that we have entered "the Asian Century"may be pre-scient as well. Xi Jinping's grand initiatives in many ways may represent the coming to fruition of the idea of the Harmonious World of shared resources, co-operative infrastructure building, and economic free trade zones across much of Asia. For China, an additional benefit is slated to be the exclusion of American influence in these areas as well as the isolation and containment of Japan. The question, however, remains open as to whether the advantages of such cooperation will outweigh the potential for exploitation by the Chinese colossus. For example, China's drive for resources in Africa sometimes seems reminiscent of Japan's blueprint for the World War II era "Greater East Asia Co-Prosperity Sphere."

While China's economy expands at unprecedented rates and Party planners attempt to steer it in the direction of sustainable growth, China watchers and commentators inside and outside the PRC have remarked on the apparent spiritual vacuum that has grown there in recent years. During the Maoist years, traditional Chinese religious and philosophical schools like the *sanjiao* of Confucianism, Daoism, and Buddhism were driven underground—to be replaced by Marxism-Leninism-Mao Zedong Thought as an ideological substitute. At times, particularly during the Cultural Revolution, Mao's teachings were preached with truly religious fervor and, as we noted earlier, a cult of personality grew around the chairman, crediting him in some cases with quasi-divine powers.

The post-Mao decades had seen something of a rebound of the three traditional beliefs, along with Christianity and Islam, but only within approved channels. For a time, the drive to develop and advance economically occupied some of the emotional and psychological space that might otherwise have been devoted to spiritual matters. As more people became affluent, however, a hunger to be connected to something larger and more transcendent than economic prosperity grew as well. Nowhere was this more in evidence than in the saga of Falun Gong. It can also be seen increasingly in the countryside as not only the *sanjiao* philosophies and Christianity and Islam are gaining ground, but also the older folk religions of hungry ghosts and local spirits are being resurrected.

Although the government finds anything that might dilute allegiance to the party disturbing, it has yet to develop a workable substitute for religion. Indeed, in 2014 the government mounted a muted campaign against Christian churches and religious symbols in Zhejiang Province and mounted a large show of force in largely Muslim Urumqi in response to a suicide attack on a market in that city that killed 43. A recent government publication advises that "religious infiltration," Western democracy and cultural hegemony, and the Internet are all serious threats to China's national security. Yet there is also some opinion within the party that religion, if managed correctly, could be a valuable resource of informal "social capital." That is, the altruistic side of the five recognized religions in China (Buddhism, Daoism, Islam, and Catholic and Protestant Christianity) may all have a role to play in fostering public involvement in philanthropy, disaster relief, social services, preserving culturally important traditions and buildings, and helping to build civil society. But the question must also be raised: since the approved religions are supported by the government, how much would their volunteerism contribute in terms of such social capital? If they are allowed a more independent role, then would they, like Falun Gong, be seen as alternatives and therefore threats?

For now, the government and party actively promote atheism as a fundamental doctrine and see their official position as fostering a secular society. Although the numbers of Chinese in the PRC who profess one of the recognized religions are large by international standards, they represent a relatively small minority of its citizens. The number of people involved in "gray" (marginal and/or unrecognized) religions or sects is unknown since they are not approved. Thus, unlike Catholicism in Poland in the 1980s or Shi'a Islam in Iran in the 1970s, where religion was integral to revolutionary opposition to the government, the many and varied religions in China are far too diffuse to mount any kind of unified alternative to the party. Within the overarching rubric of secularism, the party doctrines of Socialism with Chinese Characteristics, "the Three Represents," and, most recently (2015), Xi Jinping's "Four Comprehensives" (comprehensively build a moderately prosperous society; deepen reform; govern according to law; strictly govern the party) promote a vision of the good life as being part of building of a strong and wealthy Harmonious Society. Whether devotion to this goal can effectively satisfy the nonmaterial desires of the majority of the people is still an open question.

In 1880, during the height of the anti-Chinese movement in the United States, there appeared an imaginative work of scare literature that sounds some curiously familiar echoes among a growing number of commentators today. In *The Last Days of the Republic*, P. W. Dooner outlines a scenario in which Chinese efforts at self-strengthening lead to a Xinjiang expeditionary force moving into Russia, "setting barbarian against barbarian" among the contestants in the Great Game, followed by the piecemeal conquest of Europe. The Chinese in America, granted citizenship and voting themselves in control of California, act as a kind of electoral fifth column undermining the resolve of the United States, which ultimately surrenders to the Qing. One of the more striking illustrations in the book pictures two Chinese mandarins toasting each other with champagne against the backdrop of the Capitol dome.

What gave this alarmist screed a veneer of authenticity at the time was that Dooner cited real Qing officials such as Wen Xiang (1818–1876) in marshalling his fantasy. Given the Belt and Road initiatives, China's growing soft power, and the PRC's increasingly assertive military clout and foreign policy, one might be tempted to wonder whether a real bid for world hegemony is being contemplated. Indeed, this is exactly the thesis of American policy advisor Michael Pillsbury's controversial 2015 book, *The Hundred Year Marathon: China's Secret Strategy to Replace America as the Global Superpower* (New York: Holt). Anxious to sound the alarm for complacent Americans who misinterpret the nuances of Chinese pronouncements and aims, Pillsbury sees China's leaders employing proven stratagems from the Warring States period to play a long game and become world hegemon by the PRC's centennial in 2049.

One can certainly not dispute the current leadership's goal of being the premier political and economic power of Asia, if for no other reason than to reconstitute China's historical prestige after its "century of humiliation." Whether this will mean supplanting the United States as the world's superpower may be a different matter. For example, current Sino-Russian cooperation notwithstanding, Russia's ambition to return to great power or even superpower status seems certain to conflict with China's aims. Achieving the goals of the Belt and Road proposals may also not be quite as straightforward as the initial enthusiasm among the participants suggests.

Here, the experience of China in Africa is instructive. More than a million Chinese people now live and work in various African countries. China has poured capital and infrastructural aid into a number of resource-rich African states in return for extraction rights. In its hunger for influence and energy, China has now largely supplanted U.S. aid to Africa. Unlike American aid or loans from the World Bank, however, Chinese capital and expertise comes with no political strings attached. For African countries enduring dictatorial governments or corrupt and/or inefficient bureaucracies, China makes no demands for reform, insisting only on certain quotas for resource extraction. Although in theory both sides benefit, China generally comes out with the better end of the bargain. It gets a discount for the resources and most of the projects are staffed by Chinese engineers and workers. For many of these countries, then, China's bargain has the virtue of immediate help without troublesome political oversight, although the long-term cost of development may not be sustainable as resources are depleted.

In the case of Central Asia and the Silk Road Belt, Chinese capital and infrastructure development may be welcome, although the competition with Russian and U.S. interests may create a new version of the Great Game. The connections of the many Muslim peoples in the region to the Turkic Uyghurs in Xinjiang, moreover, will undoubtedly be troubling to Chinese security agencies concerned about support for separatist movements. For the other countries along the Belt, a large influx of Chinese workers into their regions will be cause for concern—as it has been for the non-Han peoples in Xinjiang. Similar concerns will likely arise among the countries along the Maritime Silk Road. Indonesia is largely Muslim and also has a substantial Chinese population; Vietnam has a long history of opposing Chinese hegemony; India is busy with its own rapid development and in maintaining its influence in the Indian Ocean region. Then there are South Korea, Japan, and Taiwan, all of which are "developed," nervous about Chinese power and expansion, and possess state-of-the-art defense forces. In all of these areas the United States still maintains a considerable influence and military presence. In fact, the Obama administration has announced a renewed interest in the security of the region and has already begun redeploying forces withdrawn from Iraq and Afghanistan there.

The largest factor at work in China's immediate future, however, will likely be the perception of the CCP's legitimacy and ability to rule. So far, it has proved surprisingly adaptable in this regard. Recent polls asking Chinese people to rank countries in terms of their government's legitimacy place China ahead of many of the world's democracies. The Three Represents and Four Comprehensives make an explicit bargain with the country to keep up the pace of prosperity, move to the forefront of technological and cultural modernity, and engage in vigorous reform within the party. Although many argue that the economic factors will be the making or undoing of the party's future, the aim of reform should not be discounted either.

Reform of corruption and cracking down on the exploitation of "connections" and "through the back door" practices has been a long-standing goal of the party. Discontent with corruption was a key factor in the Tiananmen Square protests, and every Chinese leader since has promised to work for party reform and attack corruption. Xi Jinping has repeatedly promised to root out corruption and place the party under tighter control. How well he and other CCP leaders are able to do this will be a powerful psychological and ethical factor in how the people see the government. This is especially true as the factions within the Party, such as the "Fifth Generation" (born in the 1950's), many of whom like Xi himself are "princelings" whose forbears had been Party officials, struggle to maintain a strong authoritarian presence in a Party whose technocrats often favor more diffuse leadership.

Perhaps fittingly, this brings us to a concept that we explored at the beginning of this text: the Mandate of Heaven. Although the emperors are long gone, the concept remains at the heart of the Chinese view of proper government. In a recent online forum on the question "How relevant is the concept of the Mandate of Heaven in today's China," most of the respondents felt that it was still very much present. One person saw it viewed by many as a kind of implicit natural force, like gravity. Another noted, "We express the same meaning in other words that sound modern." He went on to suggest that "[the] CCP has coined 'Three Represents,' which is a detailed version of a modern 'Mandate of Heaven.'" A number of contributors mentioned this as well, with one citing a recent article in the party journal *Hongqi wengao* (*Red Flag Manuscript*), "CCP Still Has Its Mandate of Heaven." Indeed, the Party's official position is one that was first articulated by Mao during the Yan'an years in 1945. "We have found a new road, which has enabled us to supersede the dynastic cycle," he said. "The new road is democracy." It is a democracy, however, in which the Communist Party retains its "permanent" position of power as it pursues what it calls "the modernization of social governance." (From Willy Wo-Lap Lam, *Chinese Politics in the Era of Xi Jinping: Renaissance, Reform, or Retrogression,* New York and London, Routledge, 2015,pp. 129, 131.)

For the Party, then, as with the dynasties throughout Chinese history, the ultimate test of this "new road" is the rectitude of the rulers in personal and public behavior and in advancing what Mencius called "the people's livelihood." Viewed in this light it is no accident that "Jiang Zemin Theory" moves away from ideology and toward development and reform and that the "virtue" (*de*) of the government and the party is increasingly cited as central to their legitimacy. Significantly, three of Xi Jinping's Four Comprehensives—deepen reform; govern according to law; strictly govern the party—deal with approaches aimed at ensuring "virtue." Whether China is currently on the upswing of a dynastic cycle—or even on a new road that supersedes it— or perhaps in a dynamic but brief fifth restoration will perhaps be the great question of this century.

GLOSSARY

Agrarian Reform Law: June, 1950 law marking the formal opening of nation-wide land reform. Landlords were encouraged, more often forced, to turn land over to their tenants; large non-government institutions such as monasteries saw their lands confiscated and distributed. Rough justice was meted out to those who refused to cooperate or those widely disliked by their former tenants.

Anti-Rightist campaign: Movement to shut down the Hundred Flowers campaign and round up the Party's critics guilty of "rightist" thinking and submit them to "re-education."

Autarky: Economic self-sufficiency. With the collapse of international trade and finance during the Great Depression, and countries frantically raising tariffs to protect their home industries, many countries retreated into themselves to try to create self-sufficient economies to weather the storm. China, whose basic industry had always been agriculture was in reasonably good shape. Japan, which relied so much on exports, looked to create autarky within its empire. This helped to drive its annexation of Manchuria as a source of raw materials, a market for finished goods, and a destination for Japanese emigrants.

Axial Age: The period roughly between 600 and 400 B.C.E. when a number of antiquity's greatest thinkers are believed to have lived. First popularized by Karl Jaspers, the appearance of the first philosophers in Greece, the prophets of Israel, perhaps Zoroaster in Persia, the Buddha, Mahavira, and the Upanishad composers in India, and Confucius and Laozi in China suggested that all of these societies were faced with crises of understanding about the nature of divinity, the world, and the universe.

Bamboo Firewall: The nickname for the restrictions and impediments the PRC imposes on internet use in China. The government attempts to force large providers to block pornographic or politically sensitive sites, and some services, like Facebook, are unavailable altogether.

Banner system: Mode of tax and military organization among the Manchus and during Manchu Qing Dynasty rule in China. Under the Qing, there were eight banners representing military and ethnic divisions in the empire: Manchu, Han, Mongolian, Tibetan, and Muslim *Hui*. Families within each banner furnished men who were organized into companies of 300.

Baojia: Systems of rural social organization that appeared in various forms from at least the Song period through the Nationalist period (to 1949). Each group of ten families would choose a headman, the families of each ten headmen would choose a captain, and the leaders at the district level would be responsible to an informal official who acted as intermediary between the people and the district magistrate.

Boxers: The secret society and militia known as *Yihetuan*, "militia of the harmonious fists." Anti-Christian, anti-foreign, and at first, anti-Qing until the Empress Dowager Cixi allied herself with them in 1900, their name and exercises caused foreign observers to nickname them "boxers."

Buddha of the Pure Land: Amida Buddha, the center of the devotional Pure Land school. No immersion in esoteric scriptures or ascetic practices were necessary for salvation, which was available to all: Simply chanting the name of Amida with sincerity was enough. The bodhisattva *Guanyin* was popularly associated with Pure Land Buddhism, and often depicted as intervening to save those in peril.

Chinese Communist Party: Inspired by the success of the Bolsheviks in Russia and intrigued by the power of Marx's economic and revolutionary arguments, a small group that included Chen Duxiu, Li Dazhao, and Mao Zedong founded the Chinese Communist Party (CCP) in 1921. Though at first they hewed closely to the Bolshevik example and party line as communicated to them through Comintern, the CCP, after its purge by the Nationalists in 1927 moved to Mao's concept of using peasants as the prime revolutionary force instead of industrial workers.

Chinoiserie: The eighteenth-century European fashion for both real and imitation Chinese art and export products. European craftspeople often produced fanciful faux Chinese porcelain, lacquerware, wallpaper patterns, fabric designs, etc. to create a feeling of exoticism in interior design, landscaping, and fashionable dress.

Cohong: *Gonghang* in *pinyin*. The licensed monopoly of Chinese merchants in the Canton (*Guangzhou*) trade permitted to deal directly with foreign maritime merchants coming to China.

Coolie trade: The economic dislocation in South China following the Opium War and exacerbated by the Taiping civil war caused considerable unemployment in the region. The need for cheap labor in Latin America, especially Cuba and

Peru, and the discovery of gold in California and the railroad boom in the American west created opportunity for large scale Chinese emigration. In the United States, Chinese came by means of "free emigration"; in Cuba and Peru they were recruited, tricked, lured into debt-bondage, even kidnapped and forced into fictitious contracts that amounted to indefinite slavery. The "coolie trade"—the Chinese characters *kuli* mean "bitter strength"—went on from 1847 till the late 1870's.

Dao: Literally, "the Way," or "the Road." A fundamental Chinese philosophical concept. The Dao (Wade-Giles, Tao) is the animating principle of the cosmos. It is unlimited and indefinable, though attributes of it can be hinted at by human beings attempting to grasp its underlying principles and put themselves in tune with it.

Dujun: Military governors; during the period from 1916–1926 the term is usually rendered as "warlord."

Dynastic cycle: An idea related to the Mandate of Heaven and formalized in Chinese historiography. In this view, dynasties tend to start with ethical, energetic rulers who have received the Mandate, expand and consolidate their territory, enrich the country, and serve as proper models for the populace. Over time, however, dynasties lose their momentum, coast on past accomplishments, and usually end up with a succession of weak and/or oppressive rulers. At this point, Heaven often manifests its displeasure with weird omens, natural disasters, and ultimately rebellion. With a successful rebellion a new ruler comes in with the Mandate and the next cycle begins.

Extraterritoriality: Sometimes shortened to "extrality." In diplomacy, the practice of exempting resident citizens or subjects of a country from the laws of the host country; diplomatic immunity is a form of extraterritoriality. In China until 1943 and Japan until 1899 the practice was a centerpiece of the "unequal treaties" and the "treaty ports." In China the exemptions were extended to include territorial concessions and ultimately the Chinese converts of Christian missionaries

Factories: In this case not machine-driven manufacturing centers, but the places where merchant "factors" met to do business. In Canton/Guangzhou, these were the places where the merchants from European and American companies were allowed to live and work under strict regulations overseen by Chinese authorities. The intent was to restrict their business contacts to the Cohong merchant guild, keep them as isolated as possible from the locals, and forbid them from going into the interior of the country or into the city of Canton.

Fengjian: Often translated and interpreted as a kind of feudalism. *Fengjian* was a decentralized form of government devised by the Zhou in which individuals were granted lands and titles in return for remitting taxes, local governance, and military service.

Foot-binding: The practice among Han Chinese and some minorities within the Chinese empire and early Republic of tightly binding the feet of young girls.

This was done in such a way as to reduce the foot's size by as much as two thirds, and make walking painful and difficult for a woman throughout her life. Begun in the Song Dynasty, it was believed to enhance a woman's beauty and decrease their mobility and was generally carried out by a girl's mother.

Forbidden City: The enormous walled compound within the capital of Beijing that contained the quarters and working areas of the emperor, imperial family, imperial eunuchs, and the chief officers of the empire. The main entrance was through the Gate of Heavenly Peace, *Tiananmen*; the famous square of the same name is across the street. The Forbidden City today is a museum and tourist destination.

Four Modernizations: Program announced by Deng Xiaoping in 1978 directed at bringing China's agriculture, industry, science and technology, and military up to modern standards. Part of the program would be to gradually introduce market economics through Special Economic Zones, open the country to foreign investment, and allow Chinese students to study abroad.

Four Olds: One of the goals of the Cultural Revolution was the elimination of the vestiges of older ideas and the creation of "proletarian consciousness." Hence, a campaign was launched calling for the exposure and eradication of "the four olds: Old customs, old culture, old habits, and old ideas. In addition to the human cost of the campaign, a vast amount of China's irreplaceable cultural heritage was destroyed in the course of pursuing its goals.

Gang of Four: After the death of Mao in 1976, a more moderate leadership came to the fore with Hua Guofeng and, shortly, Deng Xiaoping. Condemning the excesses of the Cultural Revolution, the new leaders brought the so-called "Gang of Four"—Mao's widow Jiang Qing, Zhang Chunqiao, Yao Wenyuan, and Wang Hongwen—who had been instrumental in pursuing the Revolution's goals of "proletarianization," to trial in 1980. Jiang Qing and Zhang Chunqiao were sentenced to death, later commuted to life imprisonment; Wang received life and Yao, twenty years. Jiang Qing committed suicide in 1991 while stricken with throat cancer.

Grand Canal: Still the world's longest artificial waterway at 1104 miles, running from Hangzhou to Beijing. Like the Great Wall, it was initially composed of a number of smaller canals knit together, in this case by the Sui, and expanded by subsequent dynasties. Provided vital north-south transport, particularly for commercial products, food, and tribute grain for the imperial capitals of the north.

Great Proletarian Cultural Revolution: Along with the Great Leap Forward, China's greatest mass movement during the Mao years. Worried that China had drifted to far toward Soviet-style programs and bureaucracy, Mao launched the Cultural Revolution in May, 1966 to spur the country to continuous revolution and purge it of the last vestiges of feudal and bourgeois thinking. With the country torn apart by factional fighting, the movement was officially ended in 1969, though many of its policies remained in place until Mao's death in 1976.

Guomindang: Wade-Giles, *Kuomintang*: The Nationalist Party. Usually abbreviated as *GMD* (*pinyin*) or in older works and on Taiwan, *KMT*.

Hakkas: In Mandarin *kejia* or *kejiaren*. Not an ethnic group but a minority composed of Mandarin-speaking Han Chinese who migrated south from the north during earlier dynastic changes and maintained customs separate from their neighbors, who discriminated against them and sometimes attacked them. The constituted one of the core groups of the Taiping movement.

Han Synthesis: Politically, the term refers to the system put together by Han rulers in which the structural elements of the Qin government were retained but the harsh laws and punishments of the Qin were liberalized or eliminated. Philosophically, it refers to the adoption of Confucianism as the favored state ideology but with the retention of the hereditary dynastic system in place to assure stability and continuity.

Harmonious Society: A conceptual approach to policy articulated by Hu Jintao in 2006 and endorsed by the Party, in which rapid economic growth should be accompanied by efforts to reduce social tensions among classes, regions, and minorities. Economically, it calls for "sustainable development." Politically, it seeks to reduce corruption and collusion between Party members and those in the private sector. At the same time, it also strongly opposes any attempts at regional and/or ethnic minority "splitism."

High-level equilibrium trap: Still controversial theory first proposed by Mark Elvin in his *The Pattern of the Chinese Past* (1973). The theory suggests that despite having the necessary preconditions for an industrial revolution, China did not have one because its economy, though near the limits of its pre-industrial capacity, was still in equilibrium. For an industrial revolution to begin, the theory goes, the economy—like Britain's in the 18th century—must be in disequilibrium and require innovation to correct the deficit. Thus, China was caught in a "high-level equilibrium trap."

Hou: Under the *fengjian* system, the ruler of a Zhou dependency or territory. Sometimes translated as *Marquis* or Lord.

huiguan: Guildhall; an association connected with one's hometown or district that runs hostels and accommodations for its merchants, craftspeople, and others whose occupations require them to travel. *Huiguan* customarily help with local connections, paperwork, permits, sometimes even travel costs. The institution traveled with Chinese communities overseas as well.

Hundred Flowers campaign: 1956–7 drive in which the Party encouraged intellectuals to critique the government's performance. At first hesitant, the intellectuals were assured that criticism was their patriotic duty. When the criticism mounted and suggestions were made to allow an opposition party, the CCP shut the campaign down and launched the Anti-Rightist Campaign.

Junzi: In Confucianism, the "gentleman" or "superior man" who has progressed through his understanding of *li* to *ren*.

Kong fuzi: Literally, "the Master Kong": The name by which Confucius is often called in the Confucian canon. Jesuit missionaries in the late sixteenth century transliterated the title into Latin as "Confucius."

Legalism: The system of government in the state of Qin and in the first Chinese empire created by the Qin. Championed by Han Fei and Li Si and put into practice by the first emperor, it called for all subjects to devote themselves to the power and welfare of the state, for the emperor to be the ultimate arbiter of what is good for the state, for the suppression of all knowledge not approved by the state, and for a comprehensive and strict code of laws and punishments enforced equally on all classes.

Li: Variously interpreted as "ritual" or "rules of decorum." Li is the framework of action by which one may come to "humaneness" (*ren*). The proper rules of behavior based on the best moral examples, rites and rituals designed to reinforce proper behavior, just laws that not only restrict the bad but encourage the good are all part of li. Immersion in *li* in one's personal life, family, and society leads to internalizing its principles and in its full actualization allows one to know how to act morally in any situation. One's desires and *ren* then become one.

Likin: The Taiping war put enormous financial strains on the Qing government. Because the Qing were limited by the unequal treaties in how high they could raise their tariffs, they set up a series of internal transit taxes called "likin" (*lijin* in *pinyin*) to help pay the costs of suppressing the rebellion. The taxes continued after the war, even after the dynasty fell.

Literary Revolution: A part of the New Culture Movement associated with Hu Shi, in which the use of vernacular language and some of the themes of the American thinker John Dewey's philosophy of pragmatism would be used to foster a new literary consciousness and nationalism in China. Among its goals was using language reform to aid mass literacy.

Little red book: The pocket-sized volume *Quotations From Chairman Mao Zedong* that became the most prominent symbol of the Cultural Revolution. Correct interpretation and explication of the book became the chief duty and preoccupation of most Chinese during this time. It's quotations became justification for many of the period's excesses.

Loess: A light, dry, mineral-rich soil, yellowish red in color blown into North China and built up by centuries of prevailing winds. It provides the fertile silt so important to agriculture in ancient China and gives the Yellow River its name.

Long March: The year-long trek of Mao's troops from Jiangxi to Yan'an from 1934 to 1935. Desperate to break out of the tightening circle of Chiang Kai-shek's forces, Mao forced a breach and retreated with his army into the back-country, where his troops endured starvation, rugged topography, often hostile locals, and constant harassment by Chiang's forces and local warlords.

Longshan Culture: Neolithic communities to the east of the Yangshao settlements that flourished from about 4500 to 1500 B.C.E. marked by finely crafted black pottery made on potters wheels and fired at high temperatures.

Mandate of Heaven: A guiding concept of the Chinese view of history in which Heaven gives its approval to govern (the Mandate) only to leaders who are ethically fit to govern. If they prove oppressive, dissolute, or inept enough the people are authorized to rebel and replace the ruler. If such a rebellion is successful the new ruler receives Heaven's Mandate, founds a new dynasty, and the "dynastic cycle" begins again.

Mao Zedong Thought: The collective term for Mao's writings, particularly his theories on Marxism and peasant revolution. China's official philosophy includes Mao Zedong Thought along with Marxism-Leninism, and the ideas of recent leaders such as Deng Xiaoping, Hu Jintao, and Jiang Zemin.

May Fourth Movement: The movement that is usually cited as galvanizing modern Chinese nationalism. The date is from May 4, 1919, when the representatives at the Versailles Peace Conference decided to award Japan the former German concession in Shandong. The move sparked national demonstrations and a boycott against Japan and the foreign powers.

Most-favored nation: Diplomatic status conferred on a country by which any rights granted by treaty to a particular country automatically accrue to the "most-favored" country. For example, Britain signed such an agreement with China in supplementary treaties following the Treaty of Nanjing. Thus any rights that China might grant to another country that they have not already granted to Britain are now *automatically* given to Britain as a most favored nation.

Neo-Confucianism: The philosophy developed over several centuries during the Confucian revival of the Song, and subsequent refined during the Ming and Qing periods, when it became China's official ideology. Taking the ethical ideas of older Confucian self-cultivation and synthesizing them with Buddhist and Daoist speculative thought, the brothers Cheng Hao and Cheng Yi, and especially Zhu Xi during the 11th and 12th centuries, added a cosmological strain of thought and a distinctive epistemology (approaches to acquiring knowledge) to Confucianism.

New Culture Movement: The movement among intellectuals in the early years of the Chinese Republic and Warlord Period to discard Confucianism, the old literary language, and old customs in general in favor of the latest trends in Europe and the US, science and democracy, and vernacular language.

New Life Movement: Concerned that the modernizing China taking shape under the Nationalists in the late 1920's and early 1930's lacked a unifying ideology now that Confucianism was in decline, Chiang Kai-shek attempted to craft one that combined modern ideas with more traditional ones. Inspired by the apparent success of the fascist regimes and his own experience with military discipline, the New Life Movement emphasized nationalism and loyalty to the state, self-discipline and personal hygiene, and a revival of Confucian ethics: as Chiang saw it the best of East and West.

New Youth: The emblematic literary journal of the New Culture Movement. Its title was popularized as the French *La Jeunesse*, and its early contributors included some of China's greatest writers of the twentieth century: LuXun, Hu Shi, Li Dazhao, and Chen Duxiu.

One Child Policy: As part of the overall trends springing from the Four Modernizations, China put into place in 1980 a policy restricting families to one child in an effort to curb population growth. Although a number of exemptions were introduced over the years—a second child was permitted if the first one was a girl; second children were also permitted if one of the parents was an only child; most minorities were exempt as well—the rate of population growth has been curbed. Loss of benefits and fines were imposed for violators and abortion mandatory for a third pregnancy. With China's demographics skewed increasingly toward the elderly because of the program, however, restrictions are being loosened up. Nonetheless, a 2008 poll showed a 76% approval rating for the policy. The One Child Policy was effectively ended in November, 2015.

Oracle bones: The shoulder blades of oxen or plastrons (bottom shells) of tortoises used in Shang divination. Questions are asked of the heavenly ancestors, the bones are heated and tapped with a rod to induce cracks, which are then interpreted as answers. The questions and answers are then inscribed on the bones. The caches of thousands of such bones near Anyang are the closest thing archaeologists have to a Shang historical archive.

Peking Man: Fossils of *homo erectus* hominid found in the 1920's at Zhoukoudian, near Beijing, estimated to be as old as 780,000 years

People's Liberation Army: The military of the CCP and, since 1949, the People's Republic of China. The philosophy behind this force was that it was initially a guerrilla army made up of ordinary citizens, who also did civilian work when they were not fighting, They cultivated the image of being at one with the ordinary people, treating them fairly, and refraining from harassing them.

Ping Pong Diplomacy: In April, 1971, the United States Table Tennis team visited China for a week after competing in the world championship matches in Japan. It was the first major cultural exchange between the two countries since the founding of the PRC and was hailed as a symbol of the new era of friendlier Sino-American relations.

Presentism: Often associated with the "Whig view" of history. Presentism is the practice of judging the past by the standards of the present. Usually considered a historical fallacy, it forces one to see the past as inevitably leading to the present, suggests that only what is important in the present is worth studying in the past, and, since the present is seen as the perfection of the past, creates an historical morality in which the past can never live up to the present, but one in which the heroes are those who advance trends leading to present conditions and villains are those who oppose them.

Qing: Minister or chief functionary of the Zhou rulers or the various feudal lords (*hou*)

qingyi: "Pure discussion"; debates conducted, usually by memorials to high officials and the throne, on a variety of subjects, but often about the course of the *yangwu* or *ziqiang* (foreign affairs and self-strengthening). The debates sometimes were used to bypass normal channels, to raise one's political prestige, or to impugn another official's patriotism.

Queue: The Manchu hair style for men, which became a mandatory sign of loyalty to the Qing Dynasty from 1645 to 1912. The forehead was shaved and the remaining hair was allowed to grow long and plaited into a braid.

Ren: "Humaneness" or "humanity" (as behavior). A fundamental Confucian concept in which the study of moral examples and principles, and rigorous self-cultivation, all lead one to instinctively act in moral way and thus move toward putting oneself in tune with the Dao.

Resist America–Aid Korea: One of the first mass mobilization campaigns of the Maoist era. It was aimed at showing solidarity with North Korea, supporting the Chinese counterattack on UN forces in Korea, and identifying potentially disloyal elements in the new state.

Scholar-gentry: The elite class in rural imperial China. Entry into the scholar-gentry required passing at least the first round of Confucian examinations or, in some cases, purchasing a degree. Since the surest route to both wealth and power was through the exams to get a government post, these men and their families generally acquired land and wealth along with their positions. Their wealth, prestige, and the fact that many of them were retired or expectant officials gave them leading status in their communities.

Shanghai Communique: The announcement resulting from U.S. President Richard M. Nixon's trip to China in 1972 stating that both sides would extend official diplomatic recognition to each other, that the U.S. would no longer oppose the PRC's entry into the United Nations, and that the U.S. would downgrade its diplomatic relationship with the Republic of China on Taiwan.

Shi: The lower officials, some of noble families, some of commoner households. Confucius was a member of this class.

Shujing: Known variously as "the Book of History" or "the Classic of Documents," it is a detailed compilation of historical materials allegedly from 2357 to 631 B.C.E., much of it of questionable accuracy. It remains, however, along with oracle bones, the primary literary source of the history of Northern China in remote antiquity.

Shuren: The common people of any occupation.

Socialist Realism: Artistic, architectural, and literary style imported from the Soviet Union and popularized in the People's Republic in the 1950's and early 1960's. It was intended to elevate ordinary people to heroic proportions, depicting them marching bravely against capitalist imperialism, singing on their way to fields, and so forth. The most widely recognized painting of this genre is the giant portrait of Mao that still hangs over the Gate of Heavenly Peace in Beijing. During the Cultural Revolution, the style was pushed out in favor of the more severe and restricted Socialist Idealism, or Revolutionary Romanticism.

Special Economic Zone: As part of Deng Xiaoping's Four Modernizations, older collectivist forms of agriculture and industry were to be dismantled in favor of more privatization, market economics, and "the responsibility system." Special Economic Zones were set up in various places in order to experiment with different ideas, the most effective of which would then be adopted by the country as a whole. One of the earliest and most famous of these was Shenzhen, near Guangzhou, now one of China's larger cities.

Spiritual pollution: With China's increased openness to foreign trade and technology came the increasing flow of foreign culture, much of it considered by the Party to be injurious to public morals and to Party ideology. In 1983, a campaign was launched against such things as risqué music videos, pornography, revealing fashions, and cultural exports—literature, art, film—containing potentially subversive material. Such things were lumped under the heading of "spiritual pollution."

Tanglu: The code of laws developed under Tang Emperor Taizong that tied together previous law codes and the large corpus of customary law into a body of statutes of 502 articles and commentaries and explanations. It remained the basis for imperial Chinese law and became a model code for states modeled on the Chinese system.

Tank Man: During the watershed suppression of the demonstrators in Tiananmen Square on June 4, 1989 and the following days, a lone man—whose identity is still unknown—stood in front of a line of tanks and for a time forced the column to halt. He even climbed up on the lead tank to intercede with the driver. The video and still pictures of the incident became the symbols to the world of the political cleavages in China under the Four Modernizations.

Taotie: Artistic motifs characteristic of Shang and early Zhou bronze vessels, with stylized shapes and faces, sometimes incorporating elements of real and mythical animals within them.

The Ever-Victorious Army: Although the foreign powers in China during the Taiping war attempted to maintain formal neutrality, Europeans and Americans fought on both sides as individuals. By the early 1860s the informal tilt toward the Qing had resulted in the beginnings of self-strengthening initiatives and foreigners were forming militias. The most famous of these was the Ever Victorious Army, officered, armed and drilled by Westerners, manned by Chinese volunteers, and headed by the American Frederick Townsend Ward. They were often used as shock troops by Li Hongzhang and Zeng Guofan. When Ward was killed they were led by Charles George Gordon, whose spectacular death twenty years later fighting Muslim insurgents in the Sudan immortalized him in Victorian England as "Gordon of Khartoum."

The Great Game: The strategic struggle, ultimately lasting through the nineteenth century and continuing in modified form until World War II, for control and hegemony in Central Asia among Russia, Great Britain, the Ottoman Empire, Russia and the Qing. After World War I, though the Qing and

Ottoman empires were gone, the struggle continued among Britain, the Soviet Union, and Nationalist China.

The Great Leap Forward: The drive to communize China in one massive mobilization campaign in 1958. Peasant lands were consolidated into huge communal farms, each commune was supposed to make its own implements from iron and steel tools and household goods requisitioned to be melted down into ingots in backyard furnaces. The Leap was such a catastrophic failure that Mao stepped down from Party leadership and the famine shortly after may have taken upwards of 30 million lives.

The Three People's Principles: *San min zhuyi.* The statement of Sun Yat-sen's Revolutionary Alliance, and later the Nationalist Party, of the goals for a Chinese state. Sovereignty—expulsion of the Manchus and abrogation of the unequal treaties; democracy—a constitution- based democratic republic as the basic governmental structure; and "the people's livelihood"—sometimes translated as "socialism" but based on government-sponsored division of the land and elimination of absentee landlordism.

The Three Represents: Jiang Zemin's set of principles laid out in 2000 that anchors the reforms of the previous two decades firmly in place as Party policy. According to Jiang, the Party "must always represent the requirements for developing China's advanced productive forces," represent the "orientation of China's advanced culture," and "the fundamental interests of the overwhelming majority of the Chinese people."

Thermidorean Reaction: Following the campaigns of the 1950's, especially the Great Leap Forward, the leadership of Liu Shaoqi backed away from the most radical policies of Mao and his faction. Since this was compared to the abrupt end of the French Revolution's Reign of Terror in the revolutionary month of "Thermidor" in 1794, which led to the more moderate government of the Directory, some historians refer to Liu Shaoqi's premiership during the early 1960's as China's "Thermidorean Reaction."

Three Emperors: The three most dynamic and powerful Qing emperors, Kangxi, Yongzheng, and Qianlong, who served sequentially from 1664–1795.

Three-Anti and Five-Anti campaigns: (*Pinyin: Sanfan* and *Wufan*). Like the Resist America-Aid Korea movement of the early 1950's, these campaigns, launched in 1951 and 1952 were targeted at eliminating certain practices (corruption, waste, "bureaucratism"; bribery, theft of state property, tax evasion, cheating on government contracts, stealing state economic information) and more broadly purging the disloyal, routinizing people to report on each other, and preparing to nationalize business and industry.

Tianzi: "Son of Heaven," a title by which imperial rulers were known. It symbolizes the relationship among Heaven, Humankind, and Earth, in which Humankind holds the pivotal position of keeping these three parts of the cosmos in balance. It also denotes the filial duty of the ruler toward Heaven for his stewardship of Humankind.

Treaty of Nerchinsk: 1689 agreement between the Qing and Russia in which Russia gave up its forts on the Amur River, kept their rights to the caravan trade to Beijing, settled claims in Central Asia and set up formal borders in Manchuria. The Russians also gained the right to have trade officials reside in Beijing because of its role as the caravan terminus.

Treaty of Shimonoseki: The agreement ending the Sino-Japanese War of 1894–95. It marked an historic role reversal of the two empires in that Japan, which had been regarded as a cultural satellite by China, had now soundly defeated the Qing and imposed its own version of Western-style "unequal treaties" on the empire. Japan established a protectorate over Korea, forced China to cede Taiwan, initially (until forced to return the territory through the Triple Intervention of France, Germany and Russia) acquired Manchuria's Liaodong Peninsula, and imposed a record $150,000,000 indemnity on the Qing. It marked the beginning of Japanese expansion on the Asian mainland.

Warring States Period: An interval of endemic warfare among the Zhou states dating variously from 475, 453, or 403 (depending upon the incident used to begin the period) and lasting until the final unification of the empire under the Qin.

Well-field system: A system of rural organization in which each square *li* of land is divided into a grid of nine fields of 100 *mou*. Eight families receive parcels and the ninth is farmed in common to cover rents and taxes. The term "well-field" comes from the character *jing*, meaning "water well," which is shaped like the grid in the system.

White Lotus Rebellion: Long, persistent uprising in the border region of Hubei, Shaanxi and Sichuan, originally precipitated by attempts to collect taxes from poor peasants. Starting in 1794 the fighting continued sporadically through the early 1800's. It took its name from an older Buddhist sect that the Qing derisively attached to the rebels.

xiao: Filial piety. This virtue becomes central with Han Dynasty's adoption of Confucianism as an approved ideology. Conceptually all human society—indeed, the universe—follows the fundamental pattern of a human nuclear family. From the lowest commoner to the emperor, everyone has someone above them to accord appropriate respect and obedience, and someone below them to treat with kindness and benevolence. As the "Son of Heaven" the emperor himself owes filial duty to Heaven in his responsibility for the welfare of his subjects.

Xinhai Revolution: China's Republican Revolution that began on October 10, 1911 (*xuangshi:* "double ten"). *Xinhai* is the year 1911 in the old Chinese calendar

Xiongnu: One of many Altaic-speaking nomadic groups along China's northern tier beyond the Great Wall. Some see them as related to the Huns, others see them as the ancestors of the Turks. The Xiongnu dominated Central Asia from the third century until their state was destroyed by the Han Dynasty in 89 C.E.

Yang: In Chinese philosophy, the complementary opposite of *yin*. It is the male principle, associated with the sun, light, Heaven, etc.

Yangshao Culture: Sometimes called "Painted Pottery Culture" that flourished from about 5000 to 3500 B.C.E.. Characterized by Neolithic villages like Banpo, near Xi'an. Noted for colorful pottery with geometric designs that some have suggested might be an early form of writing.

Yangwu: Literally "foreign affairs." Generally used in connection with the term *ziqiang* ("self-strengthening) to refer to the idea of using foreign technologies or institutions to help strengthen imperial China.

zhongxue wei ti; xixue wei yong: The philosophical formula of the self-strengtheners. Usually translated as "Chinese studies for the base/essentials; Western studies for practical application."

CREDITS

CHAPTER 1: pg. 2 © National Museum of China Collection/ChinaStock; pg. 12 © Wang Peng/Xinhua Press/Corbis; pg. 14 (top) © Bettmann/Corbis/AP Images; pg. 14 (bottom) Photo by CM Dixon/Print Collector/Getty Images; pg. 15 (top & bottom) © Liu Liqun/ChinaStock; pg. 16 (top) © Liu Liqun/ChinaStock; pg. 16 (bottom) Neolithic Painted pottery urn, Banshan phase of Yangshao Culture, China/De Agostini Picture Library/L. de Masi/Bridgeman Images; pg. 17 Stem cups and goblet, c. 2000 BC (pottery), Chinese School, Neolithic Period (c. 7000–1700 BC)/Collection of the Lowe Art Museum, University of Miami/Bridgeman Images; pg. 18 © Dennis Cox/ChinaStock; pg. 23 © RMN-Grand Palais/Art Resource, NY; pg. 24 China: Around two thousand years old, Yingpan man died at around thirty and was buried in elaborate clothing with a gold face mask./Pictures from History/Bridgeman Images; pg. 27 © Wiliam Perry/Alamy; pg. 30 akg-images/Osprey Publishing/Angus McBride; pg. 39 Ashmolean Museum/The Art Archive at Art Resource, NY; pg. 41 © Glow Asia RF/Alamy; pg. 47 Laozi Delivering the Daodejing (ink on paper), Chinese School, Ming Dynasty (1368–1644)/Freer Gallery of Art, Smithsonian Institution, USA/Gift of Eugene and Agnes E. Meyer/Bridgeman Images

CHAPTER 2: pg. 51 © Liu Liqun Collection/ChinaStock; pg. 56 (A) DECoxPhoto@aol.com © Dennis Cox/ChinaStock; (B) DECoxPhoto@aol.com © Dennis Cox/ChinaStock; © DECox Photo@aol.com © Wang Lu/ChinaStock; (D) Erich Lessing/Art Resource, NY; pg. 57 Juan Muñoz/age fotostock/SuperStock; pg. 61 Watch tower model (pottery & green lead glaze), Chinese School, Eastern Han

Dynasty (25–220)/Collection of the Lowe Art Museum, University of Miami/Gift of George and Julianne Alderman/Bridgeman Images; (A) China: The only surviving calligraphy of Tang Dynasty poet Li Bai (701–762), held in the Beijing Palace Museum./Pictures from History/Bridgeman Images; pg. 64 (B) China: Portrait of the scholar Fu Sheng, attributed to Tang Dynasty painter Wang Wei (699–759)./Pictures from History/Bridgeman Images; pg. 63 (C) China: Chinese script. Tang Dynasty (618–907) calligraphy attributed to Lee Yang-bing (Li Yangbing), c. 8th century/Pictures from History/Bridgeman Images; (D) The autobiography of the Monk Huai Su who was famed for his cursive style of calligraphy/Werner Forman Archive/Bridgeman Images; pg. 66 © TAO Images Limited/Alamy; pg. 71 Guanyin, Bodhisattva of Compassion Chinese, Northern Zhou or early Sui dynasty, about A.D. 580 Carved limestone (gray) with traces of polychrome and gilding 249 × 71 × 71 cm (98 1/16 × 27 15/16 × 27 15/16 in.) Museum of Fine Arts, Boston, Francis Bartlett Donation of 1912, 15.254. Photograph © 2016 Museum of Fine Arts, Boston; pg.74 © British Library Board/Robana/Art Resource, NY; pg. 78 © Liu Liqun Collection/ChinaStock; pg. 80 Kublai Khan, 1294 (ink & colour on silk), Araniko or Anige (1245–1306)/National Palace Museum, Taipei, Taiwan/Ancient Art and Architecture Collection Ltd./Kadokawa/Bridgeman Images; pg. 84 Gregory Harlin/National Geographic Creative; pg. 85 The Philadelphia Museum of Art/Art Resource, NY; pg. 89 Courtesy of ChinaStock; pg. 96 © The Trustees of the British Museum/Art Resource, NY; pg. 98 Zhao Mengfu (1254–1322). Colophon writer: Yang Zai, Chinese, 1271–1323. Twin Pines, Level Distance, ca. 1300. Handscroll; ink on paper, Image: 10 9/16 × 42 5/16 (26.8 × 107.5 cm.). Overall with mounting: 10 15/16 × 307 11/16 in. (27.8 × 781.5 cm.). Ex coll: C.C. Wang Family, Gift of The Dillon Fund, 1973 (1973. 120.5). The Metropolitan Museum of Art. Image copyright © The Metropolitan Museum of Art. Image source: Art Resource, NY; pg. 101 Courtesy Gary Lee Todd; pg. 103 Courtesy Needham Research Institute.

CHAPTER 3: pg. 106 © Reuters/CORBIS; pg. 114 China: Wufu, a Qing military officer from the reign of Qianlong (1735–96)/Pictures from History/Bridgeman Images; pg. 116 (A) Manchu Ladies, c. 1867–72 (b/w photo), Thomson, John (1837–1921)/Private Collection/Bridgeman Images; (B) China: Plaiting a man's queue or pigtail, Beijing, late Qing Dynasty (c. 1885)/Pictures from History/Bridgeman Images; pg. 117 © CORBIS; pg. 120 China: The 4th Qing Emperor Kangxi (1654 –1722), temple name Shengzu. He is considered one of China's greatest emperors./Pictures from History/Bridgeman Images; pg. 124 DECox Photo@aol.com © Qi Wen/ChinaStock; pg. 128 © RMN-Grand Palais/Art Resource, NY; pg. 130 The Hongs of Canton (oil on panel), Cantonese School/Private Collection/Roy Miles Fine Paintings/Bridgeman Images; pg. 132 Taperstick. Made in China for export to Europe. 18th century (ca. 1700). Hard-paste porcelain, H. 5 1/4 in (13.3 cm.). Purchase, WInfield Foundation Gift, 1970 (1970.266.3). The Metropolitan Museum of Art. Image copyright © The Metropolitan Museum of Art. Image source: Art Resource, NY; pg. 133 Matteo Ricci

(1552–1610), (w/c on paper), Weld, Charles (fl.1850)/By permission of the Governors of Stonyhurst College/Bridgeman Images; pg. 135 (left) Chest of Drawers (Commode), c. 1750–1765 (oak, black lacquer with raised chinoiserie decoration, gilt metal mounts, marble top) , Delorme, Adrien-Faizelot (1722–91)/Cleveland Museum of Art, OH, USA/Bequest of Mrs. Severance A. Millikin/Bridgeman Images; pg. 135 (right) Famille Rose Export Plate, decorated with 'The Doctor's Visit', after Cornelius Pronck (1691–1759) Chinese, Qianlong period, 1736–95 (porcelain)/Private Collection/Paul Freeman/Bridgeman Images; pg. 137 © John Thomson; pg. 140 Library of Congress, Prints and Photographs Division, Washington, D.C.; pg. 144 The 'European Palace' at Yuen-Ming-Yuan, illustration from 'Le Costume Ancien et Moderne' by Giulio Ferrario, published c. 1820s–30s (coloured engraving), Zancon, Gaetano (1771–1816)/Private Collection/The Stapleton Collection/Bridgeman Images.

CHAPTER 4: pg. 152 Photo courtesy of Cyrus Veeser; pg. 156 Emperor Tongzhi (1856–1875), his temple name was Muzong, Chinese School/Palace Museum, Beijing, China/Bridgeman Images; pg. 159 China: Liu Kunyi (January 21, 1830–October 6, 1902) was a Chinese official during the Qing dynasty and a native of Xinning, Hunan/Pictures from History/Bridgeman Images; pg. 166 (top) © Focus-China/Alamy; pg. 166 (bottom) © Yang Qitao/Panorama/The Image Works; pg. 172 China: The seal of the Taiping Tianguo or 'Heavenly Kingdom of Transcendent Peace', also known as the Taiping Rebellion (1850–1864) and of its leader, Hong Xiuquan (1814–1864)/Pictures from History/Bridgeman Images; pg. 178 China: Three mullahs in Yunnan, photographed in 1890./Pictures from History/Bridgeman Images; pg. 187 © John Thomson.

CHAPTER 5: pg. 194 (left) Chinese Section, Main Building, Centennial International Exhibition, Philadelphia, 1876 (albumen print), American Photographer, (19th century)/Free Library, Philadelphia, PA, USA/Bridgeman Images; pg. 194 (right) Photo by Science & Society Picture Library/Getty Images; pg. 196 China: 'Loading Tea at Canton'. The Canton (Guangzhou) waterfront is depicted from Honam Island where workers load a sampan with chests of tea. Unknown Chinese artist, c. 1852/Pictures from History/Bridgeman Images; pg. 199 China: A contemporaneous sketch of the Macartney Embassy to China (1793). The Qianlong Emperor receives a missive from Macartney, kneeling/Pictures from History/Bridgeman Images; pg. 202 (A) The Art Archive at Art Resource, NY; pg. 202 (B) Opium from Patna, India, bound for China during the Opiums Wars, Indian School, (19th century)/Private Collection/Peter Newark Historical Pictures/Bridgeman Images; pg. 204 Library of Congress Prints and Photographs Division, Washington, D.C.; pg. 207 HIP/Art Resource, NY; pg. 211 Death of General Ward in the Battle of Tzeki, 20th August, 1862 during the Taiping Rebellion (litho), English School, (19th century)/Private Collection/Peter Newark Military Pictures/Bridgeman Images; pg. 213 (left) The Collection of National Palace Museum; pg. 213 (right) Portrait of Li Hongzhang, 1871 (photo), Thomson, John (1837–1921)/

© Peabody Essex Museum, Salem, Massachusetts, USA/Frederick Townsend Ward Memorial Fund/Bridgeman Images; pg. 214 The Ever Victorious Army, c. 1863 (b/w photo), Beato, Felice (Felix) (1825-c. 1908)/Private Collection/Bridgeman Images; pg. 221 (top) V&A Images, London/Art Resource, NY; pg. 221 (bottom) Generals of the Chinese army surrendering to Japanese commanders, October 1894 (colour woodblock print), Migita Toshihide (1863–1925)/Freer Gallery of Art, Smithsonian Institution, USA/Elizabeth D. Woodbury collection of prints from Meiji, Japan/Bridgeman Images; pg. 222 © dbimages/Alamy; pg. 225 China: 'China—the cake of kings . . . and emperors'. European powers and Japan collectively carving up China in this French satirical cartoon dated 1898/Pictures from History/Bridgeman Images; pg. 226 (A) China: Kang Youwei, notable Chinese scholar and reformer of the late Qing Dynasty (1858–1927)/Pictures from History/Bridgeman Images; pg. 226 (B) China: Liang Qichao (1873–1929), Chinese scholar, journalist, philosopher and reformist during the Qing Dynasty, as a young man/Pictures from History/Bridgeman Images; pg. 228 Library of Congress Prints and Photographs Division, Washington, D.C. (LC - USZ62-25864-3a26745r).

CHAPTER 6: pg. 235 © Xia Gongran/Xinhua Press/Corbis; pg. 237 The Art Archive at Art Resource, NY; pg. 240 (top) Reproduced from Sun Yat-sen (Shanghai: Shanghai Museum of Sun Yat-sen's Former Residence,1996); pg. 240 (bottom) National Archives - Pacific Sierra Region, San Bruno, California; pg. 242 Men having their hair cut at the time of the 1912 Revolution (b/w photo), Chinese School, (20th century)/Private Collection/Bridgeman Images; pg. 247 (A) © Universal Art Archive/Alamy Stock Photo; pg. 247 (B) AP Photo; pg. 247 © China: Yan Xishan, Chinese Warlord, Shanxi Province (1911–1949), 1947/Pictures from History/Bridgeman Images; pg. 247 (D) © CORBIS; pg. 252 China: Protesters demonstrating outside the Gate of Heavenly Peace (Tiananmen) in Beijing on May 4, 1919/Pictures from History/Bridgeman Images; pg. 254 (A) China: Chen Duxiu, leading figure in the May 4th Movement, co-founder of the Chinese Communist Party, educator, philosopher, politician (1879–1942)/Pictures from History/Bridgeman Images; pg. 254 (B) Chinese intellectual who co-founded the Communist Party of China Li Dazhao (1888–1927)/Photo © Tallandier/Bridgeman Images; pg. 254 Young Mao Tse Zedong (1893–1976), July 1921/Bridgeman Images; pg. 255 (left) AFP/Getty Images; pg. 255 (right) © Underwood & Underwood/Corbis; pg. 256 Archiv Gerstenberg/ullstein bild via Getty Images; pg. 261 AP Photo; pg. 265 © Collection J.A. Fox/Magnum Photos; pg. 270 (A) China: Cai Yuanpei (1868–1940), Educator, Reformist, Revolutionary thinker/Pictures from History/Bridgeman Images; pg. 270 (B) China: The Chinese writer Lu Xun (1881–1936)./Pictures from History/Bridgeman Images; pg. 270 © Liu Liqun Collections/ChinaStock, All Rights Reserved; pg. 270 (D) Public Domain; pg. 273 (top) China: The Bund (Waitan), c. 1935/Pictures from History/Bridgeman Images; pg. 273 (middle) © Kingendai/AFLO/Nippon News/Corbis; pg. 273 (bottom) China: A studio photograph of a group of young society women in 1930s Shanghai proudly - and confidently showing off their unbound feet and modern, Western footwear/

INDEX

Page numbers in *italics* indicate figures, photos, or maps.